# The Pleasures of
# Green Lake

H. Allenger

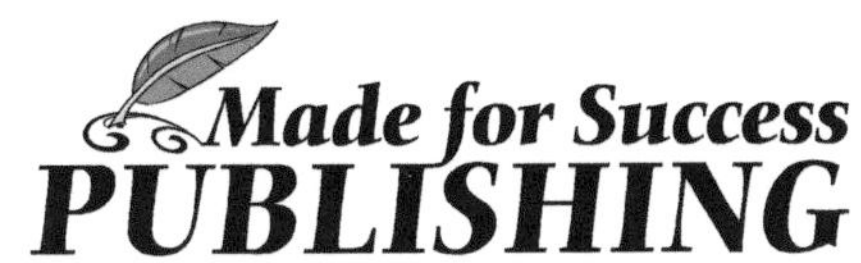
Made for Success
PUBLISHING

Made for Success Publishing
P.O. Box 1775
Issaquah, WA 98027

*The Pleasures of Green Lake*

Copyright © 2017, H. Allenger. All rights reserved.

Designed by DeeDee Heathman

No part pf this book may be reproduced in any manner without the express written consent of the author, except in cases of brief excerpts in critical reviews and articles.

**Library of Congress Cataloging-in-Publication data**

Allenger, H.
The Pleasures of Green Lake / H. Allenger
             p. cm.
      ISBN-13: 9781613398661 (pbk.)
      LCCN: 2016906523

To contact the author or publisher please email
service@MadeforSuccess.net or call +1 425 657 0300.

Made for Success Publishing is an imprint of Made for Success, inc.

Printed in the United States of America

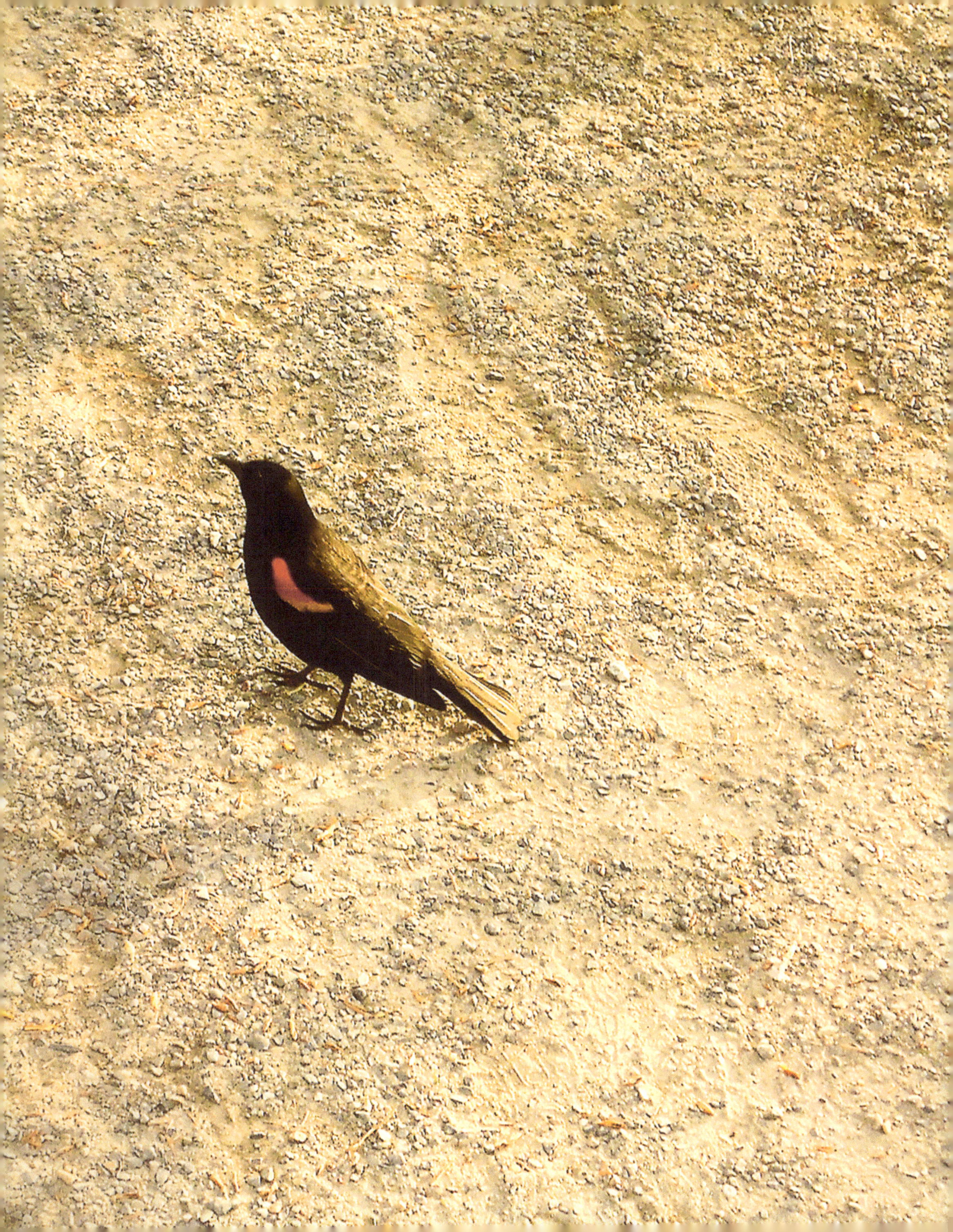

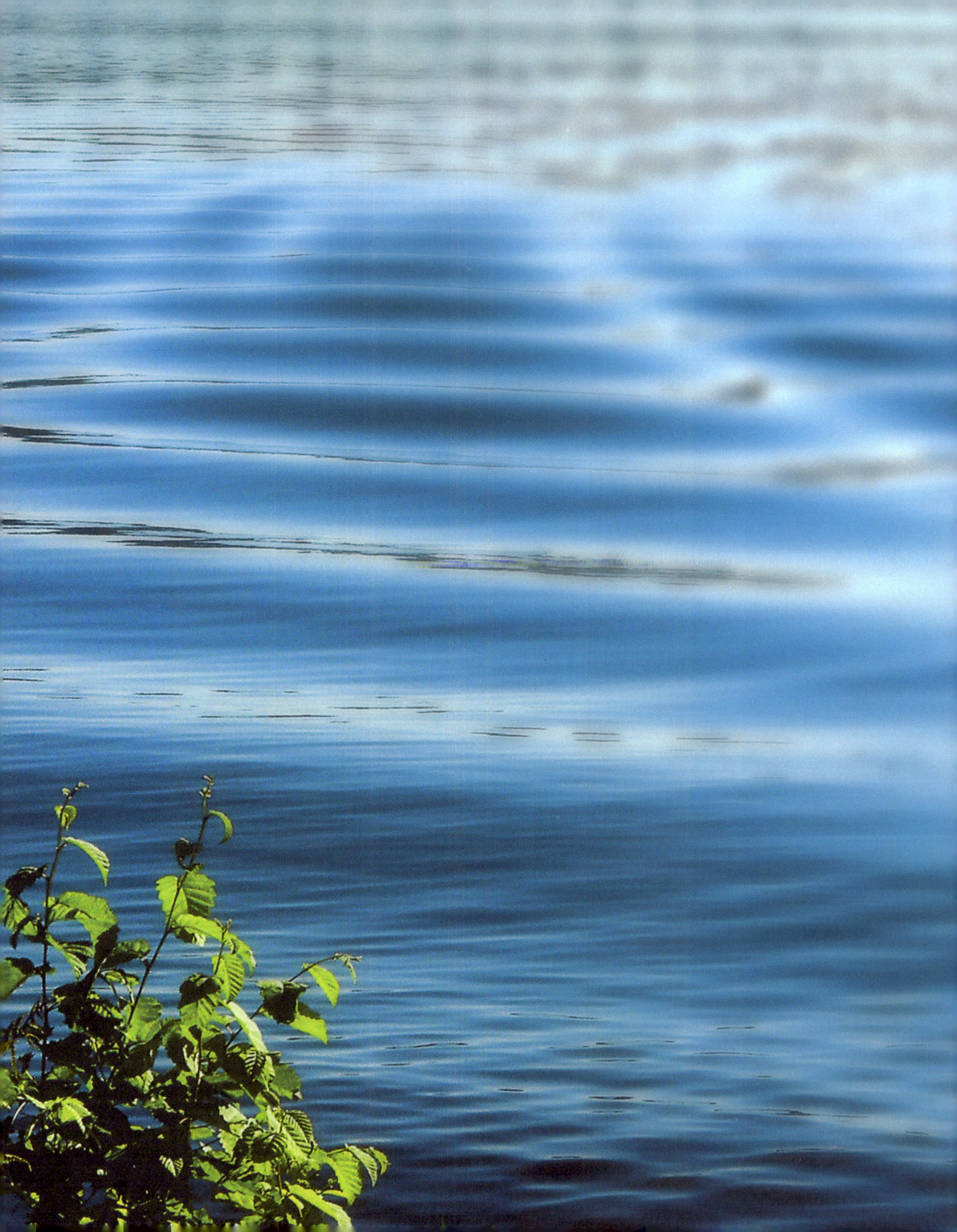

# Content

# Introduction

I live close to Seattle's Green Lake – one mile east of it– and do my daily walks around it for exercise. I used to jog twice around the lake every other day until a ruptured disc injury and its resultant surgery (in 2000) put an end to that, so since then I've hoofed it, which I'm actually enjoying more than running. That's because in walking I am more in tune with my environment and take the time to notice the smaller details of life abounding there that I failed to detect when jogging. Over the years, there have been interesting observations made by me which, I think, are worthy of mentioning and contemplating about. So, starting in the spring of 2014, I have decided to make a photographic record of the sights I come across so that I might share them with my readers. This, then, is meant to be a photographic journey of the joy and beauty I experience on my daily walks.

I am by no means a professional photographer and the pictures I have taken are with my pocket cameras, either with a Nikon Coolpix or an Olympus FE-20, cameras that would make the professionals shudder in dismay. The pictures displayed in this book are, in my opinion, fairly good and verification that it is the subject of the photographer that matters the most, not the equipment, although I would be the first to admit that they could be even better had I the right cameras and the knowledge to use them. I carry my pocket camera with me on my daily walks, mainly in my search for a target of opportunity, to use the military phrase, that I might come across. Most of the time, the camera remains unused in my pocket, but when I do use it, I am usually pleased with the result. My only regret is that the cameras I use fail me when taking the nocturnal shots I desire, even when I change the ISO settings. Sad to say, there are few night shots in this book, and that is not due to lack of trying; I've made special evening trips to the lake on a clear moonlit night in the hopes of getting the perfect shot only to be disappointed. Despite this, I think that, on the whole, the readers will enjoy what they see in this book, especially if they are familiar with the sights and recognize them from their own time spent at the lake.

Physical Features: Green Lake is located almost directly centered in North Seattle (the area of the city north of the Lake Washington Ship Canal, Lake Union, and the Montlake Cut) and is a park –the city's most popular one– covering a 324 acre site, of which 259 are the lake. It is a freshwater lake that averages 13 feet in depth with a maximum depth of 30 feet and rests 160 feet in elevation. We consider it to be a residential lake in that it is bordered by various neighborhoods –Phinney Ridge on the west; Wallingford in the south, and Green Lake in the north and east– comprised mostly of houses, although apartment dwellings are now blossoming, especially on its east side and on Phinney Ridge. The park attracts visitors from throughout the city when the days are warm and sunny, but seems to revert to a neighborhood site in inclement weather. I am basing this observation on my ability to park my vehicle there when I do my daily exercise. On a typical summer day, I cannot find a parking space within the park and have to park on its adjacent streets (unless I come at early dawn); off-season, especially when the weather is bad, this problem does not exist.

It is 2.8 miles around the lake on a paved pathway that has each quarter-mile distance marked and is level for most of this distance but rises at two major segments to the surface street elevation. One is between the three-quarter mile mark and the one and one-quarter mile mark arcing around the south end of the lake where the remains of the aqua-theater and the boathouse (moving in a clockwise direction) are located. The second rise, which is somewhat higher than the first, begins at the one and three-quarters mile mark and ends at the two-mile mark at the northwest section of the lake where the lake's Bathhouse Theater is situated. The slopes of these higher grounds are long and drawn-out and do not pose any difficulties for anyone in reasonably good shape. In short, it's not strenuous to walk around the lake if you are physically fit.

The paved pathway is divided by a yellow painted line that is slightly off center to give the inside lane a wider edge which is supposed to separate walkers from the wheels (skaters and bikers). Walkers are supposed to use the inside lane and can go in either direction. The wheels are supposed to go in a counter-clockwise direction in the outer lane, and for the most part, they do, but there are always the few who don't, which can be quite annoying on a crowded day. It creates tension when you see them coming from the wrong direction because you worry about them running into you in trying to avoid the wheels doing the right thing. Skaters also make you nervous in that they weave sideways as they move forward and I've actually been hit on the leg when one passed me and flung his leg out to get a forward push. They, or course, will tell you that walkers are often in the wheel lane, which is true, and are just as guilty of non-compliance as anyone else. The good thing is that most of the wheels are fair-weather types so on inclement weather days, which are frequent in Seattle, they tend to be scarce. Accidents appear to be rare and for the most part everyone seems to enjoy the lake.

I should mention that Green Lake Park is also an arboretum which has a hundred-some species of trees bordering the lake. Every so often, you will find an outdoor classroom with an instructor and students bunched around a particular tree. I always feel good when I see this, perhaps because I like the idea of students learning about the natural world and that this will make them good environmentalists in the future.

Brief Background: Green Lake was formed by the same glacial epoch that created Lake Washington and Lake Union about 50,000 years ago. It was named by David Phillips who surveyed the area in 1855 for the United States Surveyor General because of its algae blooms giving it a greenish look—a recurring problem to this day. One of the original homesteaders on the lake, Erhart Sarfried, sold subdivisions of his land to entrepreneurs who created various enterprises, from a park to lumber operations and even a trolley line connecting the area to the city. In 1903 the area comprising Green Lake became a part of Seattle's grand Olmstead Plan that was designed to connect green spaces throughout the city into an integrated whole – yes, by the sons of the famed Frederick Law Olmsted who helped create New York City's Central Park.

Once Green Lake became an official park, numerous facilities were built up over the years to accommodate the public. In 1927, a bathhouse was built at the northern end of the lake that eventually became the Bathhouse Theater. On the east side, the Green Lake Community Center was erected in 1929. Its nearby tennis courts were added in 1945, and its pool, named after Ben and Lou Evans, long time athletic supporters for Seattle parks, in 1955. A children's wading pool was also built at the north end of the lake.

I saw some original maps of the Green Lake area in its early days and noticed there were two or three small islets off its eastern shores. These were removed when the lake was dredged and lowered by seven feet to create Green Lake Park, an operation that removed the natural Ravenna Creek run-off into Lake Washington. Today, the lake is fed by rainfall, storm run-off, and Seattle's water supply. In 1936, an artificial island was created on the northern end of the lake as a wildlife refuge area which is now known as Duck Island and is the only one in the lake. Nobody is supposed to go there, leaving the place as the sanctuary that it was designed to be, but how strictly that is enforced is questionable. I've read that discarded human materials are found there occasionally.

The Green Lake Aqua Theater, at the lake's southern end, was constructed in 1950 where it held an attraction called Aqua Follies, a show that continued to run until 1965. This theater was host to many expositions that attracted celebrities, among them Bob Hope, but after the 1962 World's Fair, its popularity waned. The Grateful Dead held the last concert there in 1969. It has now been largely taken down, although a portion of it was retained as a sort of artificial ruin in memory if its glory days. It hugs a present boathouse facility, and itself provides storage for boats underneath the bleacher area left standing. Presently these structures are used for boating events and classes, popular activities thriving these days.

Personal Observations: In the years I have done my walks, I've seen some strange things, but I will keep my sightings confined to the animal behavior which, on the whole, I find more fascinating and wish to comment on. I'll only mention a few of these, ones that were quite extraordinary and will leave the reader mystified over how they could be. They are truthfully described as I saw them and I leave it to the reader to draw his or her own conclusion about them. My own questions about them are meant as food for thought; I'm sure animal behaviorists have the answers and might, in some cases, not even be surprised. But for me they were wonderful happenings, filing me with a sense of awe and certainly an appreciation of animal intelligence and the workings of nature.

One of the most amazing sights was that of three crows acting in unison to tip over a garbage can in order to have lid the fall open the cans top and expose the French fries inside. All three crows zoomed in against the upper removable lid of the can and flapped their wings wildly as they pressed on it, and actually succeeded in their endeavor. Thinking about this, there is some interesting speculation that might be made. For one thing: how did these crows communicate their intent to each other? Did all of them readily understand their purpose without having this told to them? Or did one of them get the idea and somehow conveyed it to the others. If so, how? Clearly they were unified in purpose and must have known their combined effort would succeed in accomplishing what they wanted. By the way, they could no longer do this nowadays because the cans are locked into place onto uprights and can no longer be tipped over.

I have a begrudging admiration for crows. By that I mean, I do not like it that they scare away the song birds whenever they seem to be present, but there is no question that crows are smart. You don't have to be around them for long to come to that realization. I'm sure nearly everyone has seen how crows often skip rather than walk (other birds do too, but not as frequently) and seem to actually enjoy engaging in this activity. I think that is exactly right —they skip because they get a pleasure out of it. They are utterly relaxed around human and are certainly not intimidated by our size or actions. They take note of you, watching you as if assessing what you are doing and even as if familiar with you. Certain crows seem to know that I regularly walk around Green Lake and won't move away as I approach them, letting me walk by within a few inches of them before their 'skip' away —and then only a few feet off. What other bird does that?

Just recently I had a rather eerie experience involving crows. I was walking along the path around the lake when a multitude of them —there must have been at least one hundred— kept apace of me by flying from tree to tree parallel to me. Talk about a weird situation —this went on for at least one quarter of a mile causing me to worry if it would ever end. It conjured up visions of Alfred Hitchcock's 1963 movie, The Birds. I've read about occasional attacks of crows on people, but until this even took place I never paid particular attention to such a possibility, but, believe me, I very much thought about that at the time —spooky.

Crows do have a temper and I've seen it demonstrated on several occasions. In one case, I saw a single crow attack a squirrel. You would expect a four legged critter to be able to fend off a bird on the ground, but it was clear that the crow was the aggressor and had the squirrel running for its life. In another case I saw one crow severely chewing out another, cawing at it mercilessly and continually —it just wouldn't let the matter rest. Whatever that crow did to piss off his or her mate, the castigation went on for almost fifteen minutes. It reminded me of the proverbial hen-pecked husband that you saw in early television sitcoms.

Ducks are a prevalent sight in most city parks and Green Lake is no exception. One day, on a clear sunny morning, I saw a mother duck leading her chain of little ducklings along the western shore of the lake where there is a sizeable area of water lily pads. As they were moving along the chain got longer and longer as one of the ducklings apparently could not keep up with the rest of the brood. When the mother duck noticed this she did something quite remarkable. She moved her brood to the edge of the lily pads and cordoned them off into a secure area by using her bill to enclose them within the pads when she moved the interlocking plants around the brood keeping the ducklings within it. She then went to fetch the lagging little duckling back to the fold.

I found this quite amazing, and heart-warming. First of all, even though there must have been as many as ten or twelve ducklings in the brood, the fact that one of them was falling further and further behind did not go unnoticed. Next, the idea that the mother would have to secure her band before going back to retrieve the laggard seems to suggest a mental process at work —I'm sure the intent behind the enclosure was to keep the brood intact and prevent its spreading out over a wide area rather than protect it from predators (of which there are few). Once everyone was together again, the mother duck removed the connecting lily barrier and the brood proceeded on its quest, whatever that was. I enjoyed observing this —a crisis situation resolved through good decision making at a very elementary level.

Another incident involving ducks was more tragic. The merry month of May, as the song in the musical Camelot tells us, is a time of high testosterone activity, and, as I witnessed, that can by trying for the females of the species. One year, I saw that one white duck, a female, was being very aggressively pursued by two males. I mean this pursuit was relentless, offering no respite for the victim, on the waters, in flight, around trees, and even if she managed to elude one of the pursuers, the other took up the cause; you could see that the effort was wearing her out. When the males caught up with her and did their thing, it still did not end there, as more came to the scene after the same reward. The next day, I saw the white duck was dead, lying below some tree not far from the pathway, with the back of its neck rubbed raw (it looked as though it had been almost eaten through). I must have come upon the scene shortly after it died and before the clean-up crews could remove it.

On reflecting over this, I am struck by its signification. Why this one particular duck? Did she exude a weakness that made her more vulnerable to being victimized than her peers, so that the males readily picked up on it and refused to give her a break? Did the act of one male pursuing it encourage others to do likewise? How many culprits were involved? My guess is that it did not end with the two initial ones, and that others joined in, and then again the same two over and over. A sober realization one comes to is that nature is cruel to the weaker members of a species. I assume that such may be the case with human beings as well —those of us who are perceived as being weak are picked upon by others as if it was invitation to abuse. The bully recognizes he or she will get away with whatever is planned, that the victim is essentially helpless in providing any defense, and this provides the encouragement to proceed with further harassment. With the ducks, such behavior is instinctive; one would like to believe that with humans it's a matter of choice, making bullying all the more intolerable.

On that note, I will end my comments on what I've observed at Green Lake and my general review of its facts and history. This sort of information tends to be of an impersonal nature and therefore runs counter to my purpose for creating this book. My intent is to introduce the reader to the images and wonder that I experience when walking on the pathway around the lake; in other words, to present a highly personalized description of what I see and how I react to it, with the hope that the reader will likewise enjoy these pleasures.

So, having given you a basic description of my favorite hangout in Seattle, let me now invite you to accompany me on my photographic journey of the place. I see beauty everywhere I look in this park, at any season and any time of day; on occasions I will make a comment on a particular scene to share with you what appeals to me about it; on other occasions I will make a comment on whatever came to my mind upon seeing a particular sight. I have broken the pictures into categories which are appropriate for them ranging from the simplest, which I call Zen, to the complex —the ones evoking a mood. Join me now, and let us together enjoy the pleasures of my Green Lake walks.

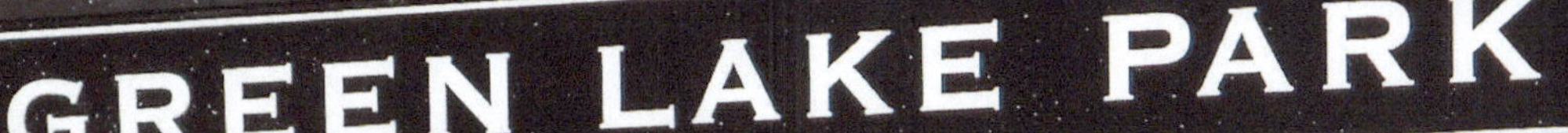

GREEN LAKE PARK


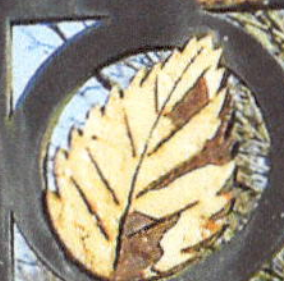

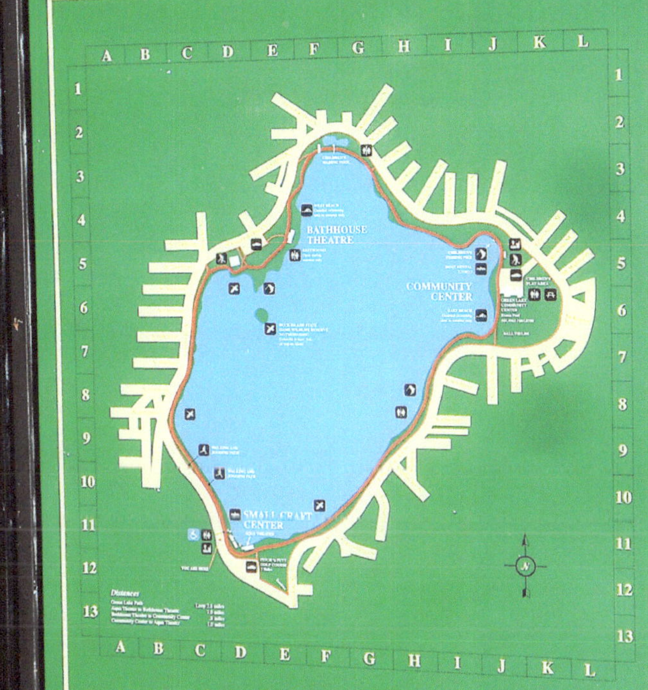

A B C D E F G H I J K L
Recreation Information
Activities          Map Grid Locator
Boating             D-11, J-5
Concessions         J-5, C-11
Fishing Piers       E-6, H-8, J-5
Parking             D-12, D-5, J-5
Paths
Picnicking          K-6
Restrooms           J-6, E-5, H-8, D-11
Swimming Beaches    F-4, J-6
Tennis Courts       D-5, J-5
Wildlife Reserve    C-8, D-5, E-6, F-11
Destinations        Map Grid Locator
Aqua Theater        D-11
Ball Fields         J-6
Bathhouse Theatre   E-4
Boat Rental         J-5
Children's Play Area K-5
Community Center    J-6
Duck Island         E-6
Evans Pool          J-6
Pitch 'n Putt       E-12
Small Craft Center  D-11
Wading Pool         F-2
Swimming Safely
Boating Safely
Seattle Department of Parks and Recreation
BATHHOUSE THEATRE
COMMUNITY CENTER
SMALL CRAFT CENTER
A B C D E F G H I J K L


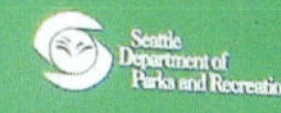


Green Lake Path Courtesy Rules
Walkers, Runners & Baby Strollers Use Inside Lane
Bicycles and Skates Use Outside Lane
STAY ON YOUR SIDE OF THE PATH
Follow the Arrows
SLOW
Maintain a safe speed
Slow down at congested areas
Obey Leash & Scoop Laws
Use Inside Lane Unless Race Training
Outside Lane:
Bicycles, Skaters - Counter Clockwise direction ONLY
Inside Lane:
Walkers, Runners - Clockwise direction recommended
Be Courteous, Respect Others

# Green Lake Zen

## In praise of minimalism: less is more.

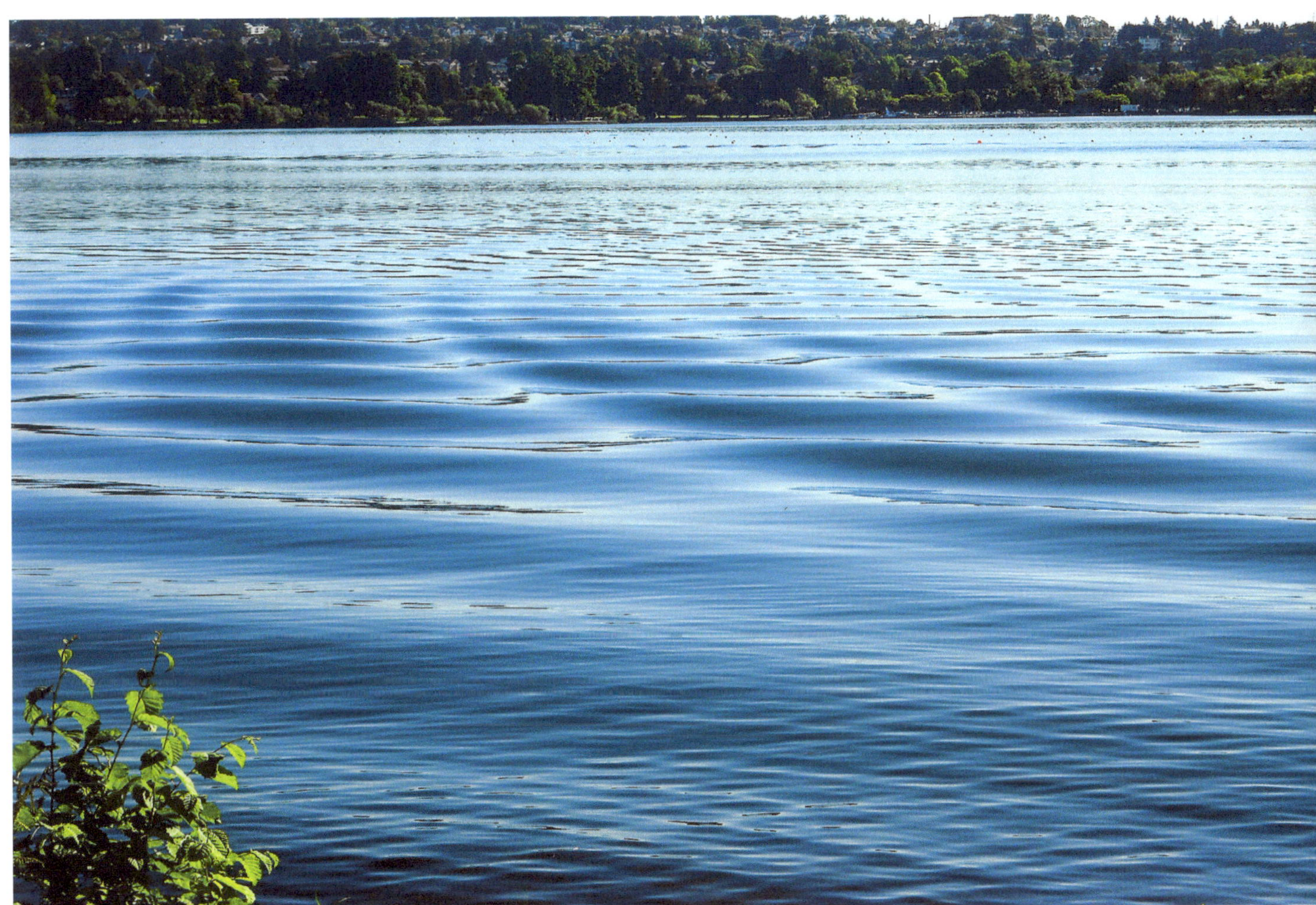

Seen here is of the wake created when a group of rowers came by in their racing boat, a common site at Green Lake. The repetitive and unusual pattern of the wave action was beautiful to see. On a clear day, the water is as blue as the sky.

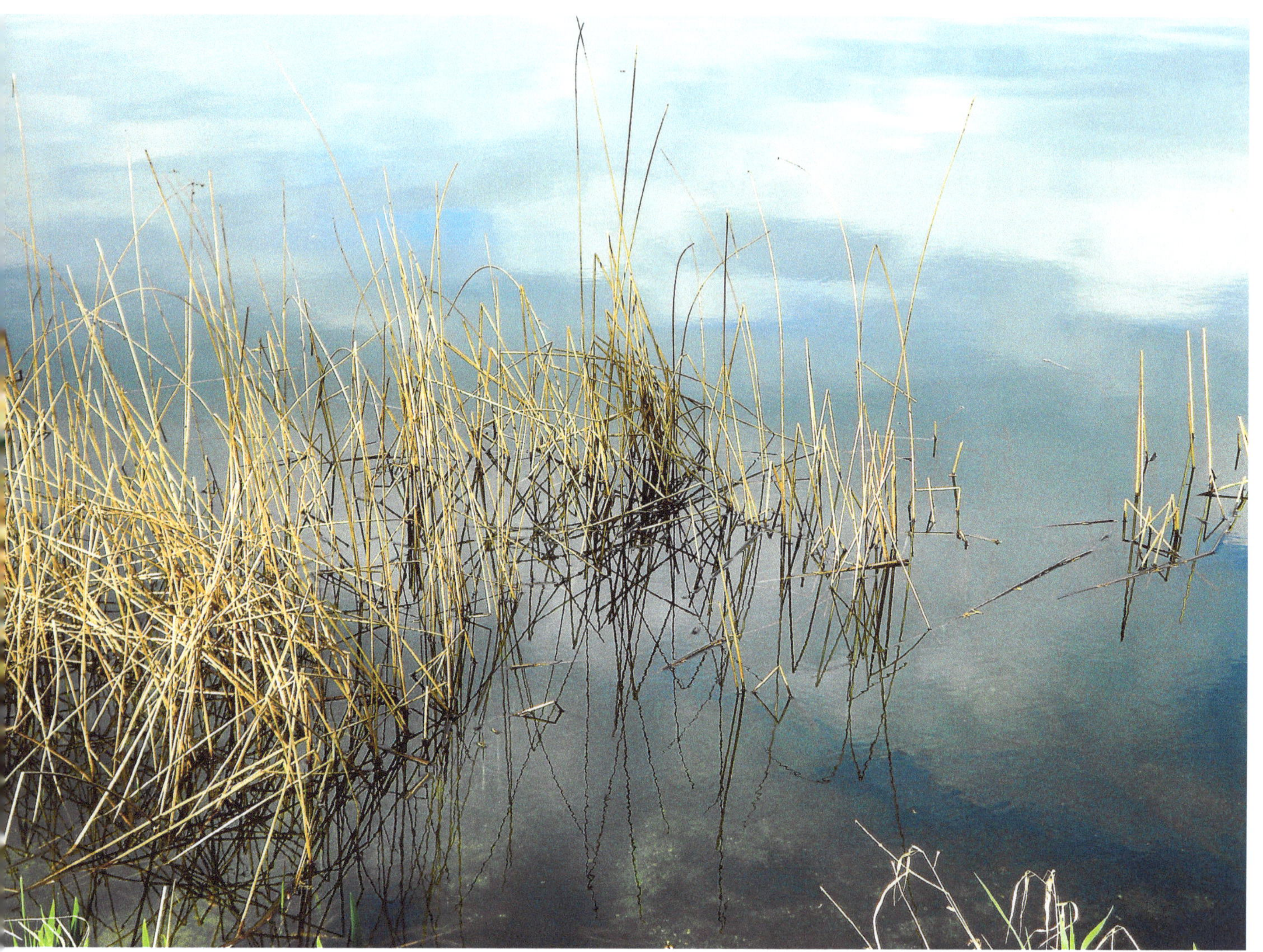

# Making the Mundane Interesting

Even these ordinary reeds create a beauty of their own. I think it is the yellow of the reeds set against the grays of the water that makes this scene interesting —a nice color combination.

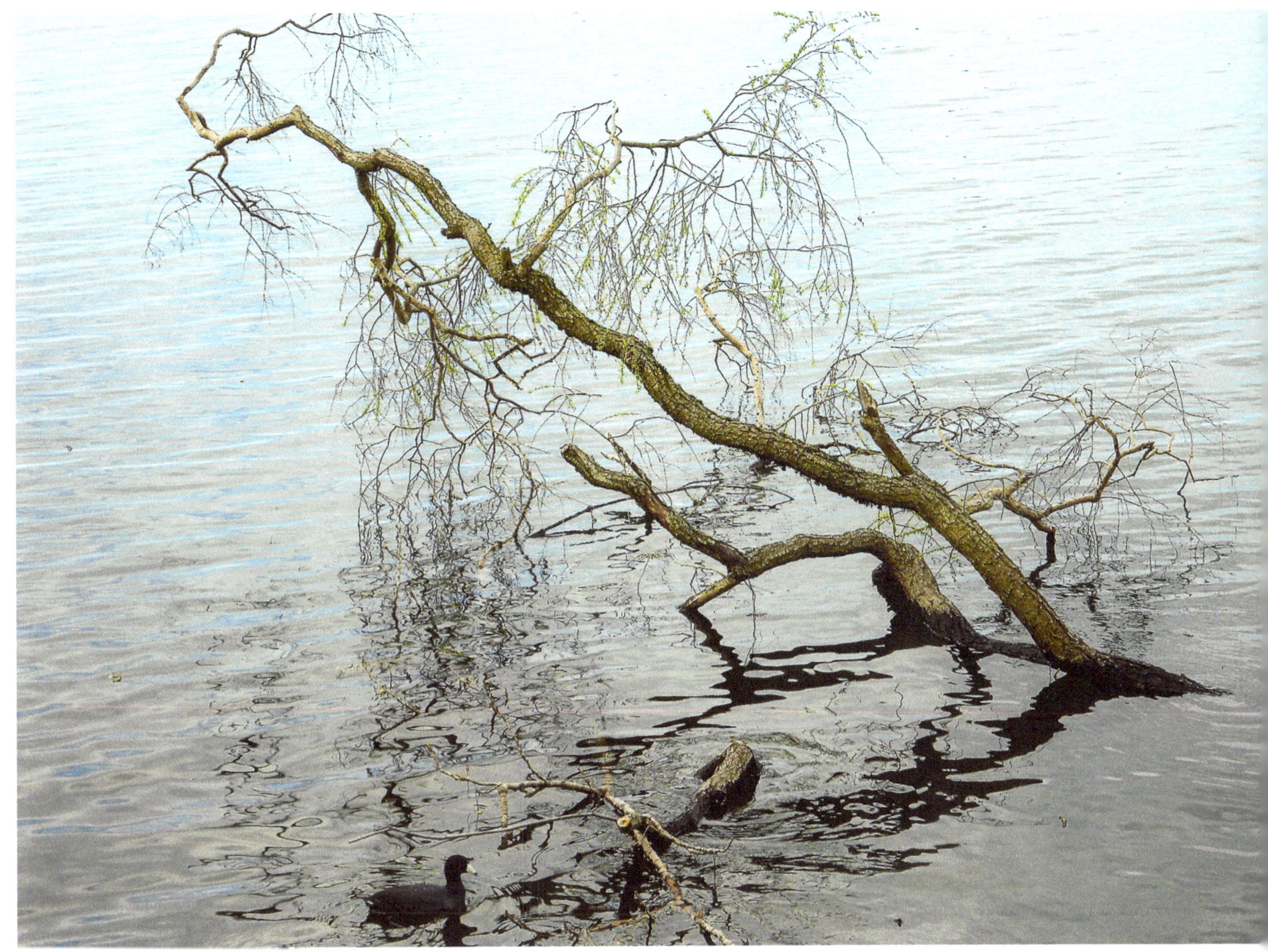

# Tree in Water

How many of us have passed by this spot on the lake? For years it was almost a landmark there, but then a fierce storm in April, 2015, finally changed its location when powerful gusts apparently ripped it loose from where it was anchored and blew it next to the shore's stone wall. It is now emplaced there.

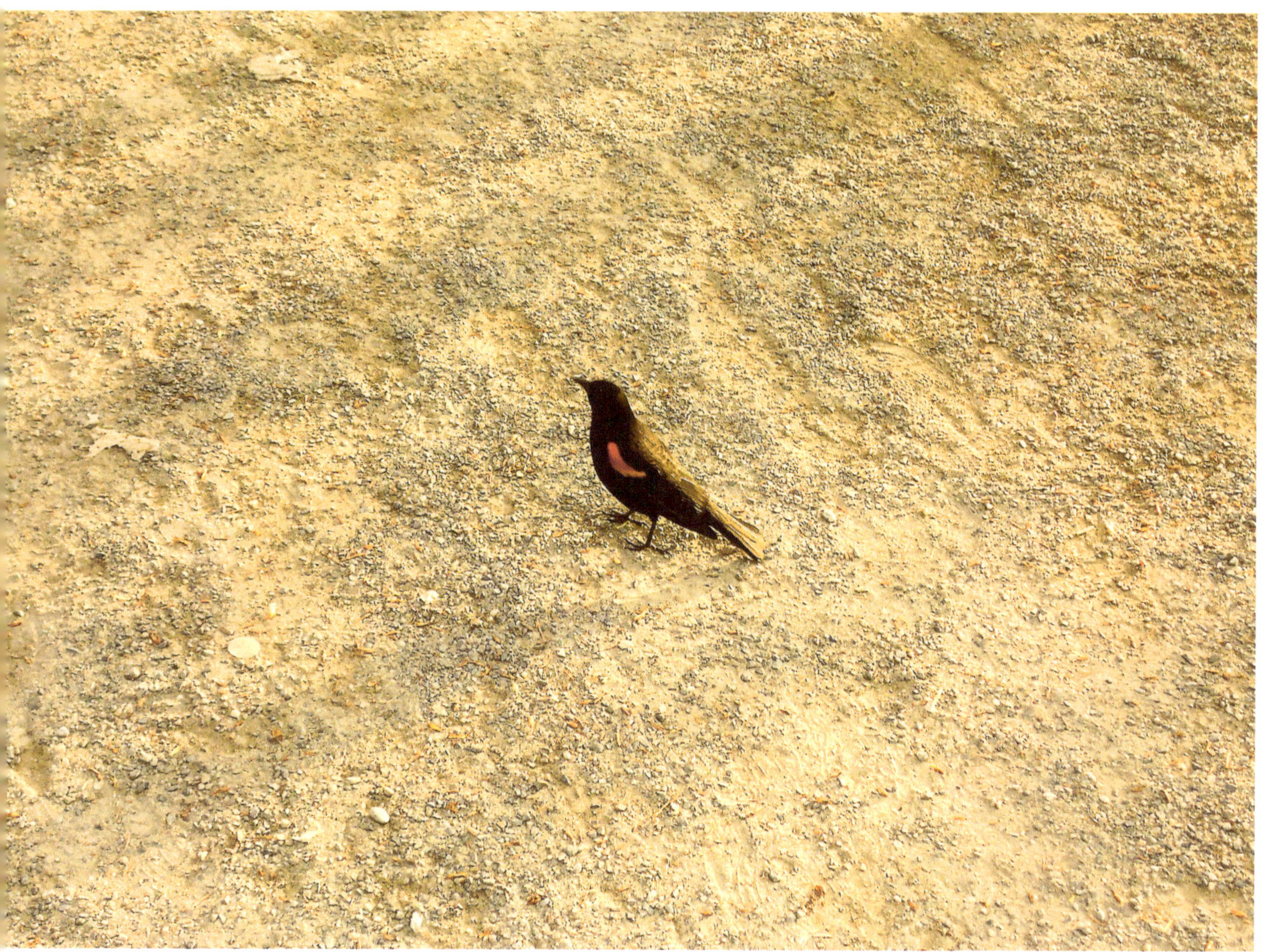

# Annual Homesteader

Each spring Redwing Blackbirds make themselves at home in the cattail marshes along the west side of Green Lake. They come to the same place year after year, but by fall they move elsewhere. Their melodic chirping is a welcome change after hearing the year-round cawing of the crows.

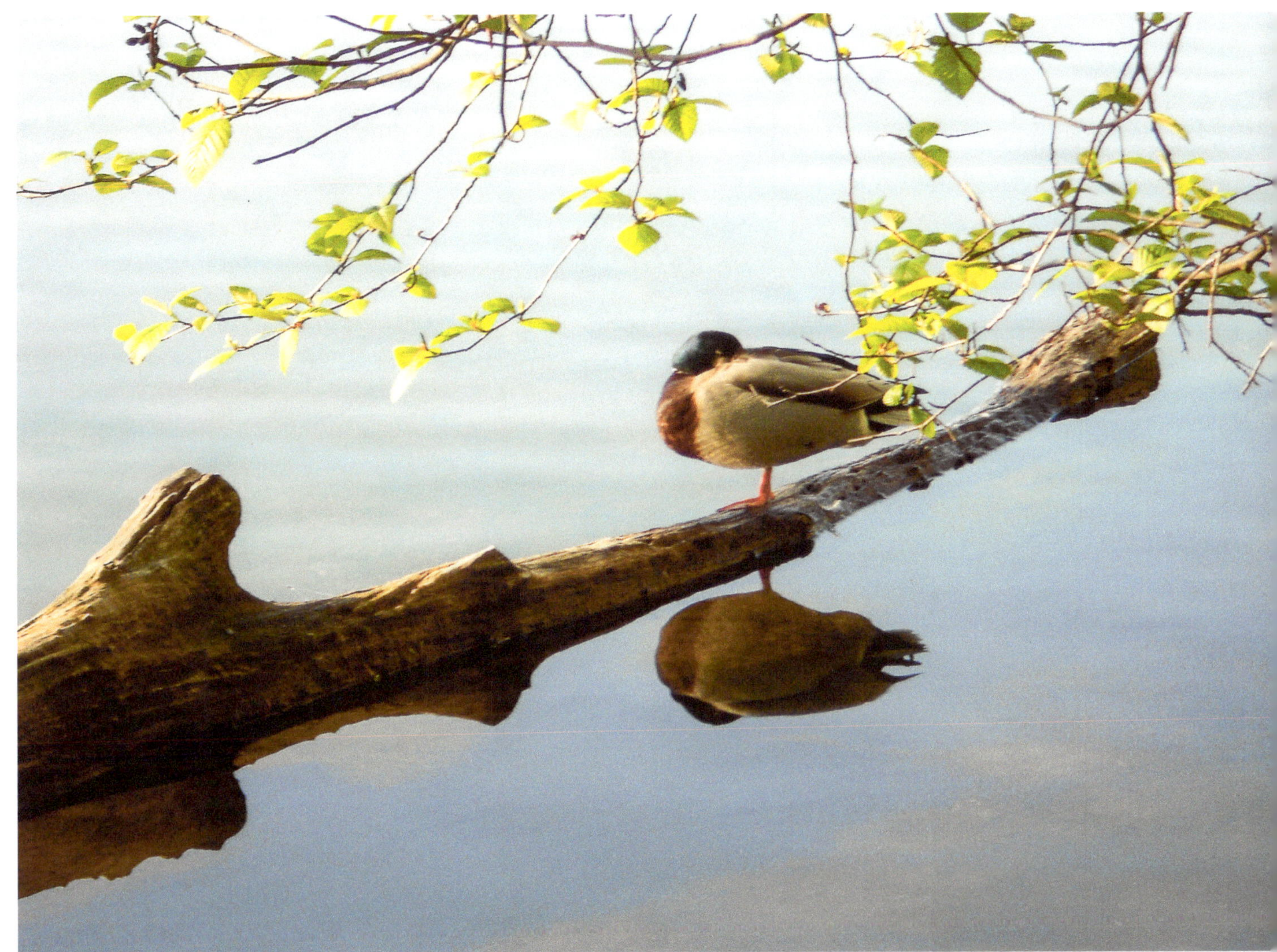

# Greeting the Dawn

This is my favorite picture that I've taken at Green Lake and remains so even after many photographs subsequent to it. It was taken on an early Saturday morning in May.  Everything about it exudes serenity and bliss. It holds the distinction of motivating me to create this book —an absolute gem.

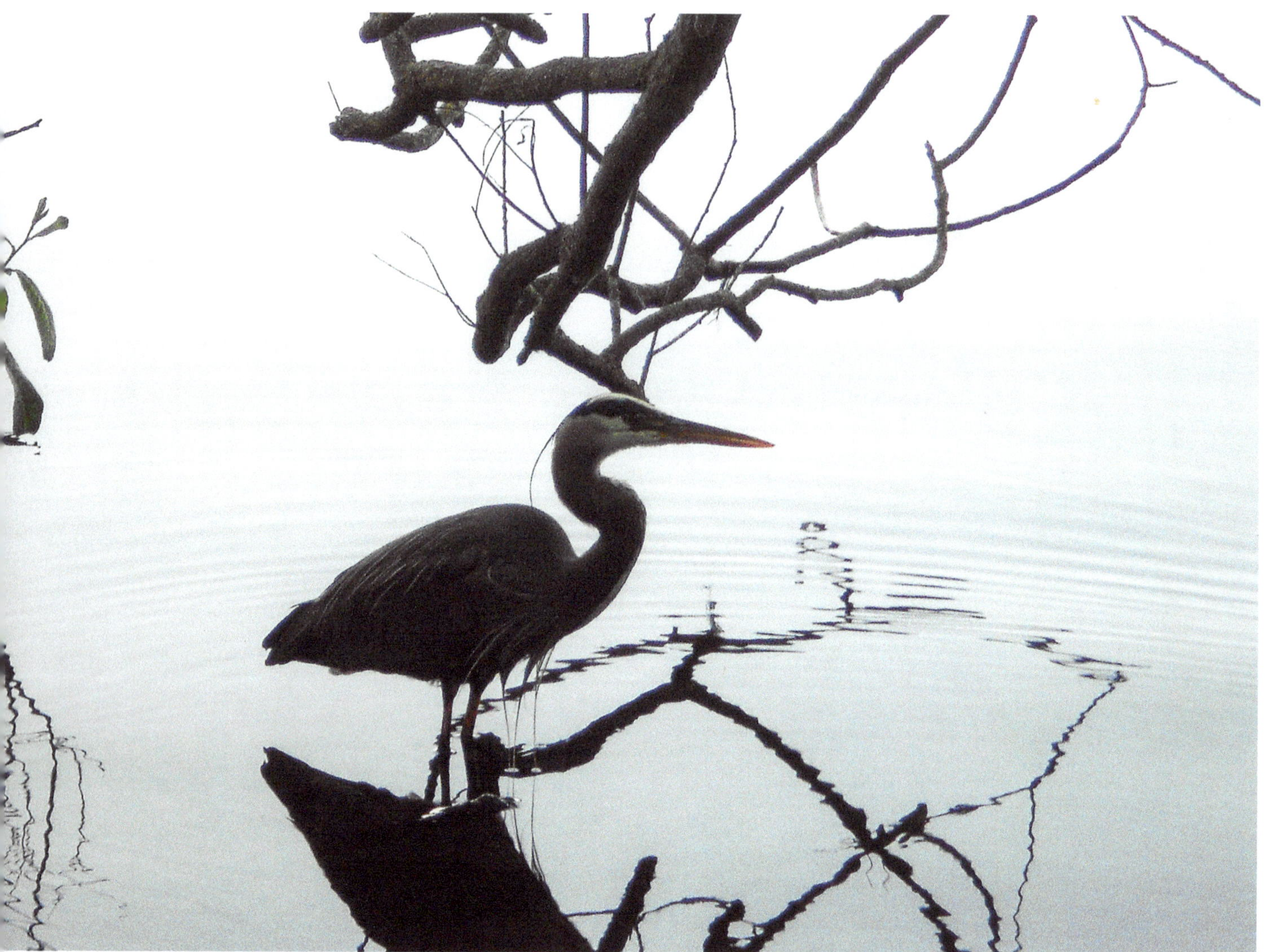

# Calligraphy

This scene reminds me of Chinese pictographs with the heron constituting part of the lettering.  There is only one resident heron at the lake that I know of and it becomes a familiar fixture when making the rounds. It can be spotted at different sections of the lake and often close to the shore. I call it my friend and miss it on the days I don't see it.

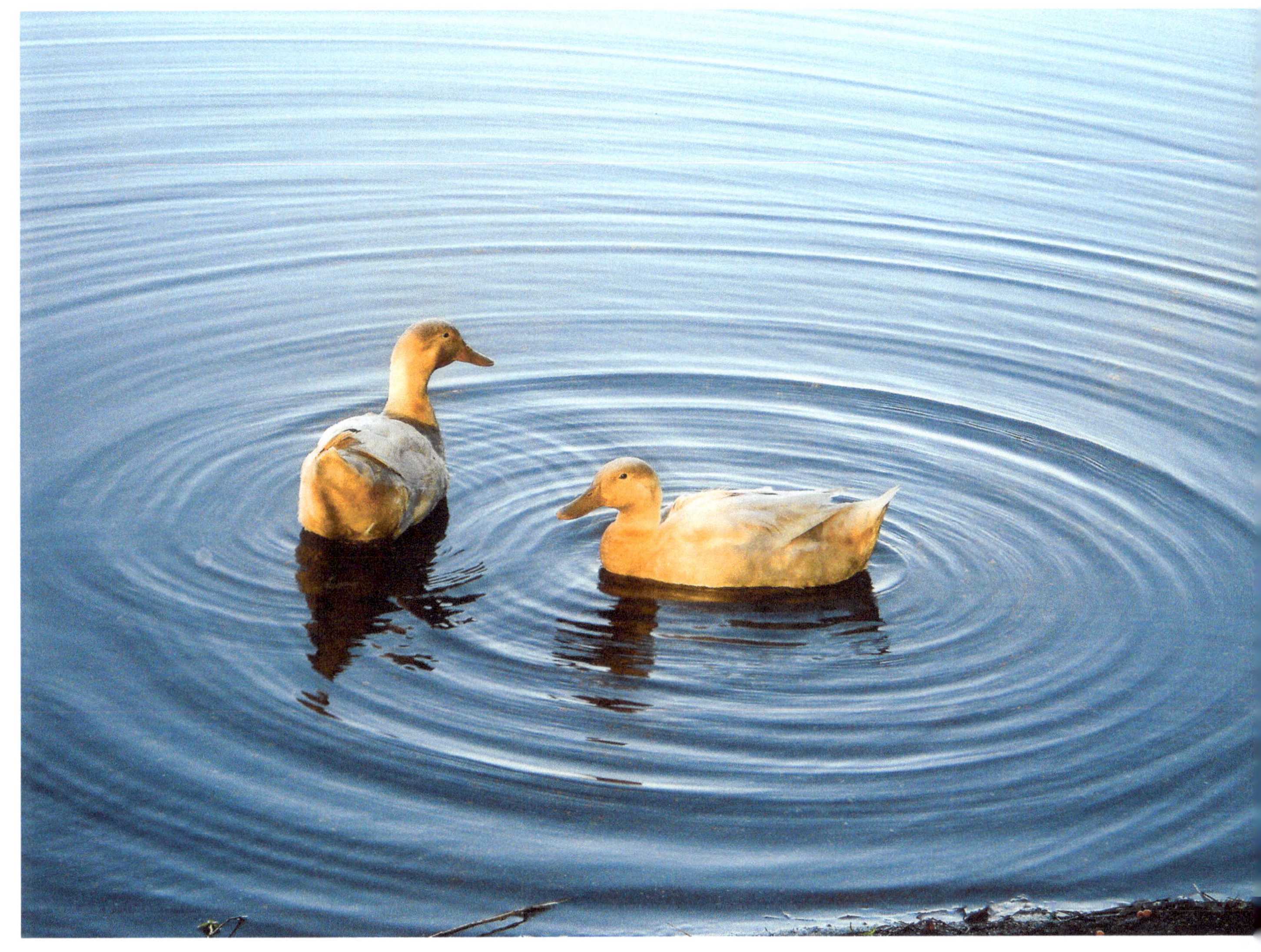

# Converging Circles

Another gem. These two ducks are constantly seen with each other's company —never apart and on their own. I've become fond of seeing them paired up like that and seek them out whenever I make my walks. It's like being witness to a happy marriage; makes you feel good inside.

# Silver Streaks

The gray hue of an overcast day reflected in the water is probably more typical than the blue of a clear day in Seattle. That's fine with me; I enjoy the lake in all conditions. A very Zen-like picture, the streaks are the wake of a boat having gone by in the distance.

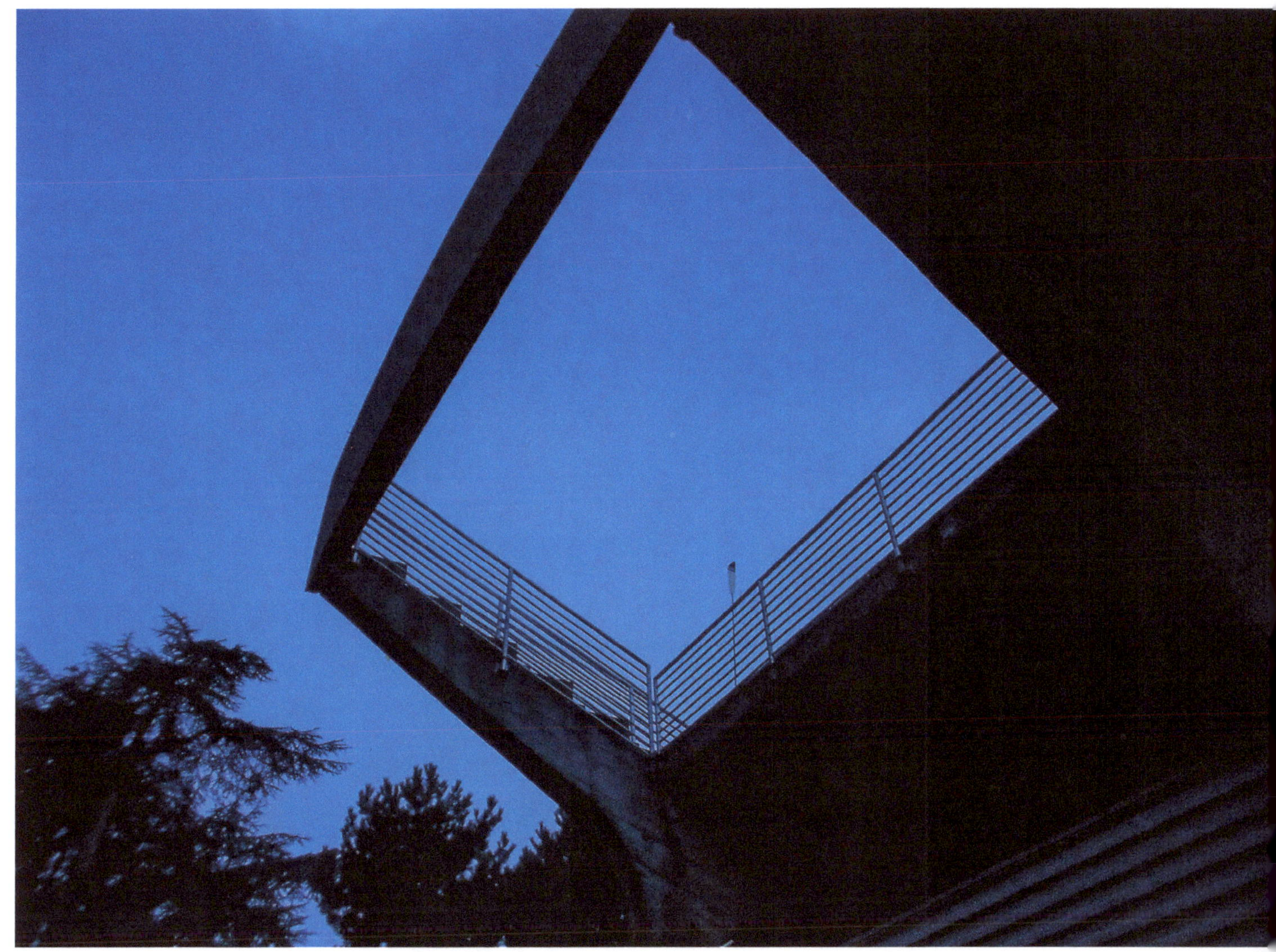

# Remnant of a Former Glory

Rather than completely tear down the Aqua-Theater that stood at Green Lake's southern end, parts of it were retained as a memorial to its earlier popularity. I'm not sure what to make of it. There is little romanticism attached to an artificially created ruin, but, to its credit, many people, especially kids, enjoy climbing up the old steps. The metal barriers were put in to protect them from falling or to prohibit them from using that area. The gaping hole you see is what's left of the former bleachers in this section of the Theater.

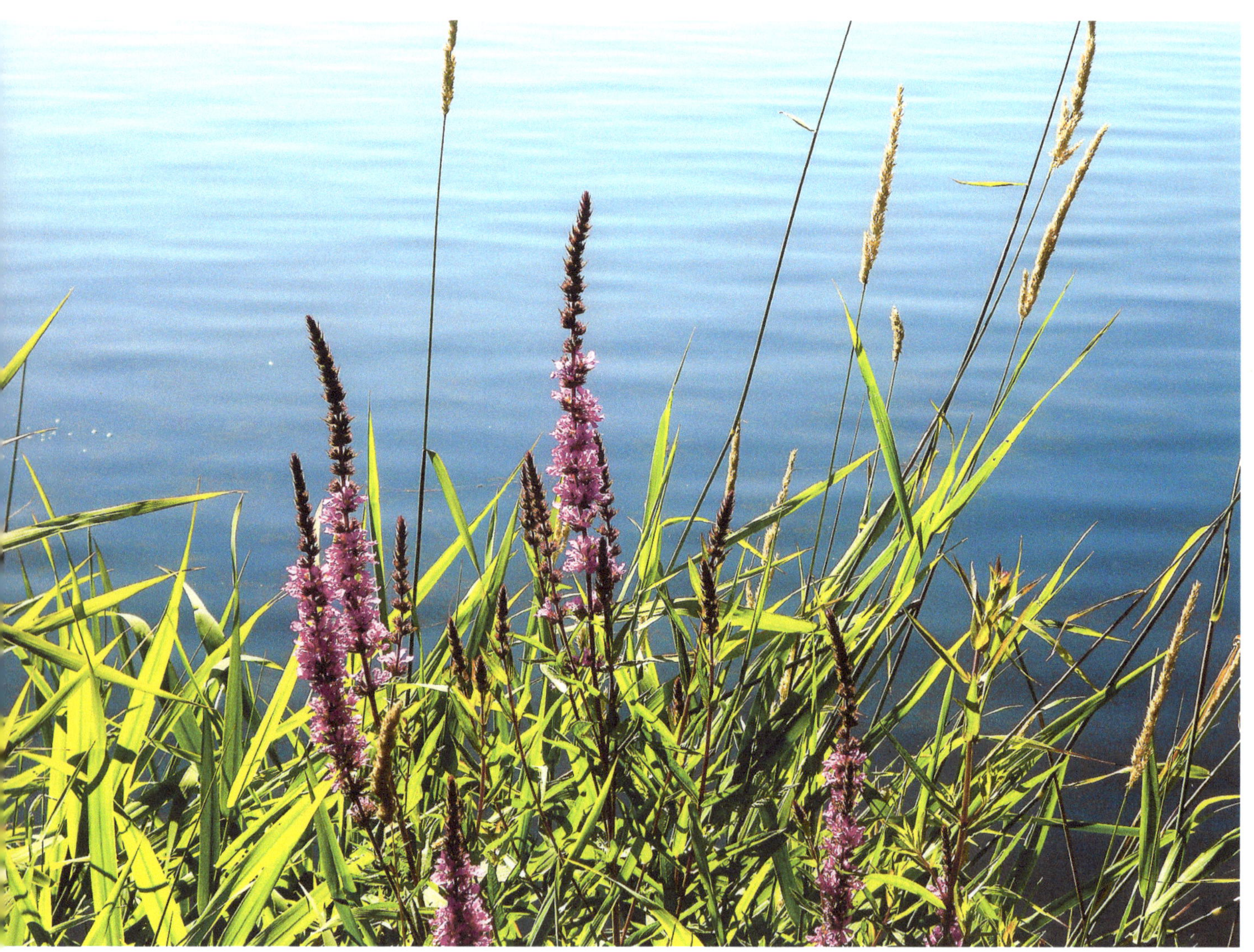

*Nature does not aim to deceive. Everything that it
produces it does so with clarity and truth.*

**–Xenophon**

I don't really think this is a true observation, as much of our
planet's flora and fauna involves life in camouflage and deception
but it goes well with this picture.

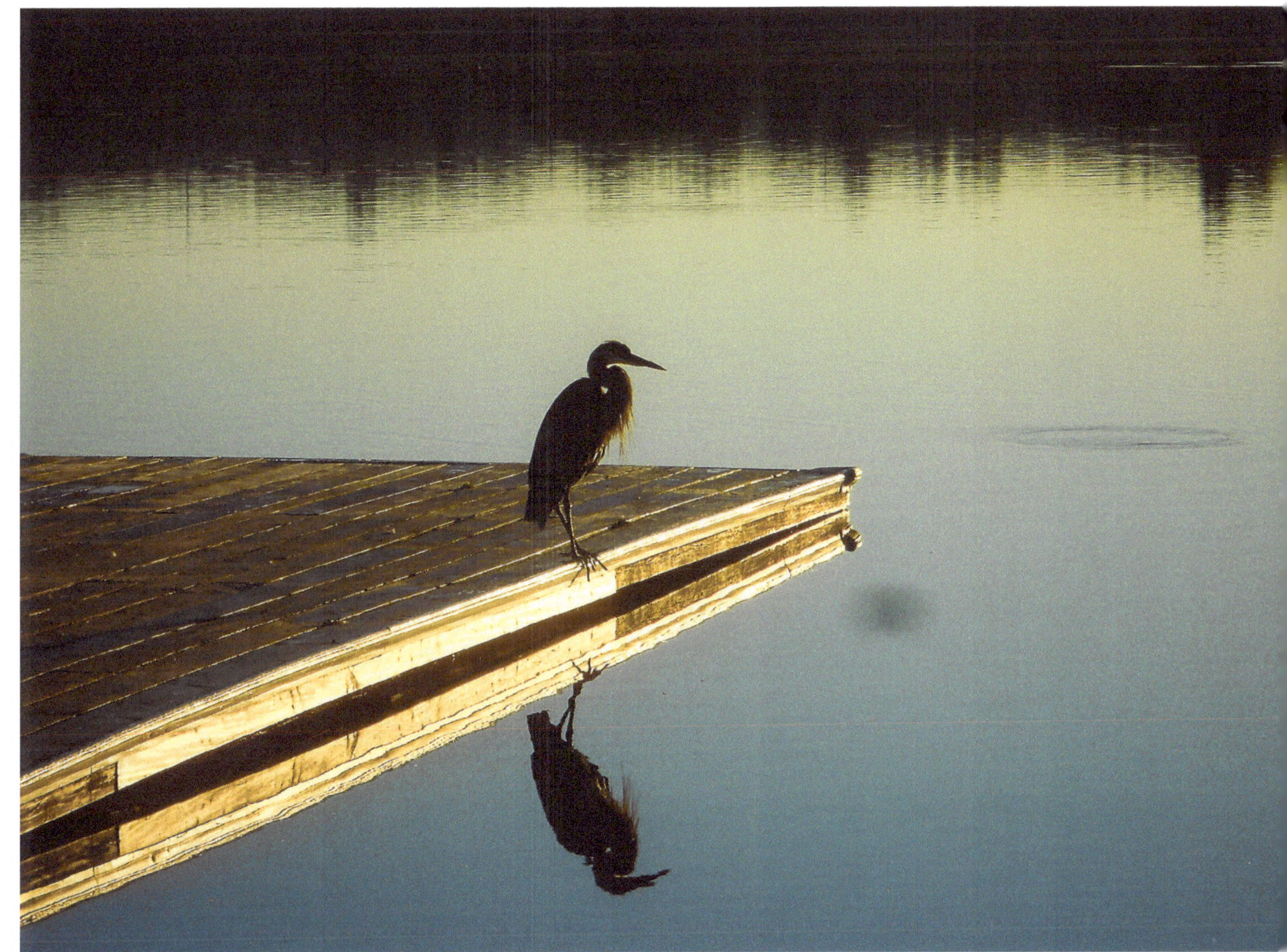

# By Dawn's Early Light

My friend, the Blue Heron, is soaking up the warmth and glory of a sunny morning. This is another one of my favorite pictures despite the smudge mark that was on the lens of my Coolpix when I took it that can be seen in the water. Composition wise, it's a wonderful photograph.

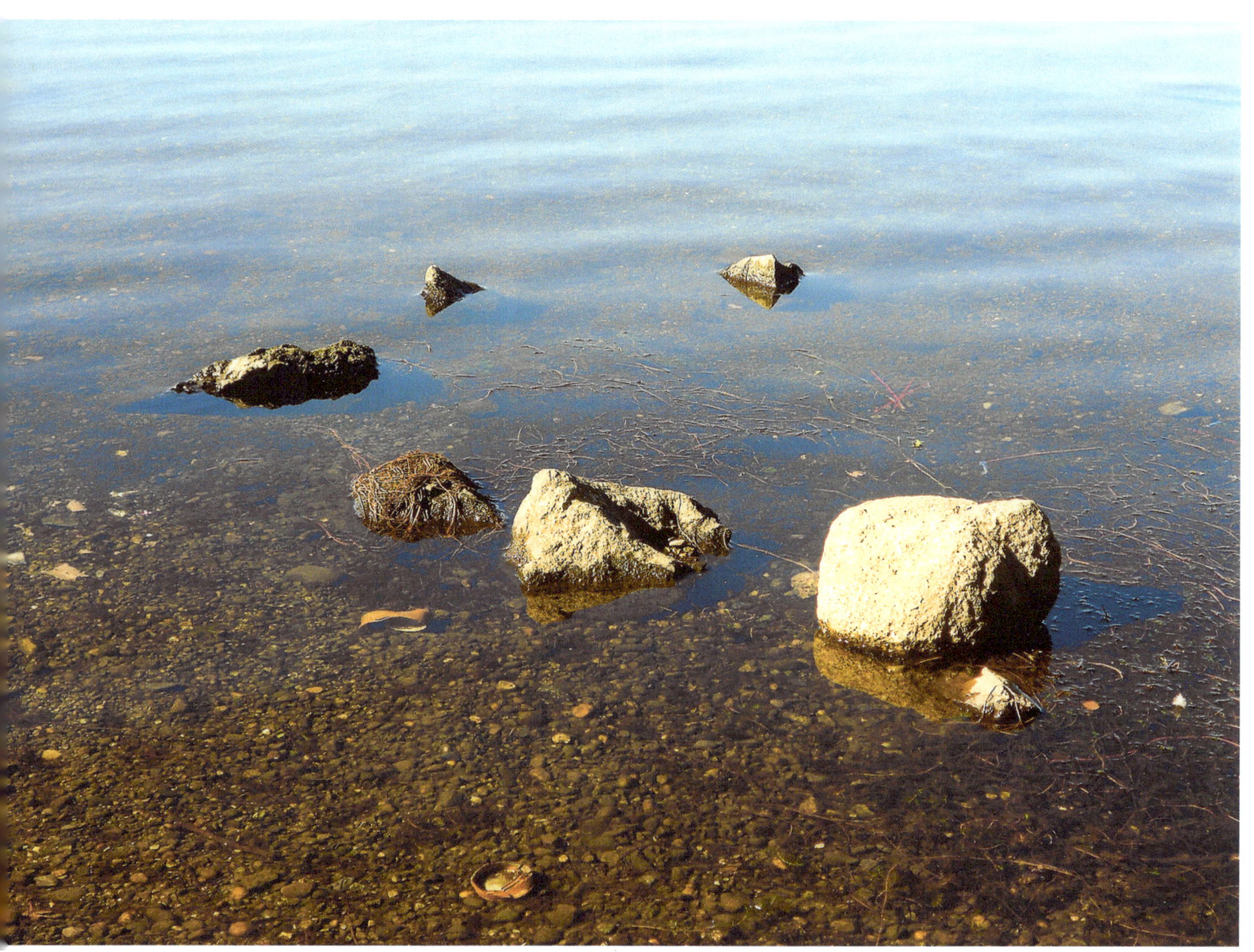

# Water with Rocks

If you can visualize the water as small crushed rocks, this would be a nice Japanese garden —actually it violates the triangulation principles entailed in these gardens but still, the idea is there.

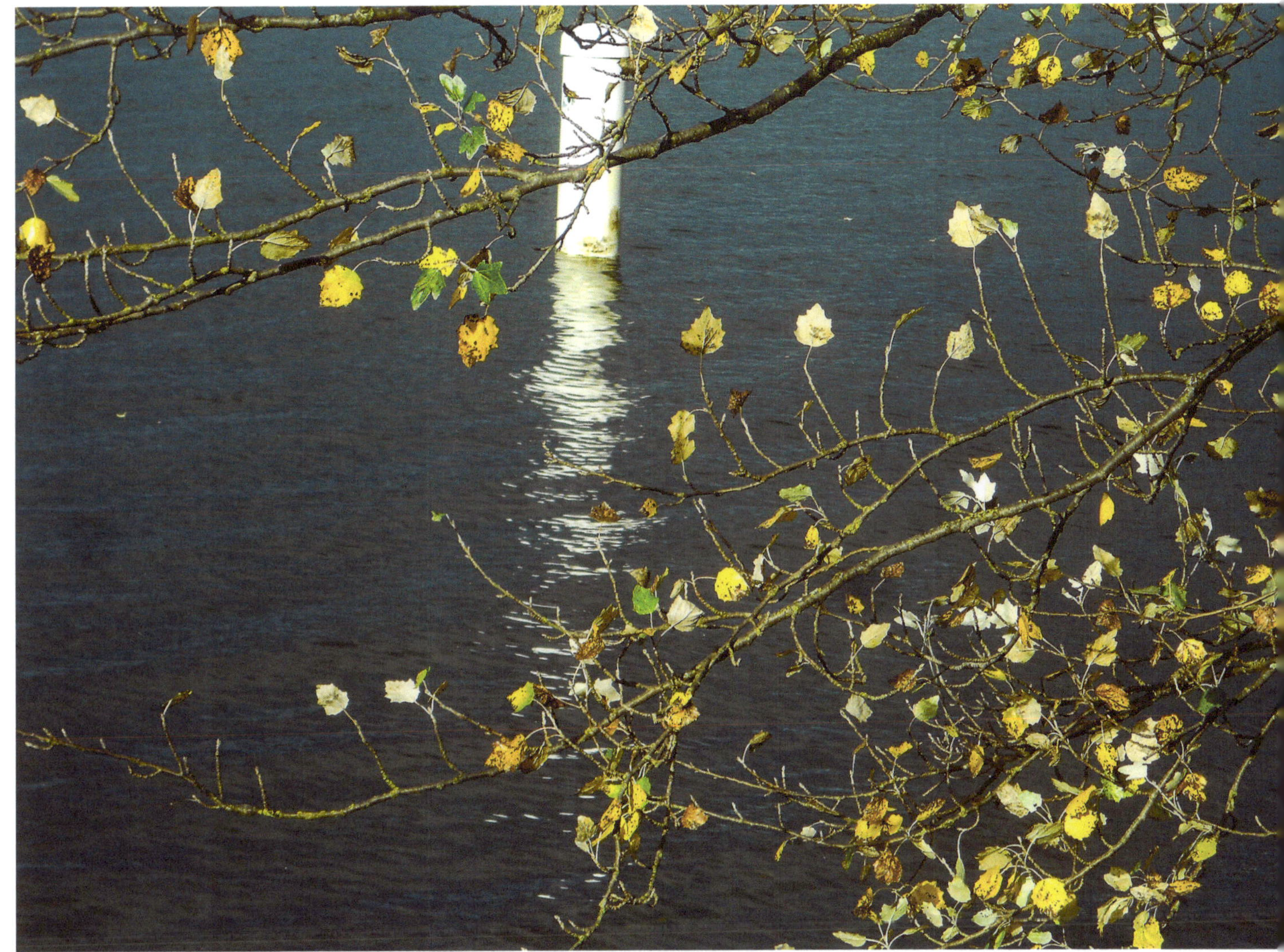

# Post in Water

These white painted posts are used to delineate the boundary of the swimming areas at Green Lake. There are two such spots, one by the Center House in the northeast and the other by the Bathhouse Theater in the northwest. A photographic gem, the picture was taken in October as revealed by with the thinning leaves and the water reflecting an overcast sky.

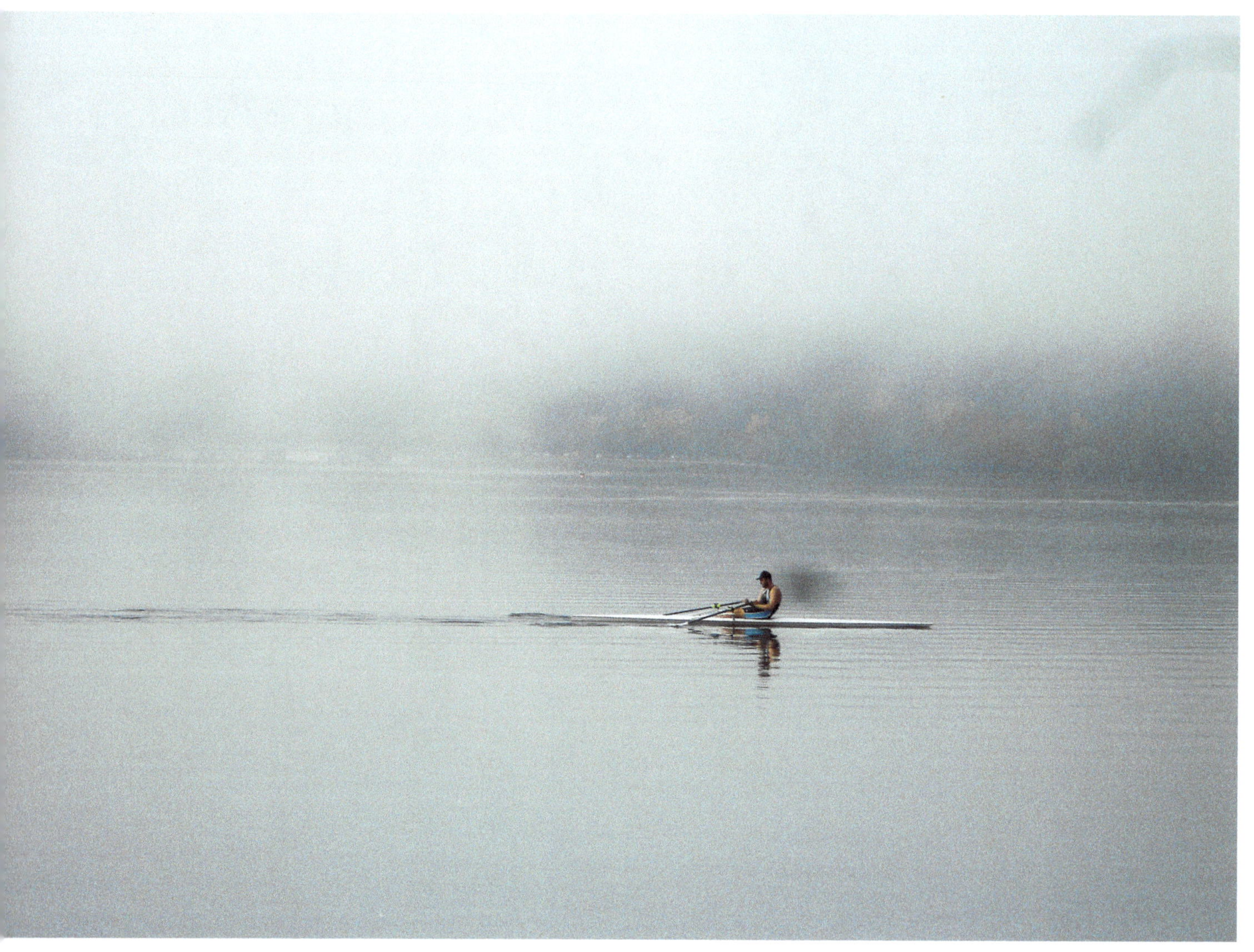

# Solitude

I like this picture for its sheer simplicity. Taken on a foggy morning, it evokes emptiness and quietness. I originally titled it 'loneliness' but that would be a misnomer; when you are engaged in this kind of activity, you want to be by yourself and are therefore not alone. Solitude is desired; loneliness is not.

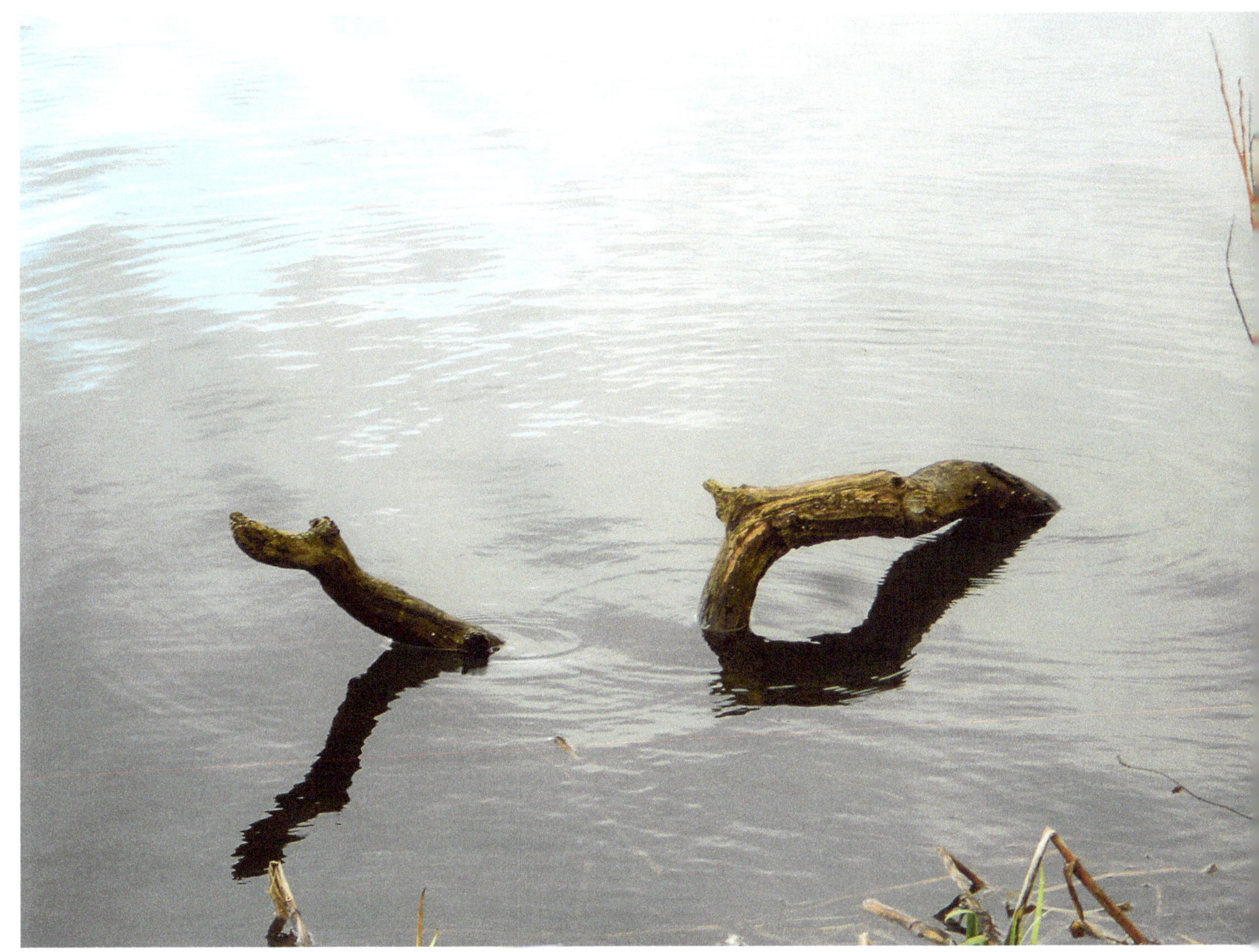

# Nessie

It's considerably smaller than Loch Ness's monster, but with a little bit of imagination this partly submerged tree branch does resemble a water snake, one with a happy smile on its face and with bulging eyes.

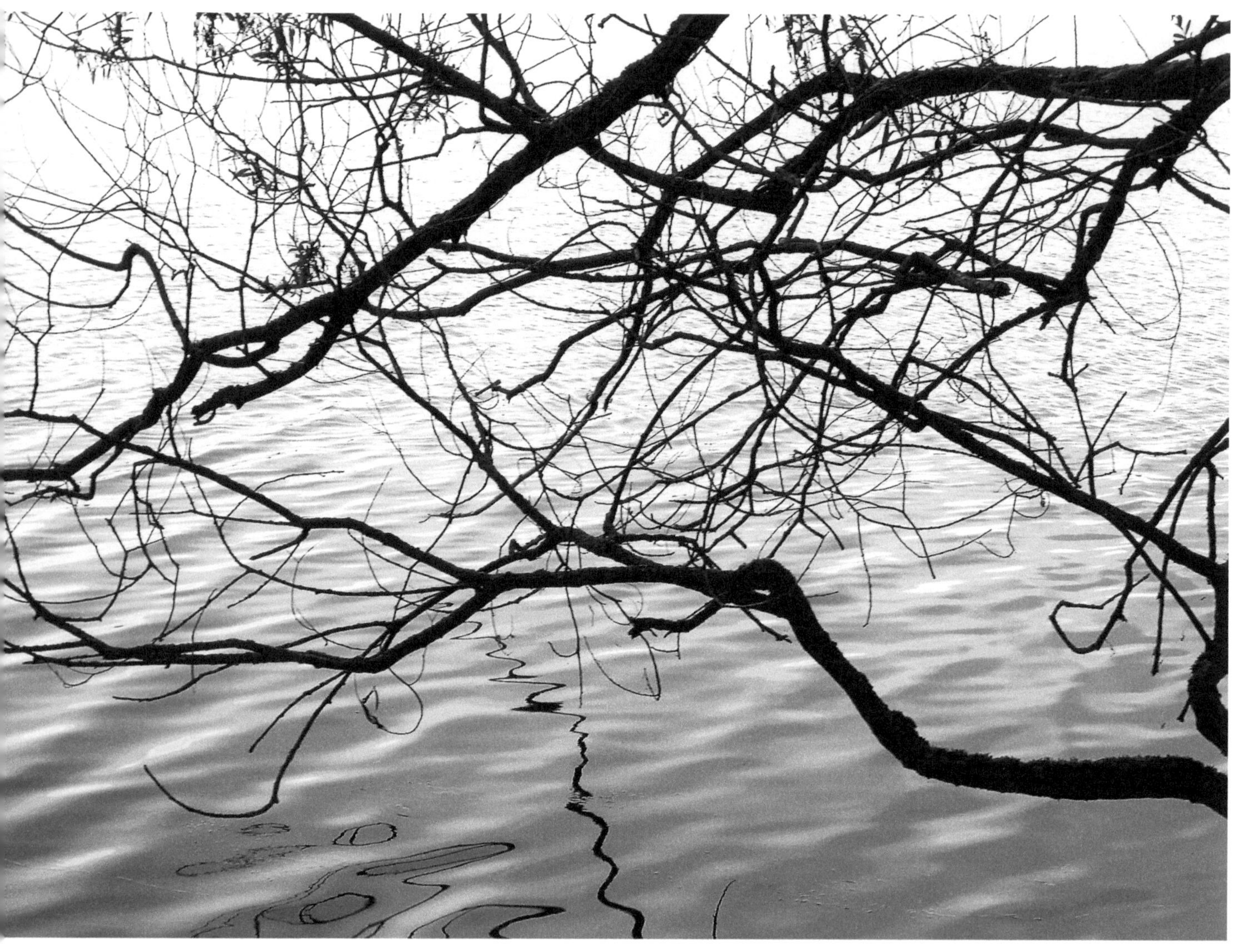

# Black on Gray

I find this scene interesting —the reflection seen in the water makes this appear like something out of an animated film. It also looks like an oil slick.

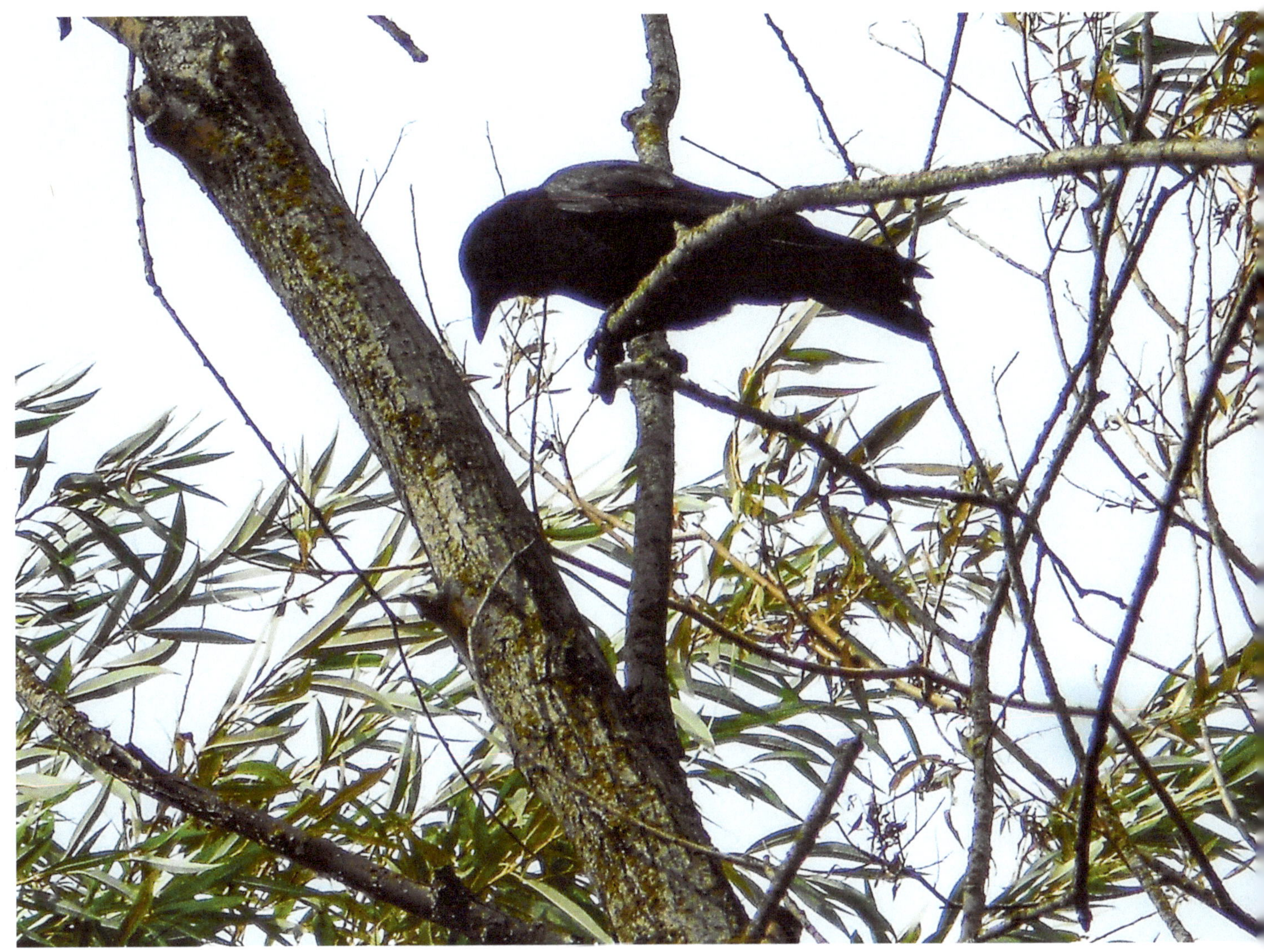

# Bucking the Wind

This scene reminds a lot of a Japanese print or what you would see on a silk screen. You can almost feel the gust of a wind tearing at the leaves —a wonderful shot.

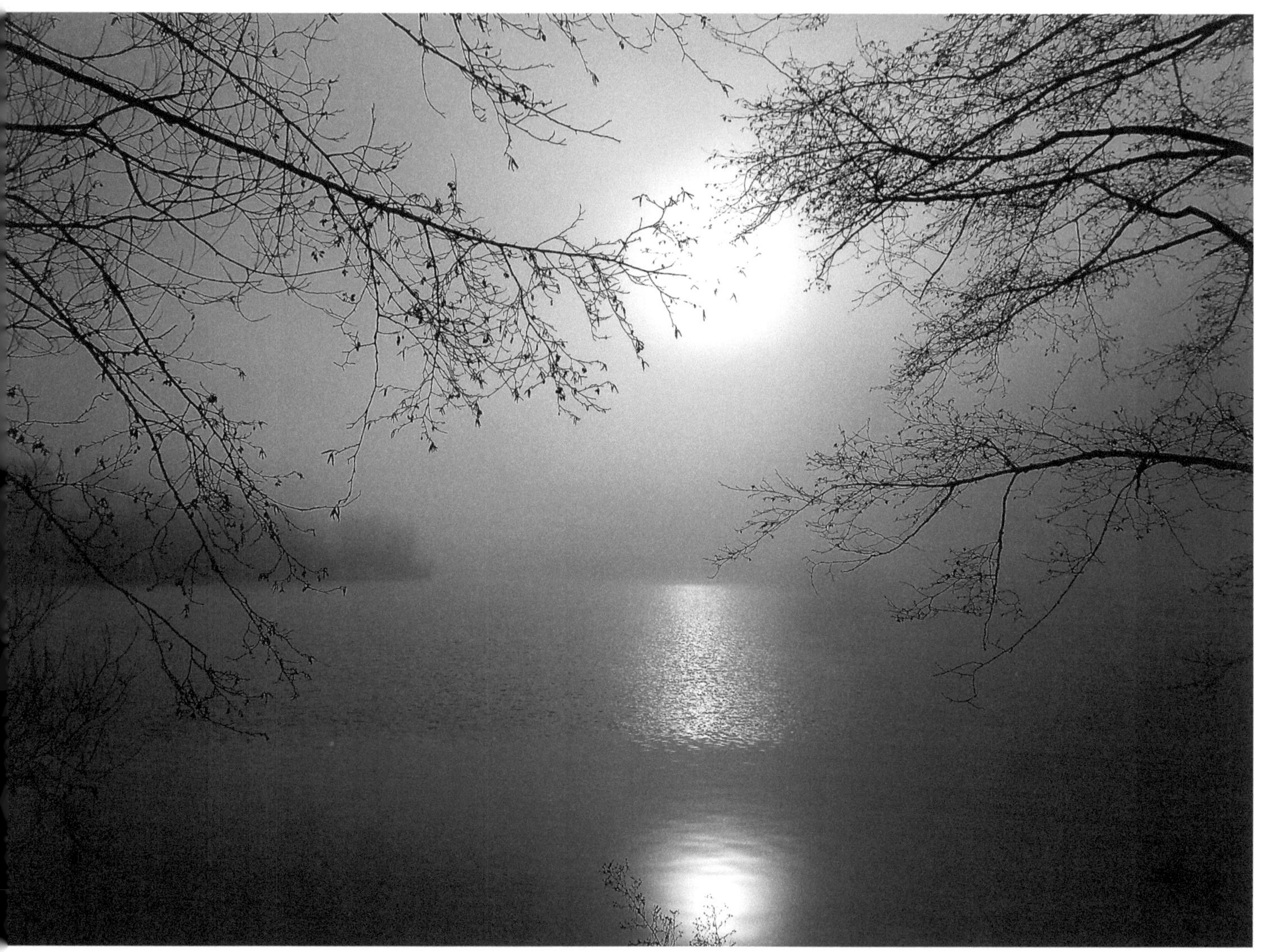

# Morning Fog

I like this scene for its bare essentials. There is little variation in the
theme and a minimum range of color, and yet is very expressive
-the essence of Zen.

# Silk Screen Print

Looking more like an artistic rendition than an actual scene, this view of the northern peninsula, called Prospect Point, jutting out towards Duck Island consists of only shades of gray. Typical of such fog-shrouded scenes, there are no other colors that can be made out.

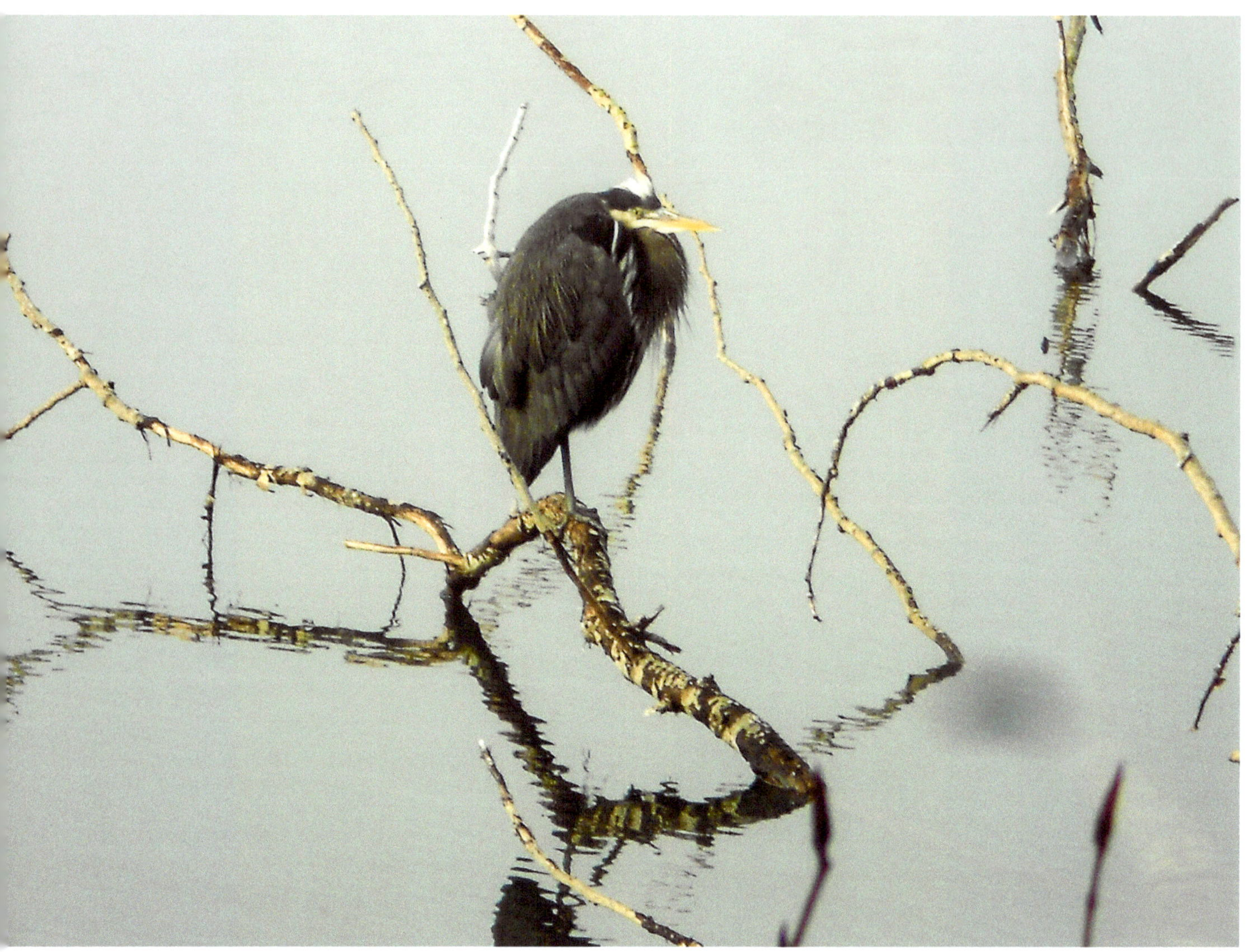

# Disheveled

There's my blue heron friend again, looking as scraggly as the winter branches he is resting on. It's interesting how they retract their long necks into almost disappearing.

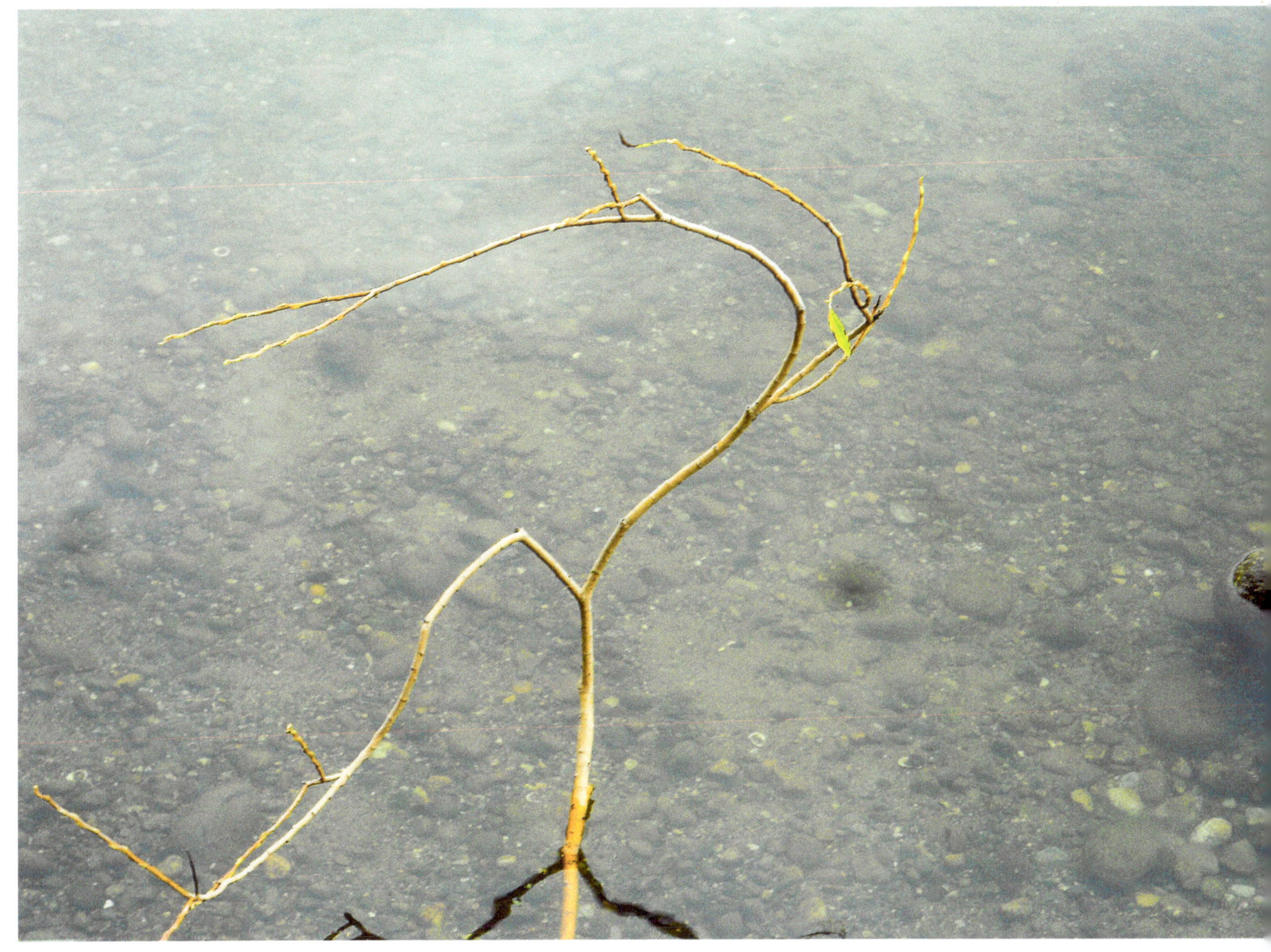

# Modern Sculpture

Probably the ultimate Zen picture, this represents a modernistic conception of my Blue Heron friend, stripped down to its most basic elements. Do you see it? Or is my imagination getting the best of me?

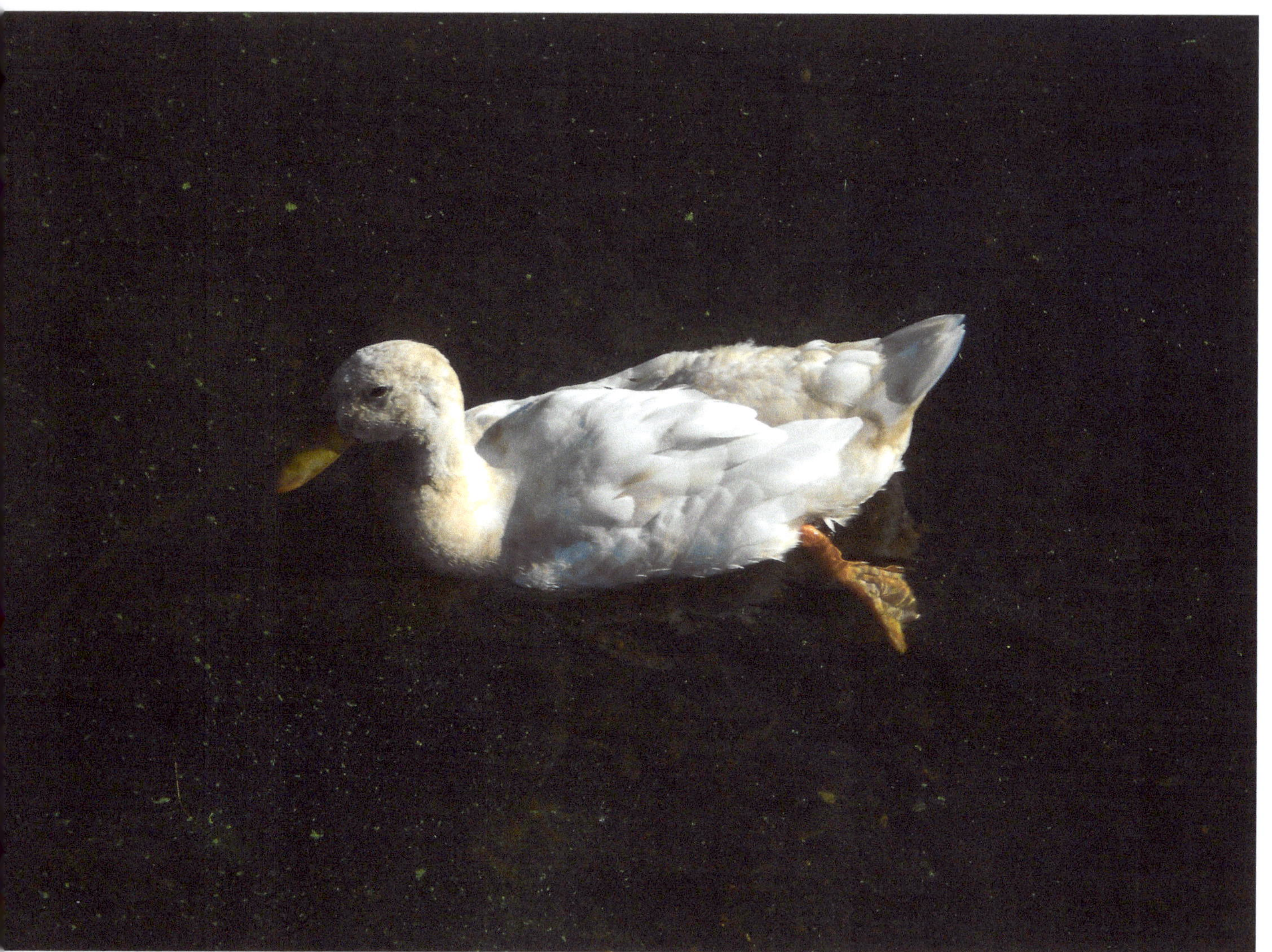

# Composition in
# Black and White

It appears like the title of a modern art piece in a gallery. I'm not sure how I got the water to look so dark, but it makes a wonderful contrast with the snow white duck. Clearly the duck is in its element, as seen by its contented look.

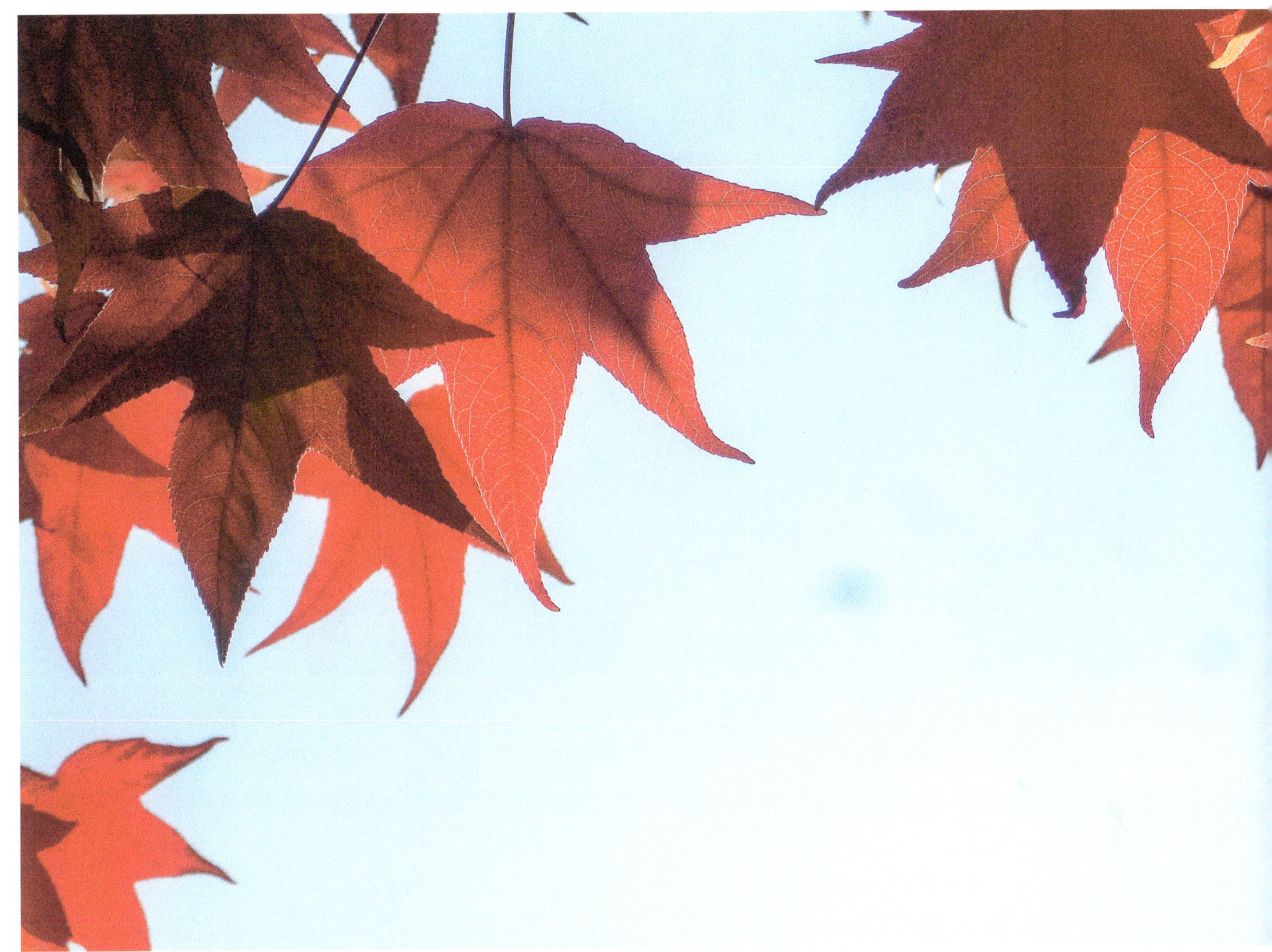

# Changing Season

Here we see a very simplistic representation of the coming of autumn at Green Lake. There are only two colors declared, although each has variations of shades.

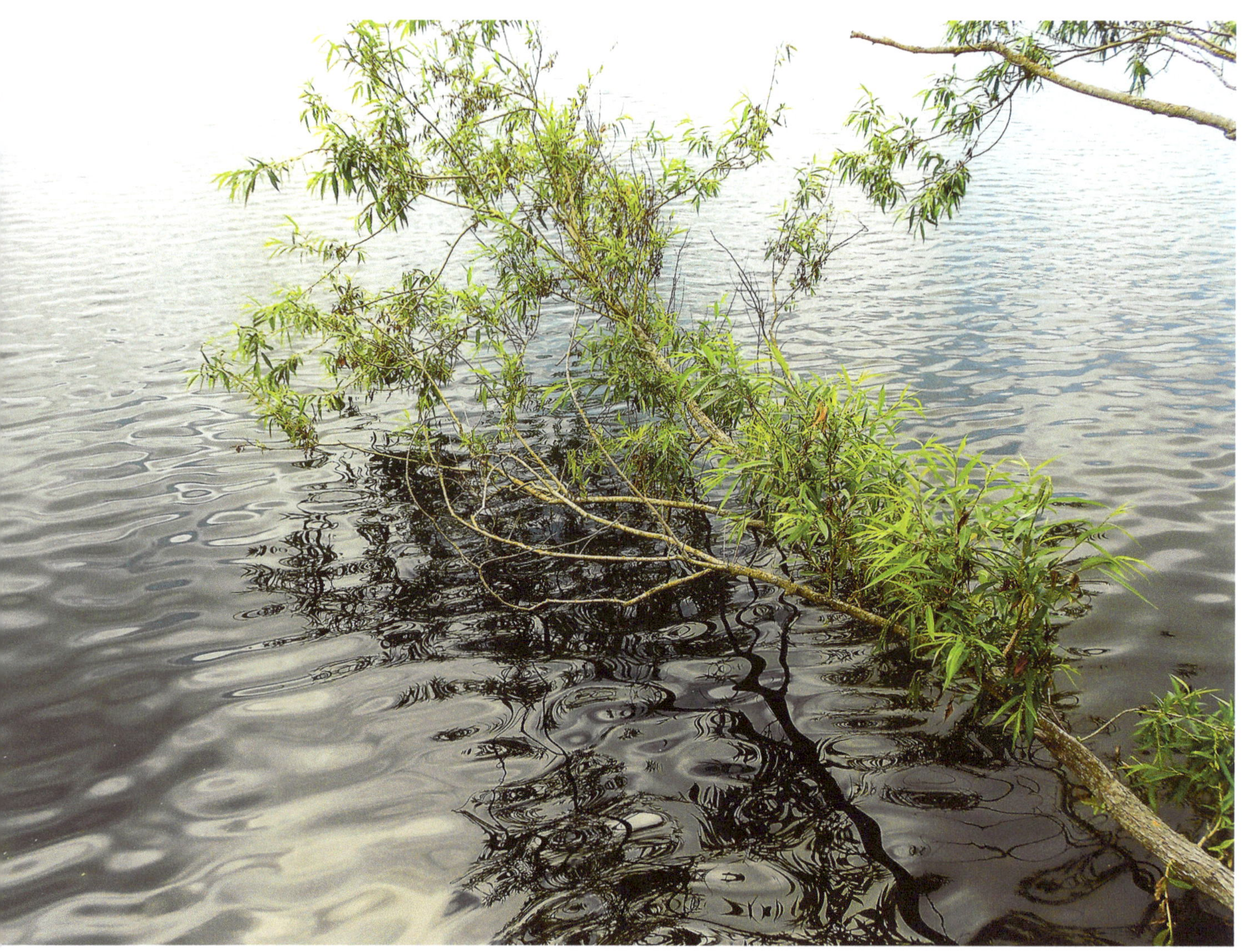

# Gooey Sludge

That's what the reflection of this overhanging tree branch looks like on the water. It has a beauty of its own despite what it appears, but that's only because I know that it isn't pollution. If it actually were, I would be horrified.

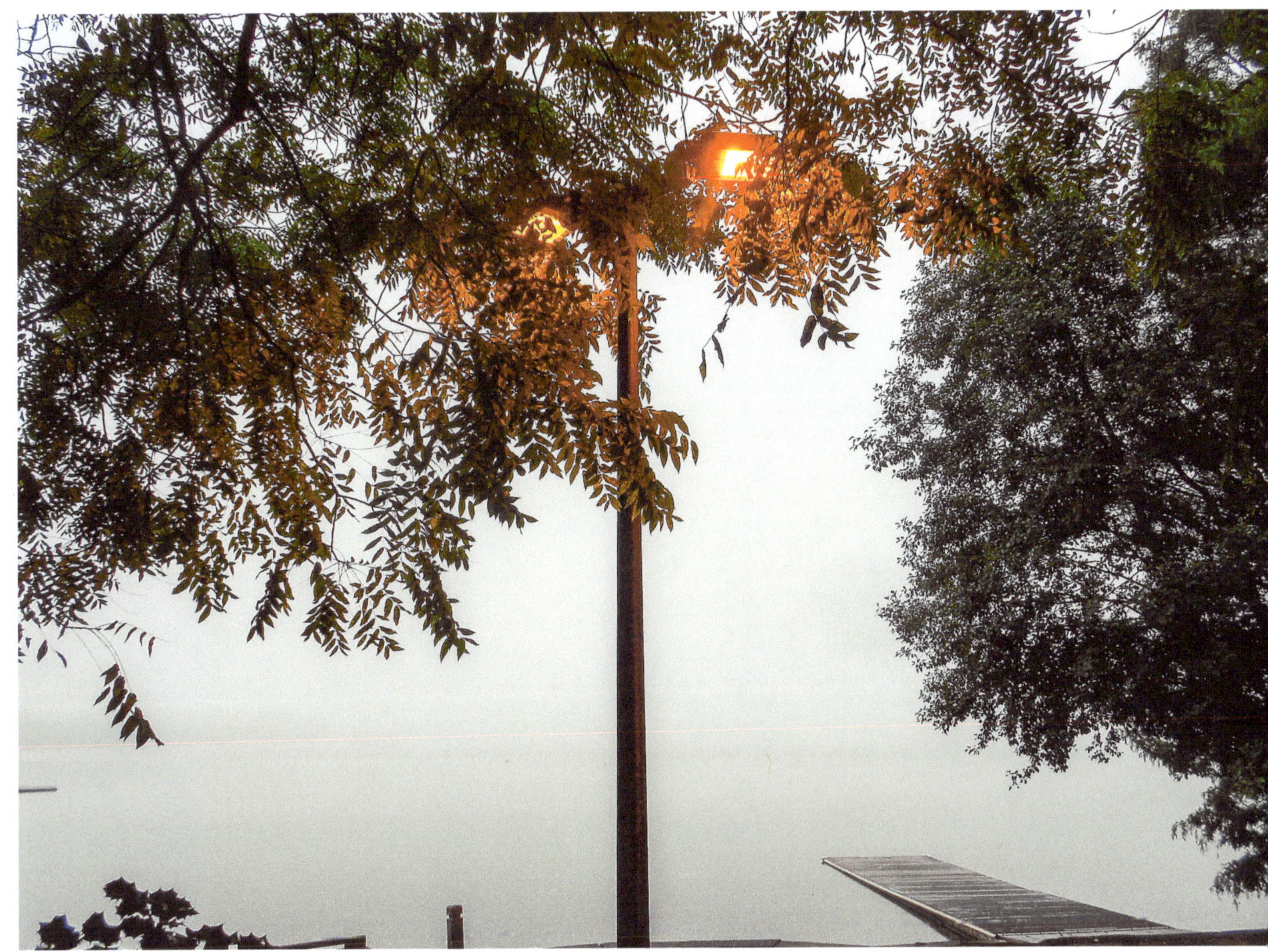

# Giant Praying Mantis

I'm letting my imagination run wild here: two protruding eyes on a long neck hidden behind some trees.

# Green Lake Tapestry

## In praise of opulence: more is more.

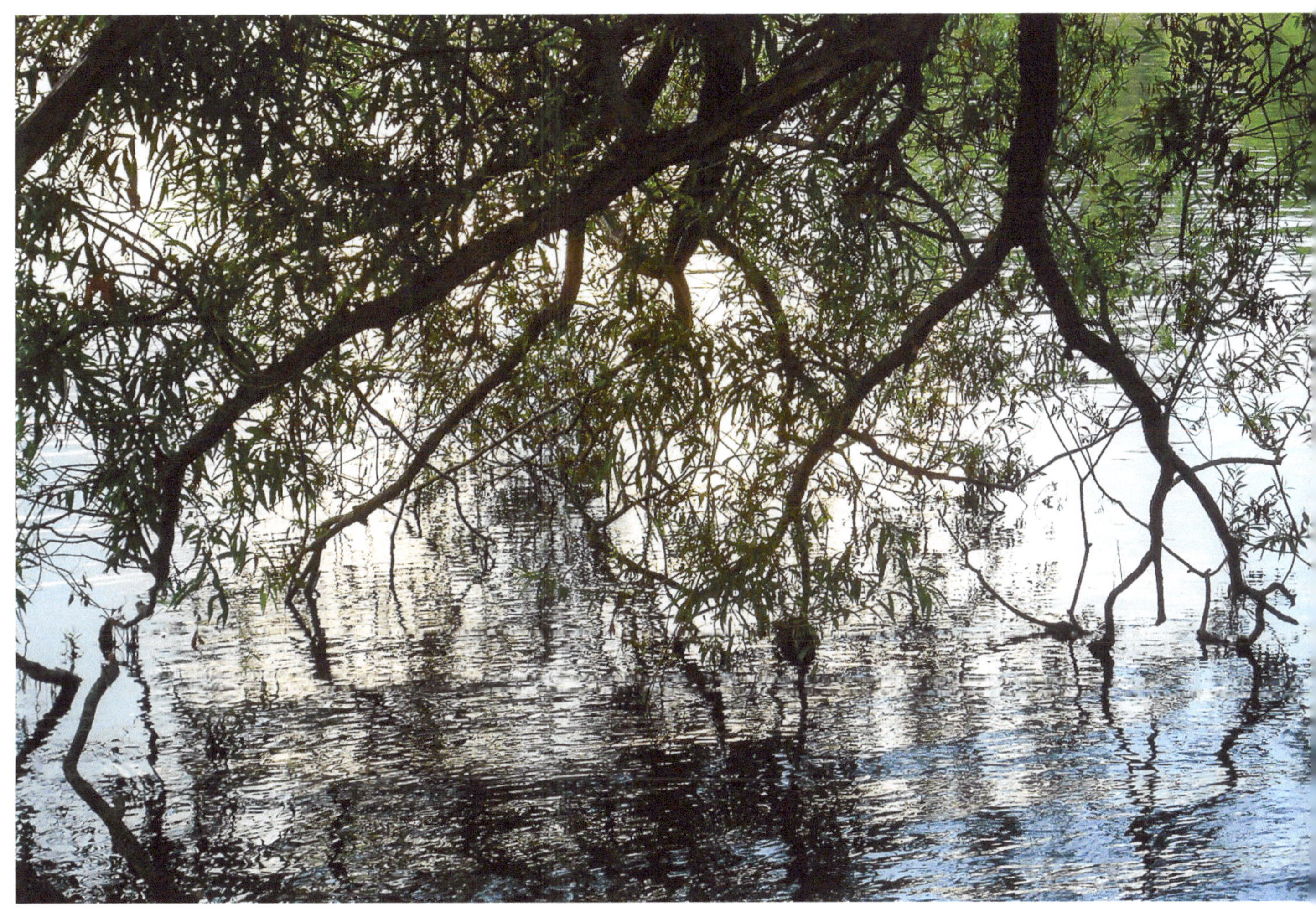

The pictures under this category are ones that remind me a lot of the kind of tapestry I saw hanging on the interior walls of castles in Europe. These works of art always seemed somewhat cluttered to me, with a lot attention paid to details and colors. They can almost be regarded as the exact opposite of Zen in their profusion of light, variations, and themes. There is a lot to see in these pictures.

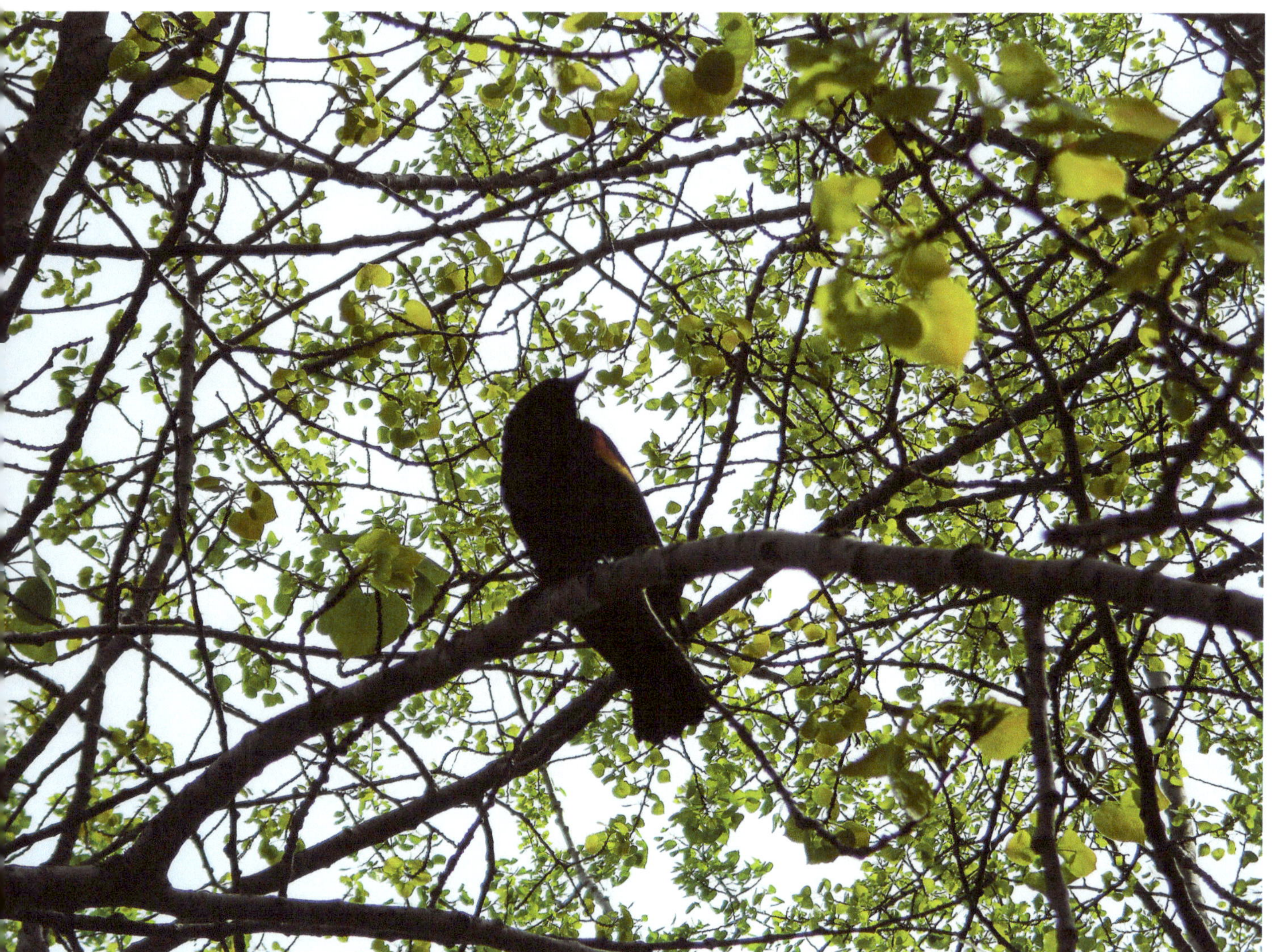

# Enjoying the Day

Here we see a Redwing Blackbird caught against the backdrop of tree leaves and branches. I think of the wallpaper designs in older homes when I look at this picture; the theme is simple but it is cluttered enough to merit my tapestry designation.

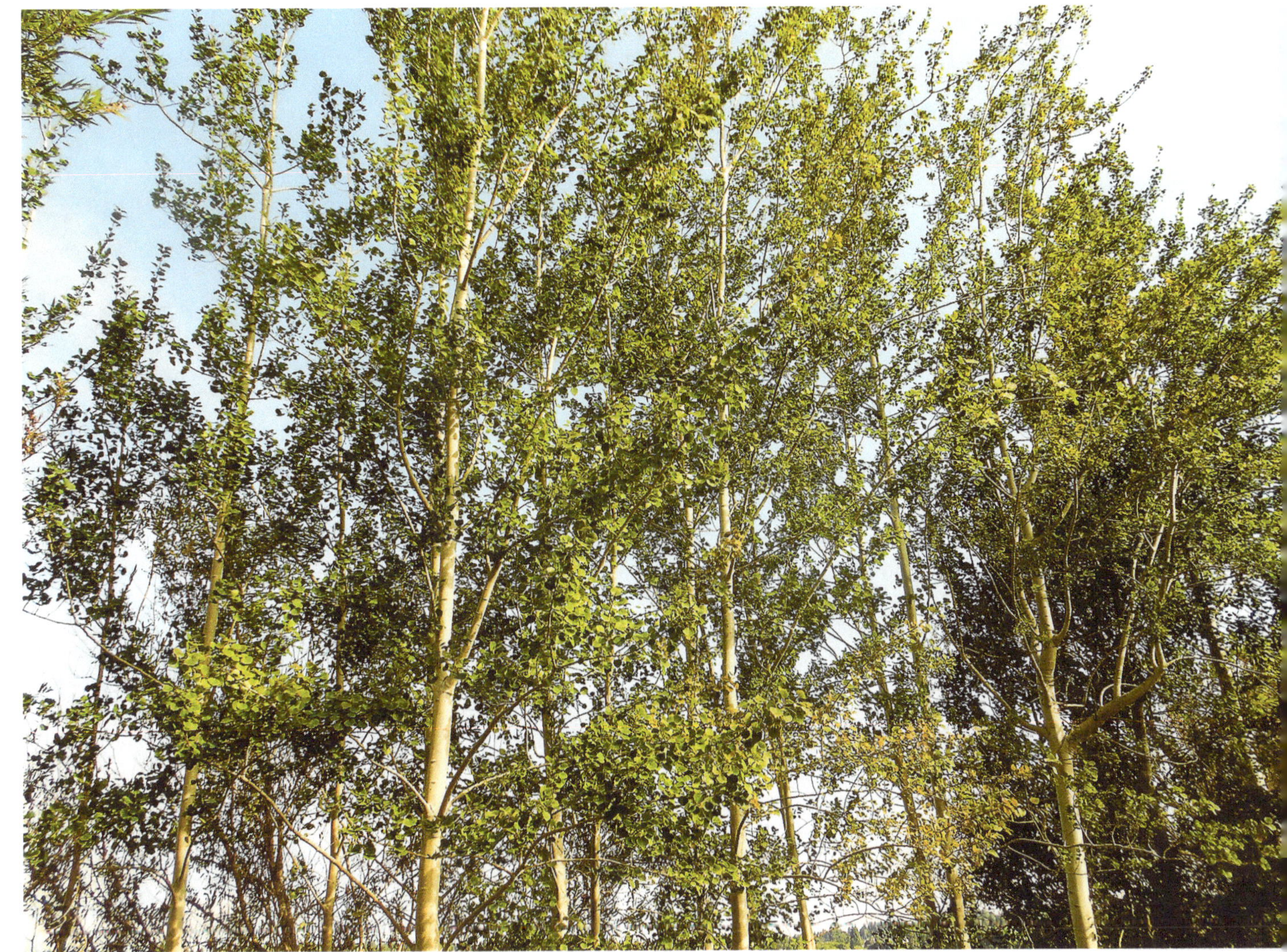

# Trees in Formation

These trees, standing straight and erect, reminded me of a military unit at attention in a dress right dress formation. I like the seeming loftiness in which the trees greet the sky —very impressive.

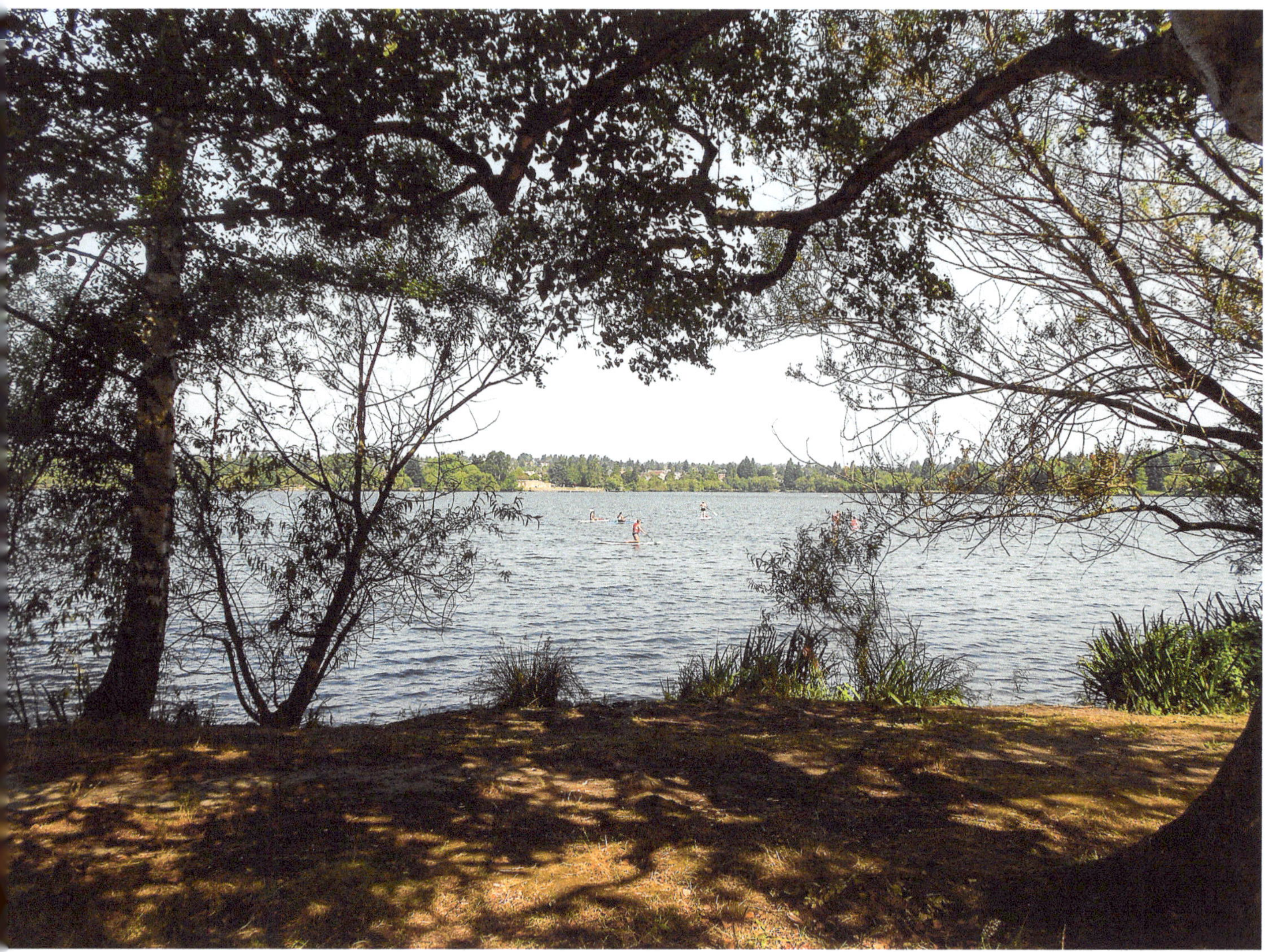

# Near Summer End

As summer goes into its later weeks, the ground along the shore turns to more brown which makes a nice contrast with the blue of the lake.

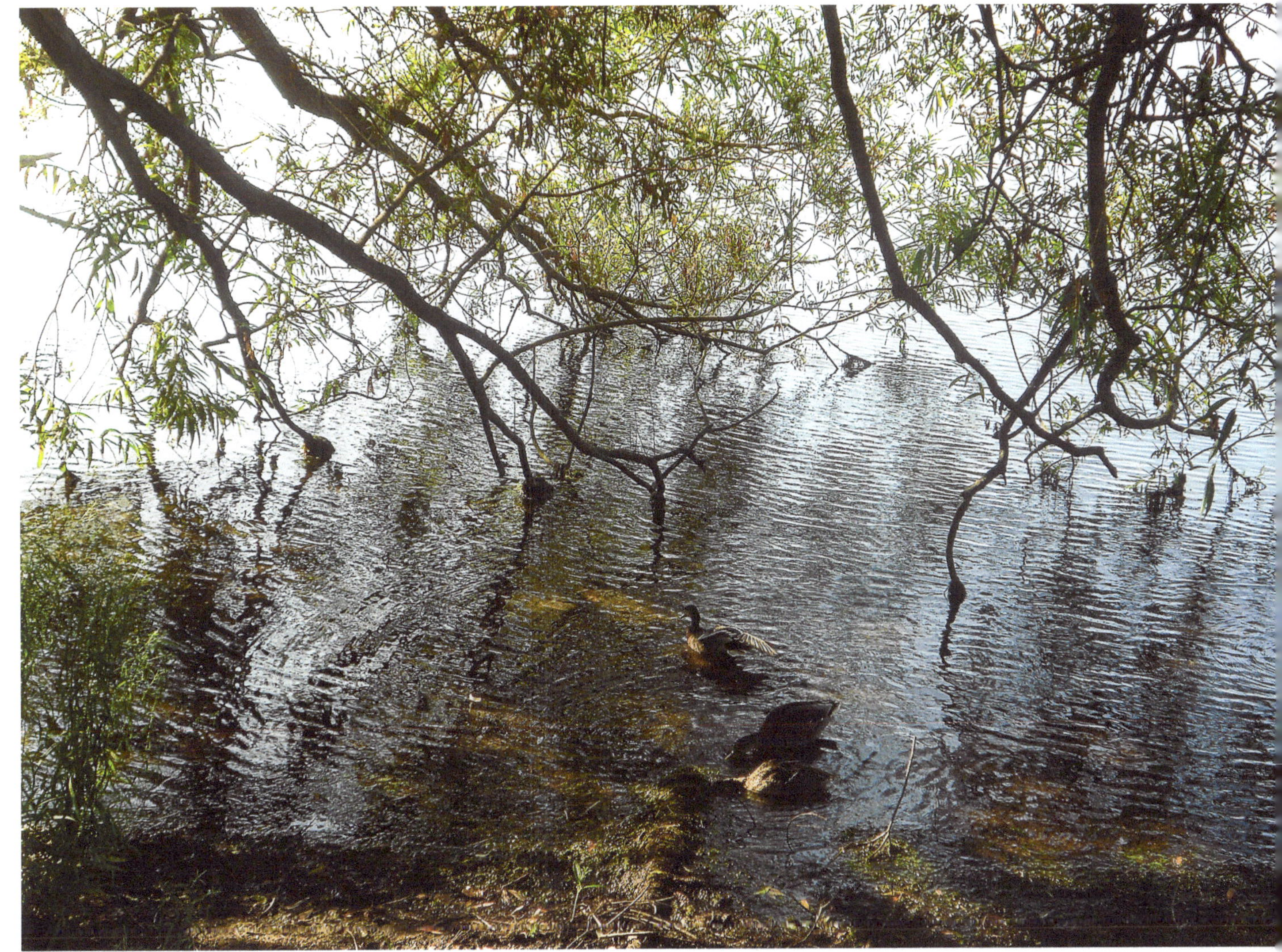

# Relishing the Shade

This is probably the best example of my tapestry category pictures.
There is such a myriad of colors and shades in both the water and
the tree. The ripples in the water greatly add to that effect.

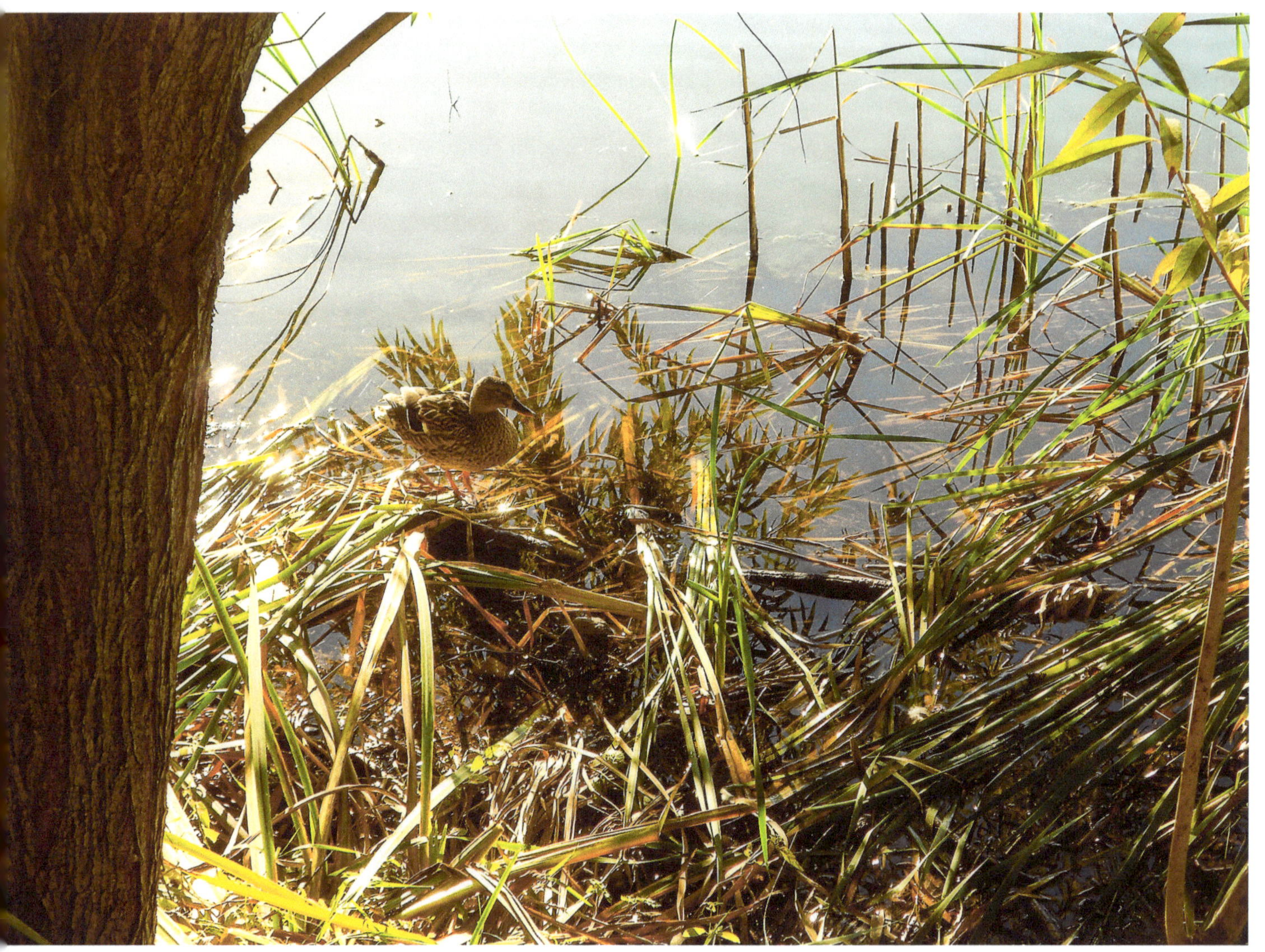

# Reedy Haven

There's a thicket of reeds in this setting that seems to provide a
refuge for the duck that's quite well-camouflaged within it. I like
the clarity of this picture, taken at mid-morning on one of those
crispy clear days that are so exhilarating.

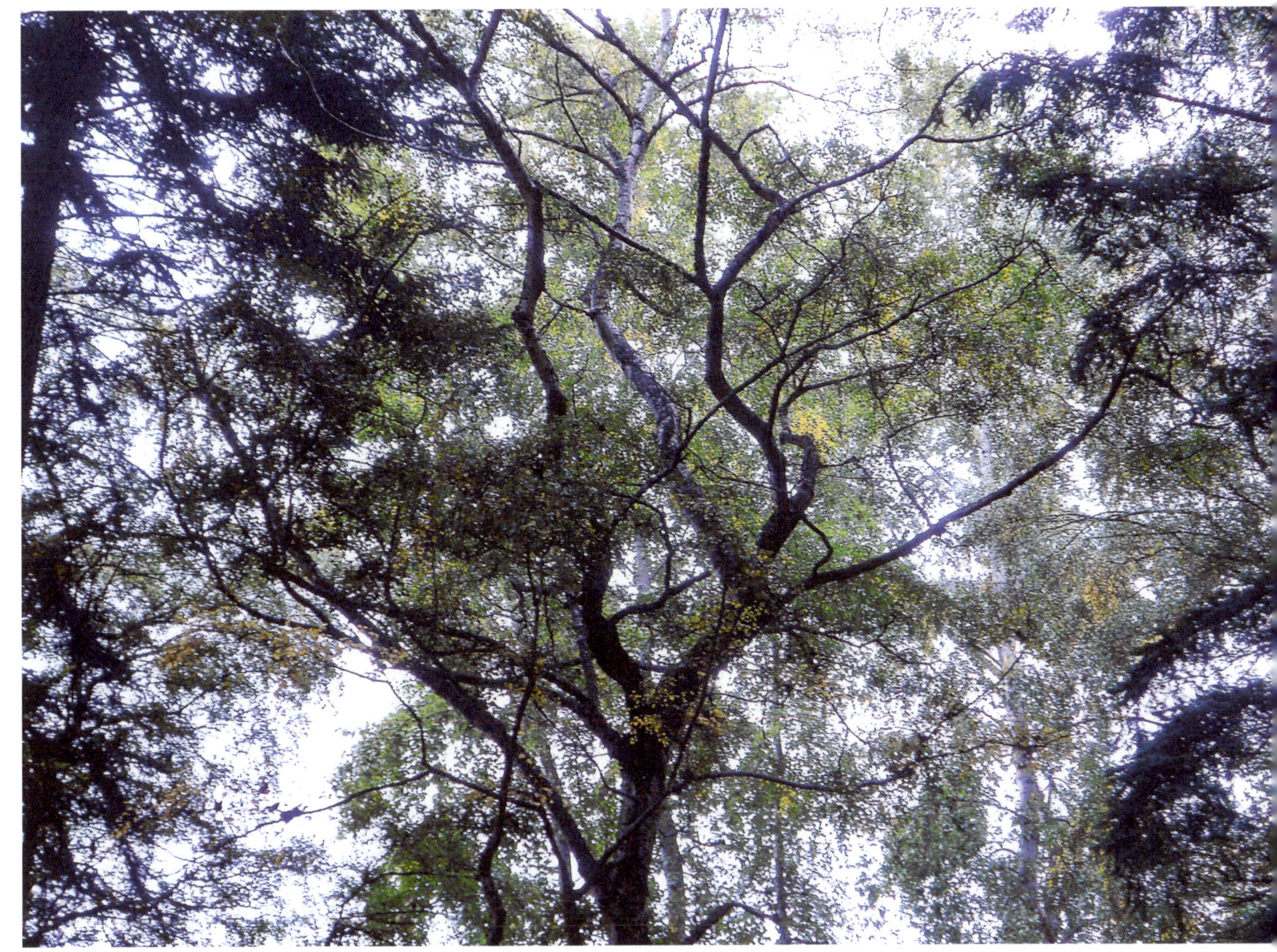

# Twists and Turns

This is one of those pictures that borders on the surreal. For one thing, the bluish tint was somewhat off of its actual coloring and I'm not sure how I achieved it with my camera. Yet the effect is intriguing, giving an alien presence to the scene —the bent and curved branches add to this other worldly character.

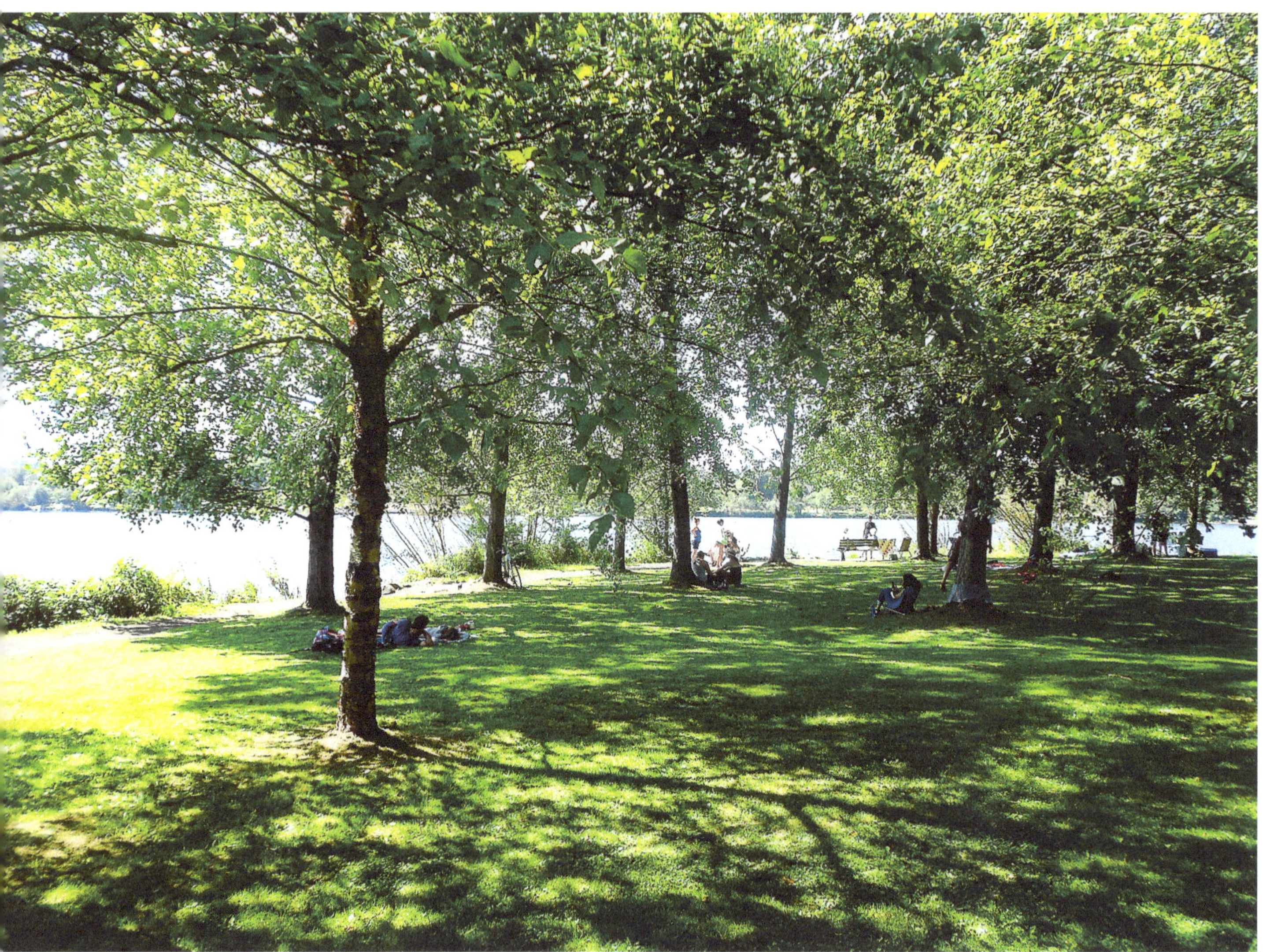

# Shaded Bliss

I'm reminded of a Georges Seurat painting when I look at this. To me the speckled light drops on the leaves and grass resemble his Pointillism style. Finely detailed, there's no question about its cluttered look.

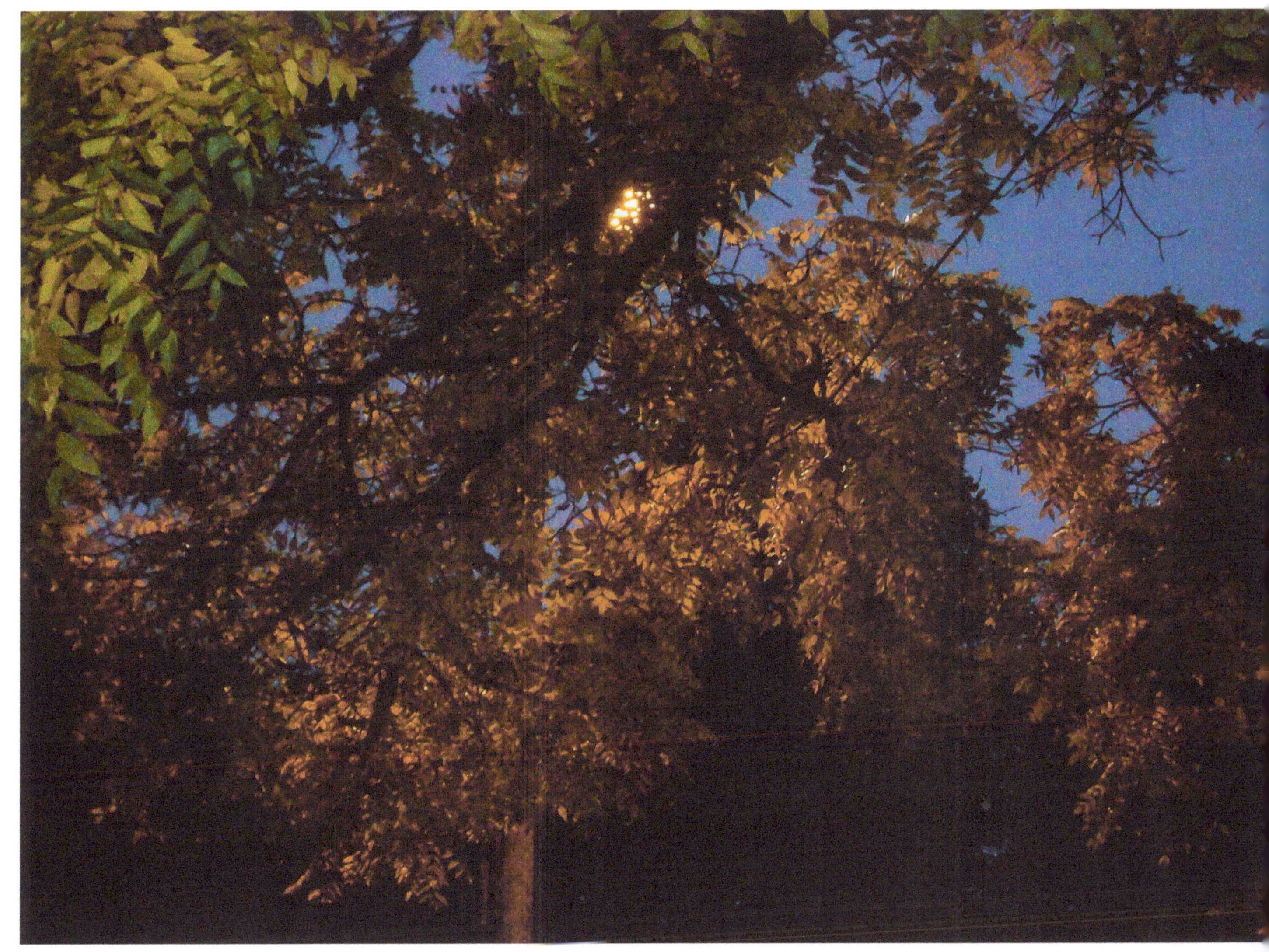

# Light Post by Tree

I like the tawny colors of the trees, but it also looks like a long neglected piece of hanging tapestry that is in dire need of cleaning.

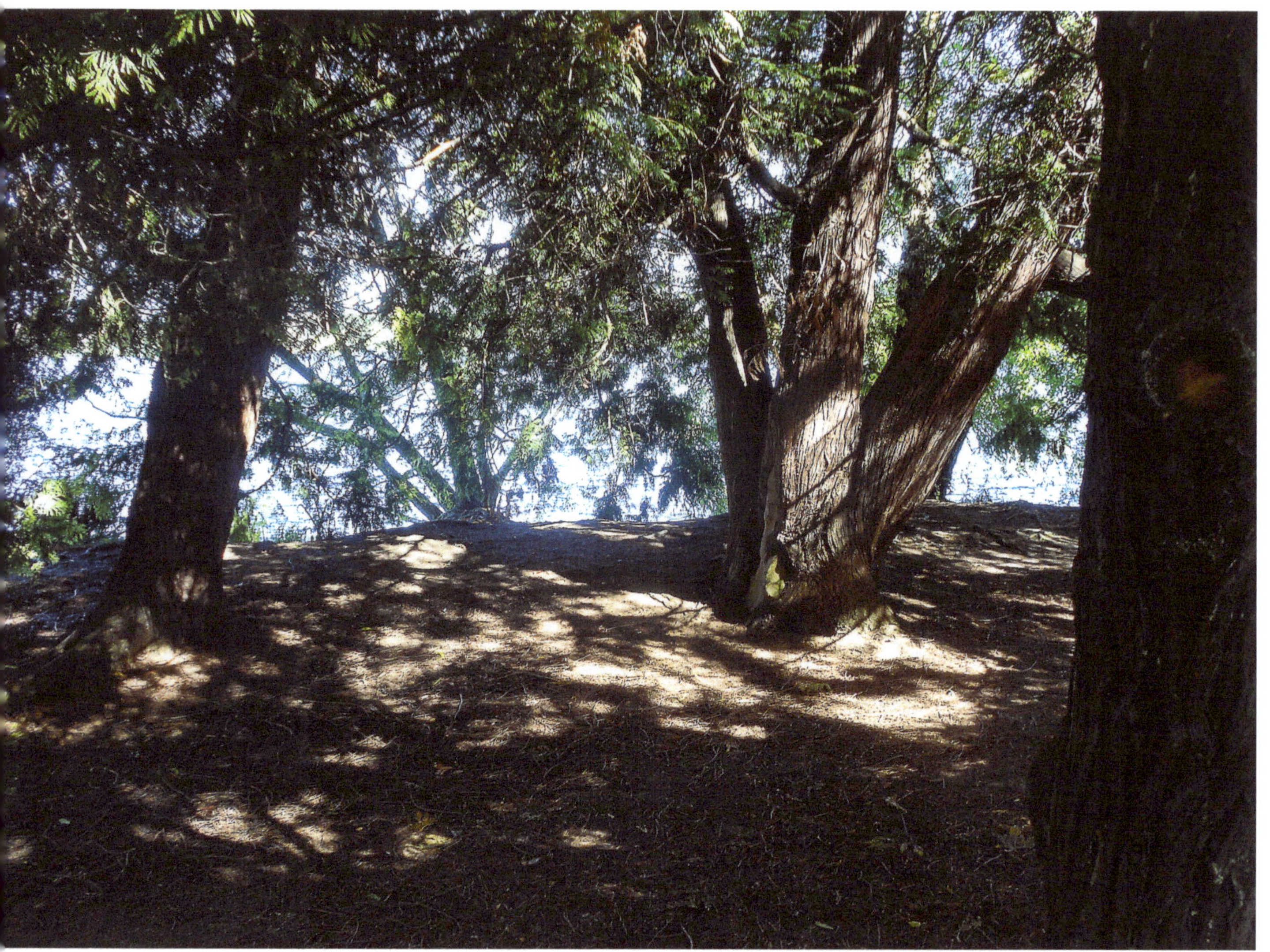

# Burnt Umber

I think of the opening lines of Longfellow's Evangeline when I look at this: "This is the forest primeval. The murmuring pines and hemlocks, Bearded with moss, and in garments green, indistinct in the twilight, Stand like Druids of old...." It was a passage introduced to me early in childhood that I have never forgotten.

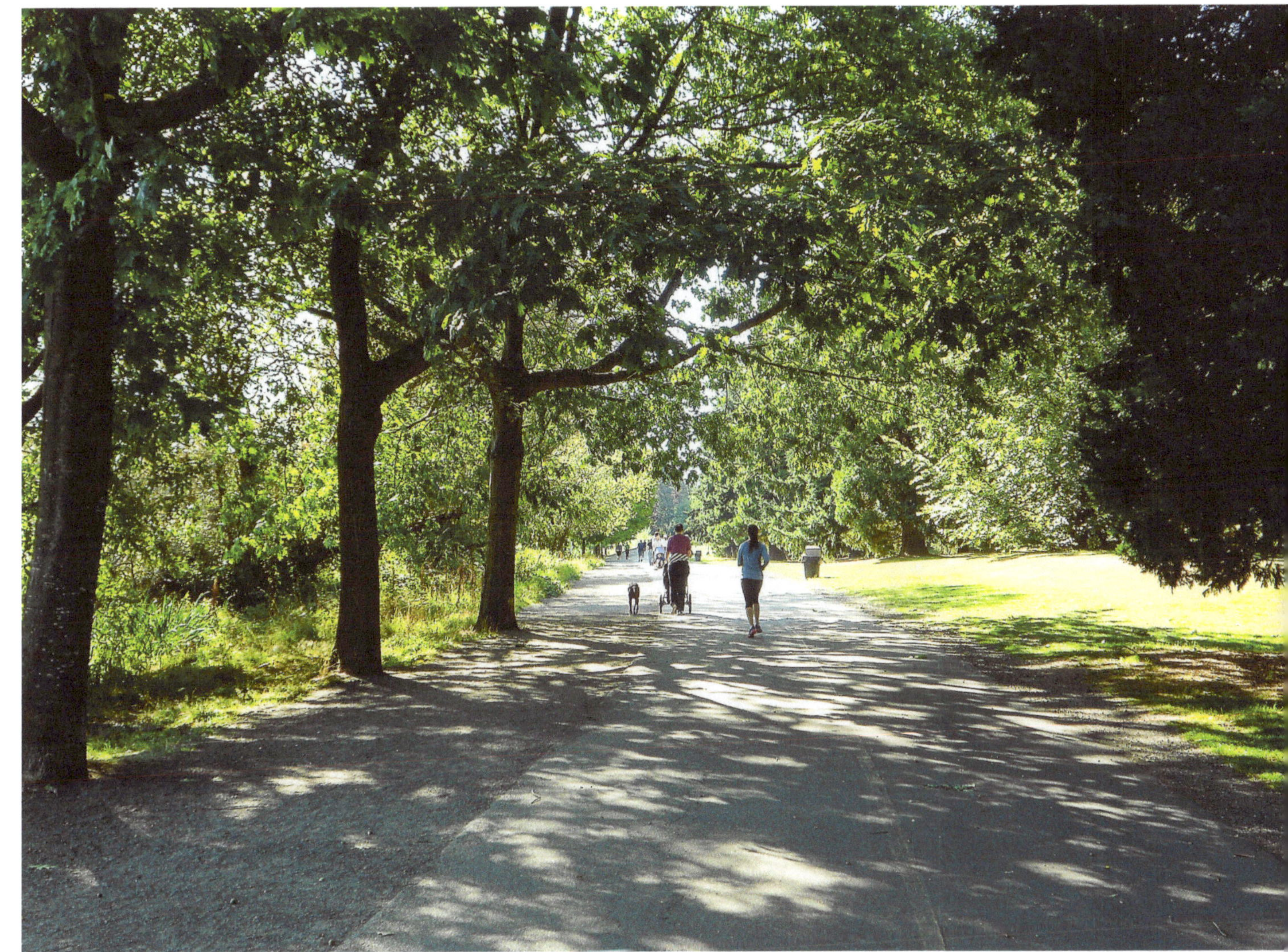

# Enjoying Exercise

This scene, with a jogger and a woman pushing a baby carriage and her dog adjacent to them is one of the more common sights at Green Lake. It epitomizes what this park is all about and why it is so popular. The graveled pathway inside of the paved one is for those joggers who prefer a softer running surface. Both circle the lake covering a distance of 2.8 miles. There is no better way to get your daily exercise.

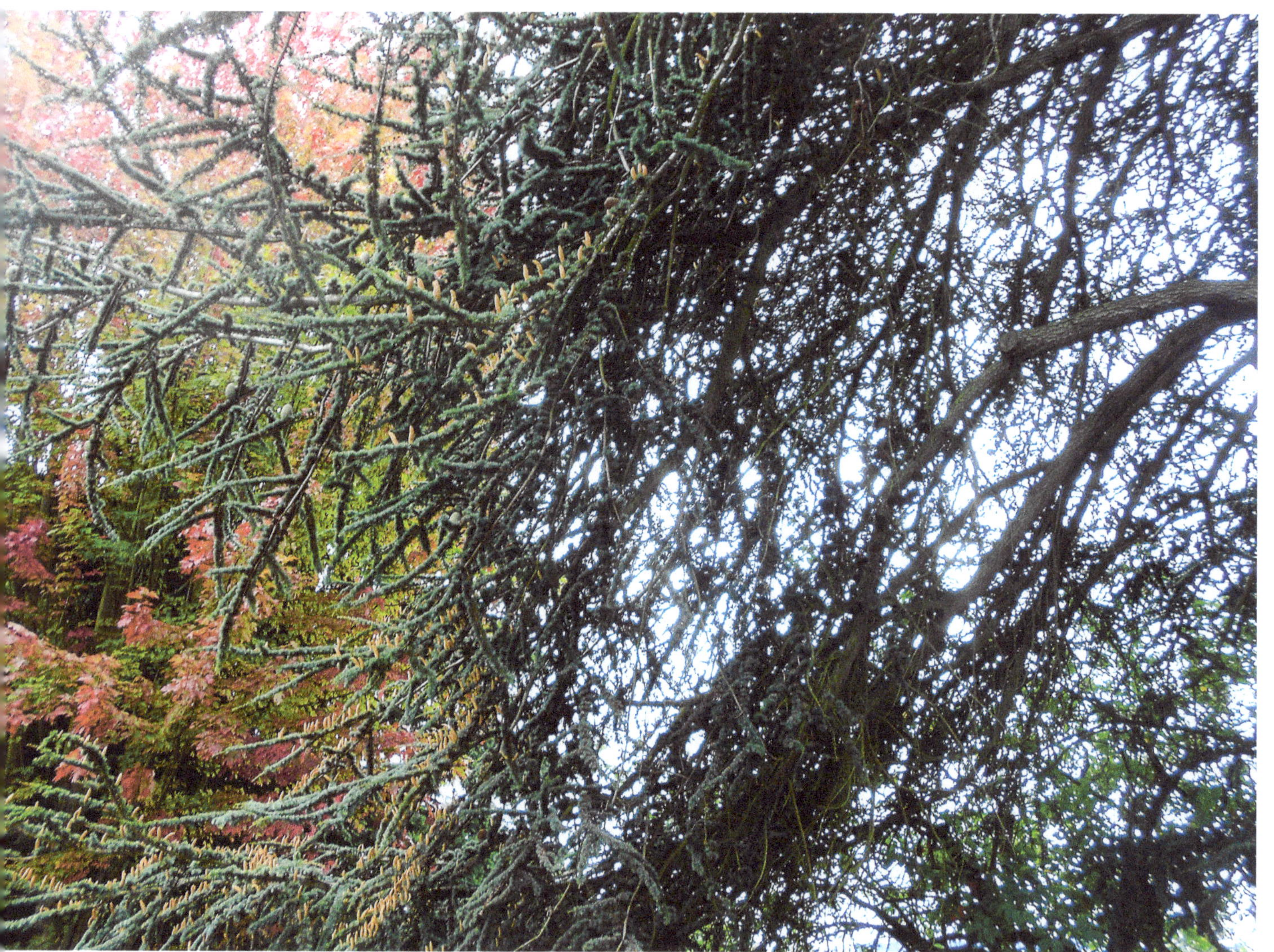

# Jumbled Mess

Here we see the branches of an Atlas Cedar Tree with its convoluted, gnarly, and twisted features that readily identifies the species. It has the appearance of an intricate lattice work run amok that almost overwhelms you in its detail.

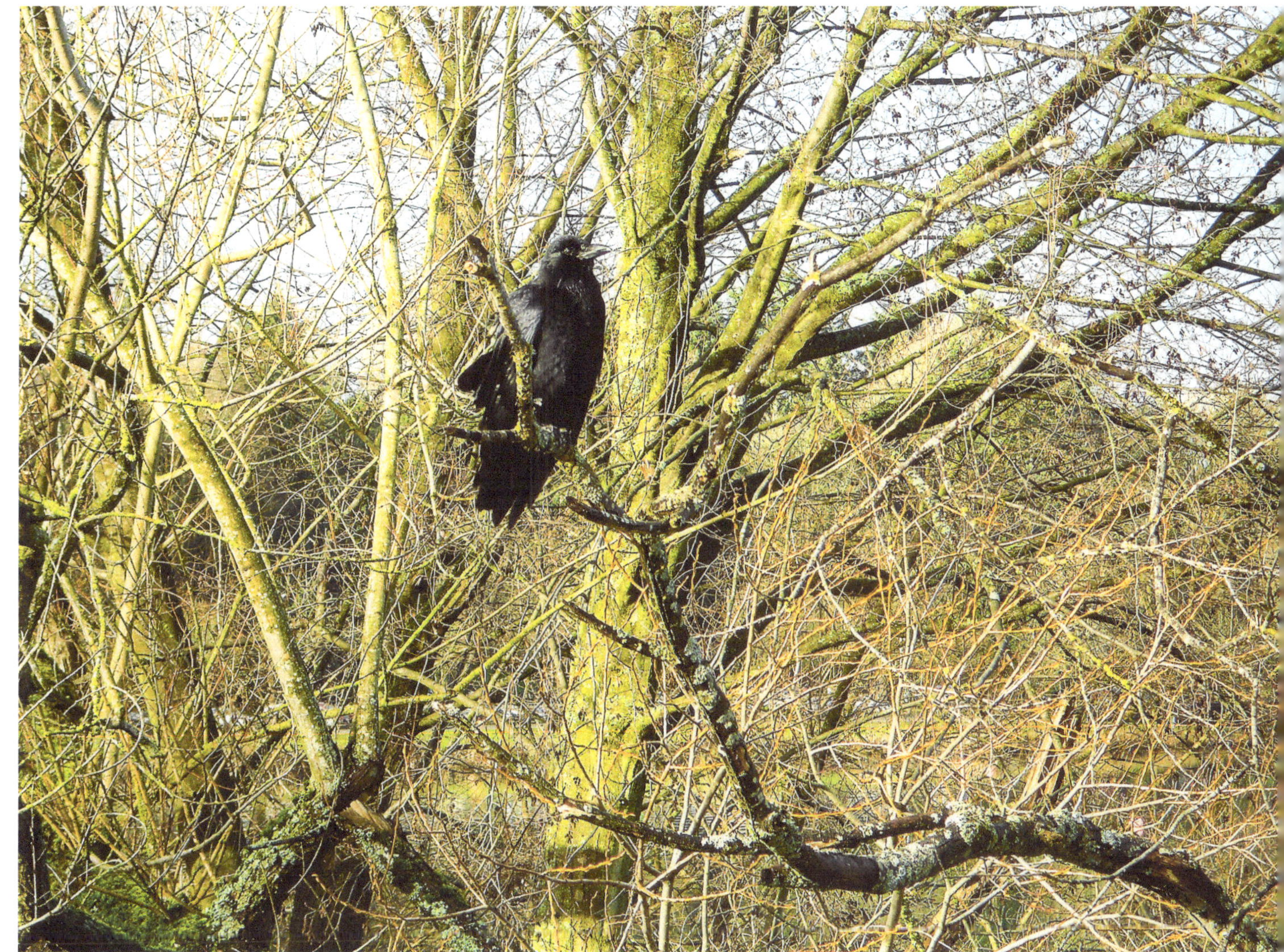

# Leafless Branches

This picture was taken in mid-January when there are no longer any leaves left on many of the trees and is a good representation of the beauty you see at Green Lake in all seasons.

I think it is the monochrome setting that renders the scene interesting. I do like it.

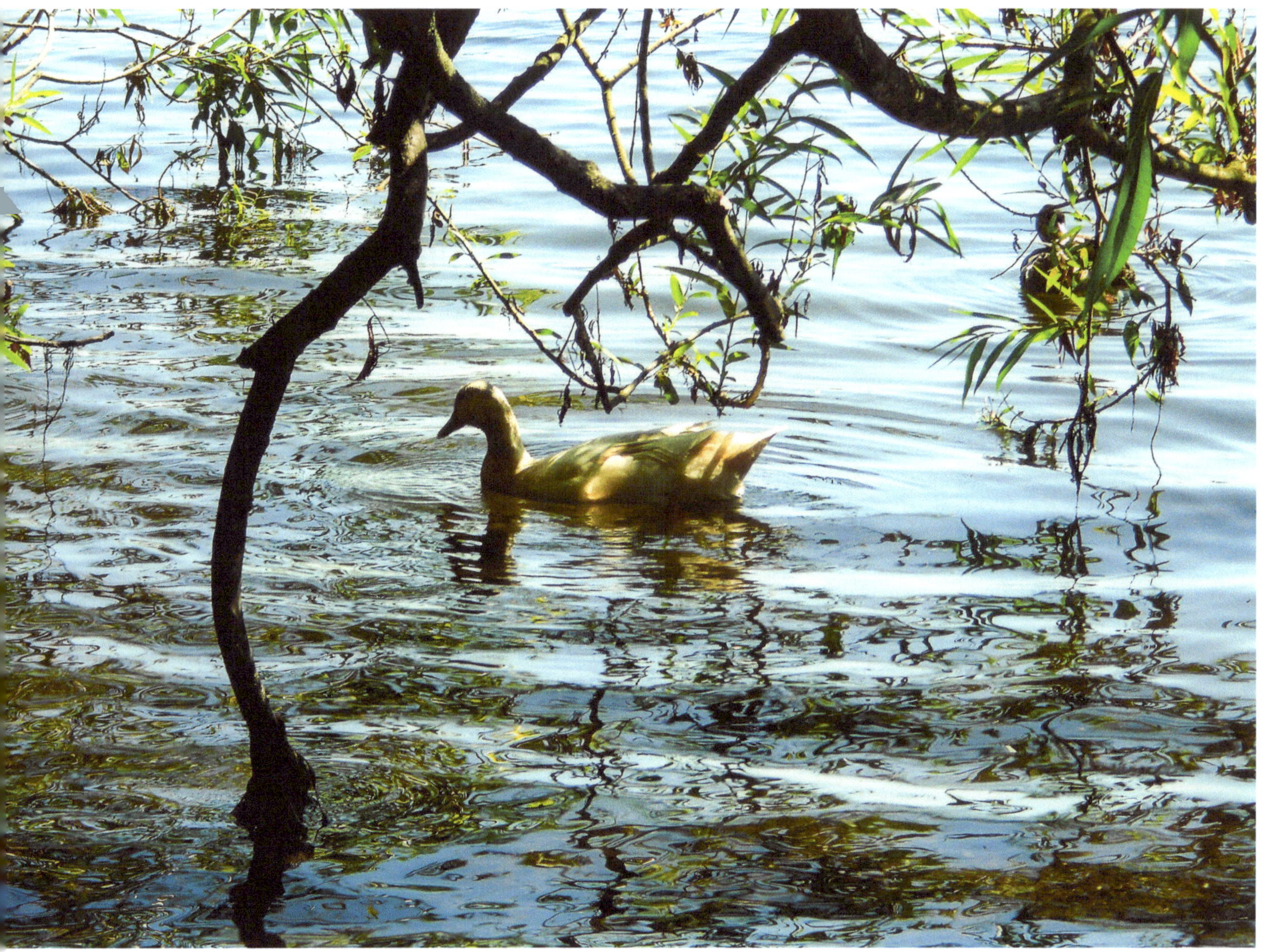

# Duck in Water

Seemingly simple, there is a lot of detail in this picture. The wave action, the reflected greenery in the water, the splashes of sunlight on the branches and the duck all contribute to making it a fully integrated scene. It is one of my favorites. I caught this duck separated from its mate; actually it is camouflaged behind the descending branch on the right.

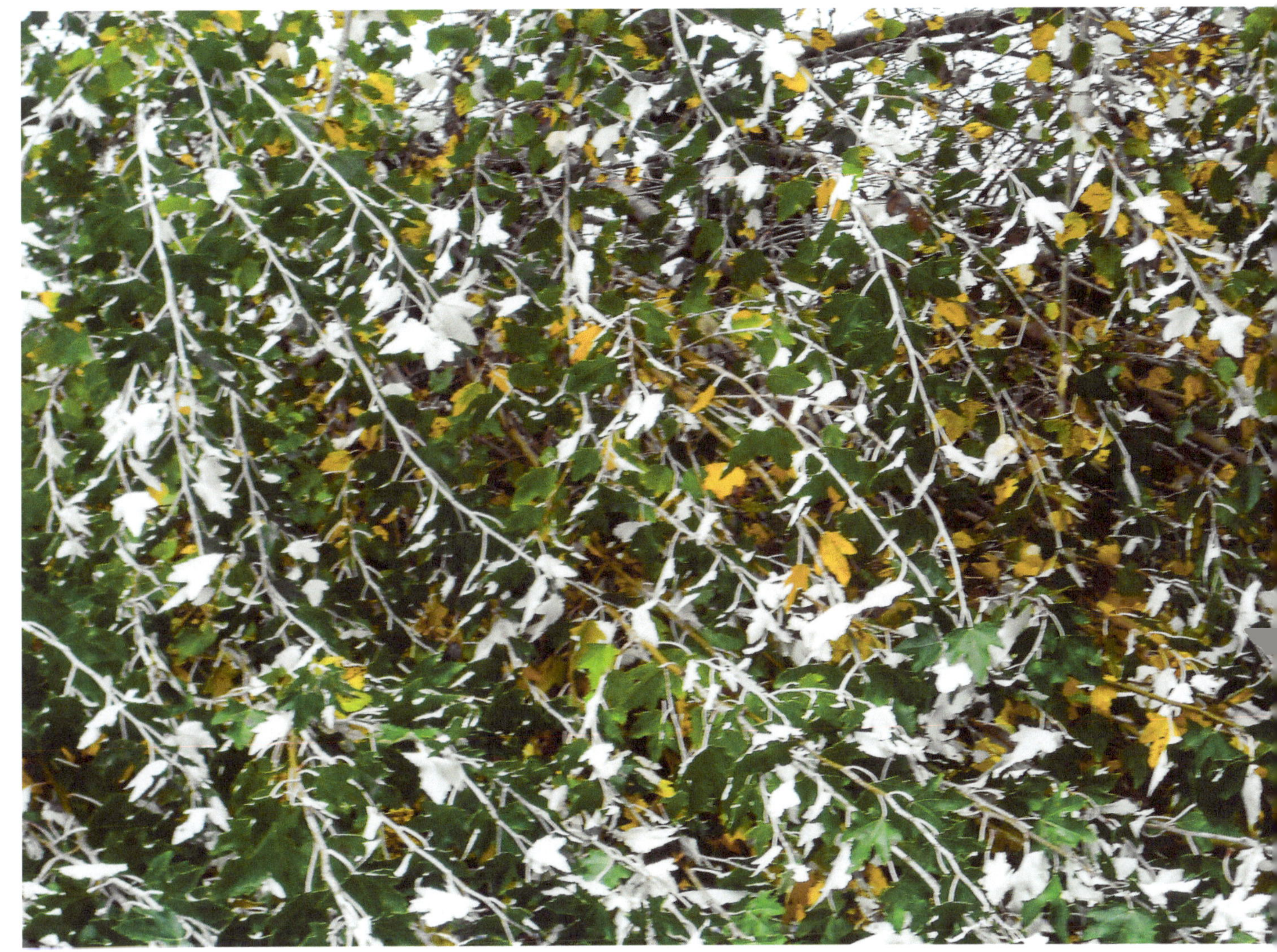

# A Jackson Pollock Work?

No. It's a shrub at the eastern end of the lake next to the Center House as seen in the fall. Although more symmetrical, it does bear some resemblance to the artist's works which have a spilled paint look with their array of colors covering all of a canvas.

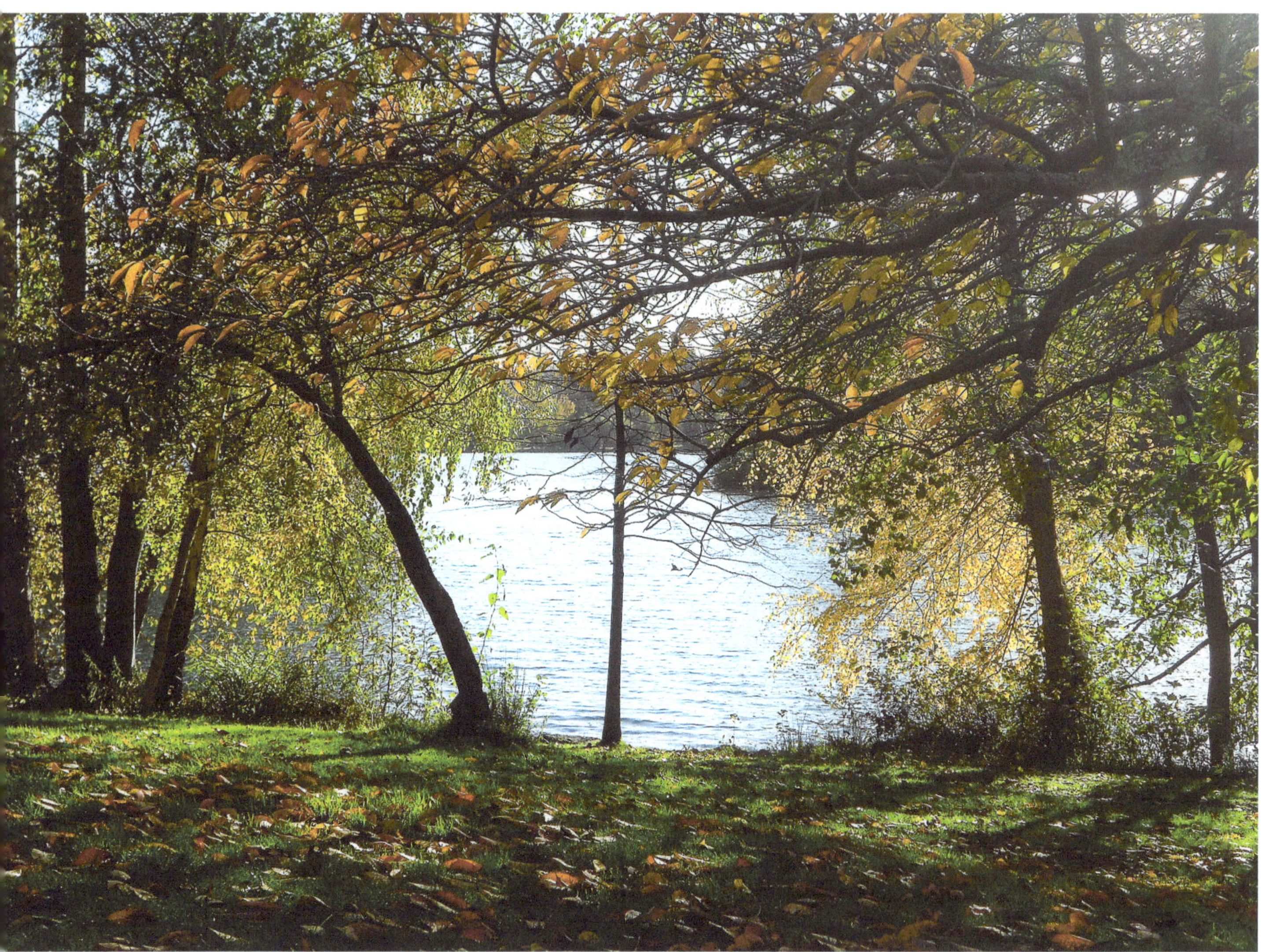

# Autumn View

The straight tree in the center of this picture makes it appear as the spine of a book with each side capable of being folded as two separate pages. Anyway, that the first impression I get in seeing this. It's a magnificent scene, and a good preview of what you will see under the Green Lake Color chapter.

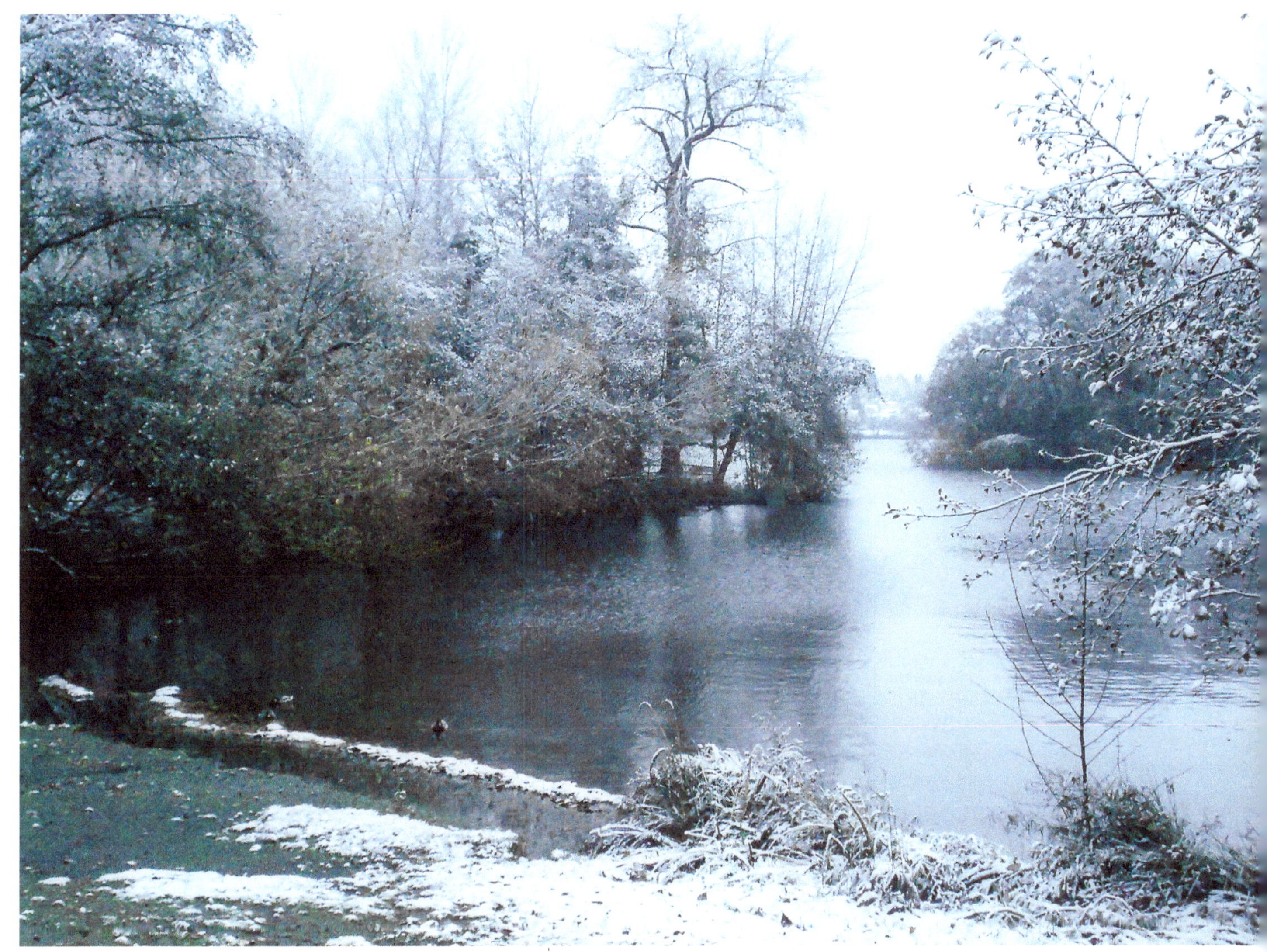

# Quiet Beauty

This winter scene is made quite busy by all its details, enhanced by the prevalence of the snow blanketed branches.

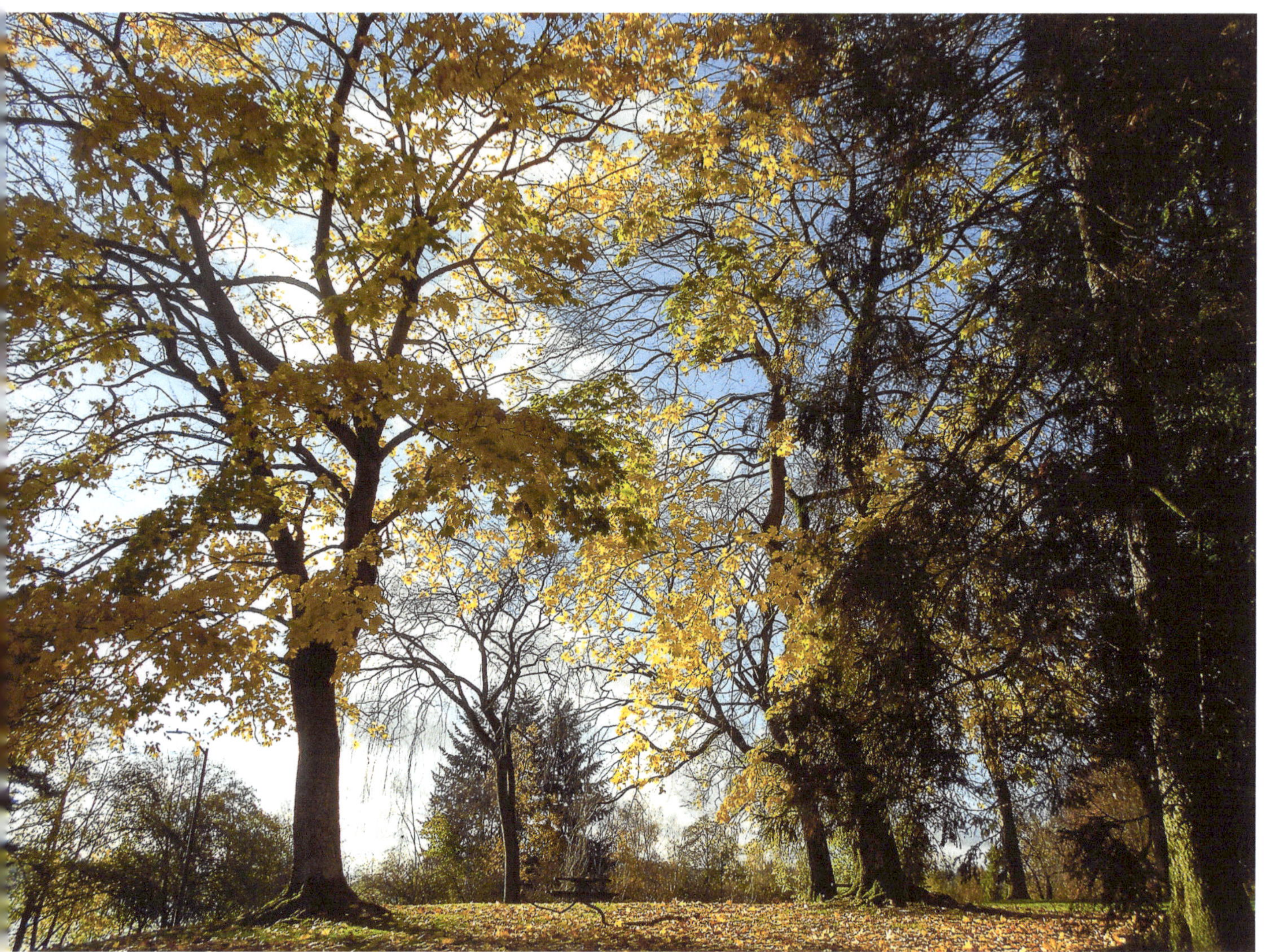

# Sunshine

In this wonderful autumn shot, you can see the dramatic effect created by the sun's rays penetrating through a cluster of trees. I think of Joyce Kilmer's opening lines of Trees:

I think that I shall never see A poem lovely as a tree.

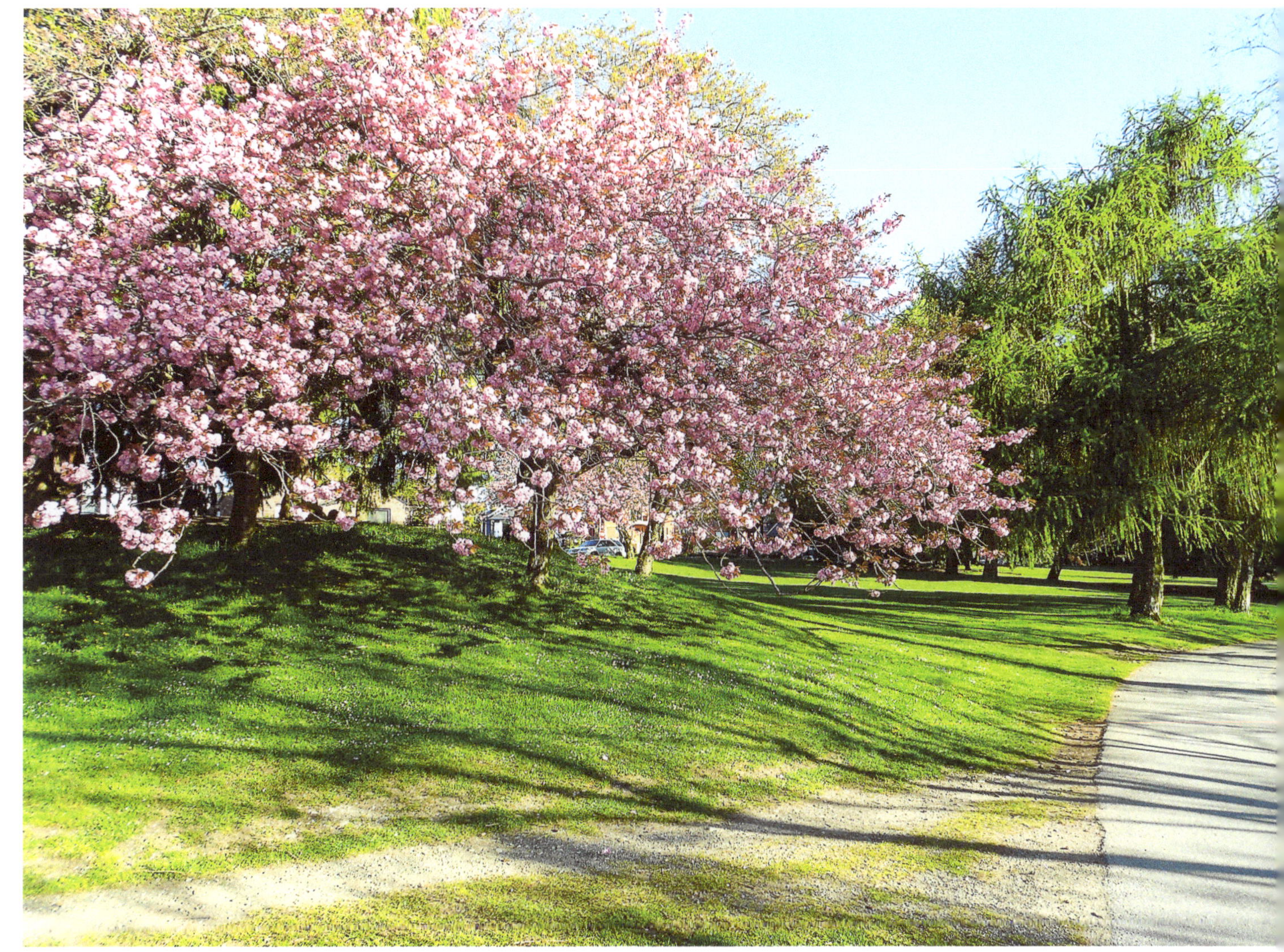

# Springtime

A wonderful time to visit Green Lake Park is in the spring. Blossoming trees abound in the north end of the park as seen here. It's also a time of pollen so care must be taken by anyone sensitive to that.

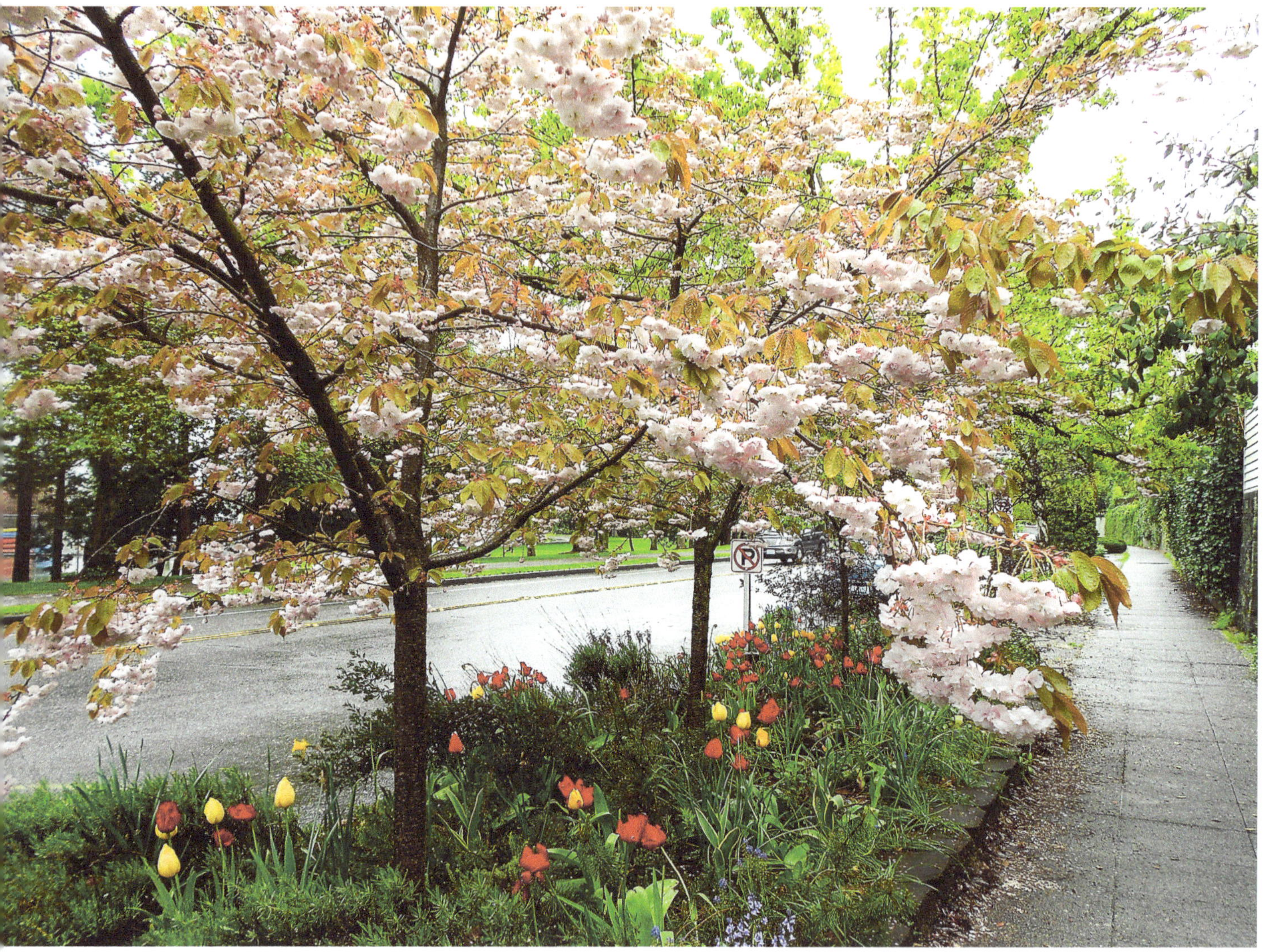

# Across the Street

This picture probably should not be included among my Green Lake photos, but the beauty seen in it is reflective of spring time in the park. We are looking at East Green Lake Drive North (there is also a West Green Lake Drive N) across the street from the main east entrance of Green Lake Park.

# Green Lake Wild

## In praise of living things

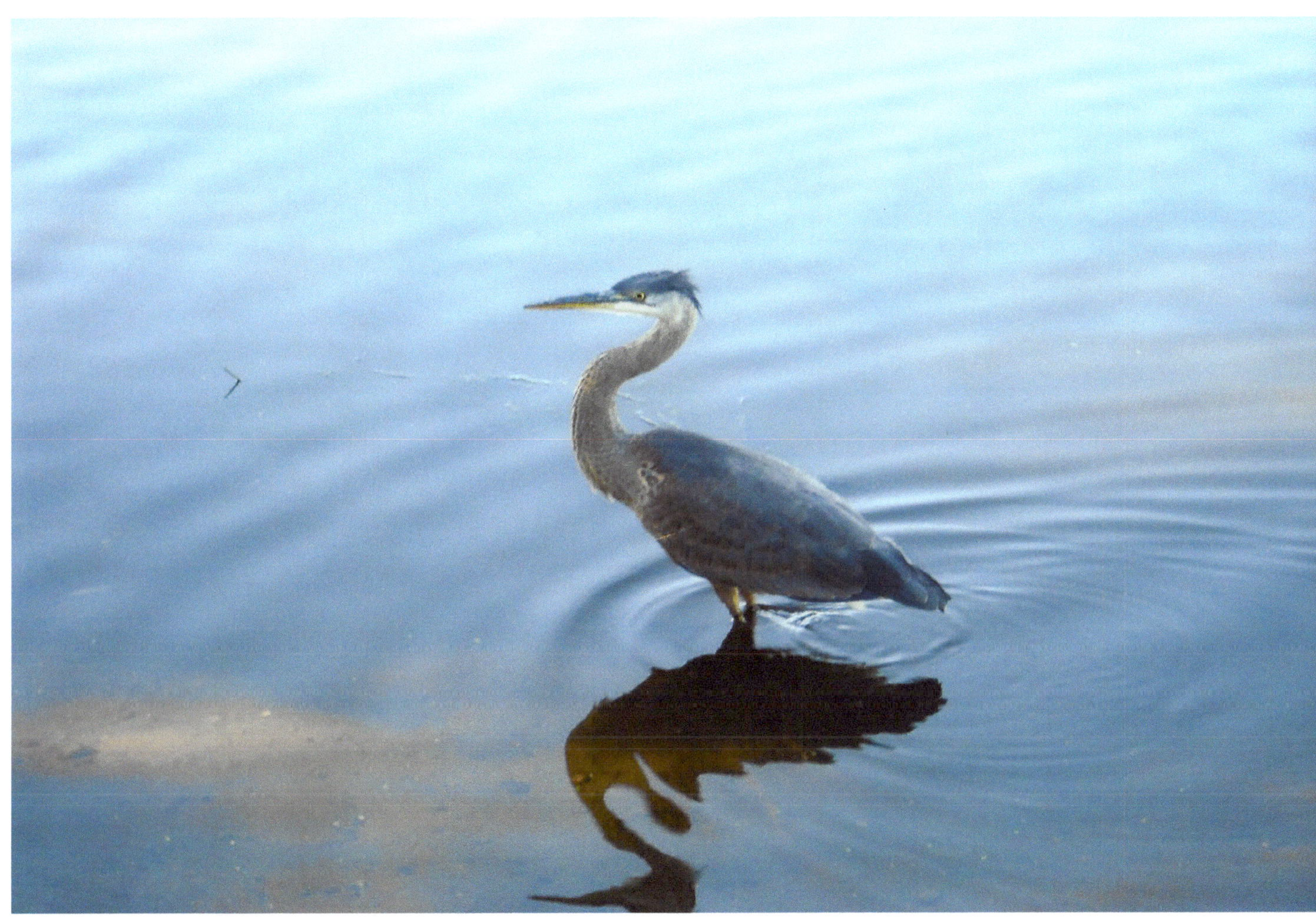

Wildlife abounds at Green Lake Park. Birds, ducks, and squirrels are the most prevalent, but there are also rabbits and raccoons which can be seen if making the rounds early in the morning, usually before twilight. Every so often a bald eagle (I've never seen more than one at a time ) will visit the lake and is easily spotted as it will rest upon the upper most branch of a given tree (usually a conifer) overlooking its domain. These visits draw the crowds.

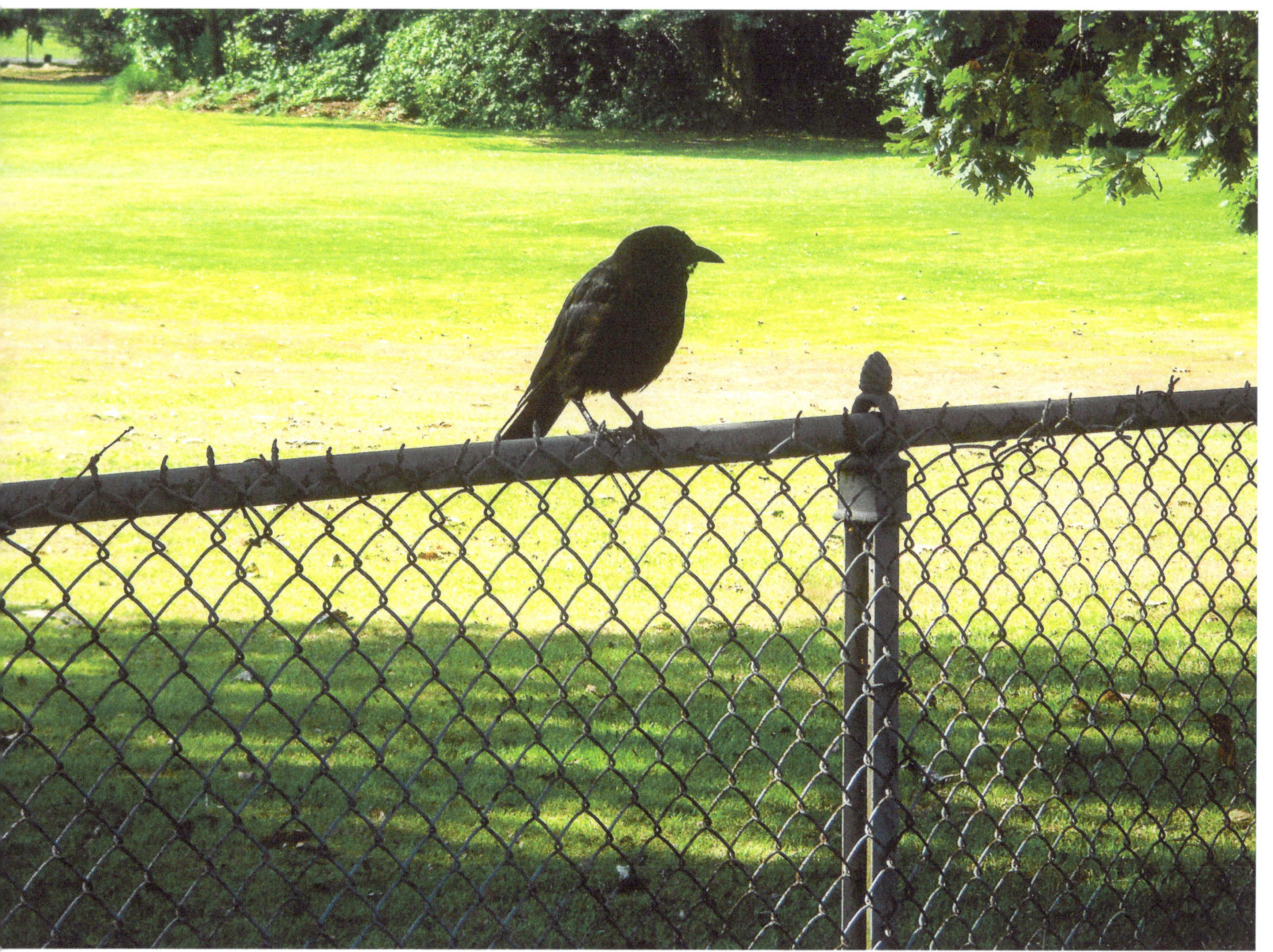

# The Ubiquitous Crow

Crows are prevalent at Green Lake, seemingly everywhere and often seen in groups even though I suspect they are highly individualistic. They have adapted so well to human presence that they will not even get out of the way when you approach them, often passing within a foot of them, meriting a sobriquet as 'cool' birds. I have a begrudging admiration for them; they scare away song birds but display signs of intelligence and seem to know you. When you see too many of them flocked together, it can be a bit unnerving, conjuring up images of Alfred Hitchcock's movie 'The Birds'.

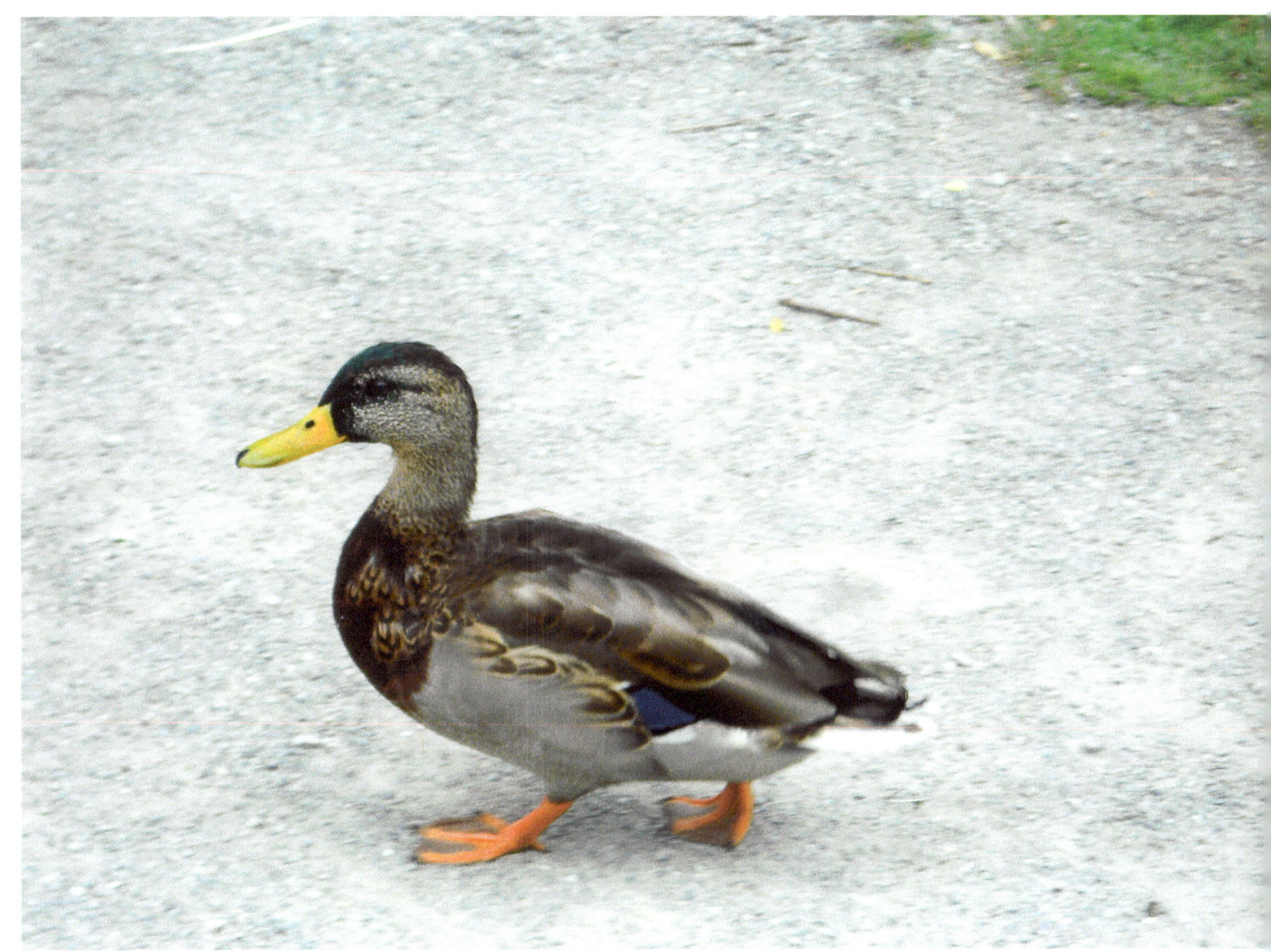

# Stepping Out

I like ducks —not Oregon, but the fowl type (I'm an ardent UW Husky fan)— because of the way they look and move about. This one flunks the walking test. Ducks aren't supposed to actually walk, they're supposed to waddle, that is, shift their body weight over the foot that hits the ground thereby swaying from side to side as they proceed. Only penguins are better at waddling than ducks.

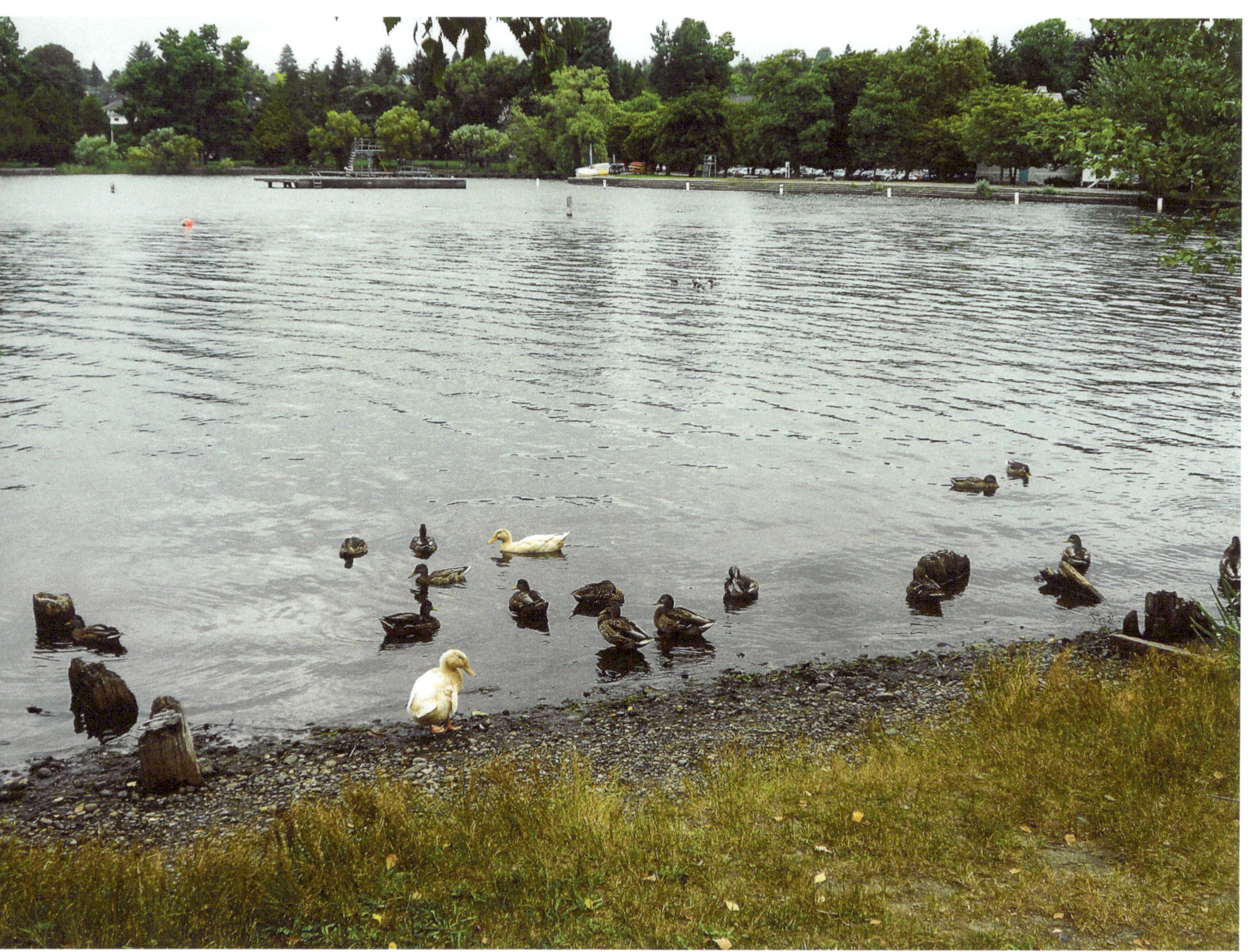

# Sociable Ducks

I've noticed that ducks like to assemble in groups, even if of different species, especially when they snooze for the night. During the day they can be seen in nearly every section of the lake, and often by themselves, although generally they are partnered up, but when they bed down for the night they tend to cluster in a select few spots. I suspect they find security in numbers.

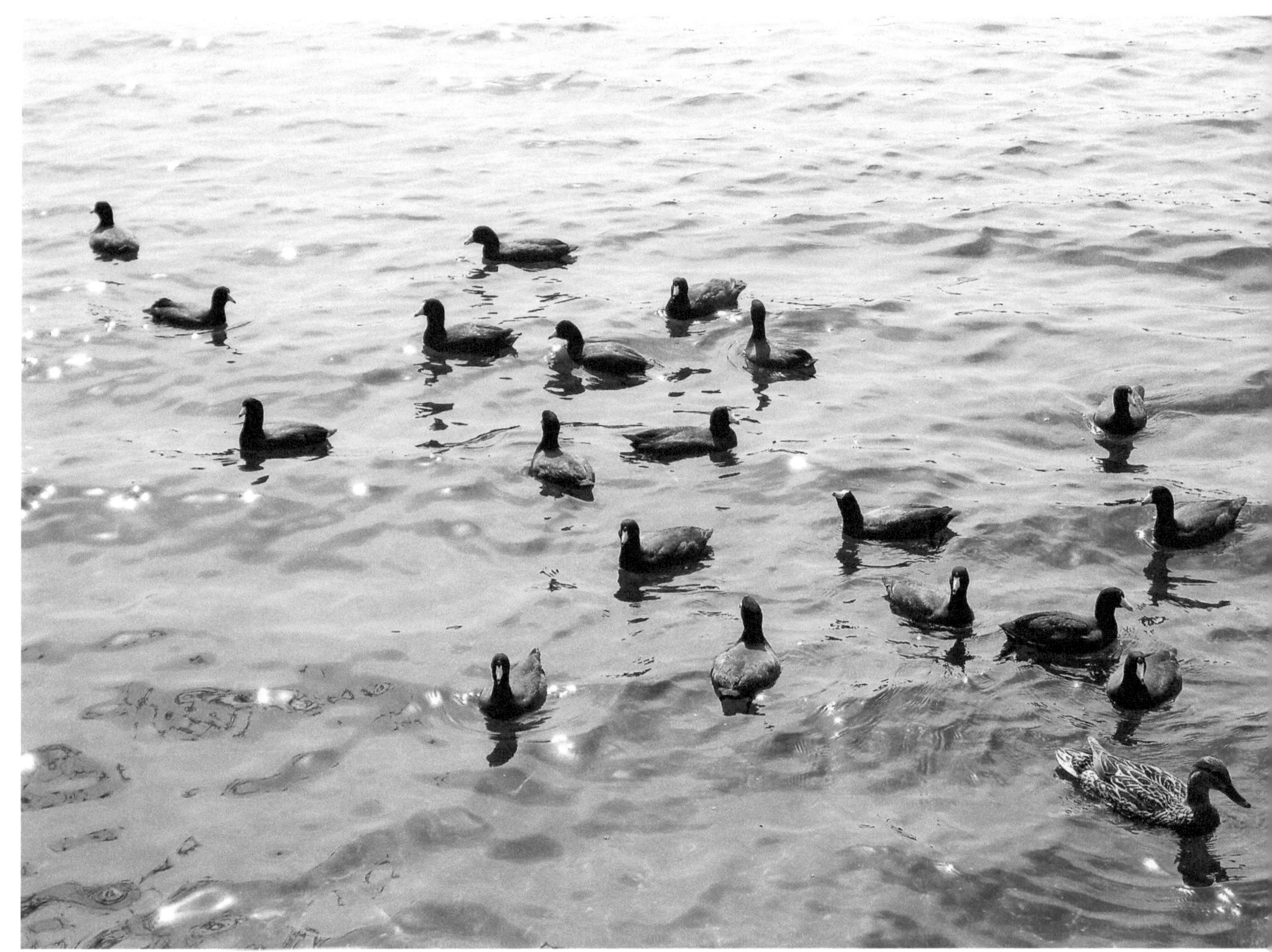

# Where Are We Going?

Remember Monty Python's spoof on game shows called 'Spot the Looney'? Obviously the looney here is the duck in the lower right that seems to know what it is doing or where it is heading; the rest of the coots all behave normal, that is, disoriented and confused.

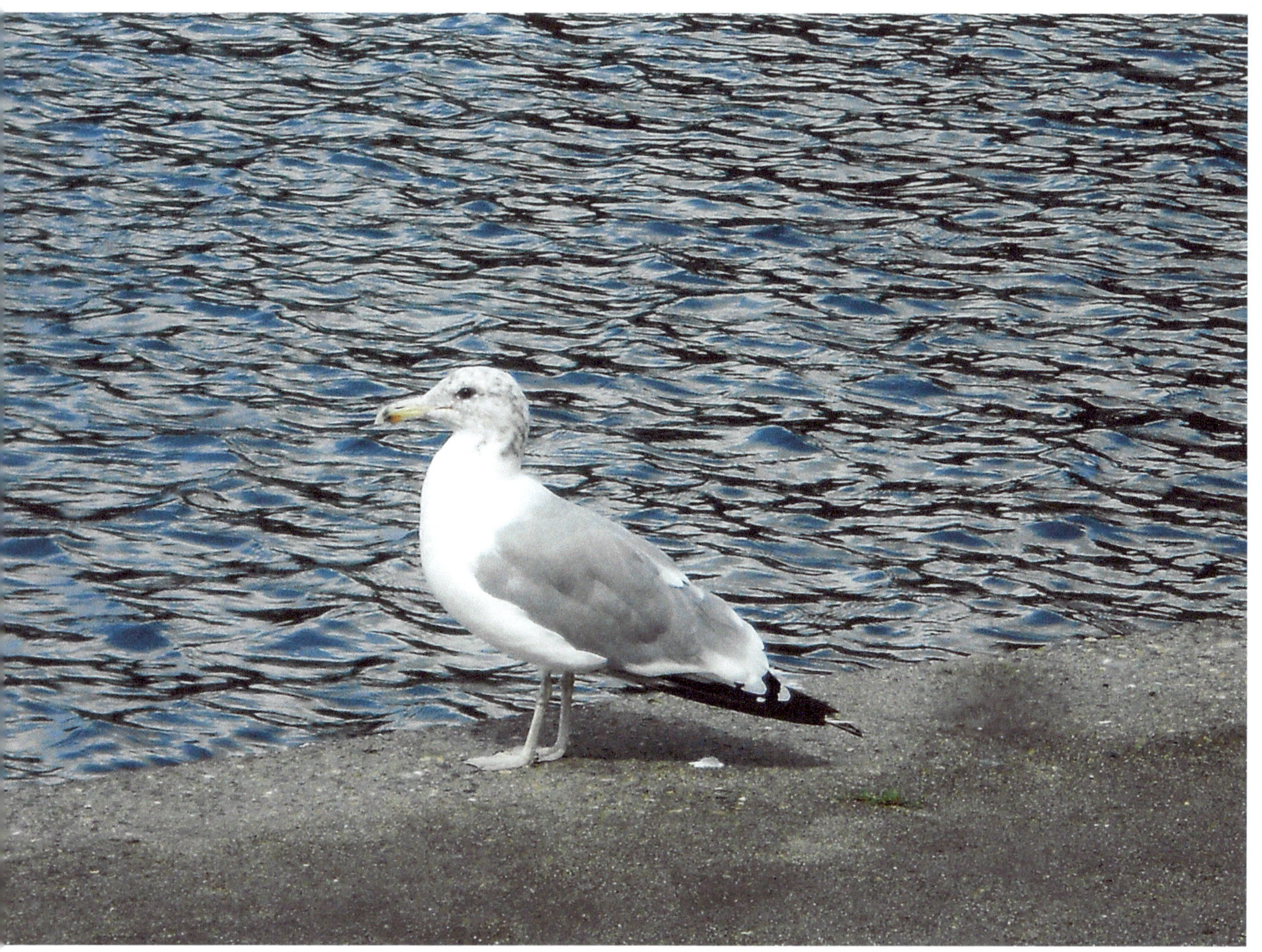

# Shades of Gray

A number of sea gulls have made their home at Green Lake and
are permanent fixtures there. They like to roost on the wooden
piers when vacated by swimmers after the summer season. This
one has just finished doing his thing. In the fall and winter they
become more abundant and are seen in flocks.

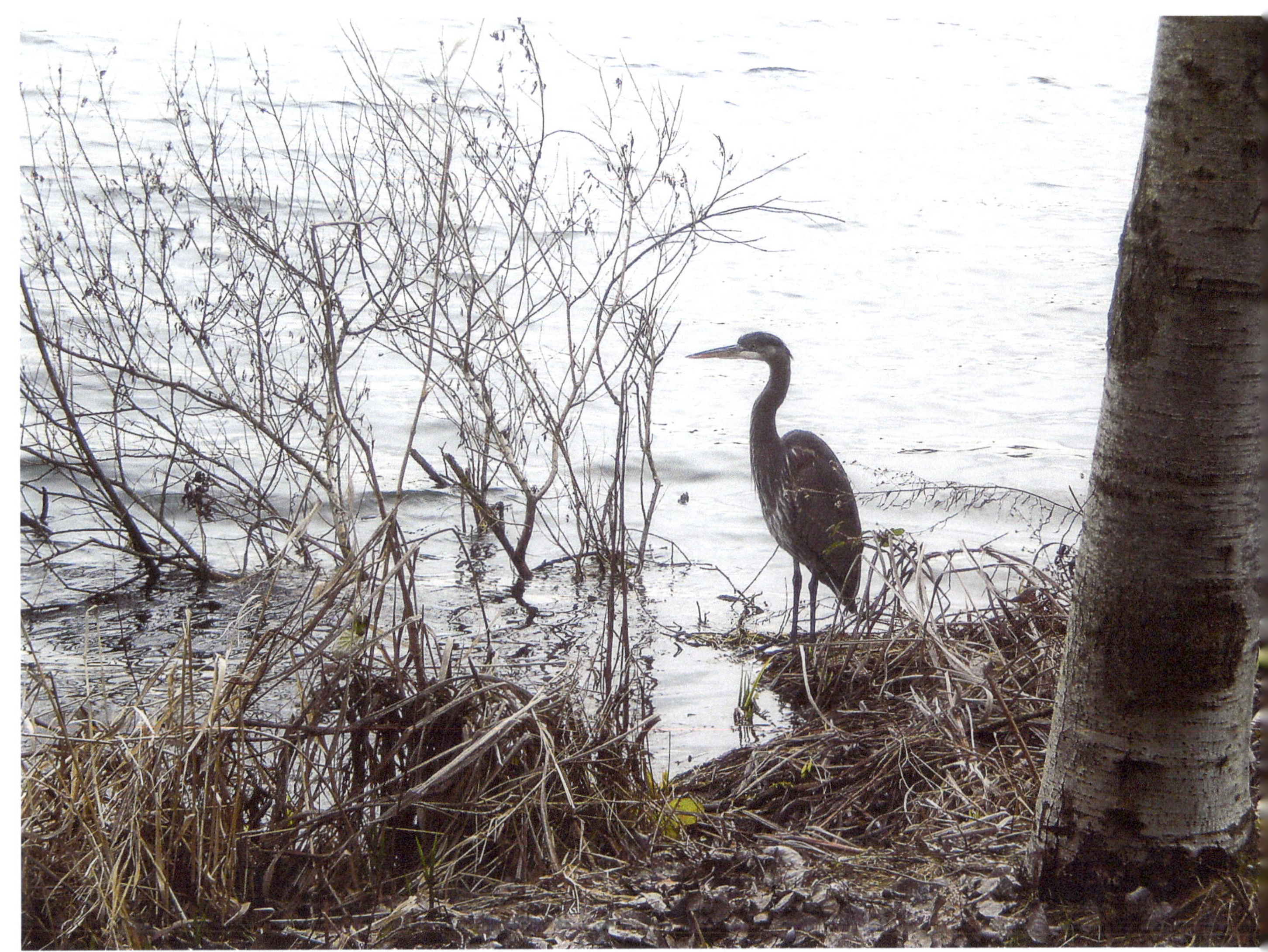

# Natural Setting

It's my friend, the Blue Heron. Looking at this picture, you think
of being out in some remote river edge rather than in a city park.
I like it for that reason.

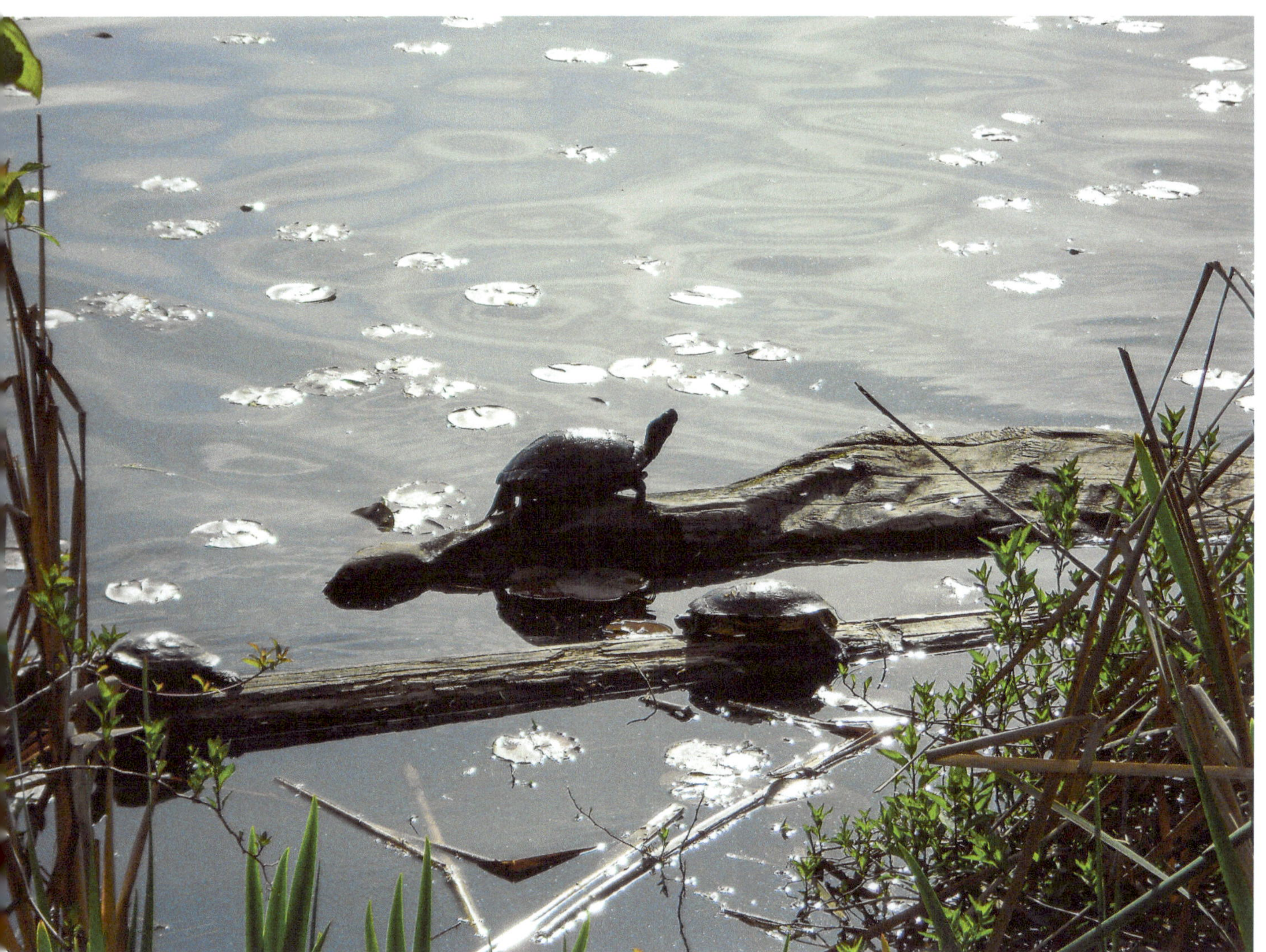

# Enjoying the Sun

In spring, a number of turtles can be spotted resting on the floating logs at the west side of the lake amid the growing lily pads. For some reason they cannot be seen by the time mid-summer arrives. Where can you migrate to in a lake?

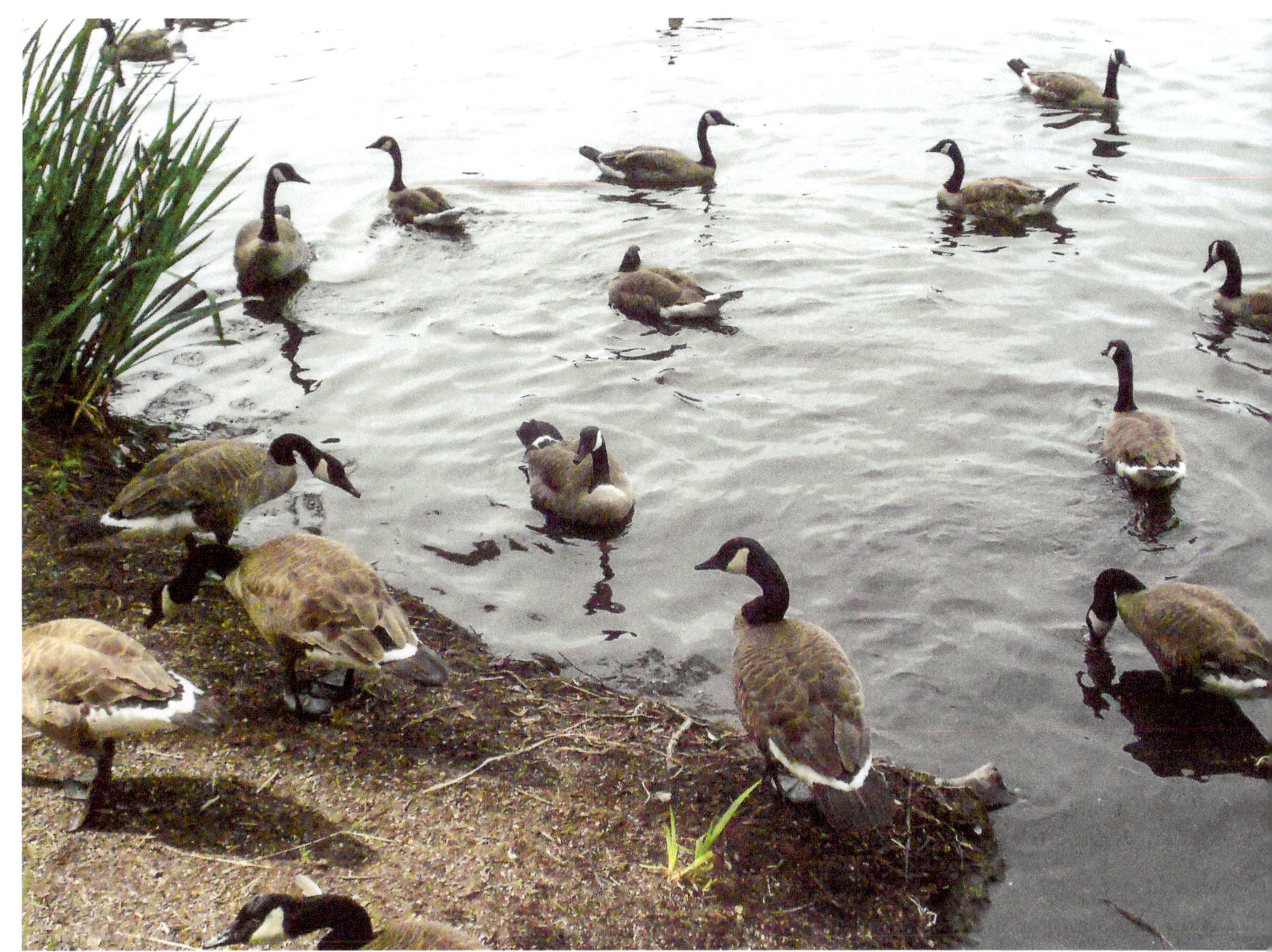

# Just Visiting

What park isn't frequented, or should I say plagued, by Canadian Geese along their migration routes? I call them excrement machines because they do make a mess of things. But in all fairness, I've observed some of their behavior patterns and find them fascinating. They appear to have a distinct leader —an alpha Goose so to speak— and designate lookouts when feeding or resting as a group. Green Lake appears to be an annual resting stop in their journeys.

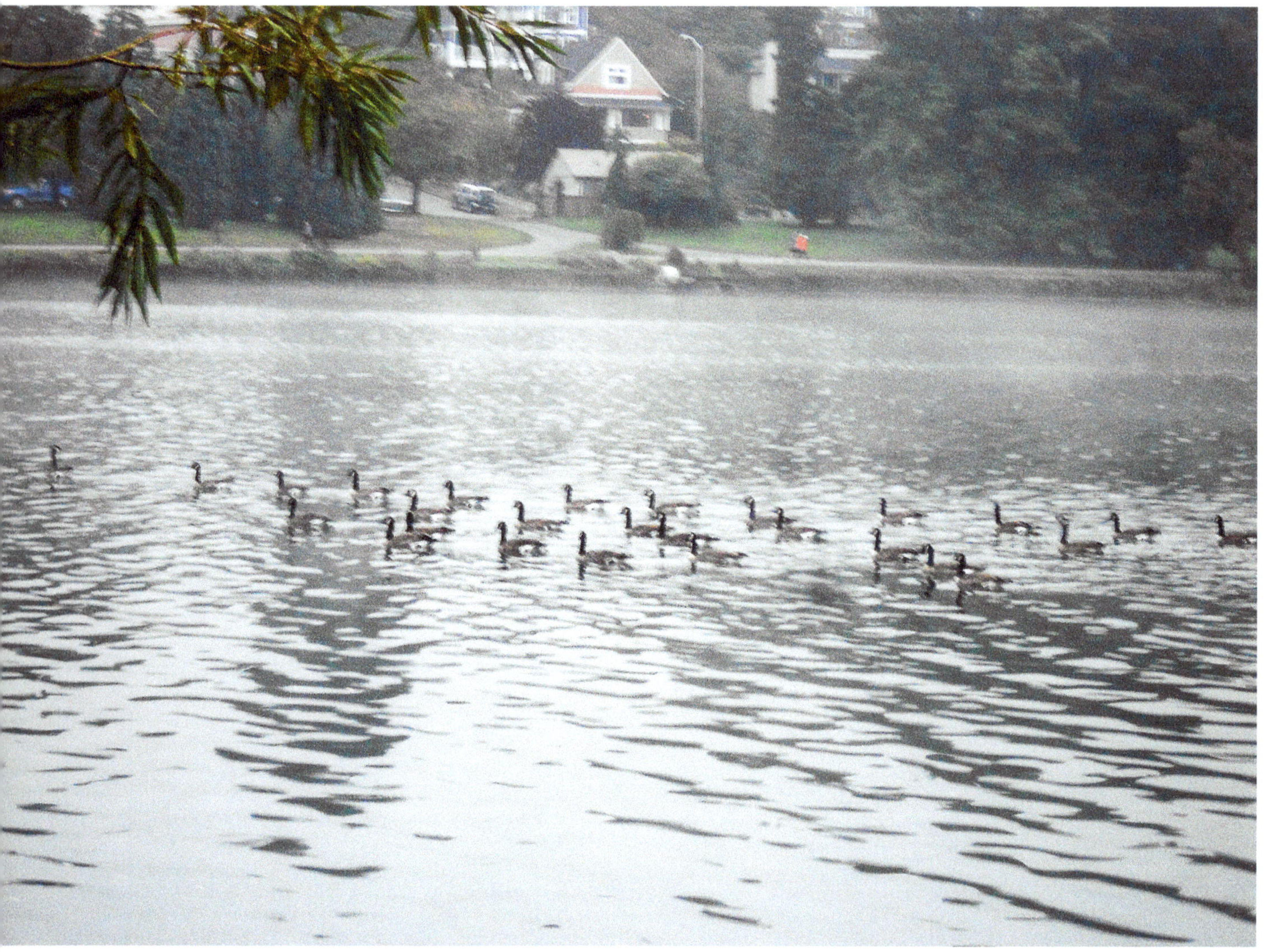

# Call to Assembly

While resting at the lake, Canadian Geese may scatter into smaller groups that stake claim to particular areas in the park. When ready to continue, an interesting development takes place. One Goose trumpets a call —so sonorous that I've actually heard it from my house a mile away— giving out a signal for all the geese to assemble at a certain place. There they congregate from every part of the lake. The alpha goose appears as if actually taking roll call. When every goose is accounted for, portions of the massed group, in a cacophony of honking, begin flapping their wings and taking off so that instantly they form into a 'V' formation, each goose knowing where it belongs. Once airborne, they fly off in a giant loop with amazing swiftness and are gone within seconds. A second group then takes off (I've never seen more than two). So if you see Canadian Geese gathering in large numbers on the water, stick around: you're in for a terrific show. This shot was taken during an early morning fog.

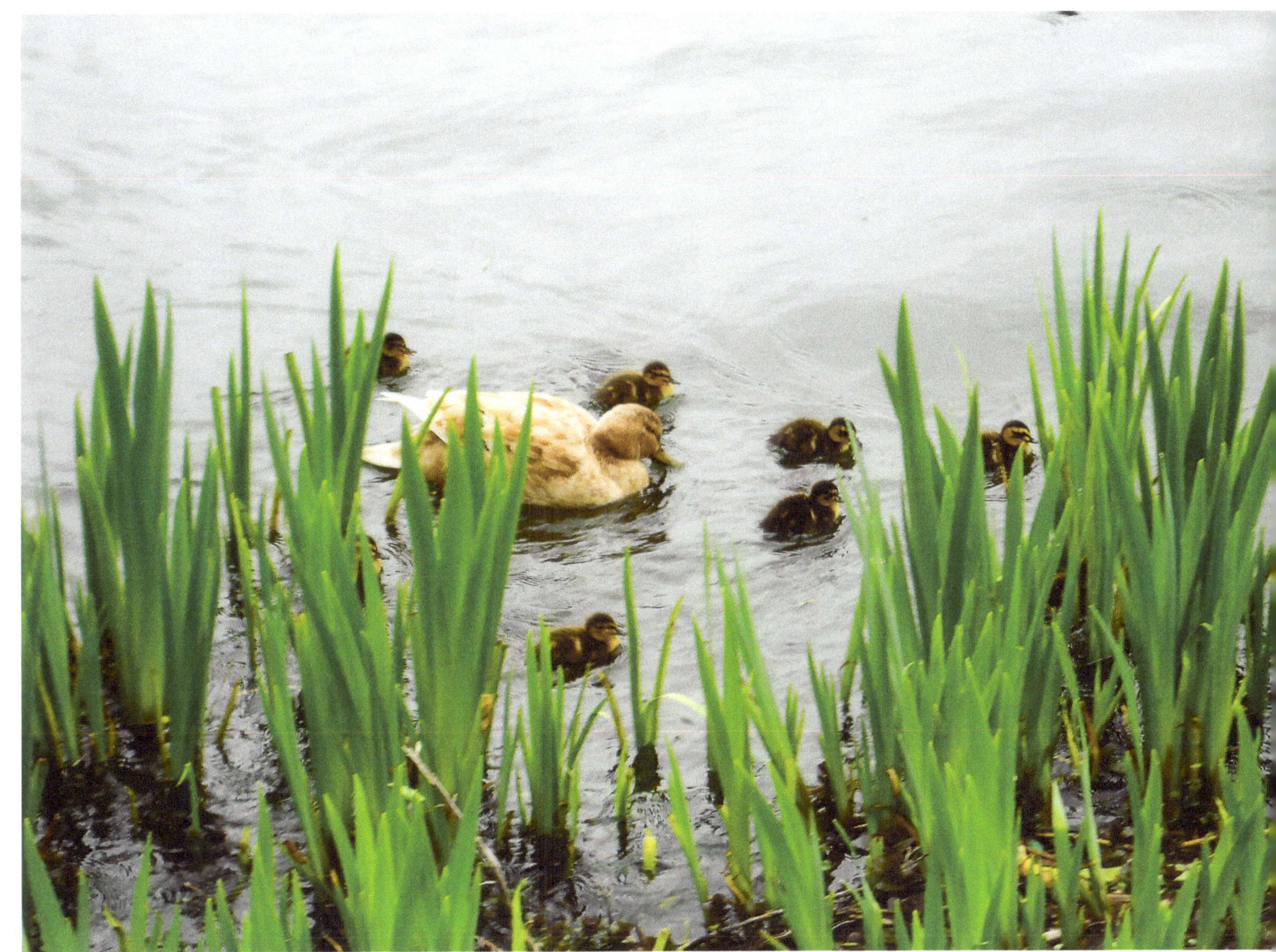

# Life Goes On

This is obviously the female of my two favorite ducks at the lake (the only two golden colored ones there). It's clear the male hasn't wasted any time in doing what he is supposed to do. I like the contented look of this mother, as if immensely proud of her accomplishment.

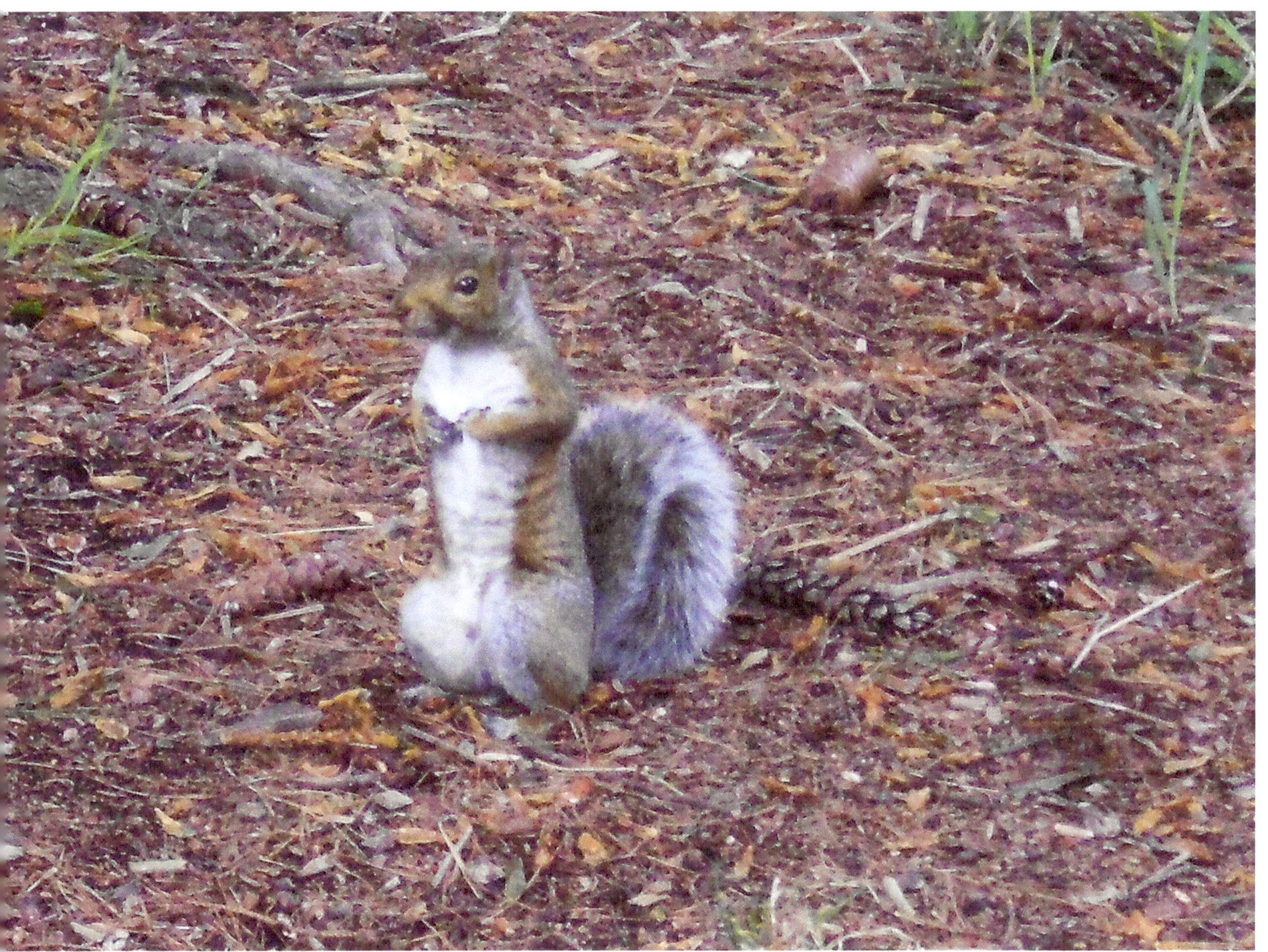

# Well Camouflaged

Squirrels are abundant everywhere in the park. They are very animated creatures and difficult to catch in a standstill position or motionless for any length of time as this one. By the time you get your camera set, they will have moved. They run by hopping with both front legs and rear legs together when hitting the ground. They're fun to watch.

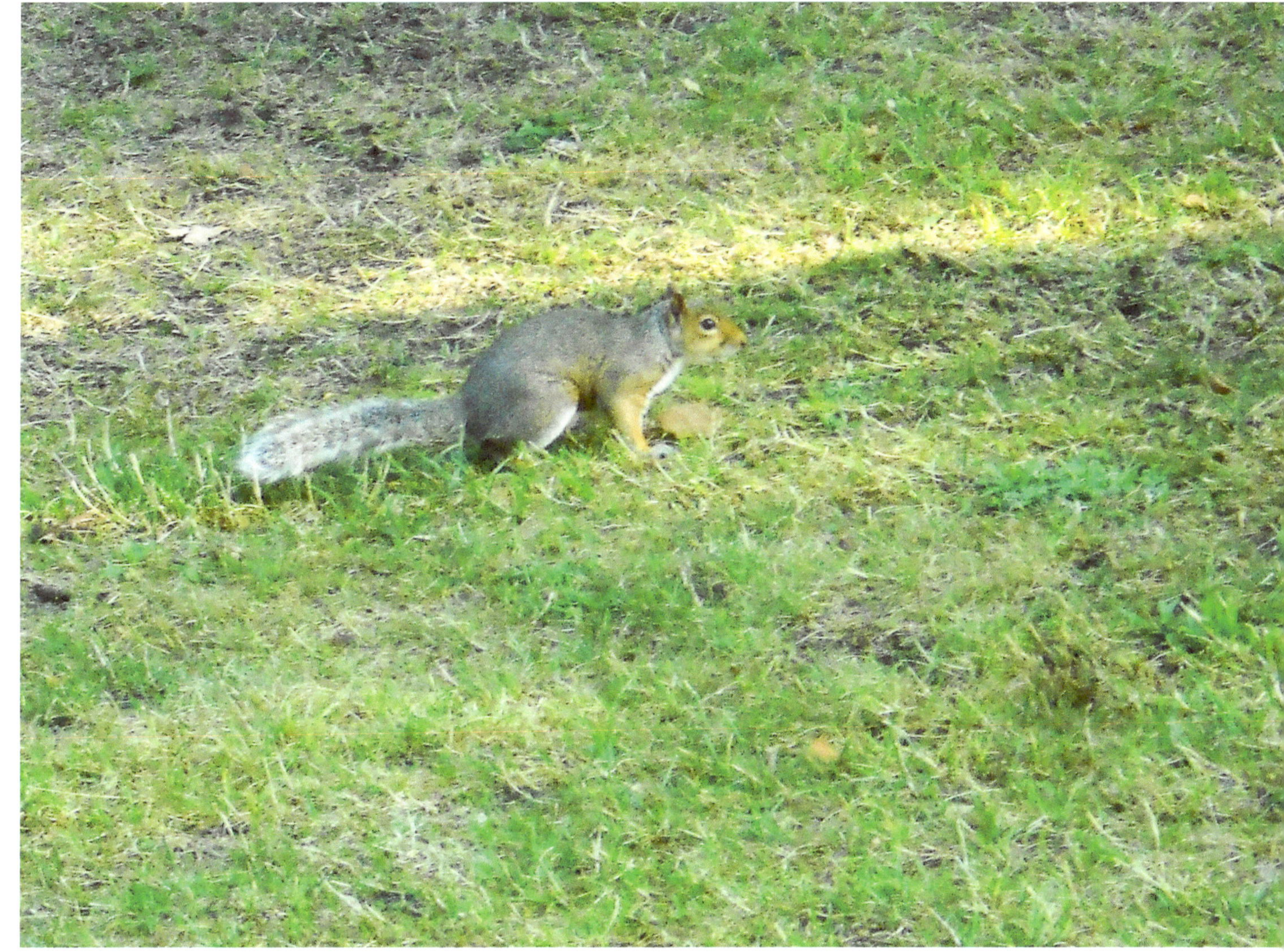

# Pausing, Perhaps to Think

If they didn't move, you would have a hard time seeing them. Squirrels blend quite well into their background, whether in grass or at the base of trees as in the previous picture. I once heard that they are nothing more than rats with a furry tail. That may be, but rats are associated with sewers and gutters, squirrels with lawns and parks and, to me, that sets them worlds apart.

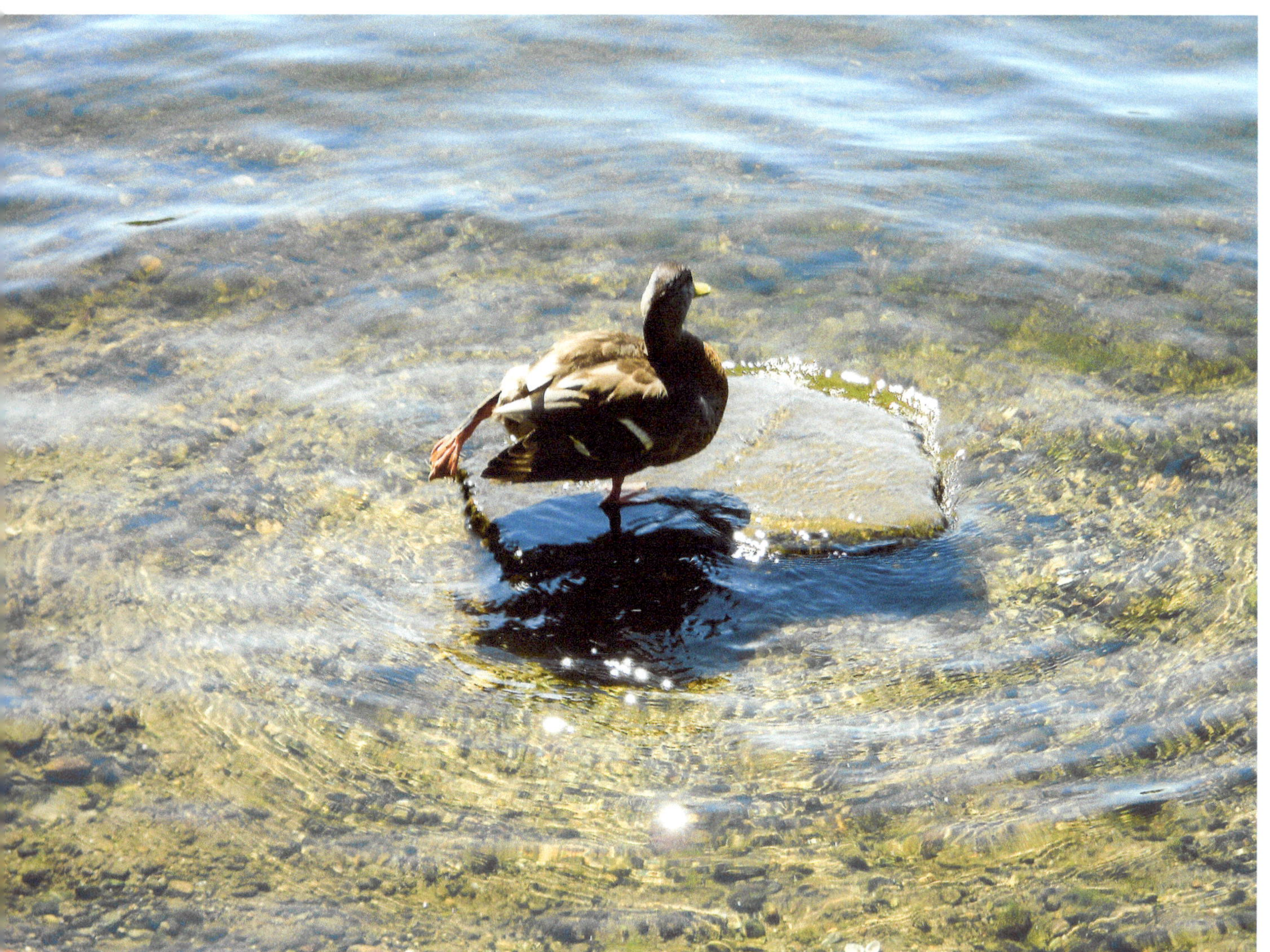

# Testing the Water

This duck wants to make sure the water temperature is just right before taking the plunge.

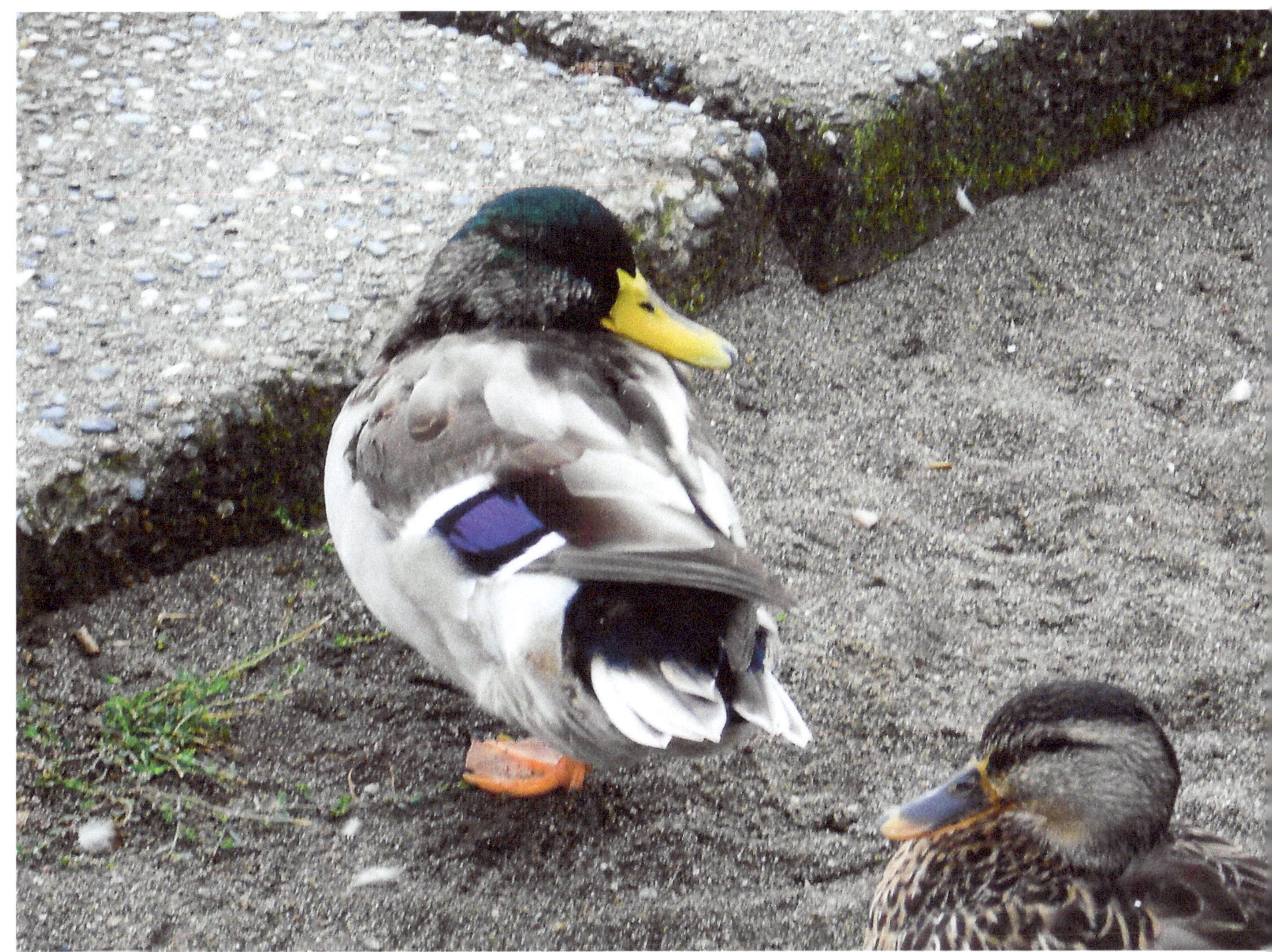

# If I play it cool, she'll be impressed with me.

Actually this duck needs to be told it's not cool to keep looking at her, but who can blame him? She's so lovely.

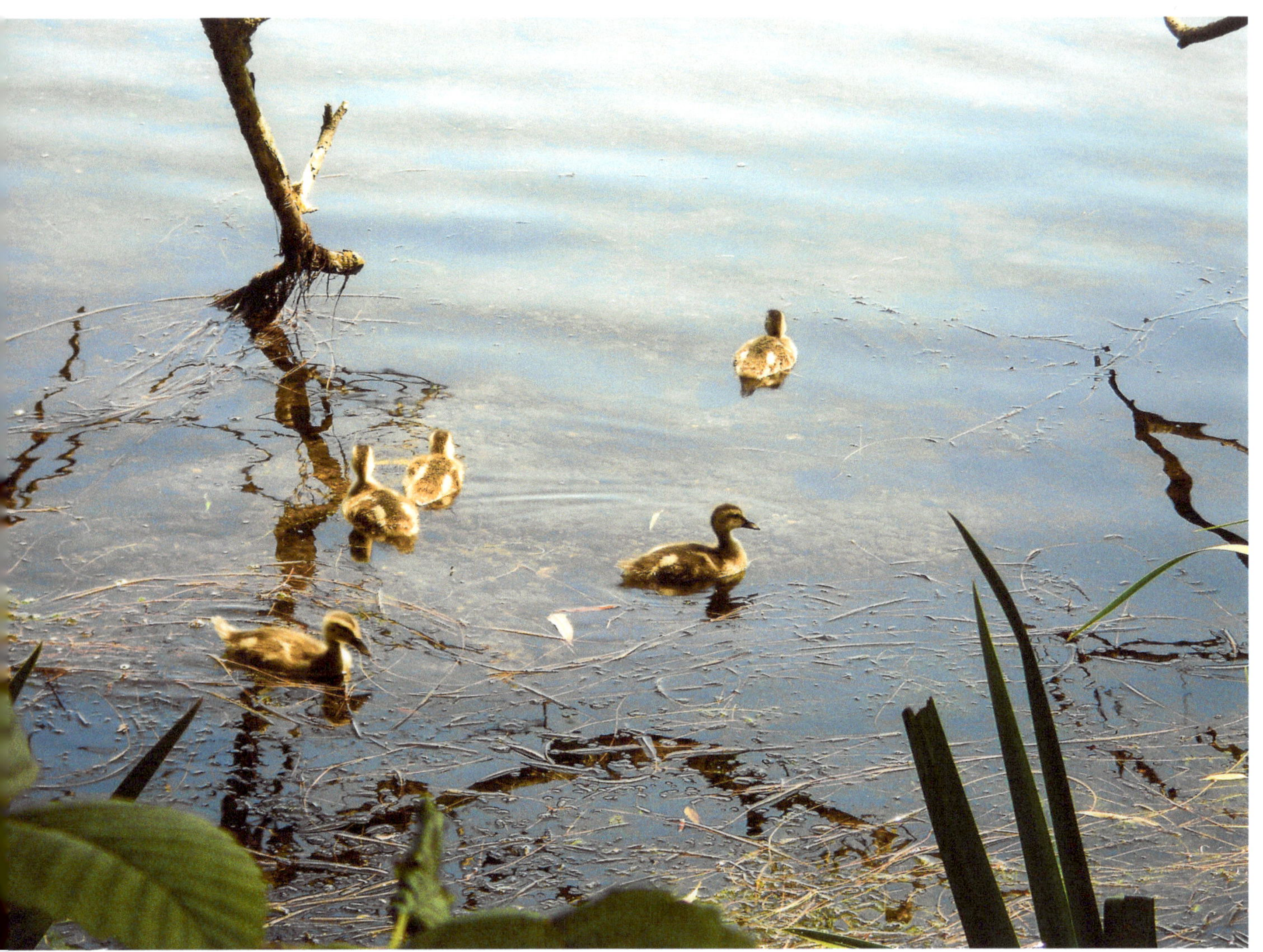

# Where's Mother?

Somehow these ducklings got separated from their mother. They're probably teen-agers now and think they can make it on their own, but still seem unsure of which way to go. That has a familiarity to it.

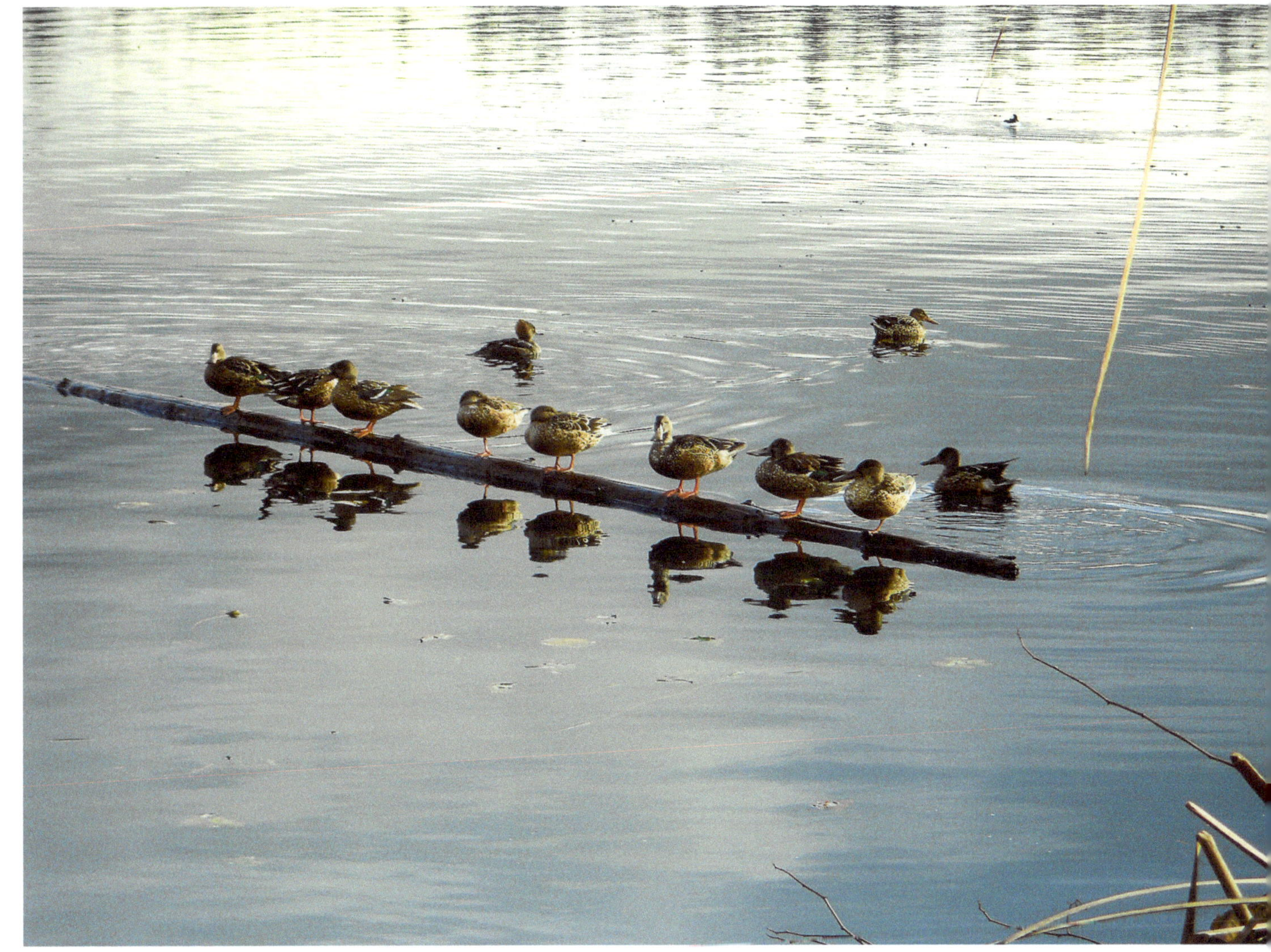

# Getting Your Ducks in Line

This picture gives a whole new definition to that old phrase. As usual there's one in every crowd that doesn't follow the rules (the second duck from the left). What I like about this picture is its clarity, especially the reflected ripple effect on the water

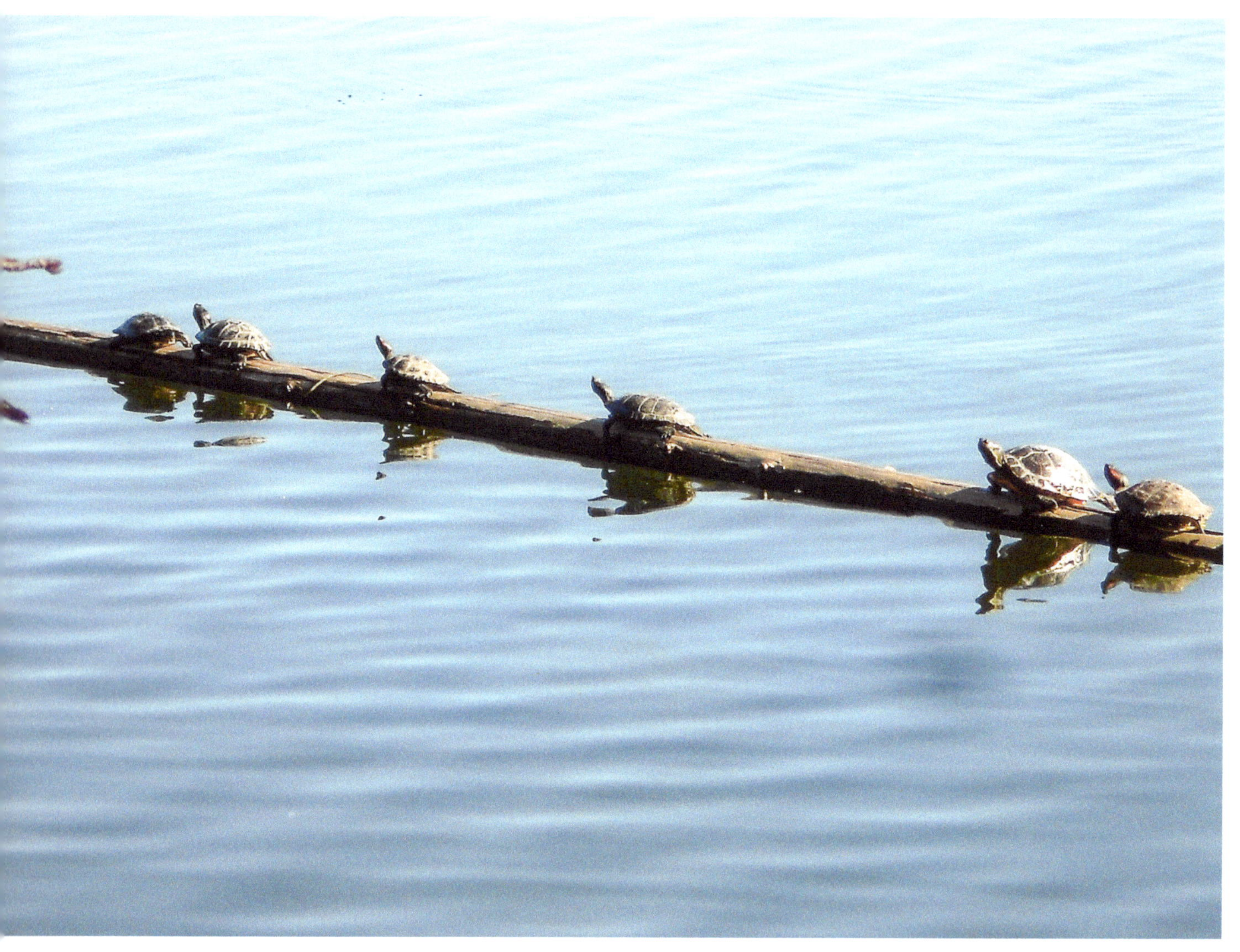

# Getting Your Turtles in Line

That just doesn't sound the same. When turtles bask in the sun they seem to always stick their necks out as if reaching for something in the air. As with the ducks, there's always one that doesn't toe the line.

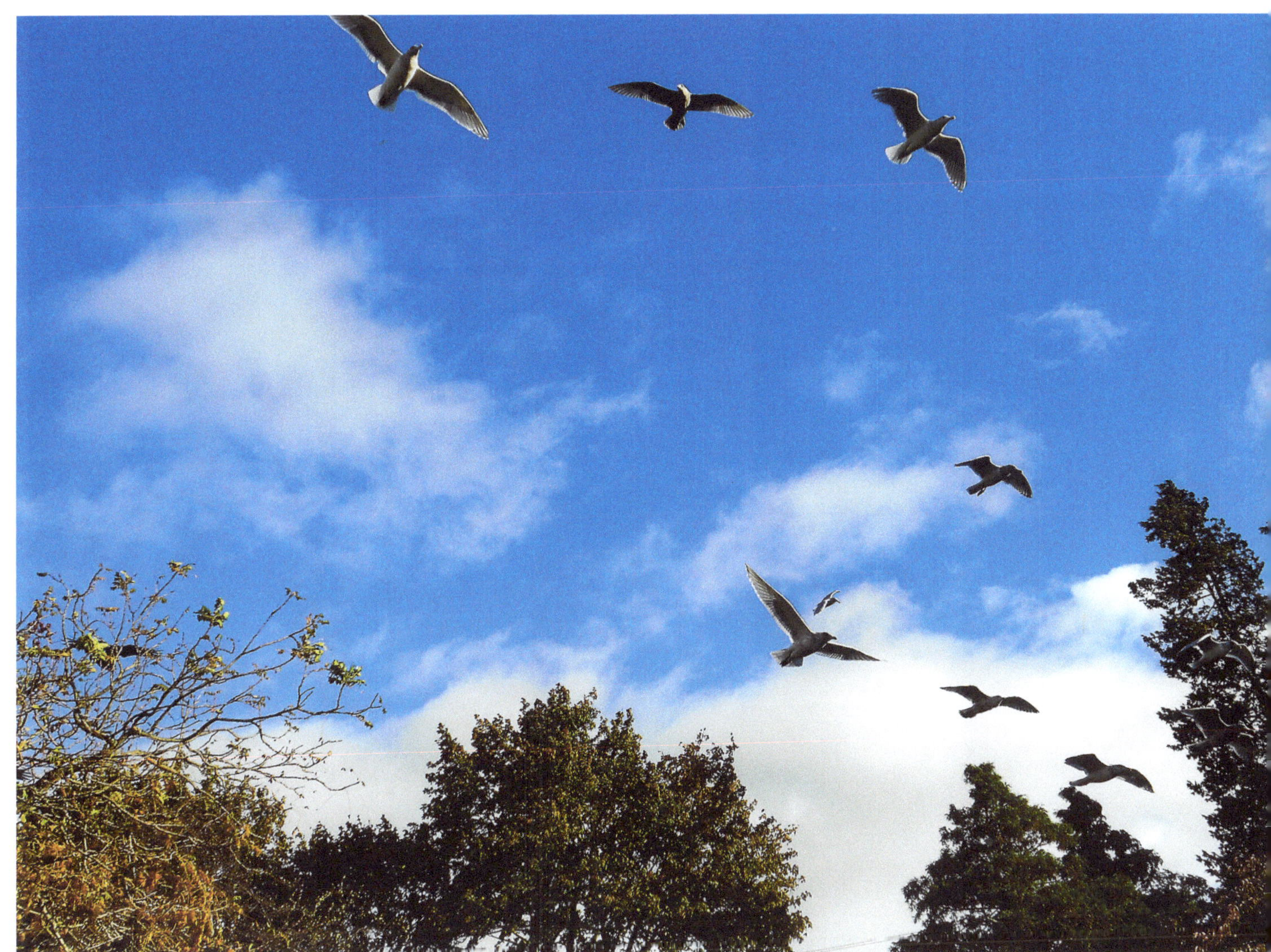

# Bopping up and down

These gulls are actually stationary, letting a strong wind weave them up and down in the air. I think they do this because it's fun for them, much like us riding a roller coaster. You see such a sight often when you have a stormy day.

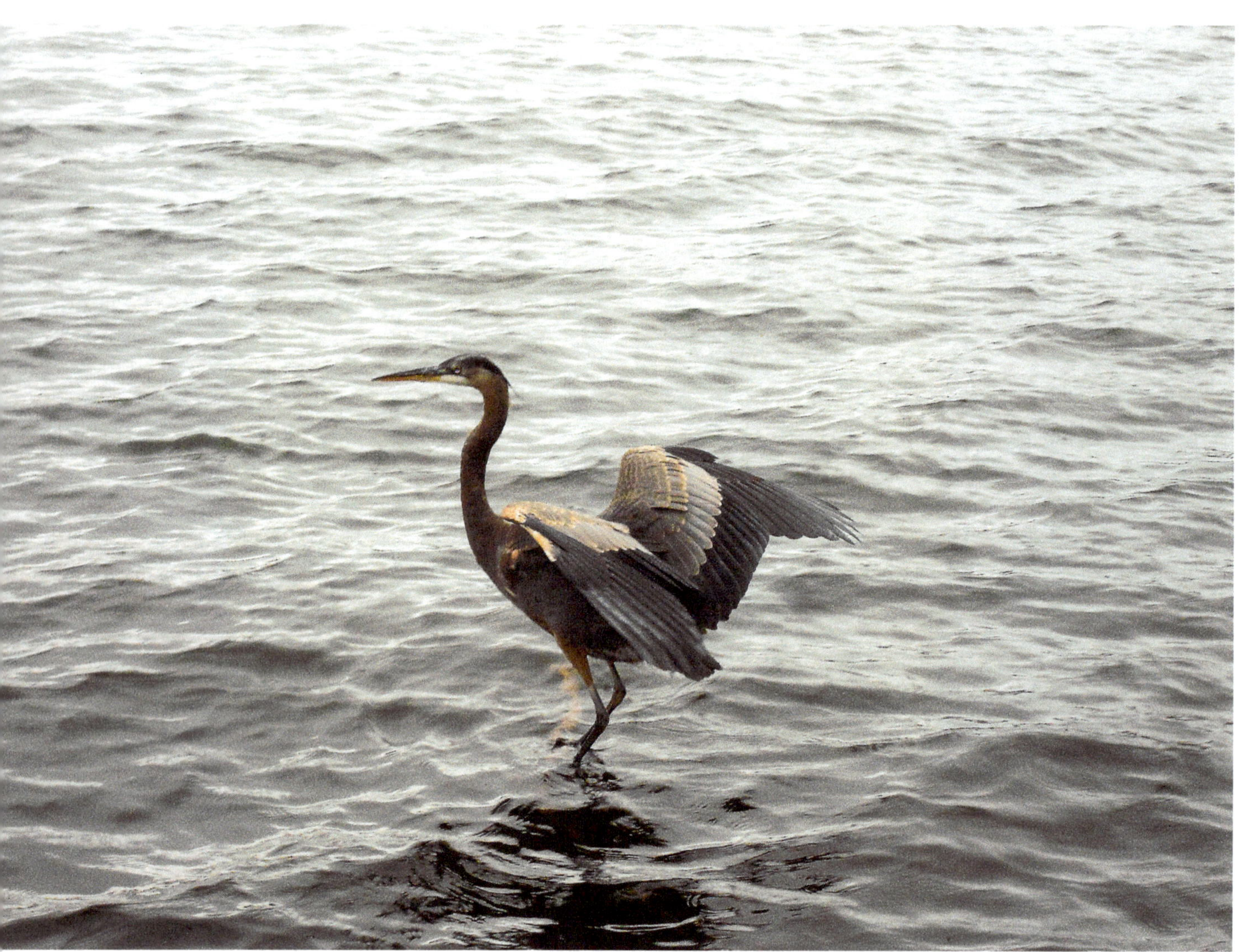

# "Blue Heron One —You are now cleared for take-off."

This is the closest I have come to getting the resident Blue Heron in flight. Once airborne, it moves too fast for my camera. You will have to take my word for it that it is a magnificent sight to see a Heron flying, sheer grace and swiftness all in one.

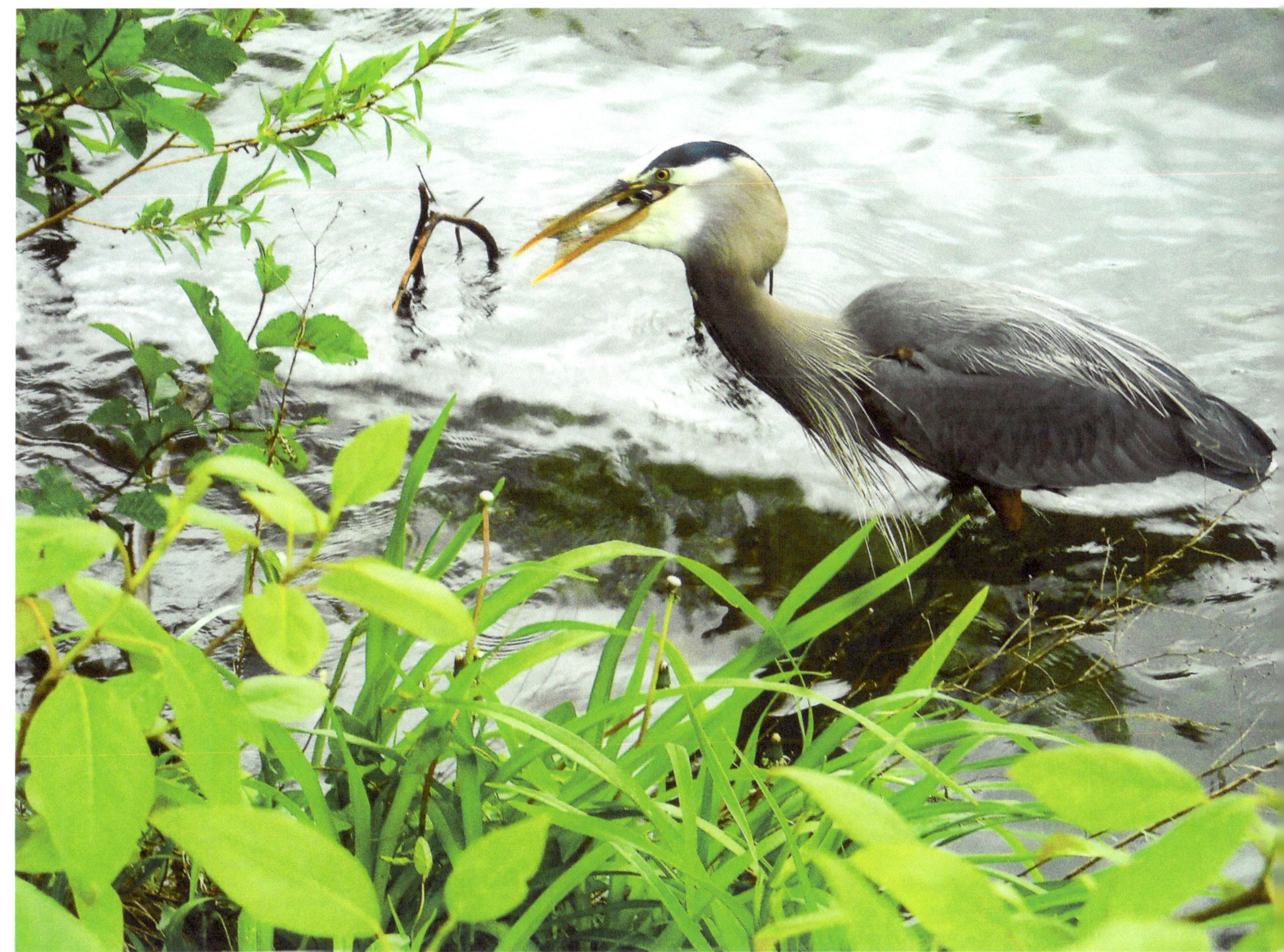

# Caught in the Act

This is a Gray Heron devouring a fish. I saw it only once at Green Lake. Considerably more bulky than its Blue Heron cousin, its proportions seem awkward to me with an overly sized head and neck and stubby tail; not exactly handsome, but very unique —and rare.

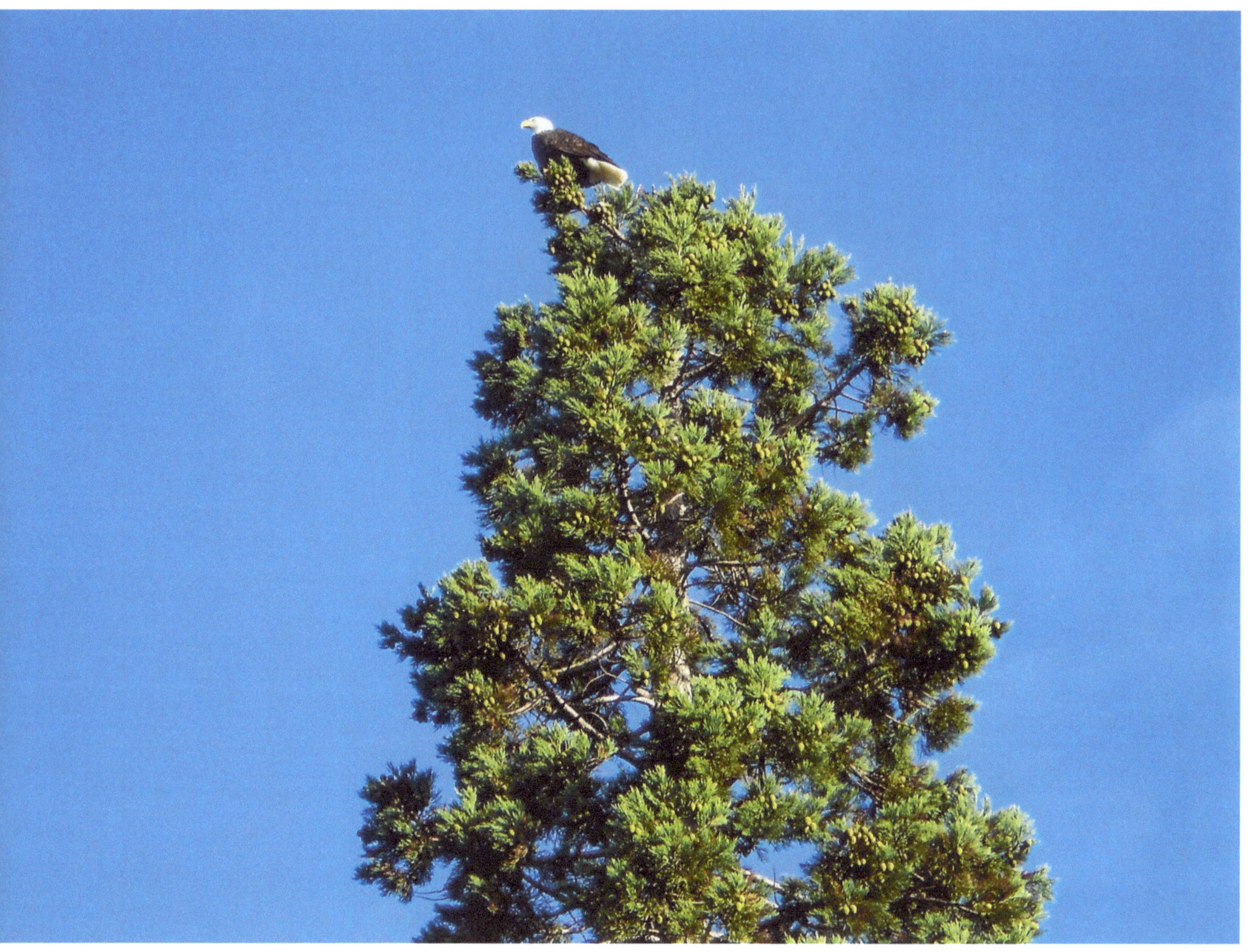

# Visitor

Occasionally a Bald Eagle will visit Green Lake. When it does, it generates considerable excitement and draws a crowd. Usually the bird will perch on the upper most branch of an evergreen tree and is therefore easily seen from below, much like the star on top of a Christmas tree. When you're on top of the predator bird chain, there's no need to be inconspicuous.

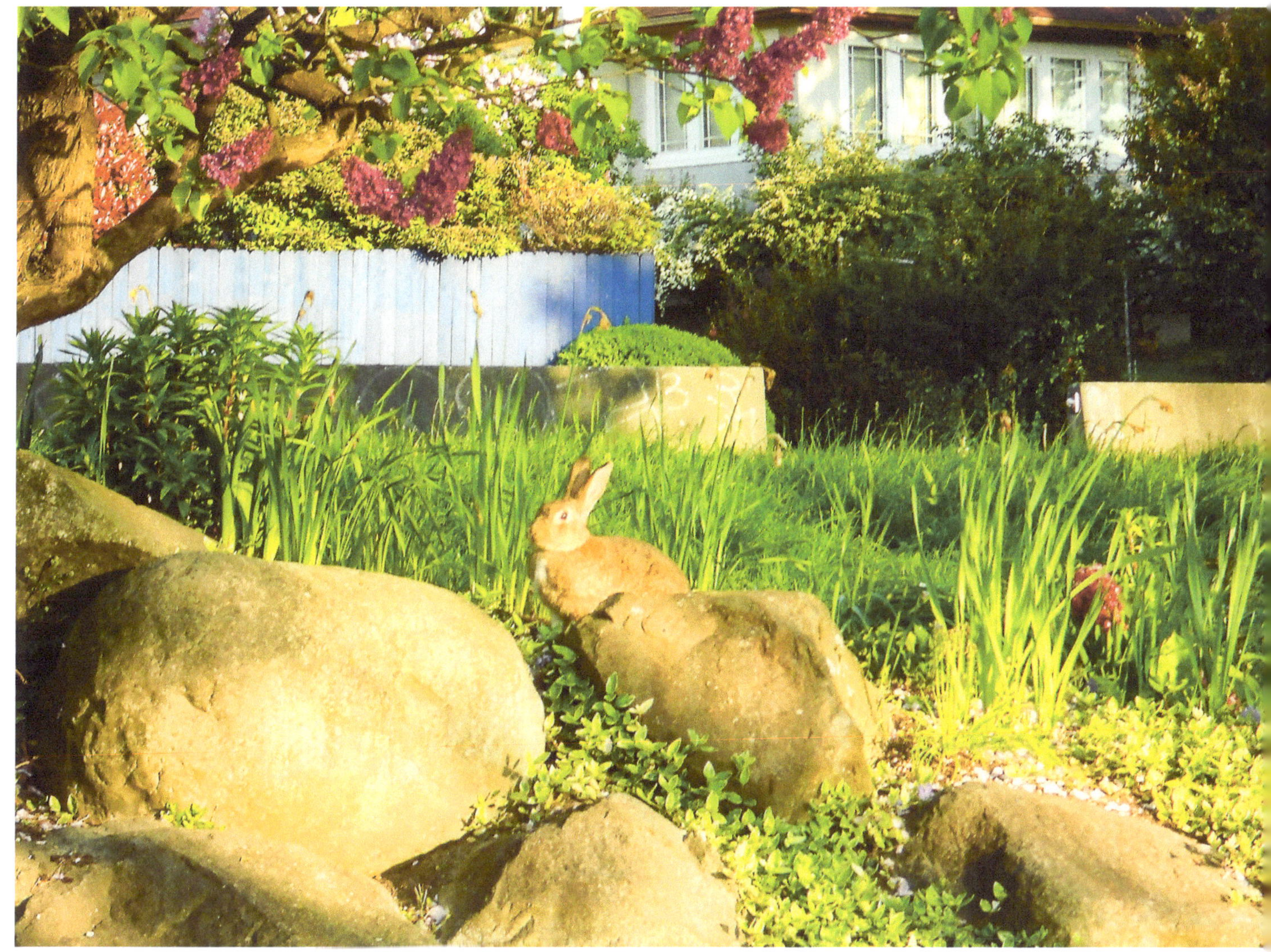

# Peter Cottontail

Here we see a rabbit looking as big as the boulder in front of it which resembles a beaver. Rabbits can be seen occasionally at early dawn; they used to be more plentiful and one year it even seemed as if they threatened to take over the lake as its most abundant fauna. The house in the background is across Aurora Avenue bordering the west side of the lake.

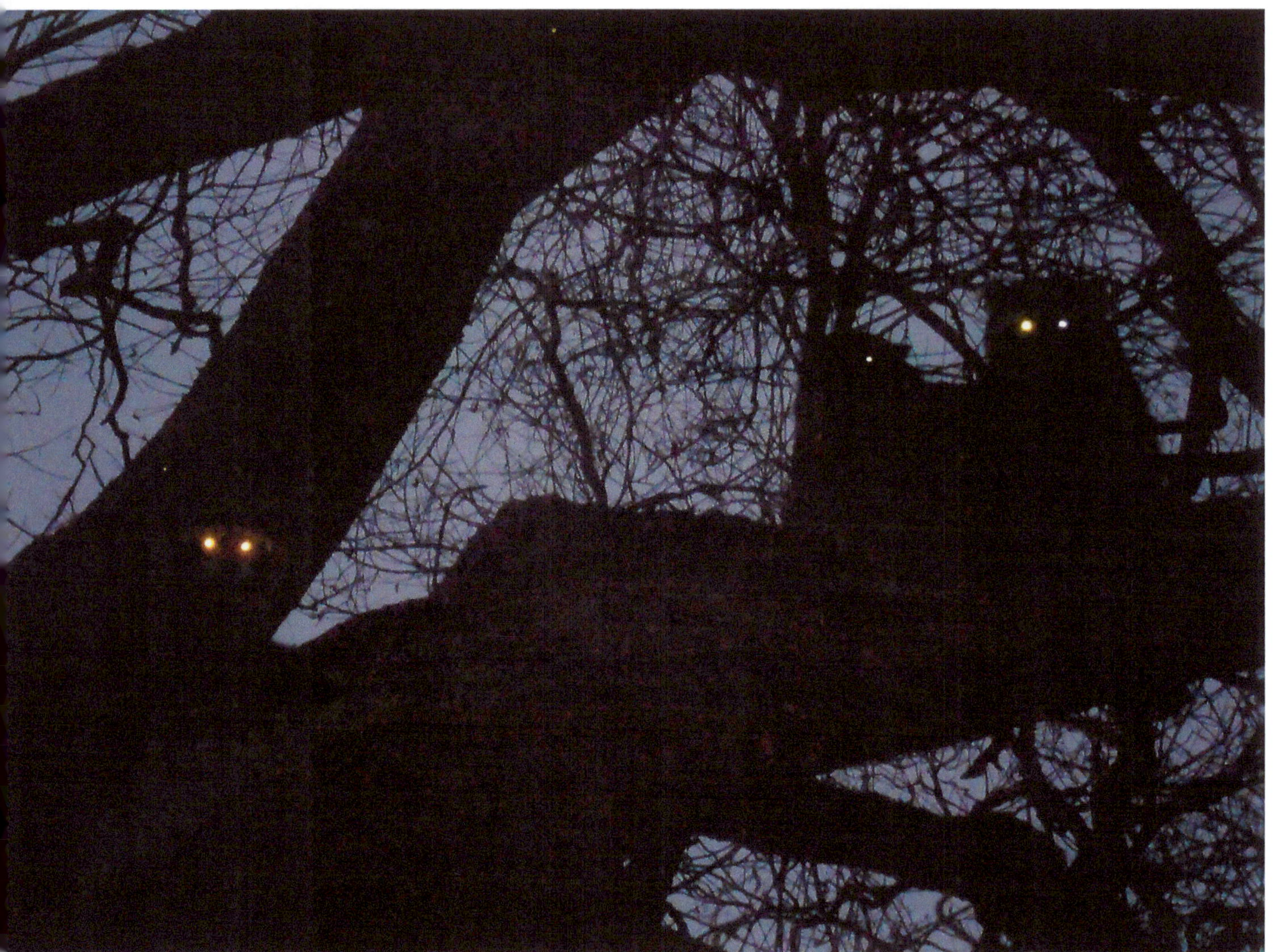

# Hoot! Hoot!

Looking more like owls than raccoons, this trio of the furry critters was caught atop a tree adjacent to the main parking lot of the Green Lake Center facility. Raccoons are typically seen early in the morning before the sun comes up and during the winter months. Where they hide during the day, I don't know, but I suspect it's at Woodland Park Zoo (attached to Green Lake Park at its south end). They have absolutely no fear of humans.

# Green Lake Dawn

## In praise of each coming day

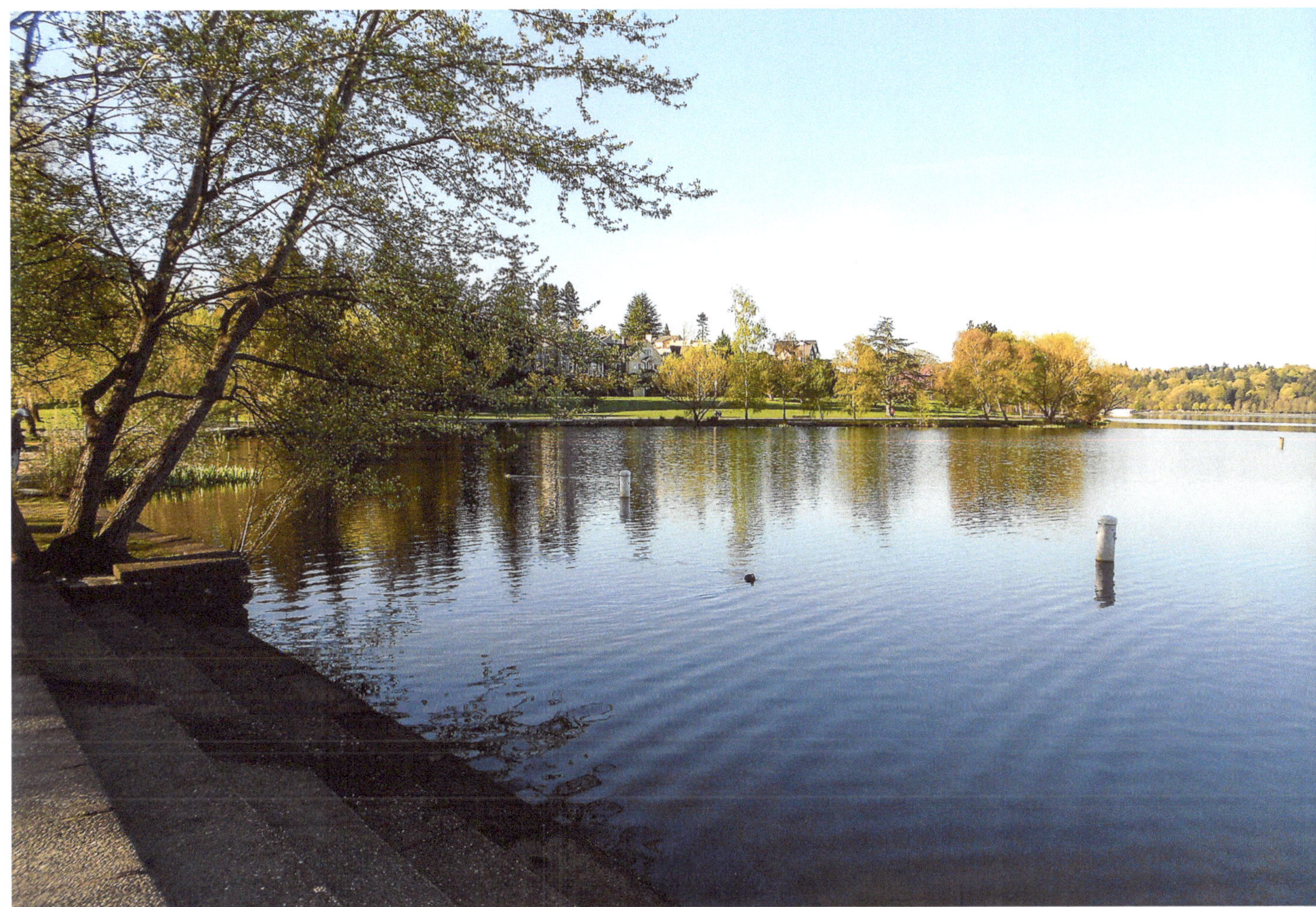

The shadowed steps facing west reveal this to be a glorious morning scene common during Seattle's dry season –yes, we have one– during the months of July, August, and September. This category has some of my favorite pictures. On weekends I usually take my walk early at dawn, especially in the summer, mainly to avoid the crowds that gather later in the day. I prefer my walks to be solitary: it places me more in tune with my environment and I see things I would otherwise not notice.

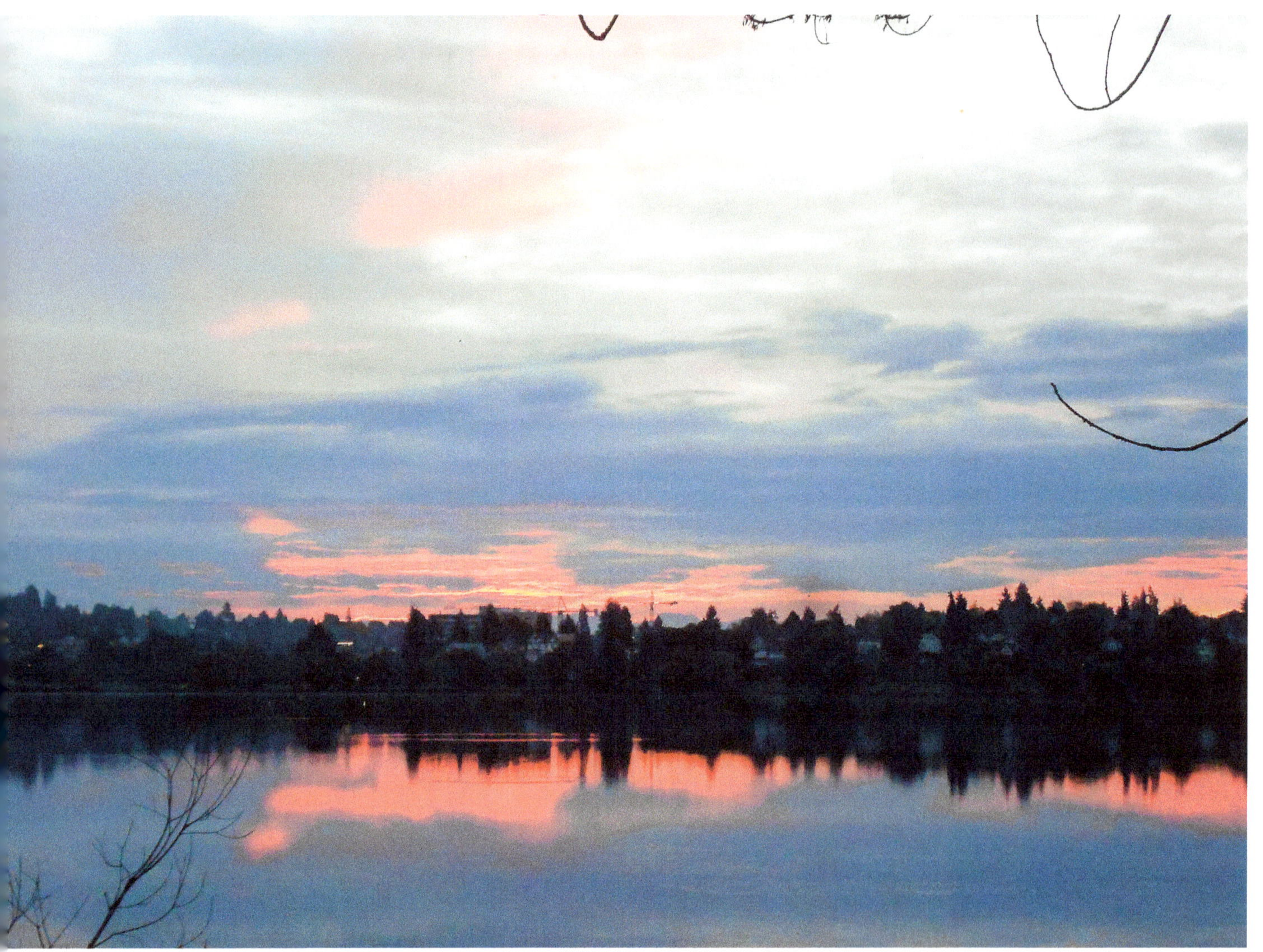

# Dawn's Early Light

I have always been a lark, not an owl, so many of my photos are of sunrises. I like the cool, crispy clearness of the morning air which always seems fresher to me than that of the ending day. This scene nicely depicts such a setting, evoking a quietness characteristic of mornings rather than evenings. It also looks like a cheap oil painting.

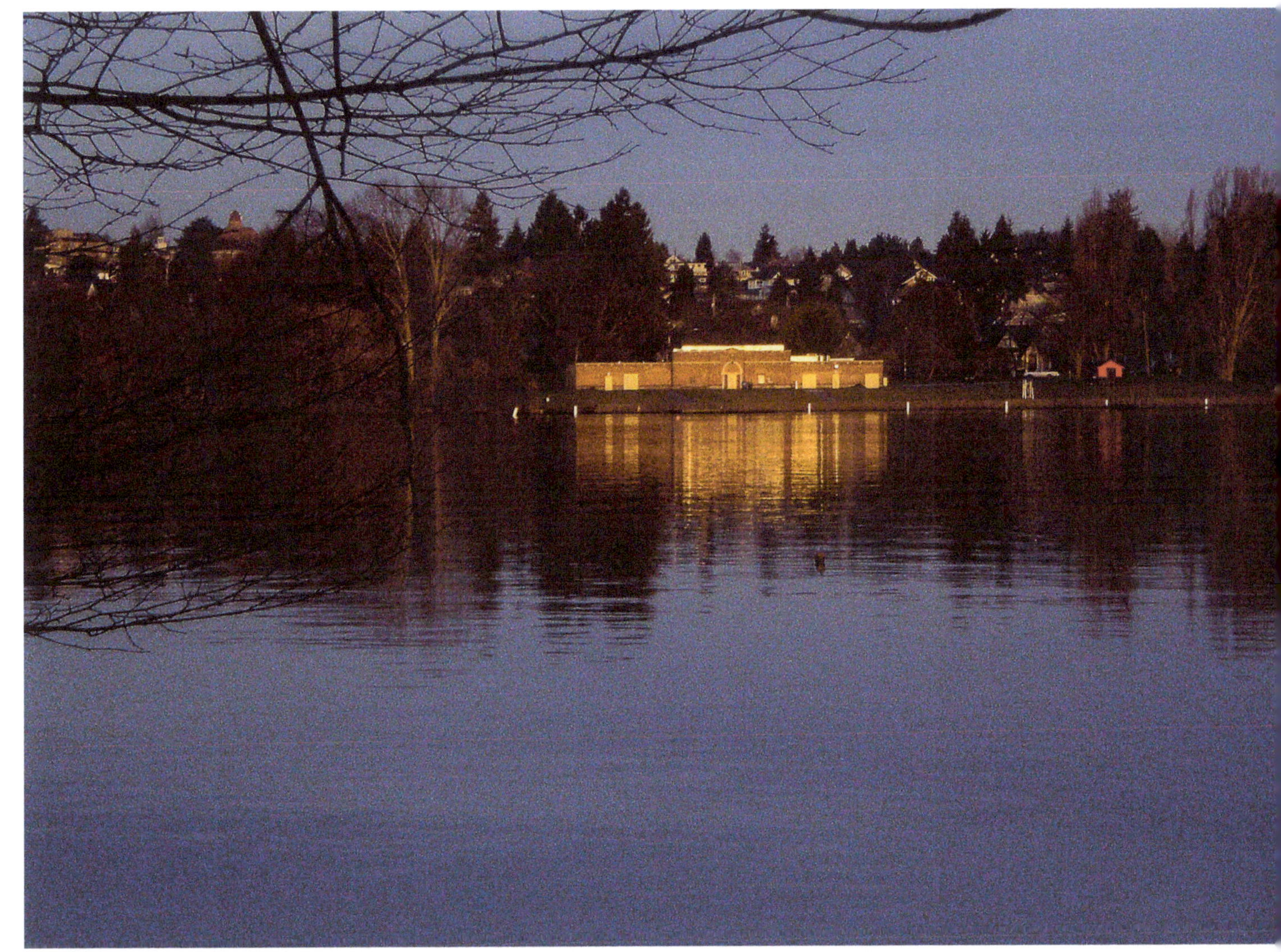

# Another perfect day

Stage productions are held at Green Lake's Bathhouse Theater, located on its northern shore, throughout the year. I've only attended one —an abridged version of Shakespeare's 'A Midsummer Night's Dream' with a teen-age cast. I enjoyed it thoroughly. It's usually the first building to receive the sun's rays. Built in 1927, this was one of the first structures put up at Green Lake, and initially served as a bathhouse only.

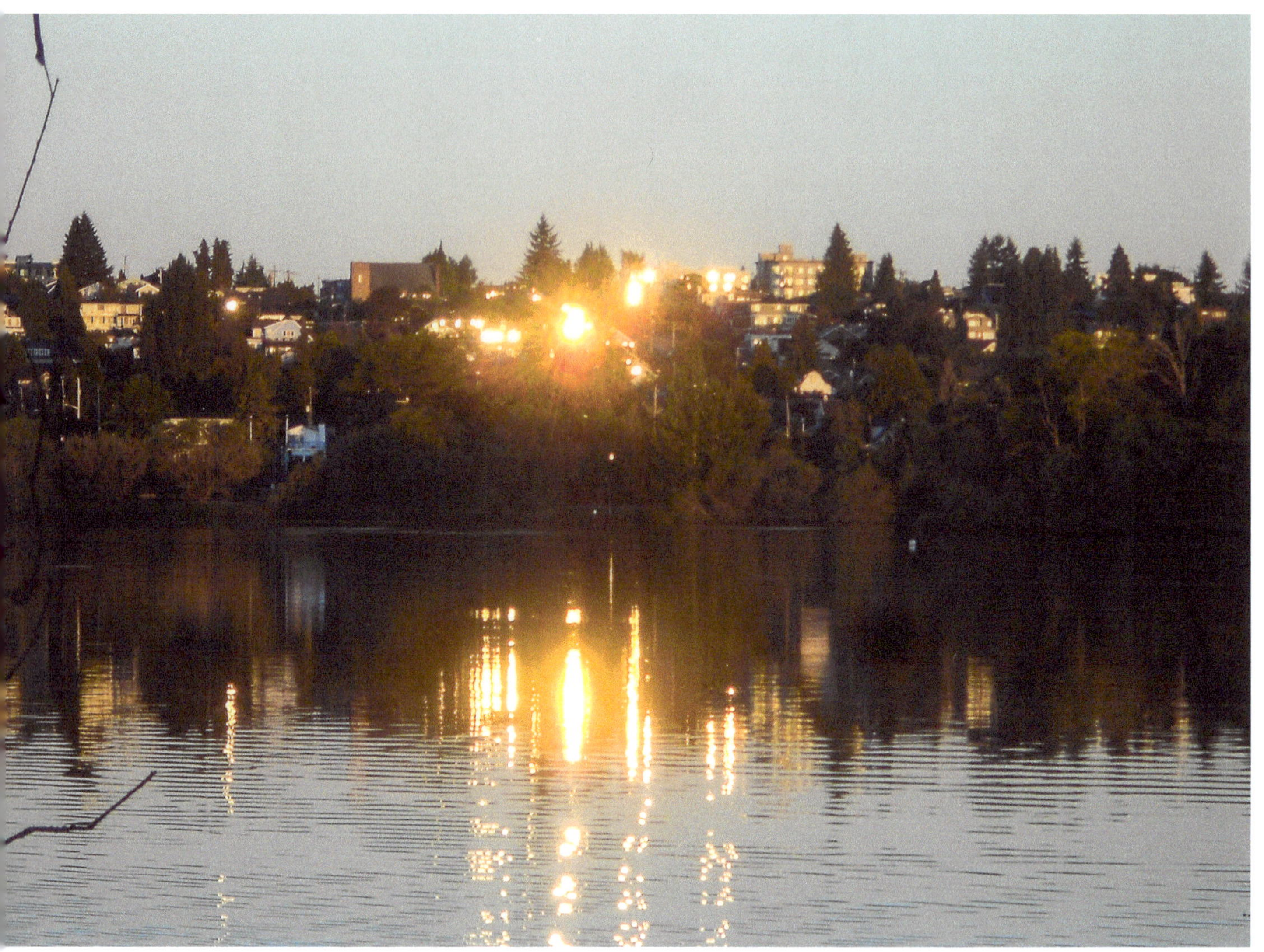

# Reflections

Here you see the sun's rays being reflected off the glass windows of the structures on Phinney Ridge at the west end of the lake. The telephoto setting in my Coolpix makes this area appear nearer than it actually is. For an impressive view of Green Lake, it should be seen from the top of Phinney Ridge.

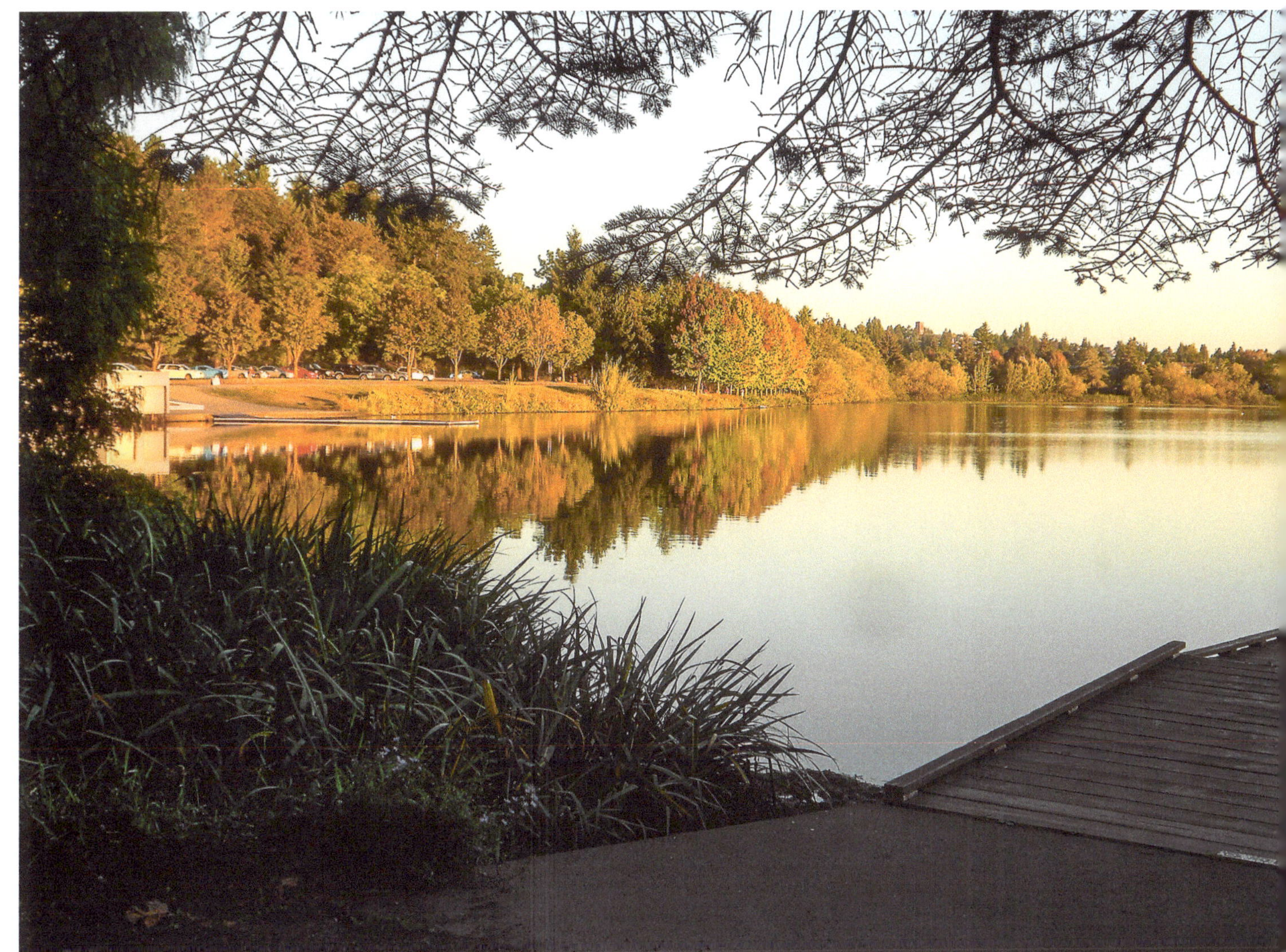

# Feeling the Warmth

This scene is near the boathouse and aqua-theater at the southern end of the lake. The sun's light has not yet reached the pier but has nicely brightened the western shore. The calmness of the water indicates there is no wind and that this will probably be a warmer than normal summer day.

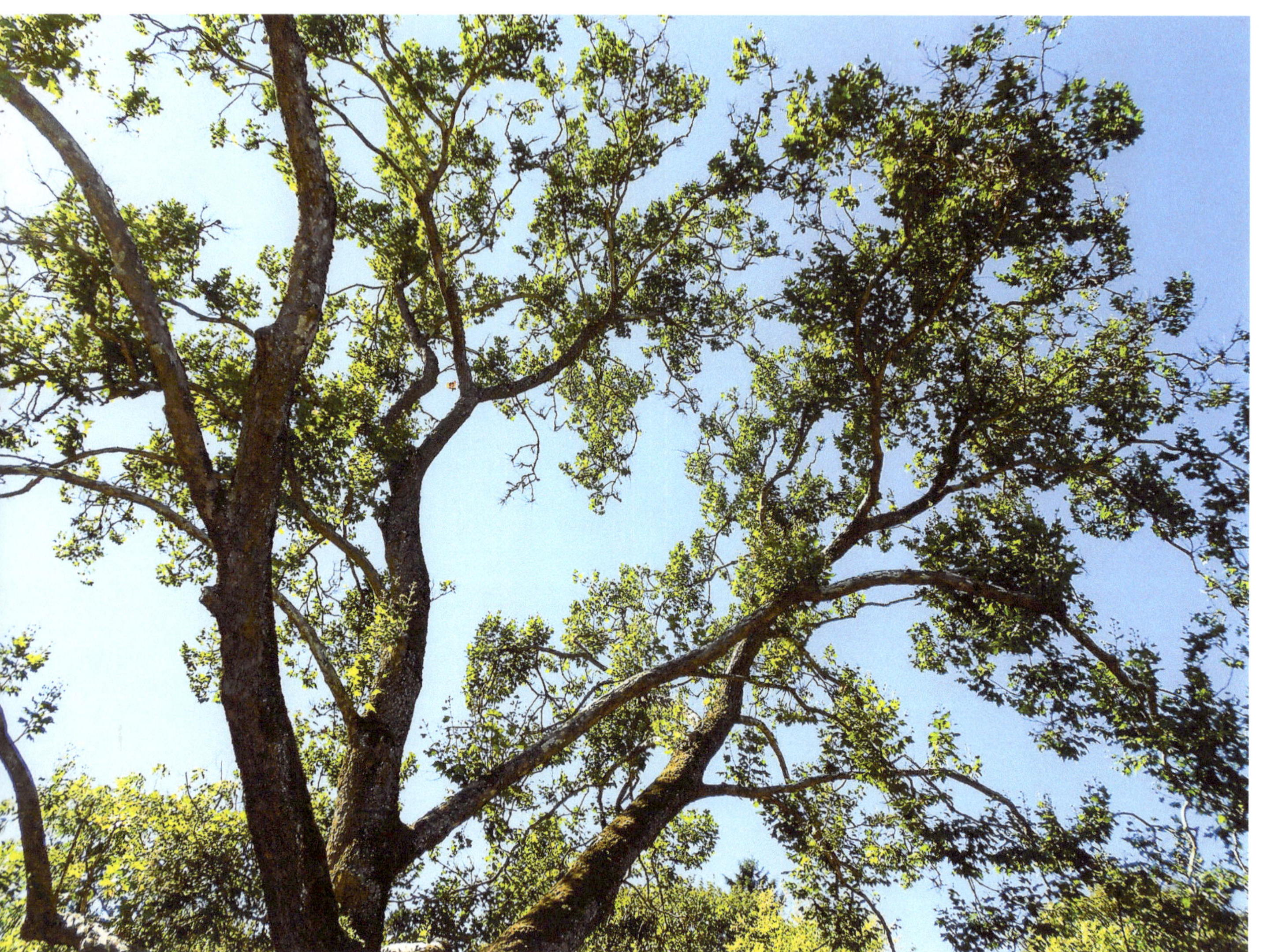

# Capturing the Light

This conjures up the lyrics of the old Perry Como song 'The bluest skies you've ever seen see are here in Seattle', that is, when you can see it. I've read that we have the most overcast days in a year of any major city in the country. This tree is located at the southern end of the park near the boathouse.

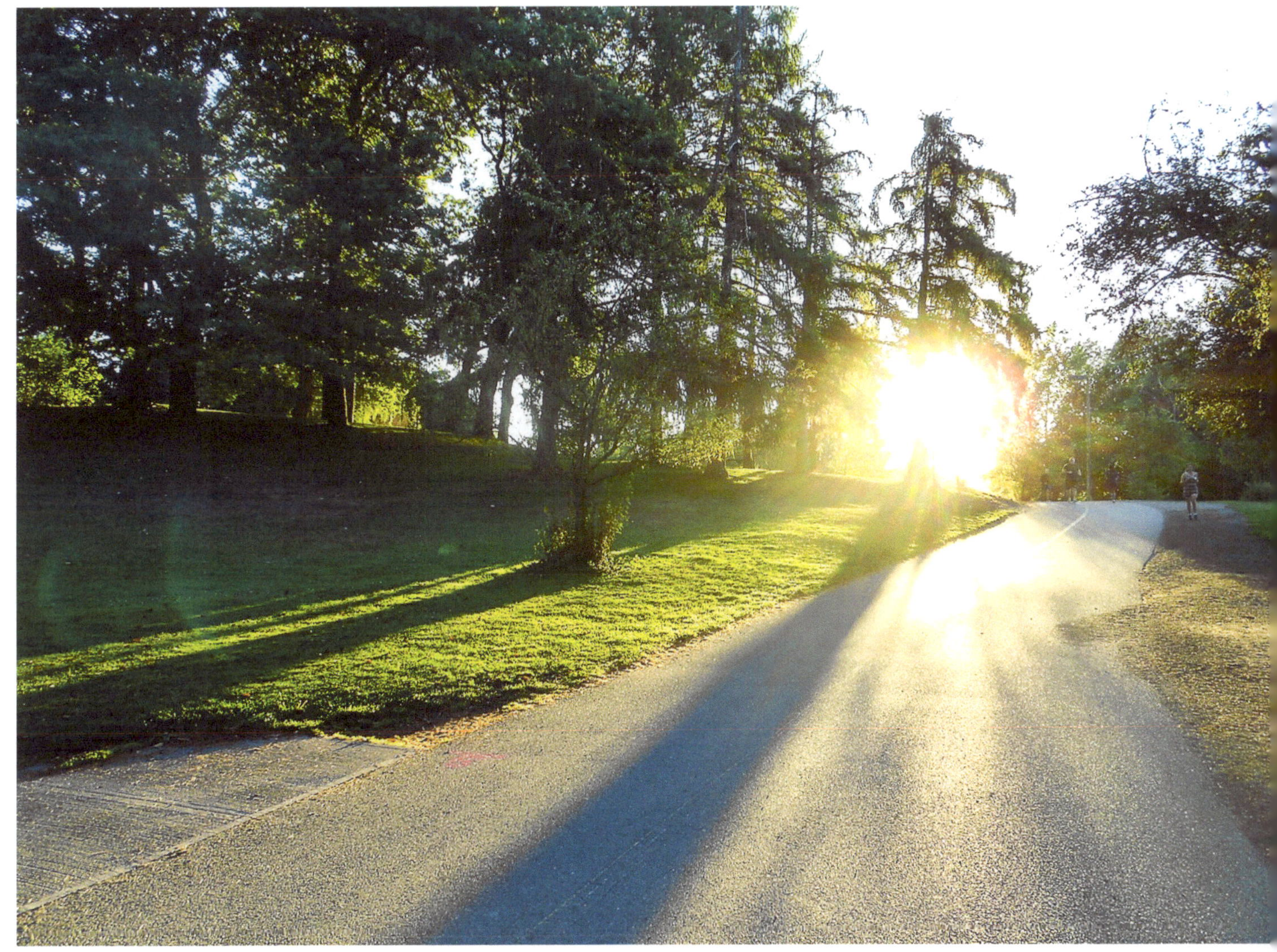

*"The sunshine is a glorious birth...."*
**—William Wordsworth**

I like the sharp shadows that are cast in the early and later parts of the day. We're at the northern end of the lake here where that path rises in elevation as it turns from west to east and leads toward the Bathhouse Theater. I was pleased to see that this picture turned out as it did; usually the colors are distorted when facing a camera into the sun.

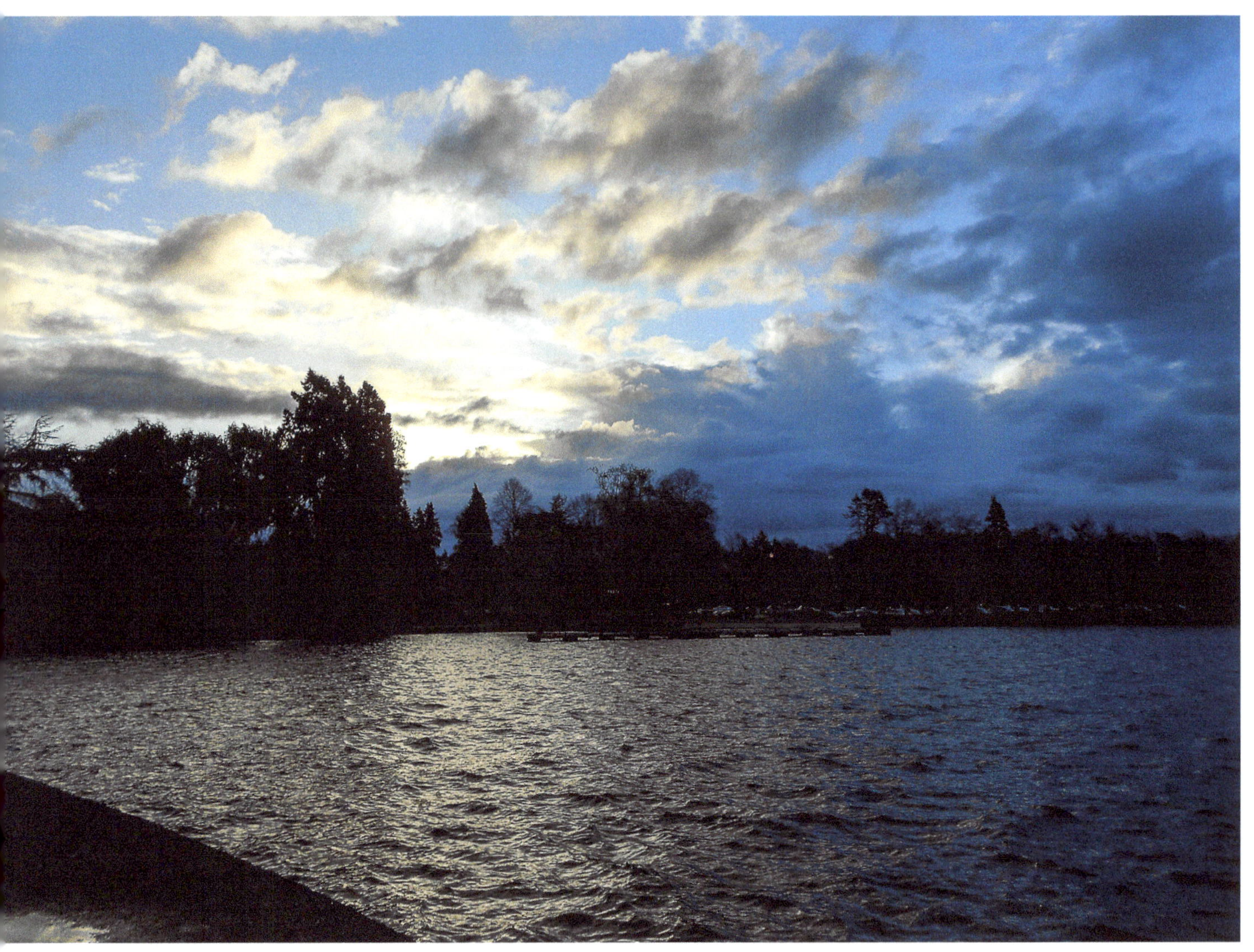

# Hiding the Sun

Clouds often obscure the sun's light from brightening up the shores of the lake at early dawn. Clearly they are featured in this scene, which is rendered somewhat chilly by their hanging low on the horizon and preventing warming things up.

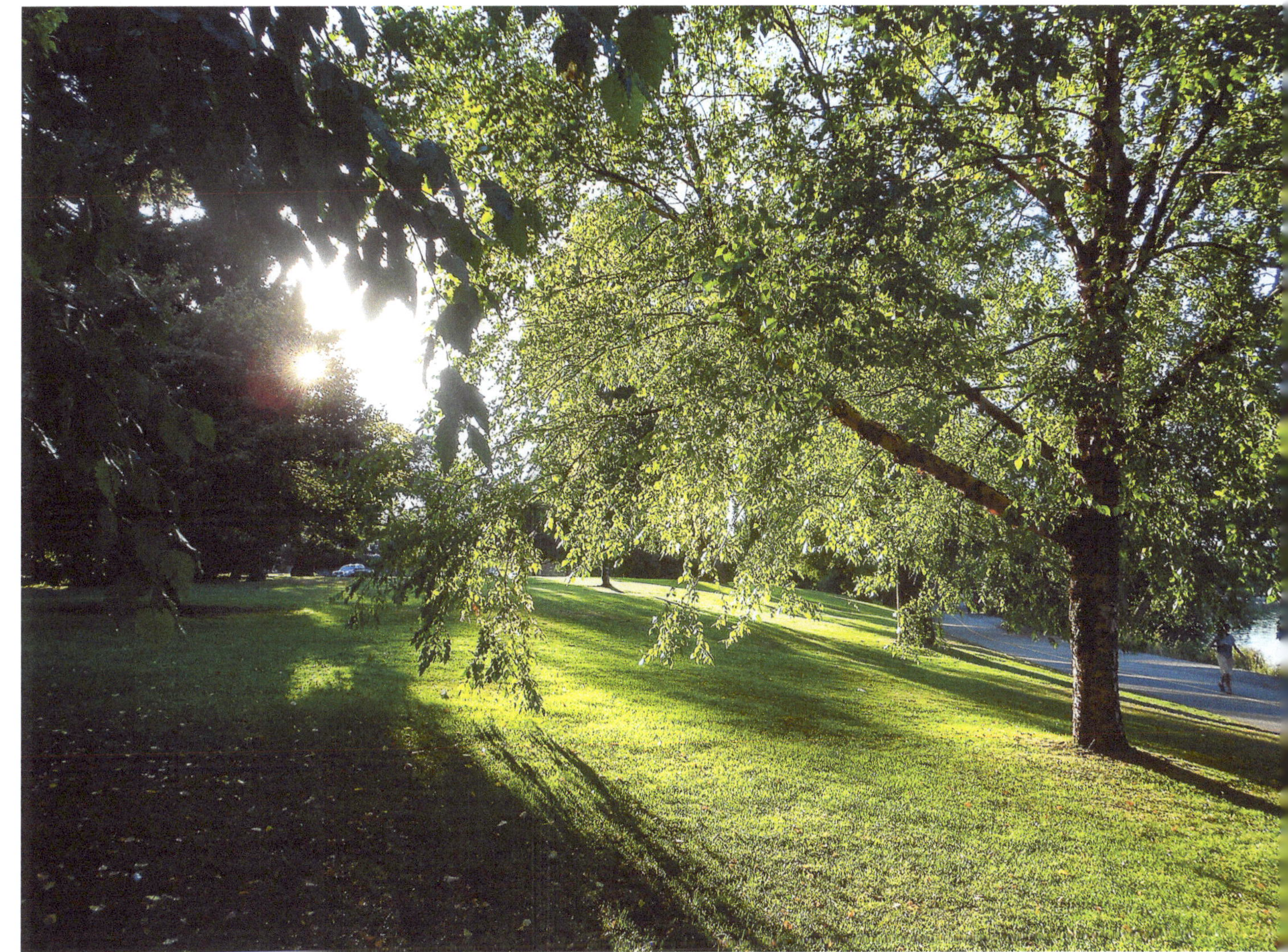

# Shimmering Light

I love this picture. When you see the sun's rays illuminating the edges of leaves in a tree like seen here, you can't help but marvel at the sheer beauty of nature. I really enjoy walking around the lake in the early hours to bear witness to such magnificence.

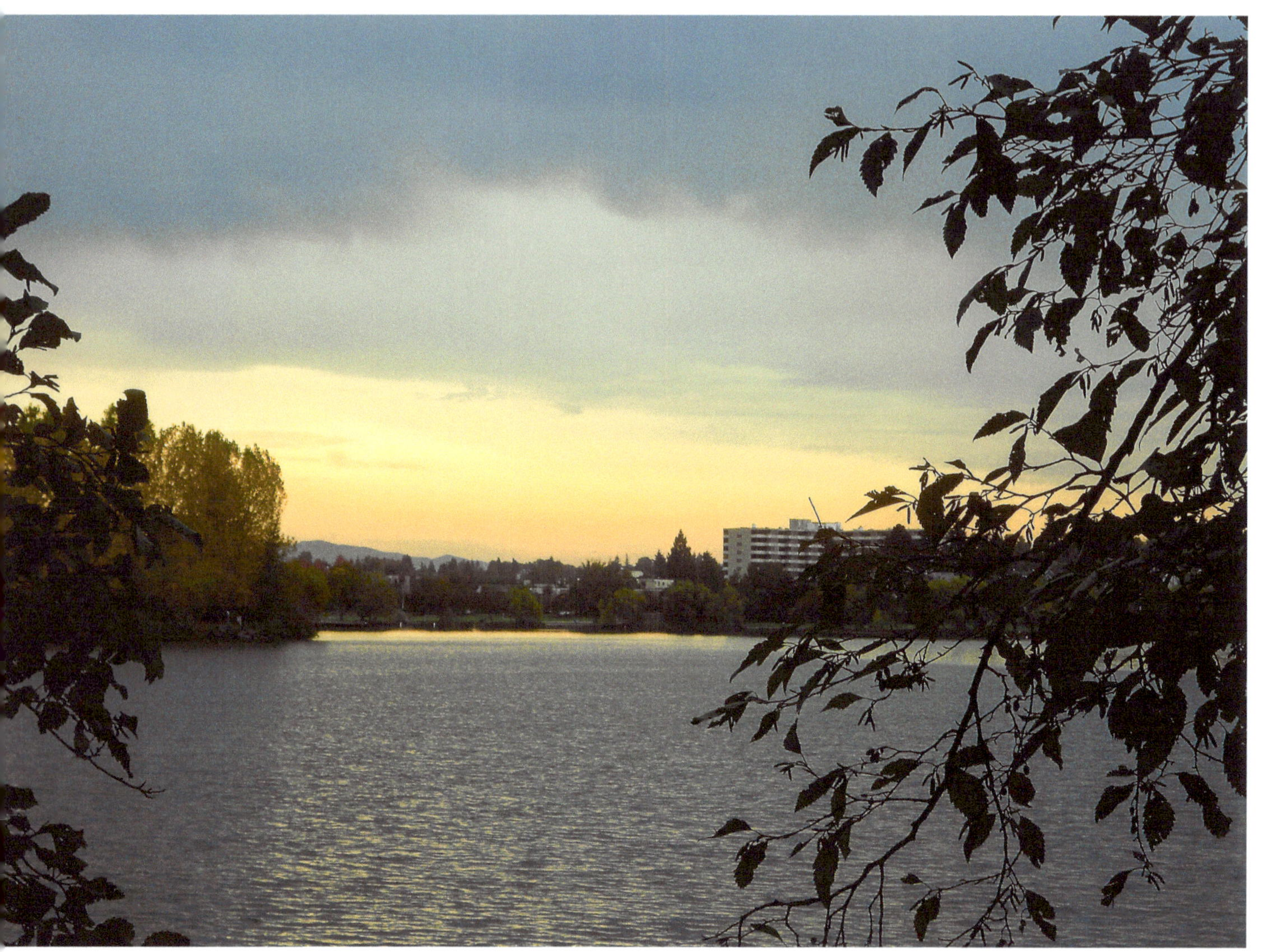

# Band of Gold

The eye seems to naturally focus on the golden hue between the darker layers of the water and the clouds. I very much like this picture for its variations of colors that seem to complement each other. I'm thinking these are the colors I would like my next car to be.

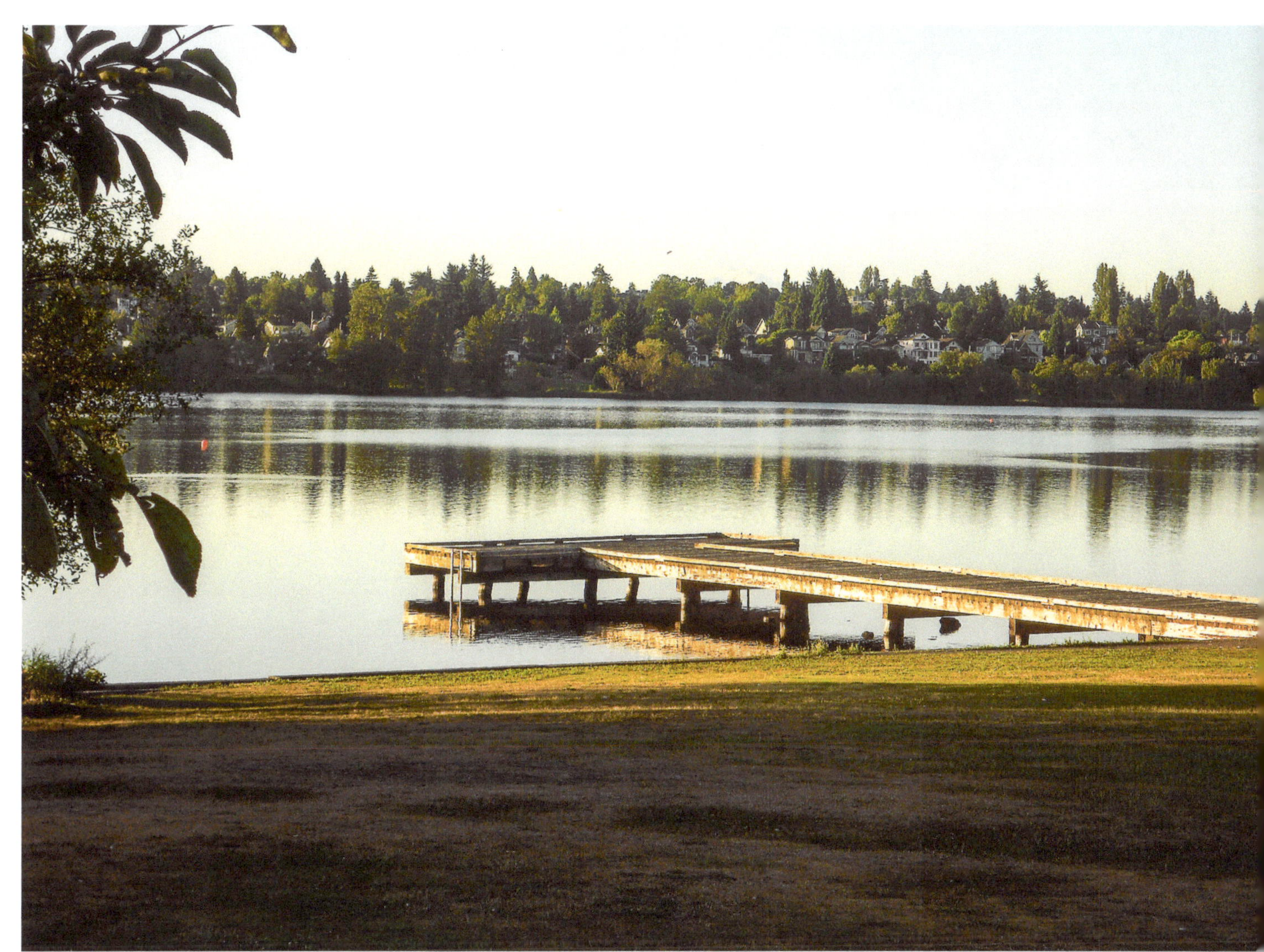

*As the morning's glow grows bright,*
*And shadows shrink in passing light.*
*A comfort comes with such a sight,*
*On earth everything seems just right.*

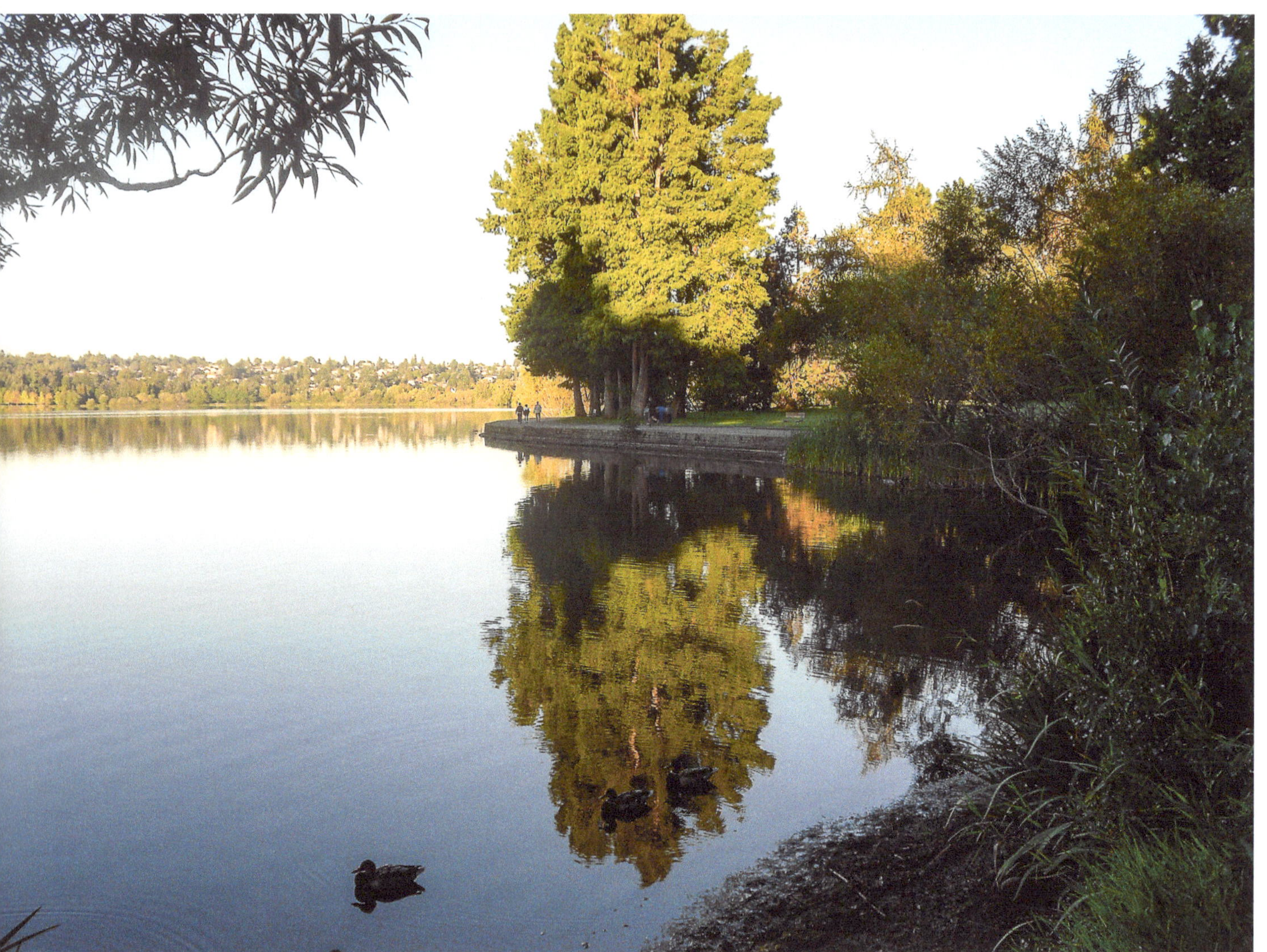

# Cloned Tree

Here again you can see how the sunlight has bathed the rest of the lake except for its eastern shore. Clearly it is morning in what looks like is going to be a balmy day. There's serenity in this scene, contributed in part, I think, by that single duck looking peacefully stationary in the calm water, creating not the slightest ripple.

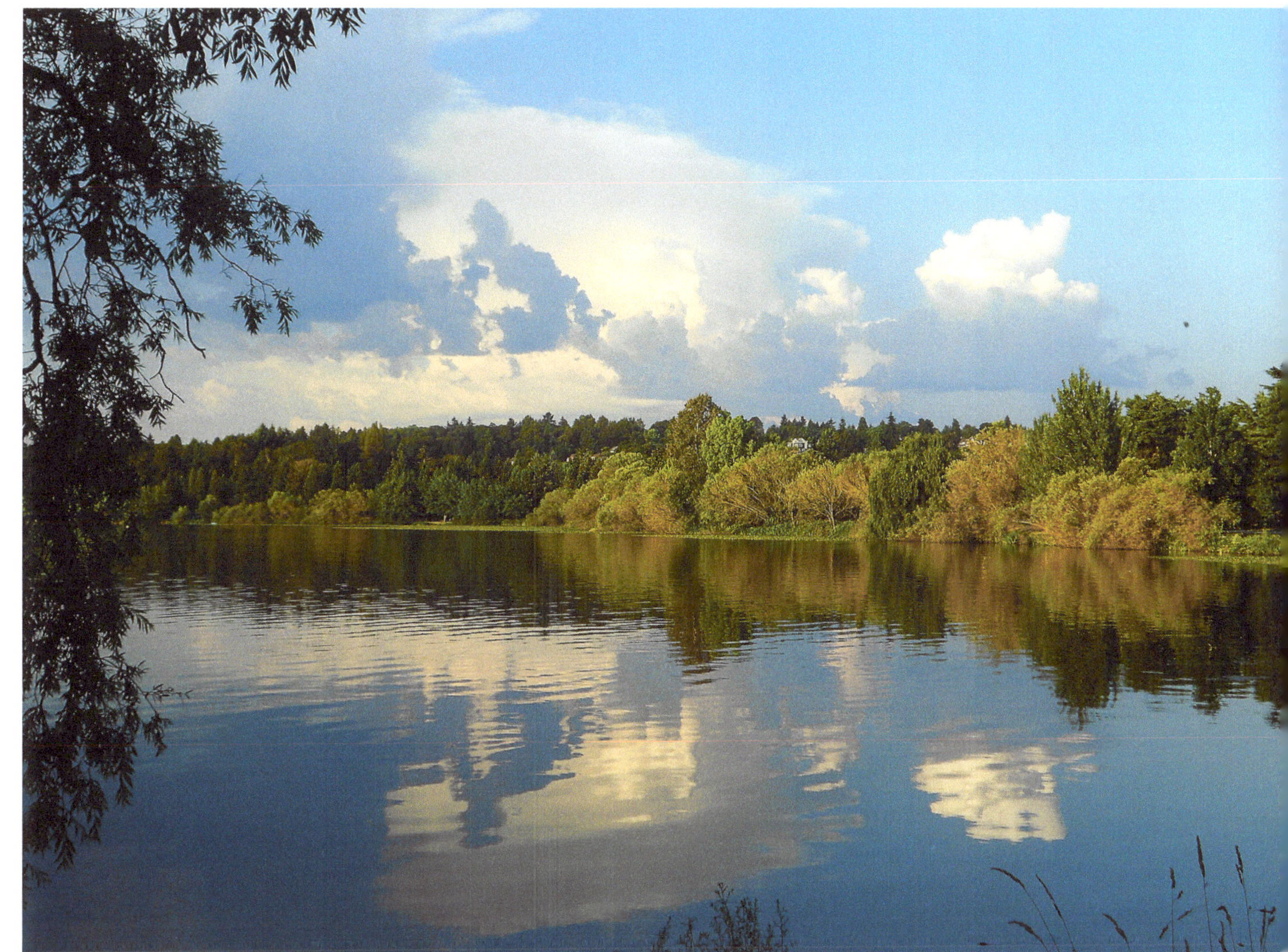

# Looking West

The sun's light rising in the east is being reflected off the thunderclouds hovering over the southwestern sky. It definitely is a dawn picture, and a good one at that. I like its clarity.

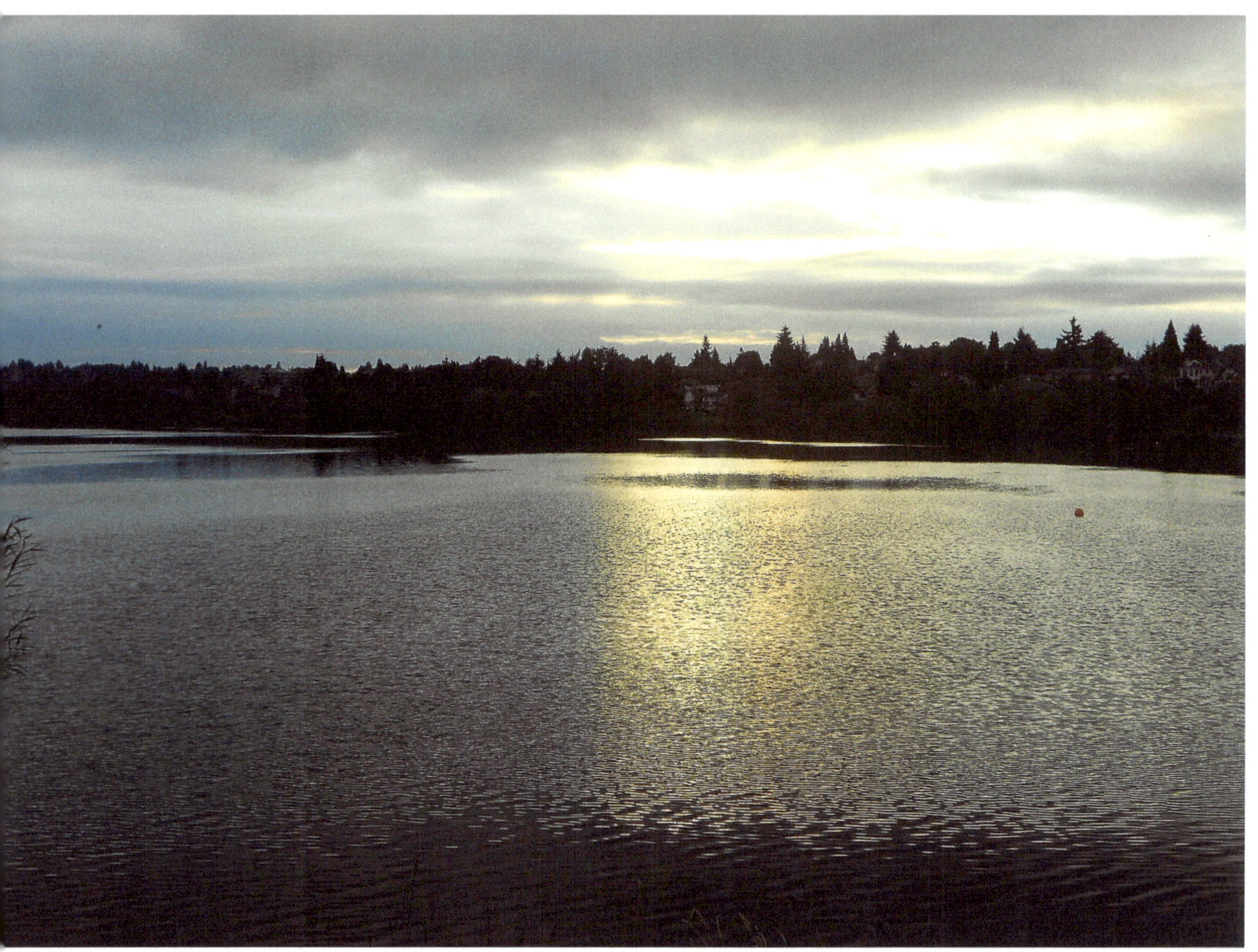

# Half and Half

Seeing the lake on a cloudy gray day is all too common, but it is not common to see the nearly perfect demarcation between dark and light as shown here. You can read a lot into this. It's a rare sight.

# Green Lake Grandeur

## In praise of nature's artistry

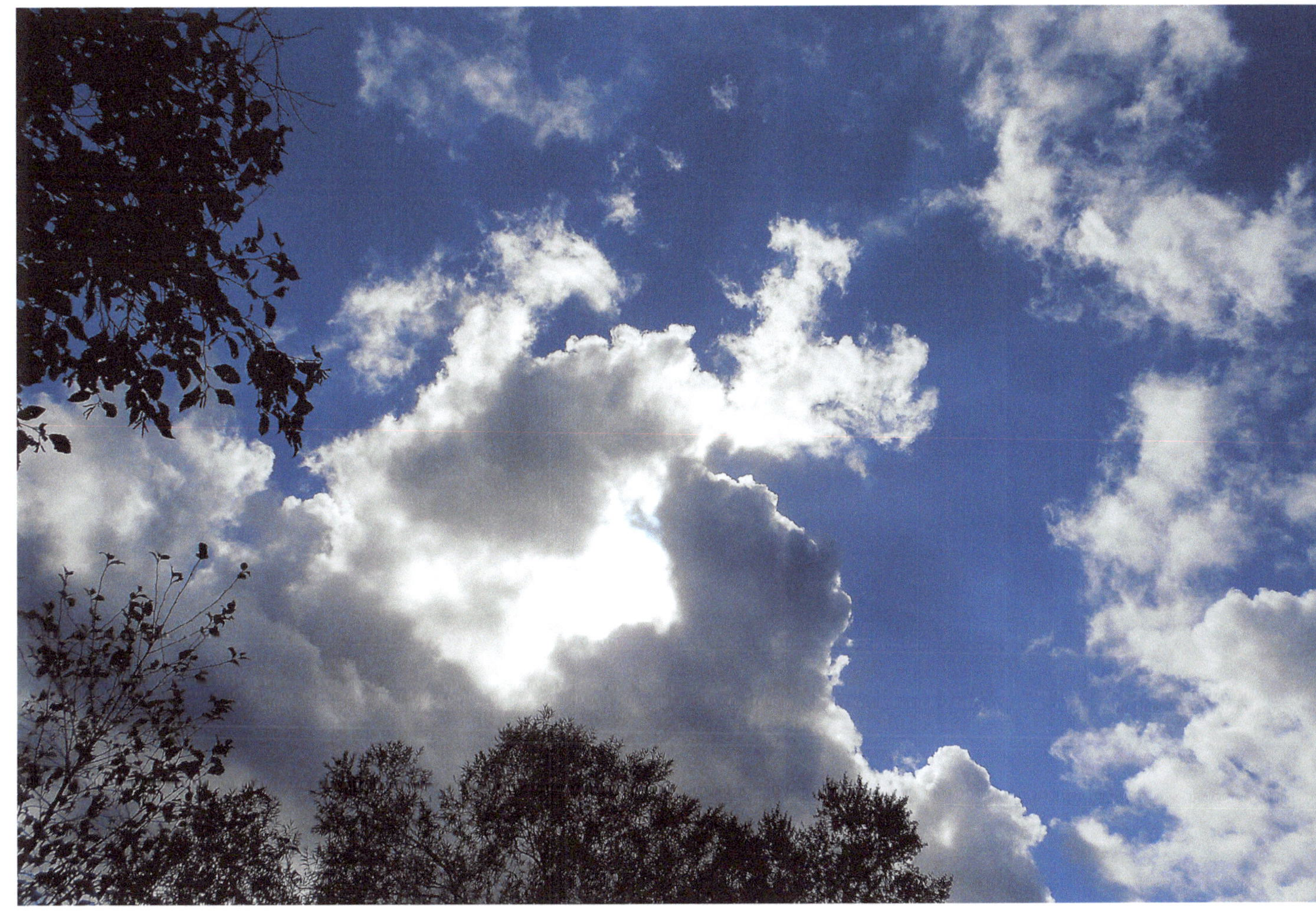

Scenes under this category are ones that evoke a sense of the dramatic that nature provides in abundance at Green Lake. Clouds are a major feature of such presentations and they can be truly awe-inspiring, often seen at their most spectacular best here. I am lucky to live close by so I can observe such beauty on a recurring basis because in seeing this I am overcome with a feeling that it's good to be alive. That is highly rewarding for me —it makes life a joy.

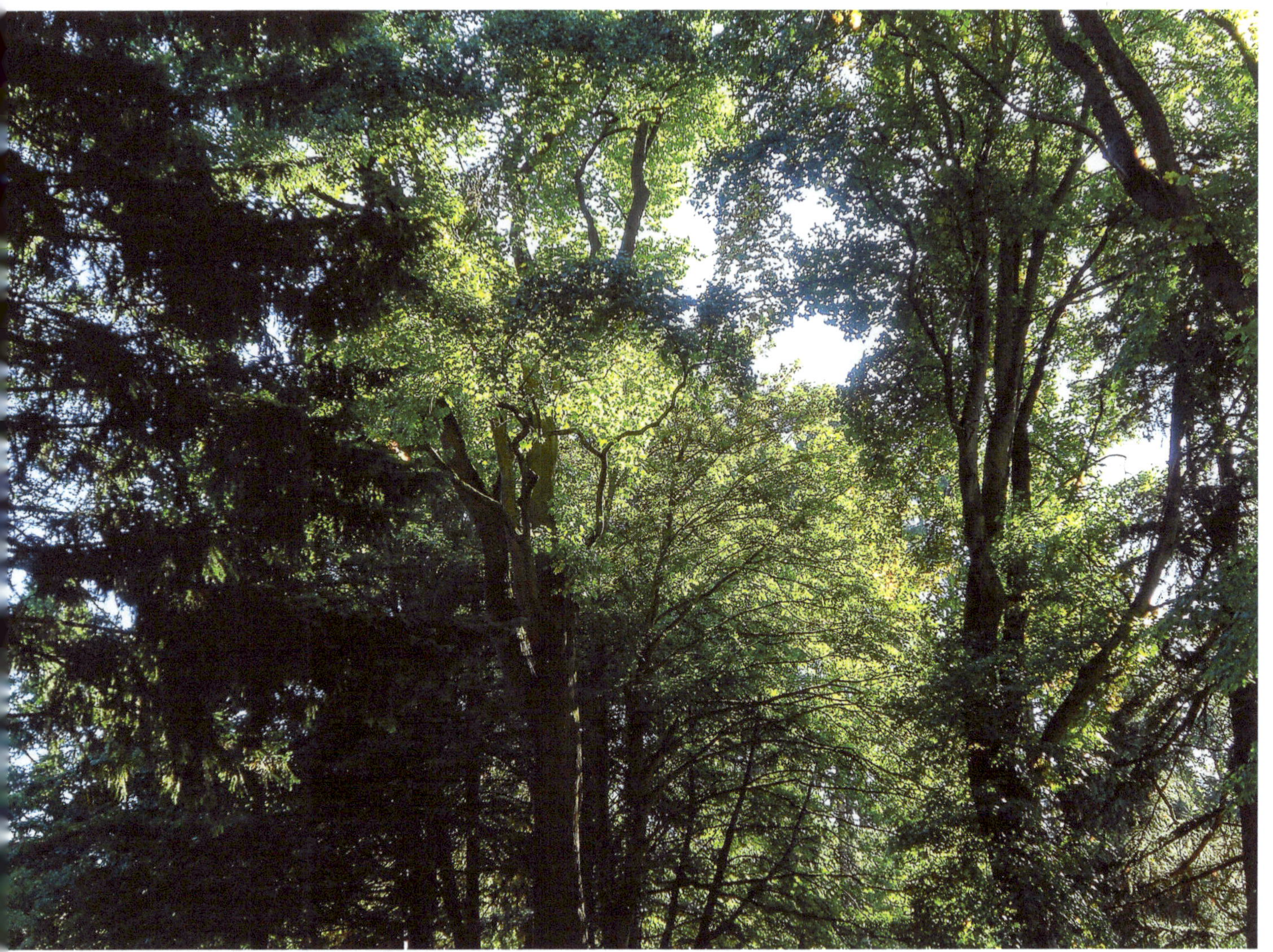

# Sunlit Trees

Green Lake Park is also an arboretum with around one-hundred some different kinds of trees ranging from the stubby to the lofty as seen here. On a sunny day they are magnificent to behold, giving off a myriad of verdant shades, especially when sunlight hits them. The ones captured here are at the southern end of the lake.

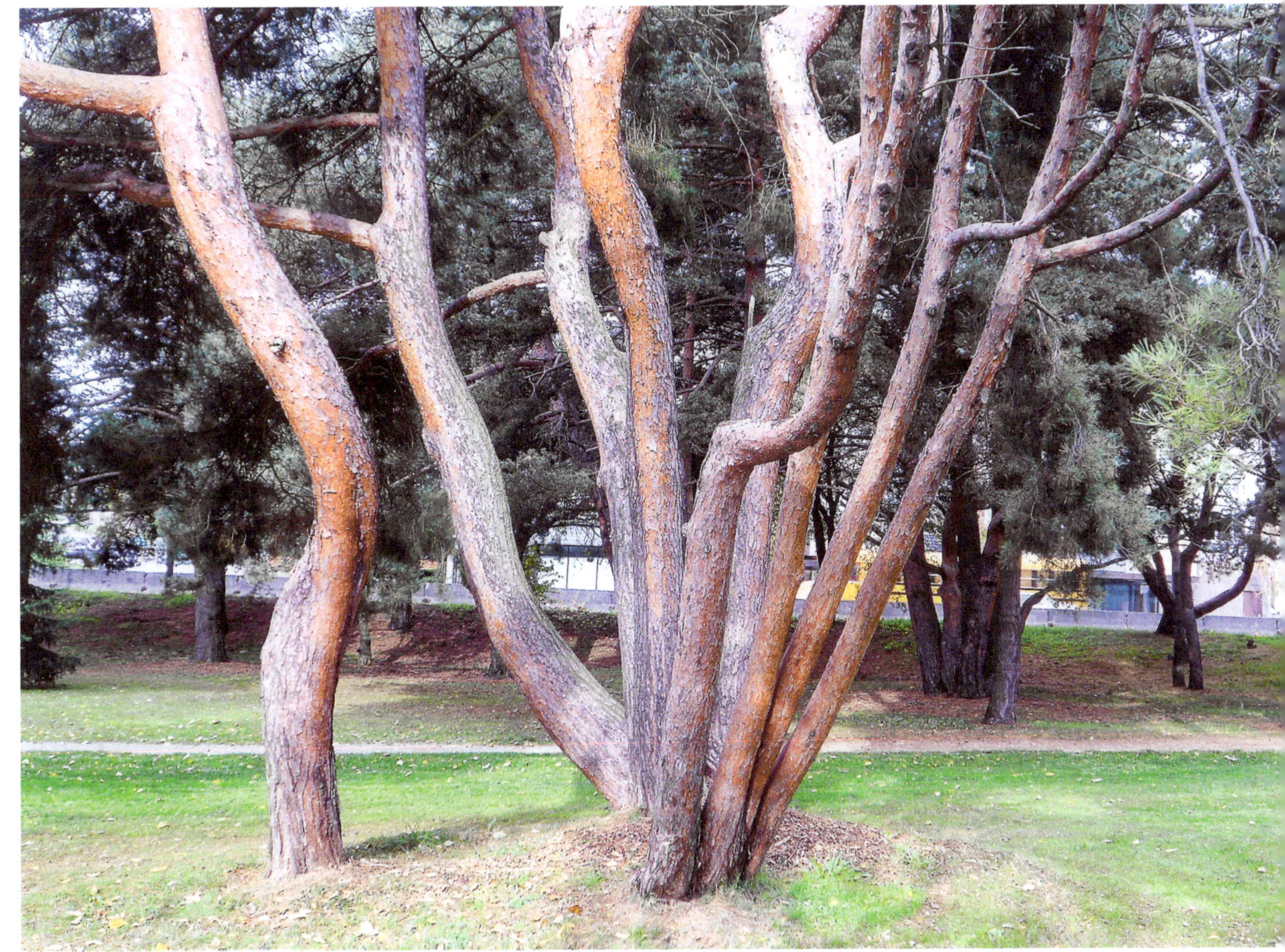

# Bronze Sculpture

Looking more like artificial tree trunks than natural ones, this tree resembles a giant size sculpture that should be in a modern art gallery. It's the smoothly shaped bark that creates this effect. The tree can be seen at the northwest end of the park.

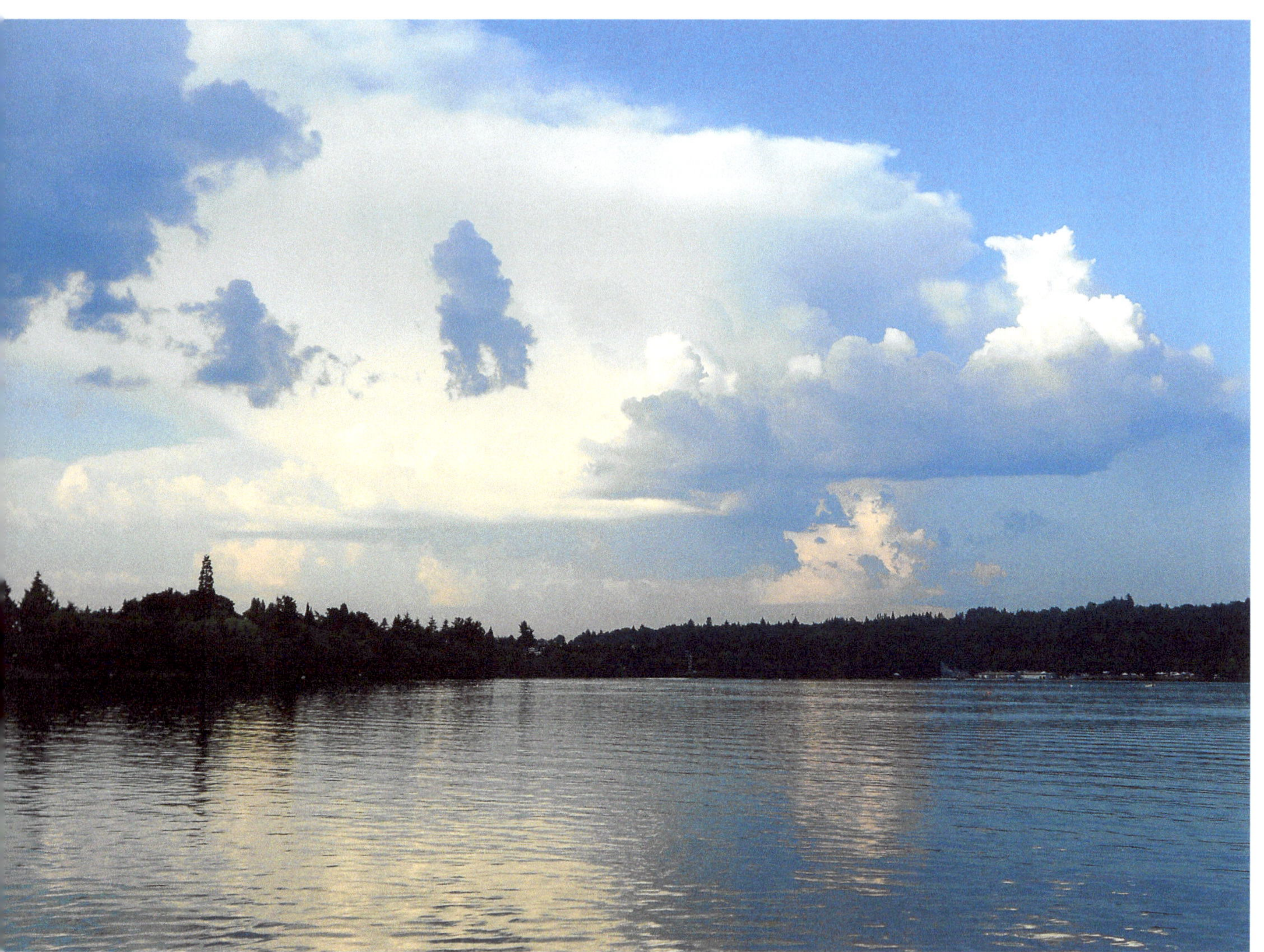

# Thundercloud

Thunderstorms behave strangely in Seattle. After a lightning flash occurs you may have to wait for a long time before another one happens. Also we can have thunderstorms in winter, which is not that common. Seen here is an impressive formation looking south across the lake. I like the nearly vertical darker clouds in the foreground.

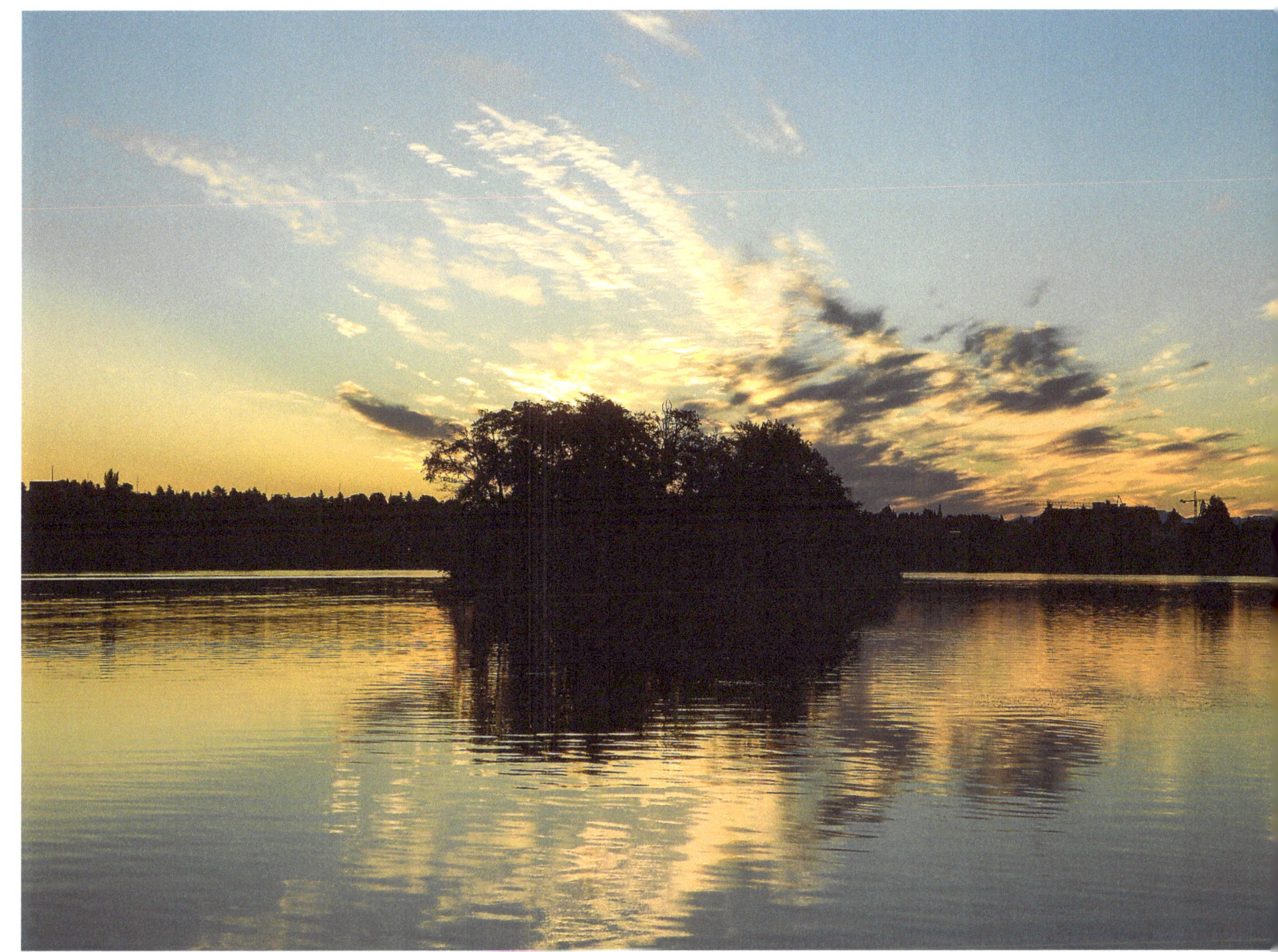

# Duck Island

Here is a stunning view of a sunrise behind Duck Island at the northwest end of the lake. This artificially created island is the only one on the lake; originally a number of small islets existed along its eastern shore. The island remains somewhat pristine in that nobody goes there except for the birds and ducks. At times it can appear quite mysterious.

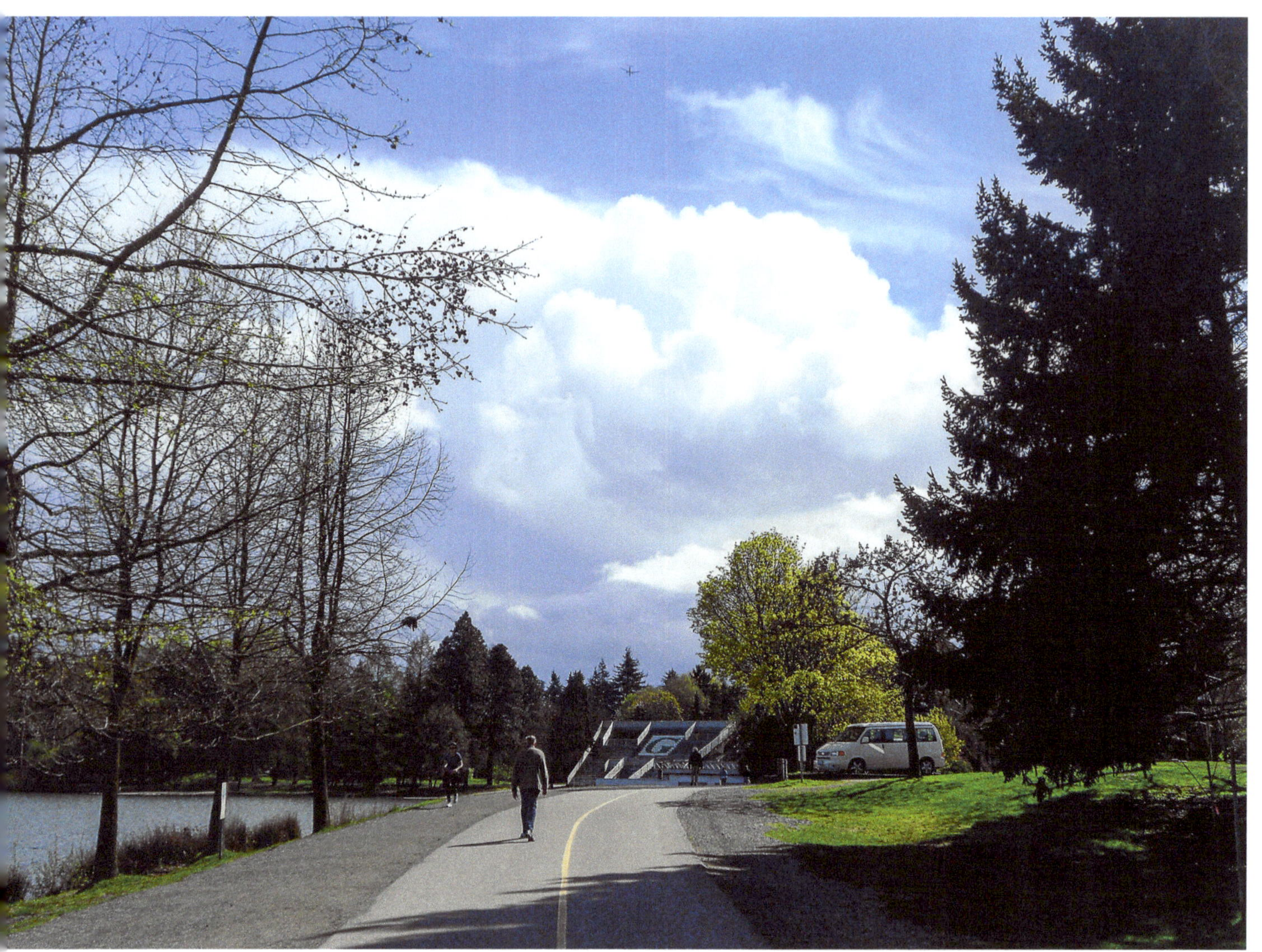

# Facing a Thunderhead

As we learned in elementary school general science classes, this is a cumulus-nimbus cloud, which is characterized by its billowy look and huge mass. Here we are looking at one that dwarfs its surroundings.

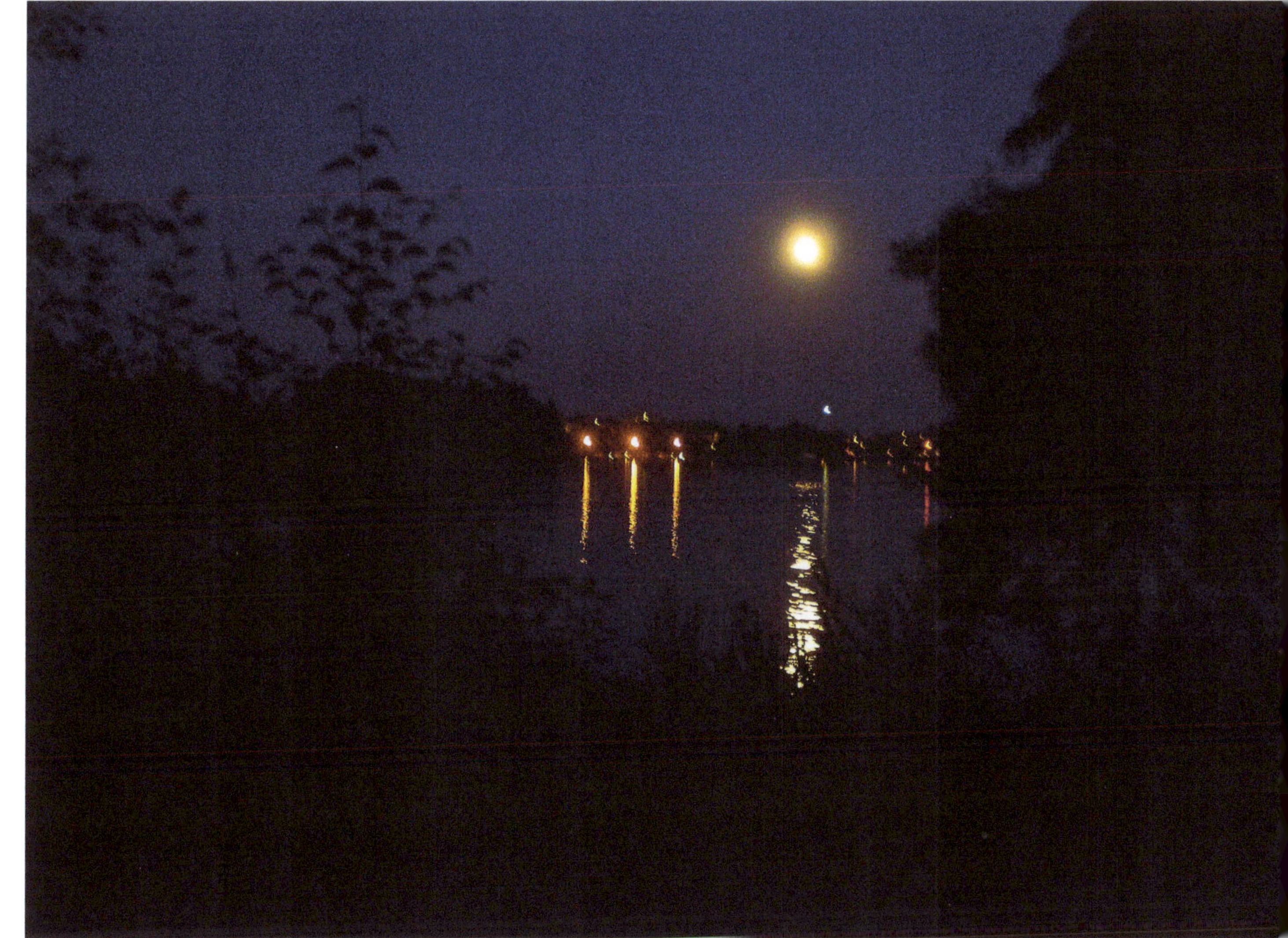

# Moonlit Night

Here is one of my few successful nocturnal shots. It's difficult to capture such an image with a Nikon Coolpix, but this one is actually quite faithful to how things look late at night under a full moon. No matter what time of day or night you go to the lake, you'll run into at least some people.

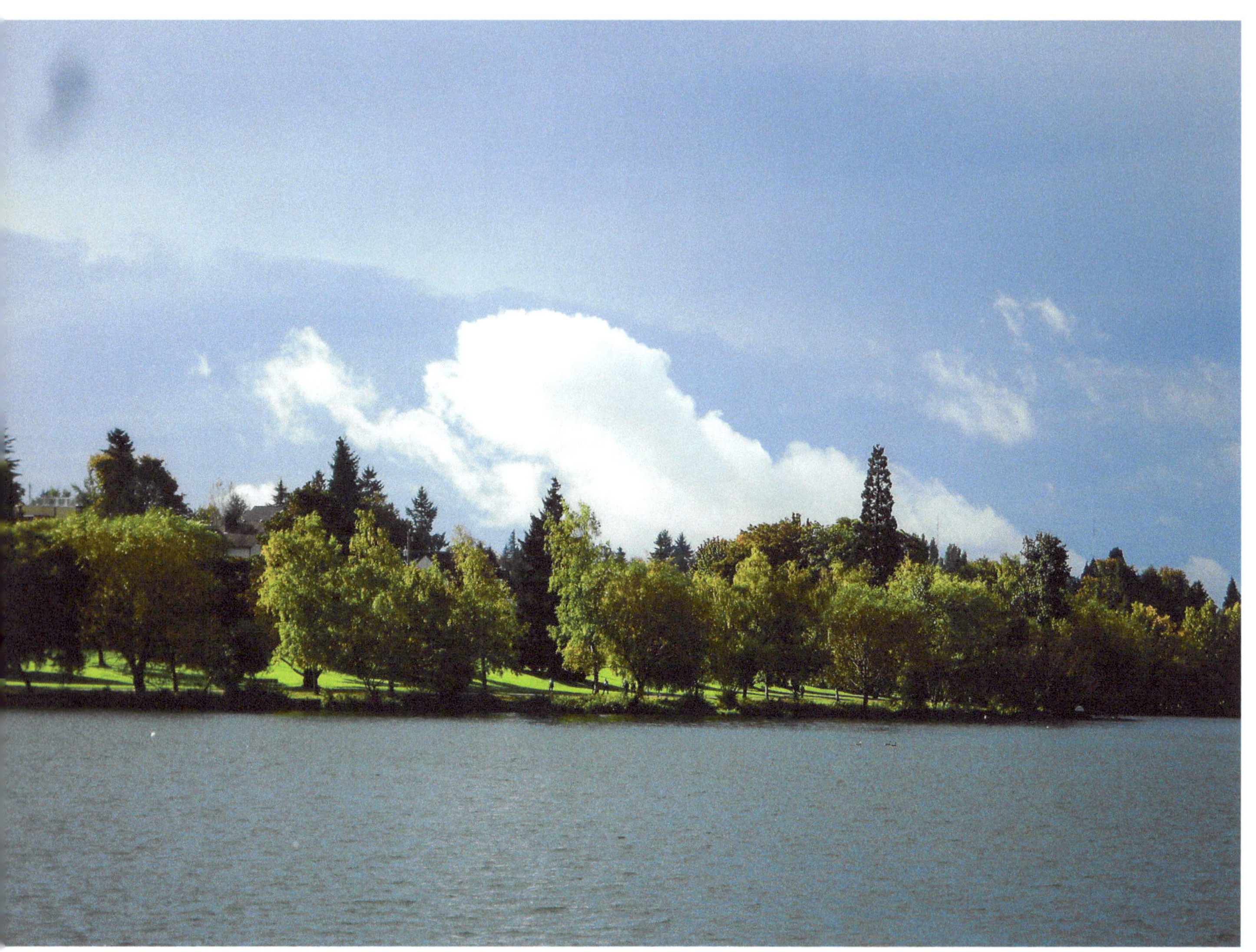

# Low Hanging Cloud

I like the contrast created by this white billowy cloud set against the bluish-gray backdrop clouds. It's not often that you see this so vividly expressed and when you do, it's truly a magnificent sight.

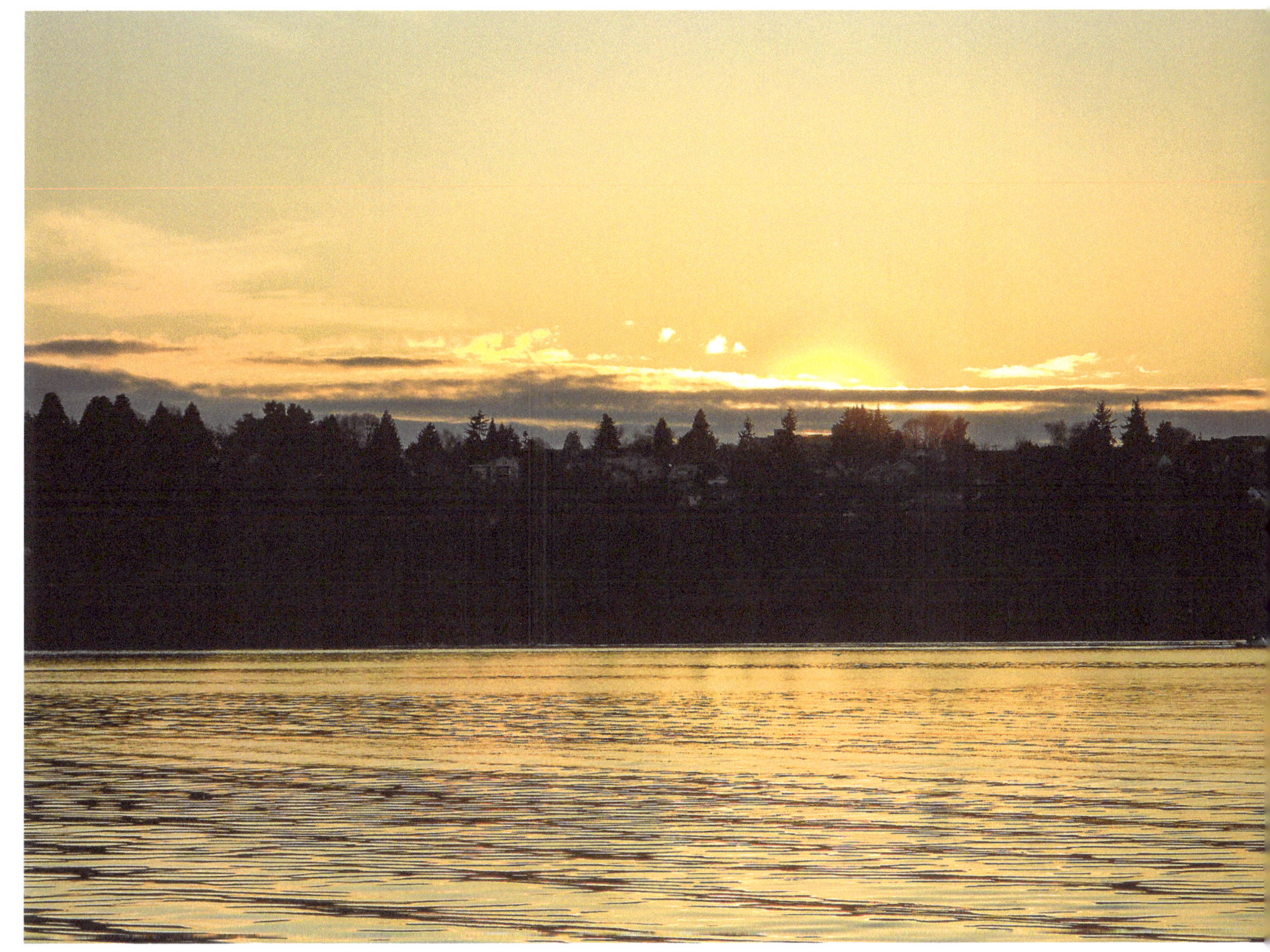

# On Golden Pond

Gold is the color that dominates this scene, the sun setting over Phinney Ridge with its warmth reflected on the water. What I think of when I see such a sight is: nature remains our best artist.

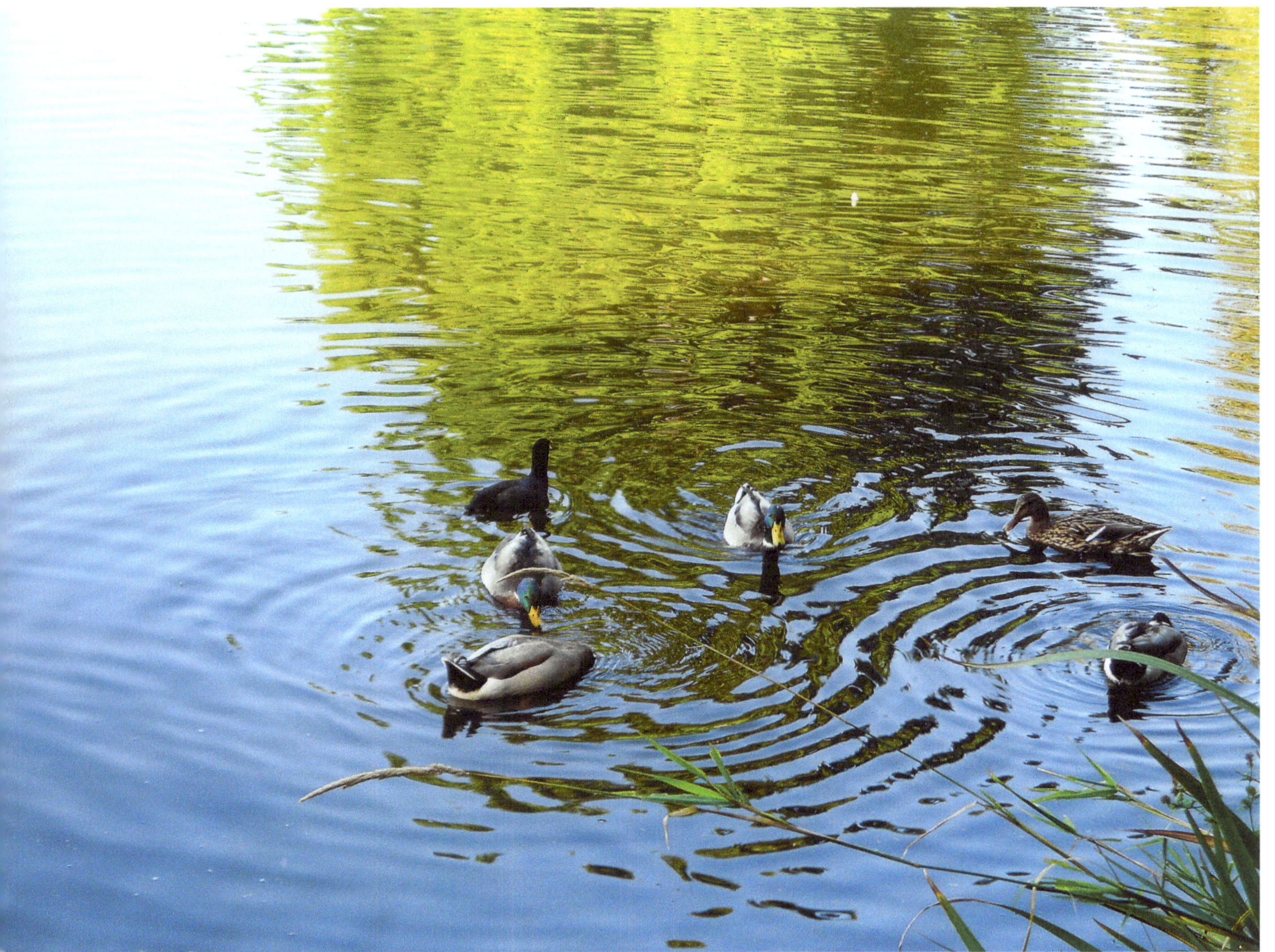

# Impressionism

This scene reminds me of a Claude Monet painting with its swirling motion of water and shimmering reflection of tree leaves. Monet is one of my favorite artists and I very much like the impressionist school of art. It's interesting to see that you can achieve a similar effect with a camera.

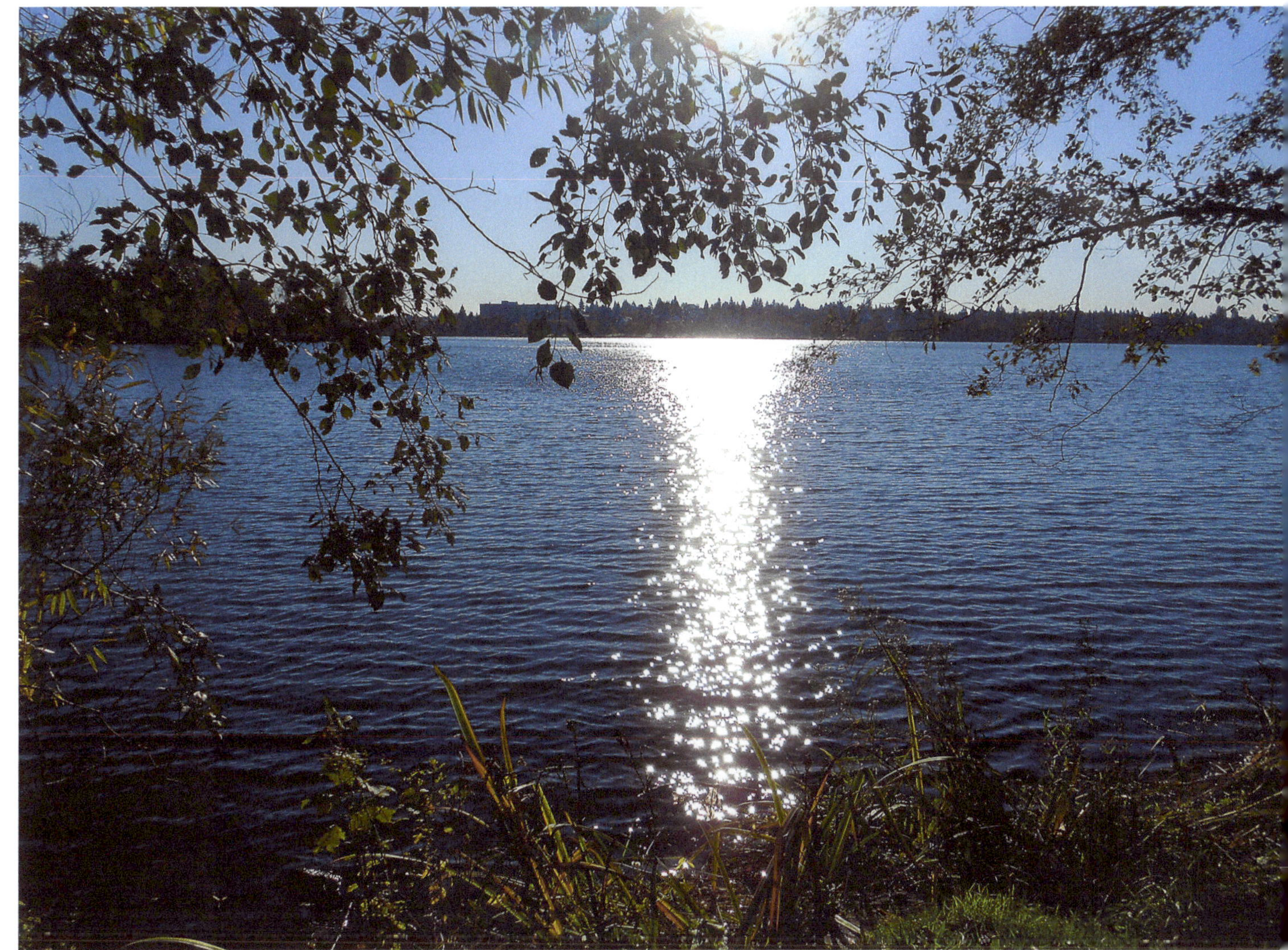

# Glistening Reflection

On a crystal clear, somewhat cold morning, the sun's rays reflect like a shiny vase of sparkling light on the water. The coloring is somewhat distorted because the camera is facing into the glare, so it looks like as if wearing sunglasses.

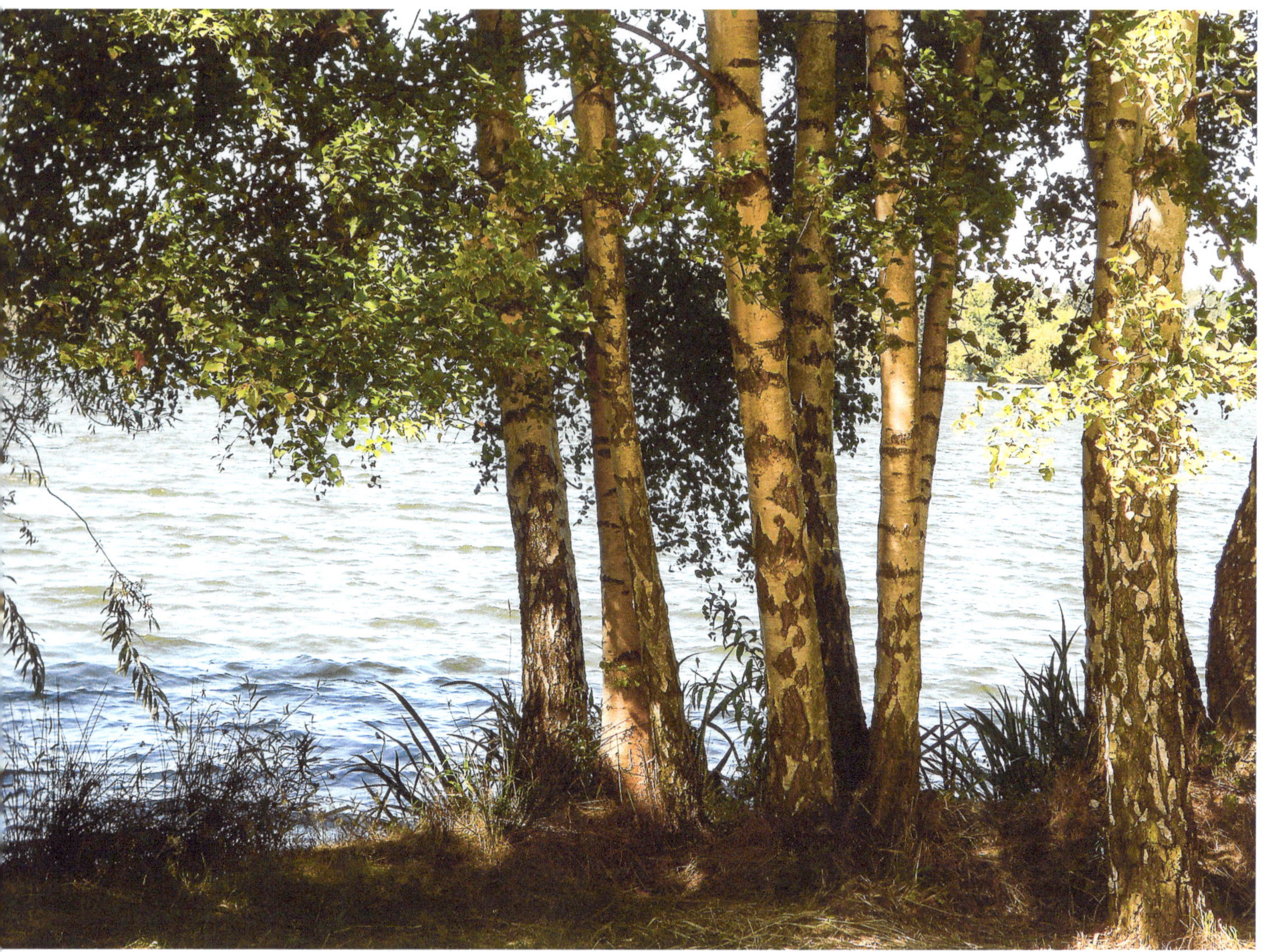

# Splashes of Light

This is a nice scene revealing the effect of sunlight breaking through the clusters of thick leaves to create a speckled look.

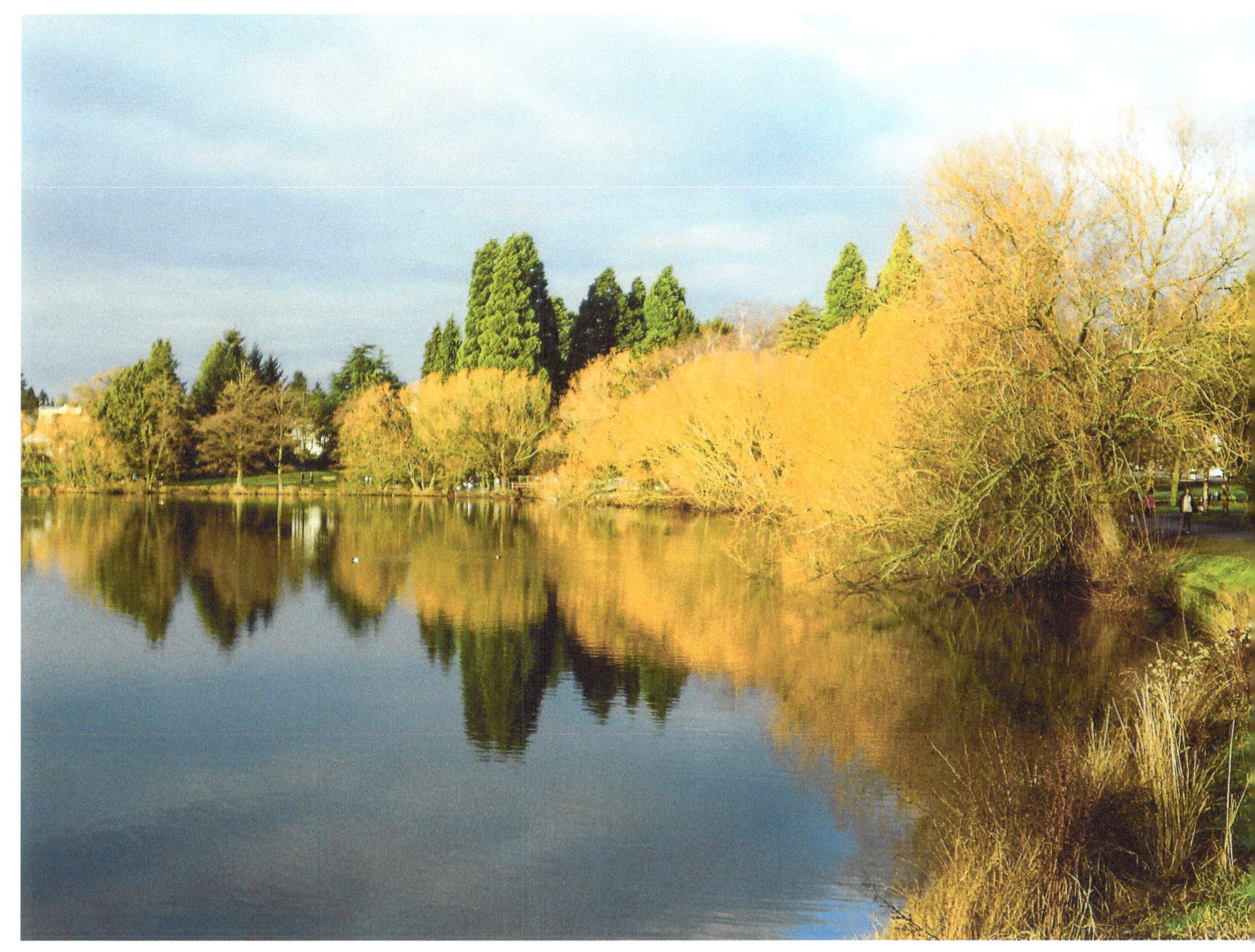

# Winter's Hues

I like the tawny look of the shrubs and trees during the winter months as so splendidly demonstrated here. An overall orange hue dominates the shore of the lake giving it a warm glow even though the temperatures might be quite chilly. We're seeing the lake's northern shore.

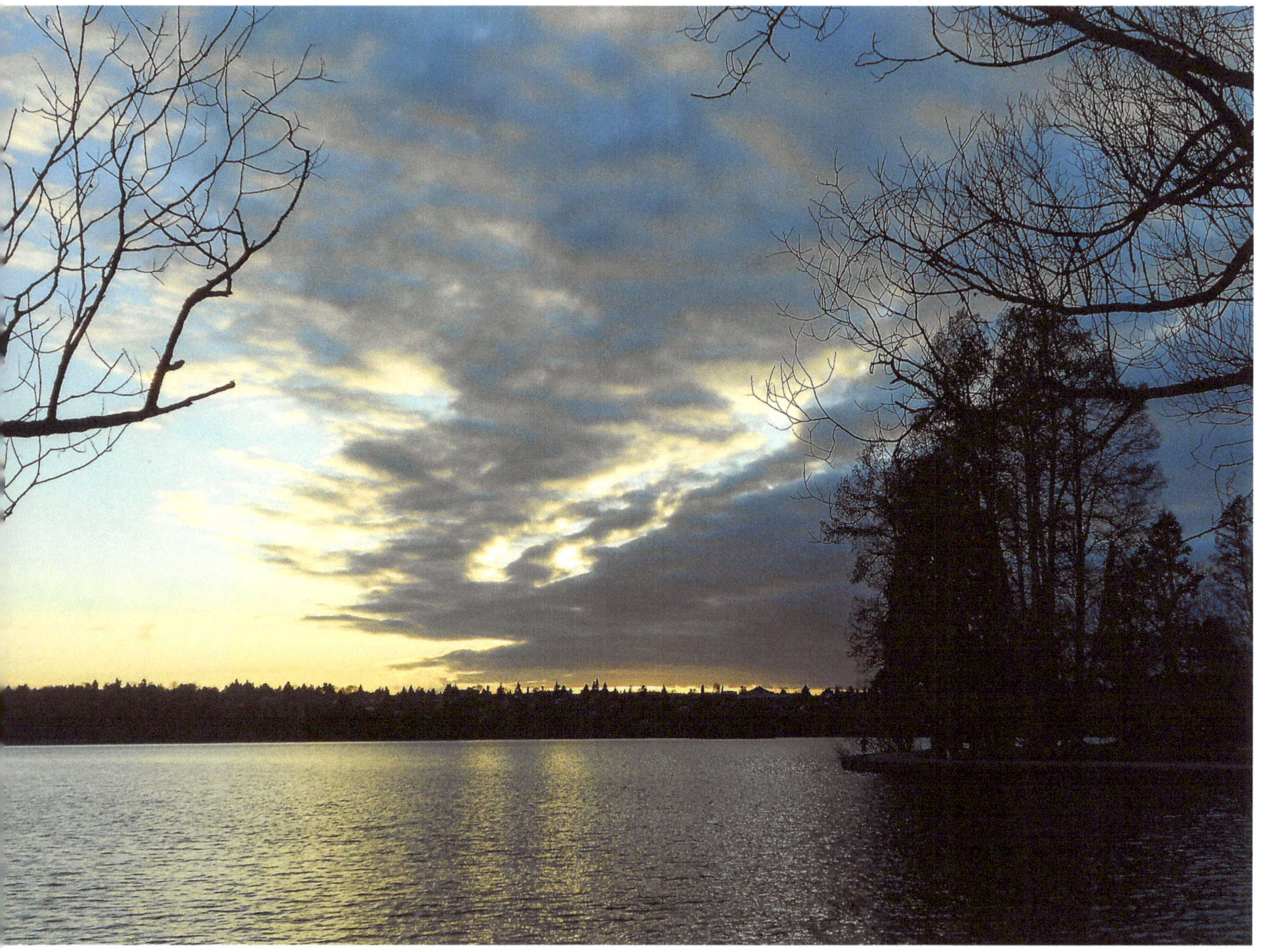

# Early Stages of a Sunset

The sun has not yet reached the horizon and is obscured by the dark cloud. The puffy clouds had me anticipating that the ensuing sunset would be spectacular, but, as seen in the next page, while interesting, it fell somewhat short of my expectations. I like the clarity of this beautiful view and how it turns from light to dark as you scan over it.

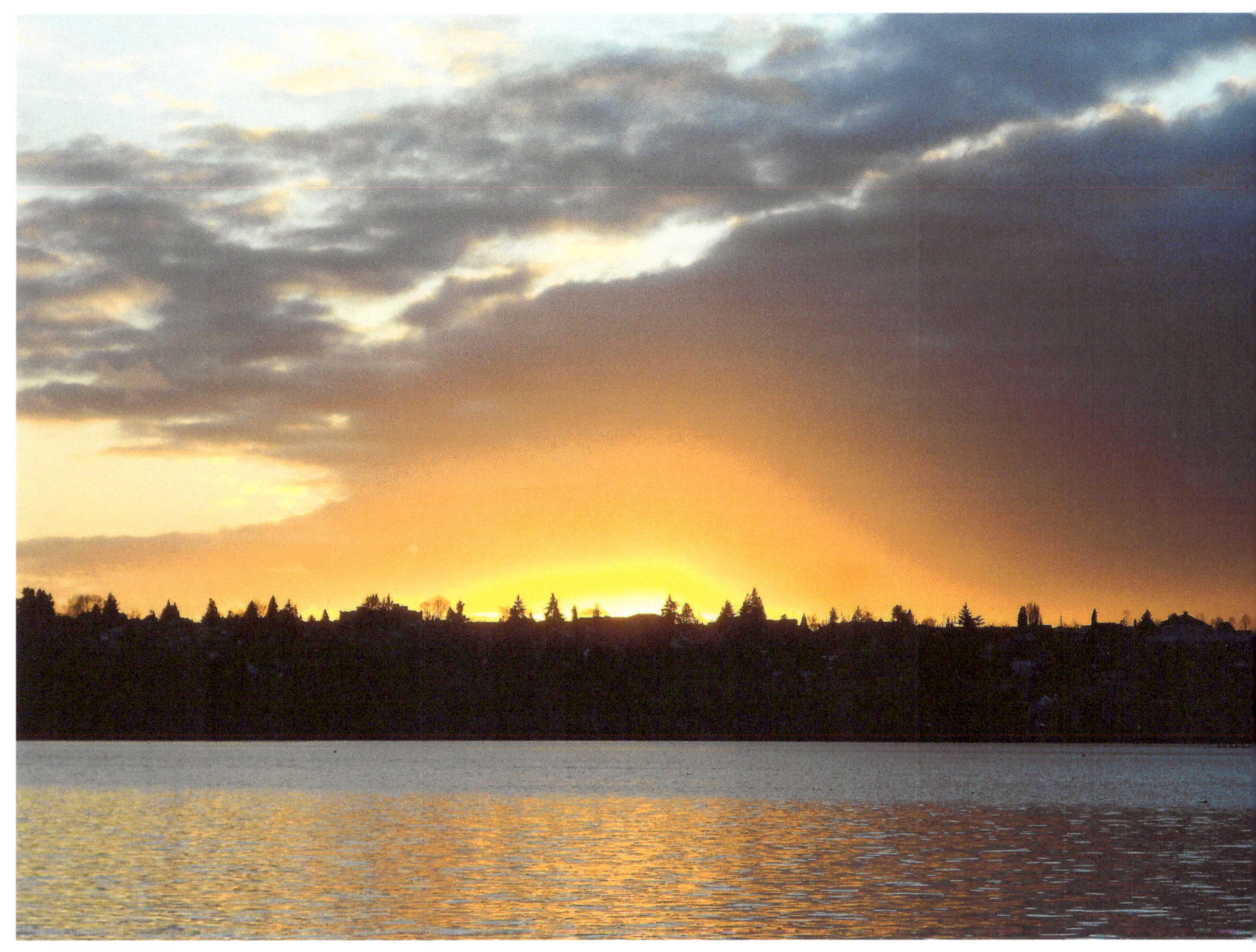

# The Awaited Sunset

Here's what the actual sunset looked like from the previous scene. Quite impressive, to be sure, but I have seen more spectacular ones. Still, it confirms that nature's beauty is boundless.

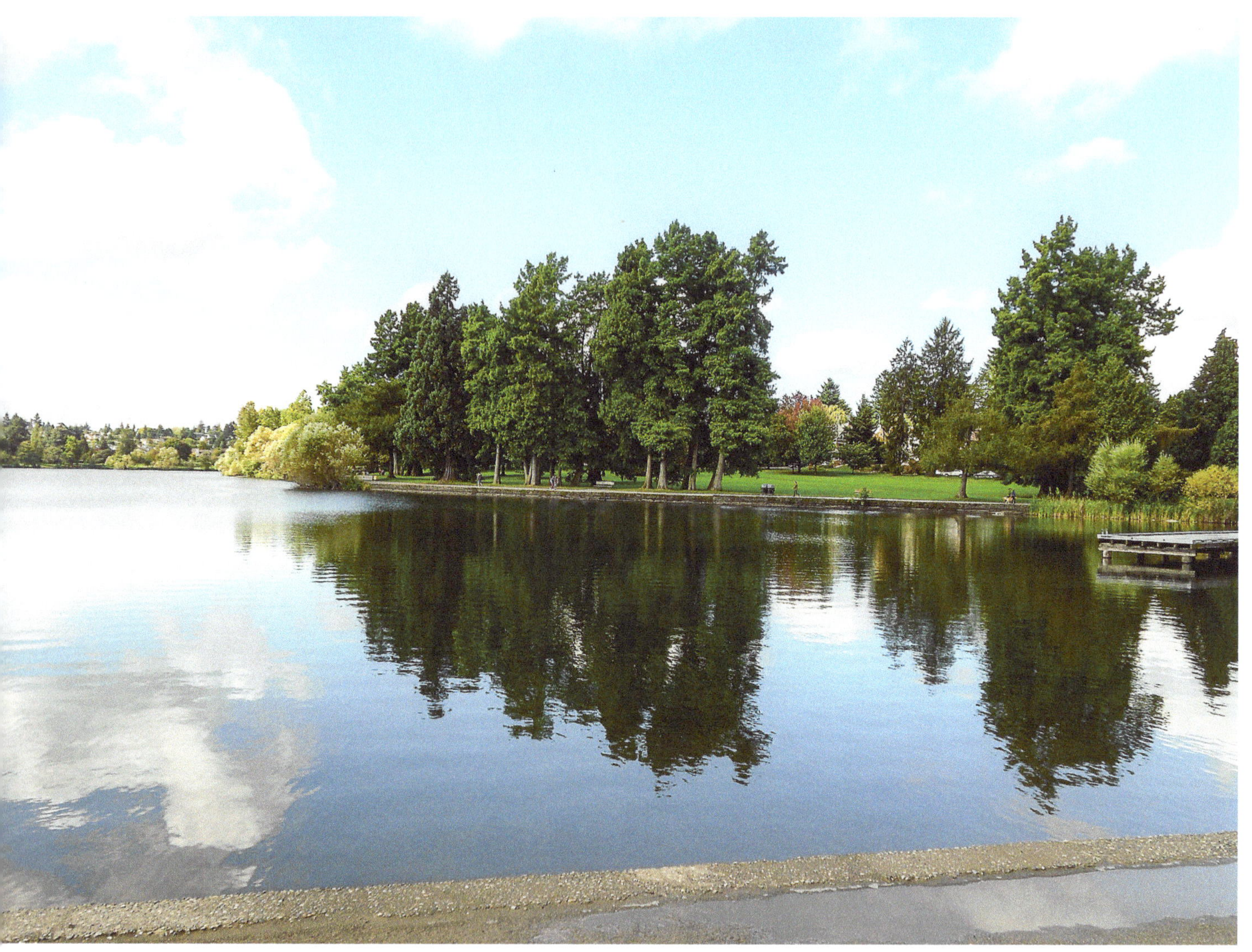

# A Hudson River
# School Landscape

This placid scene is reminiscent of the Hudson River School of Art
that specialized in landscapes. It does appear more like a finely
detailed painting of that genre than an actual picture, especially
with the billowy clouds and the reflections in the water —a splendid
midsummer sight.

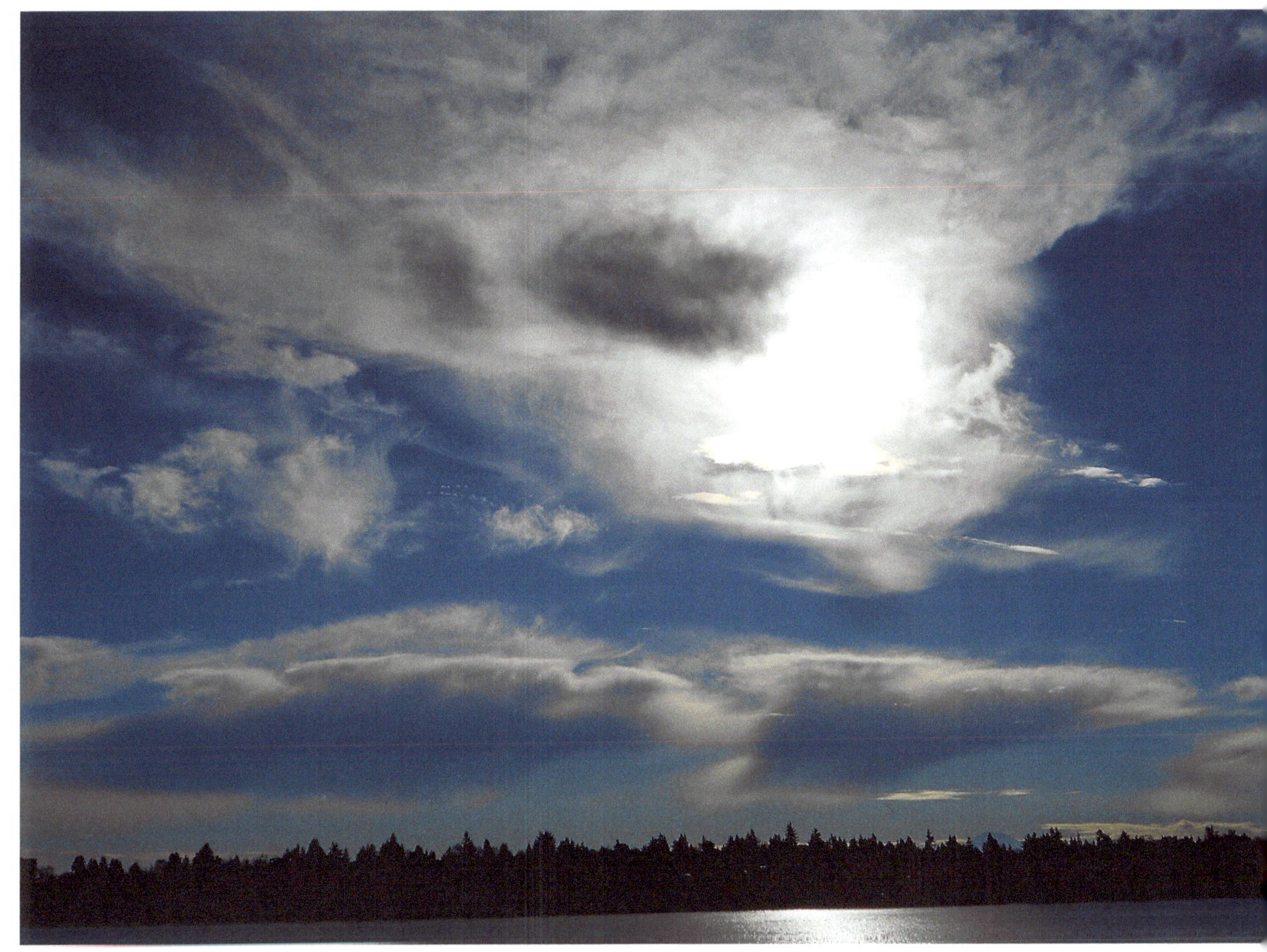

# Surreal Clouds

This has to be one of the strangest cloud formations I've ever seen, resembling an amateurish attempt at painting a sky with both vertical and horizontal brush strokes. I'm expecting a UFO to come out of the bright spot.

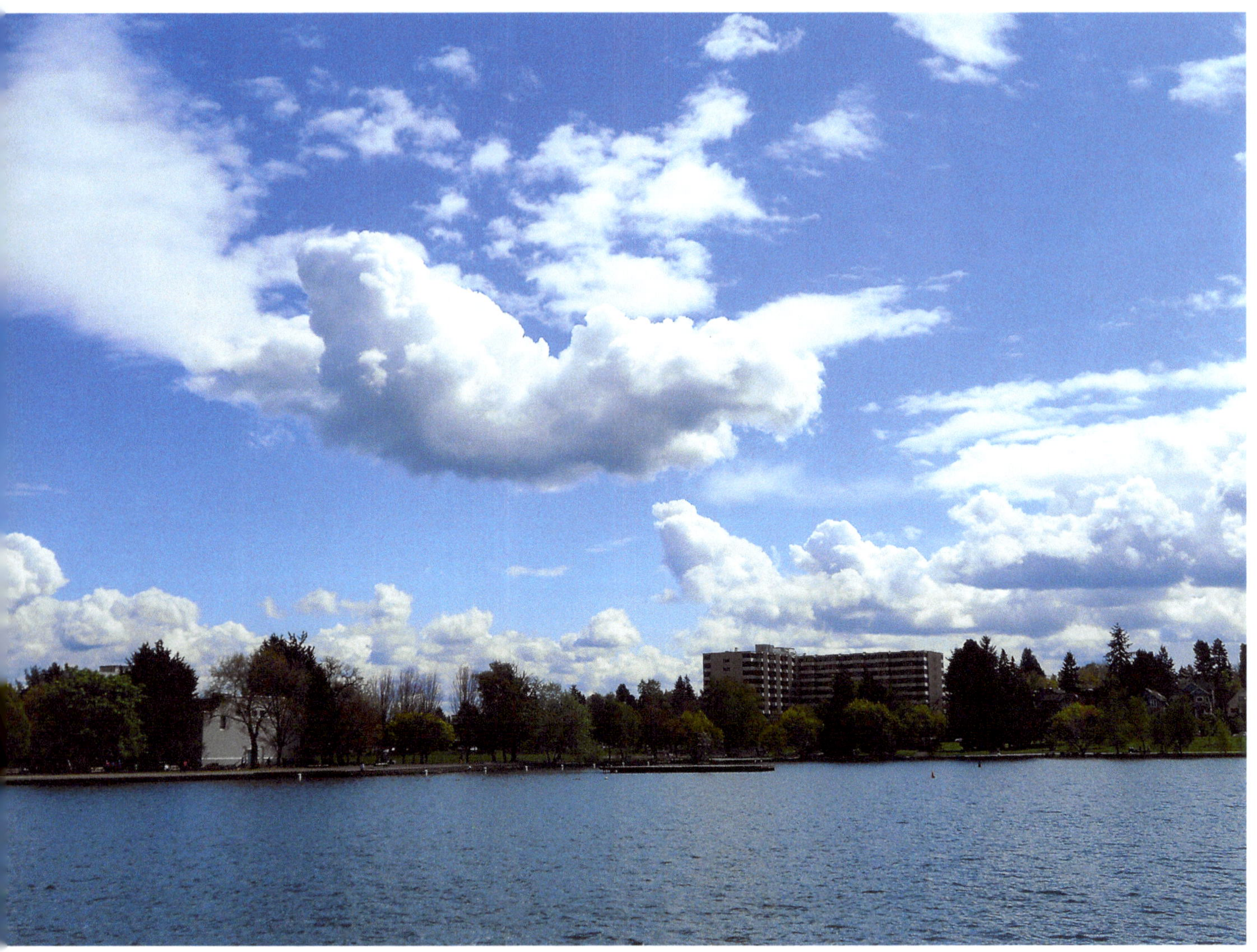

# More Clouds

Seattle is blessed with many cloudy days —some would question if that's being blessed— but whatever you might think, it creates beautiful scenes, such as seen here. You can't deny that's not impressive. These clouds appear heavy to me as if they shouldn't be able to float in the air.

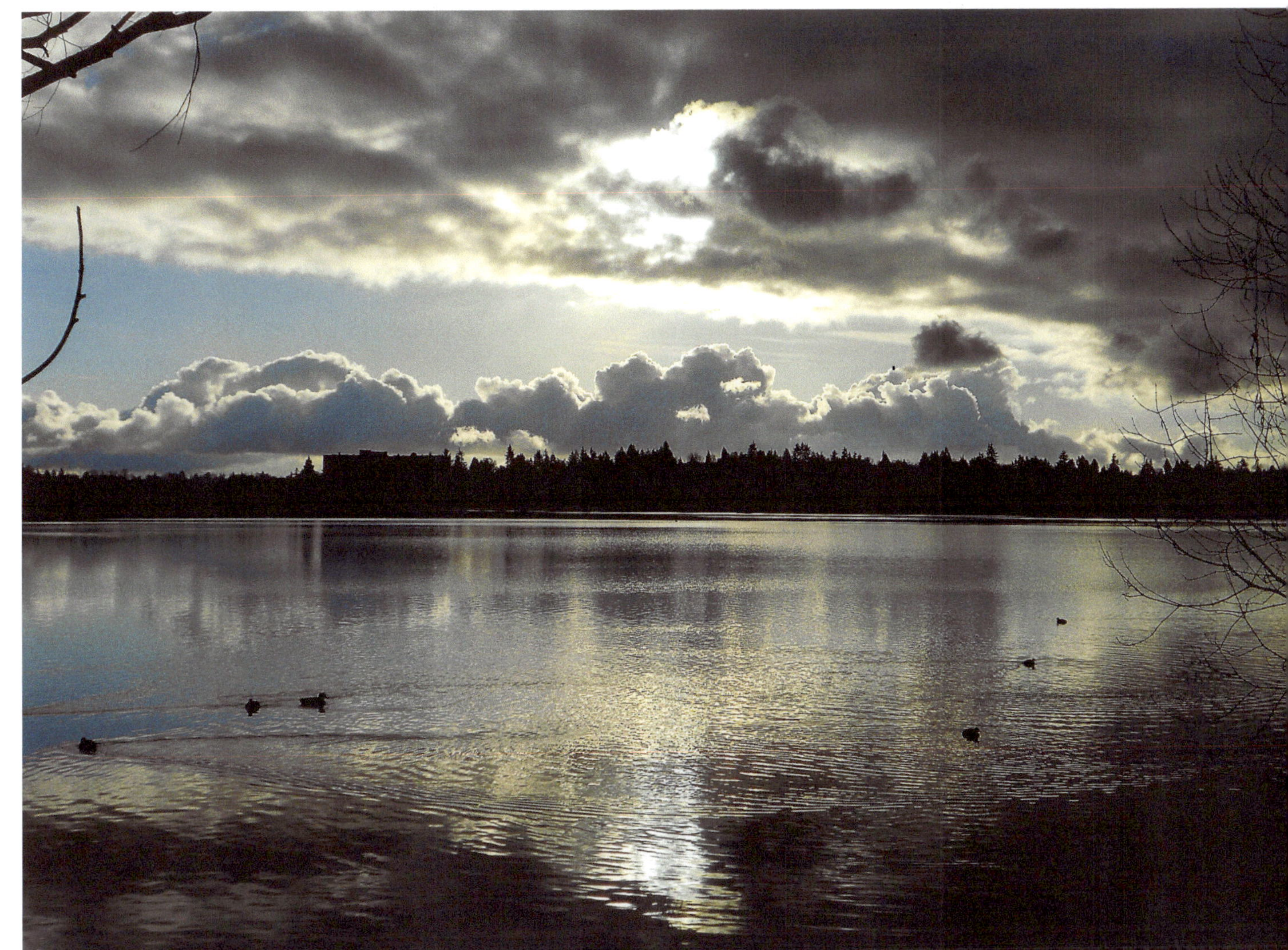

# And More Clouds

Looking to the east, this monochromatic scene was taken on a winter morning. I like it for its lack of variation in color but that is exactly how it appeared (best revealed by the hue of the sky). I love the reflection seen in the water.

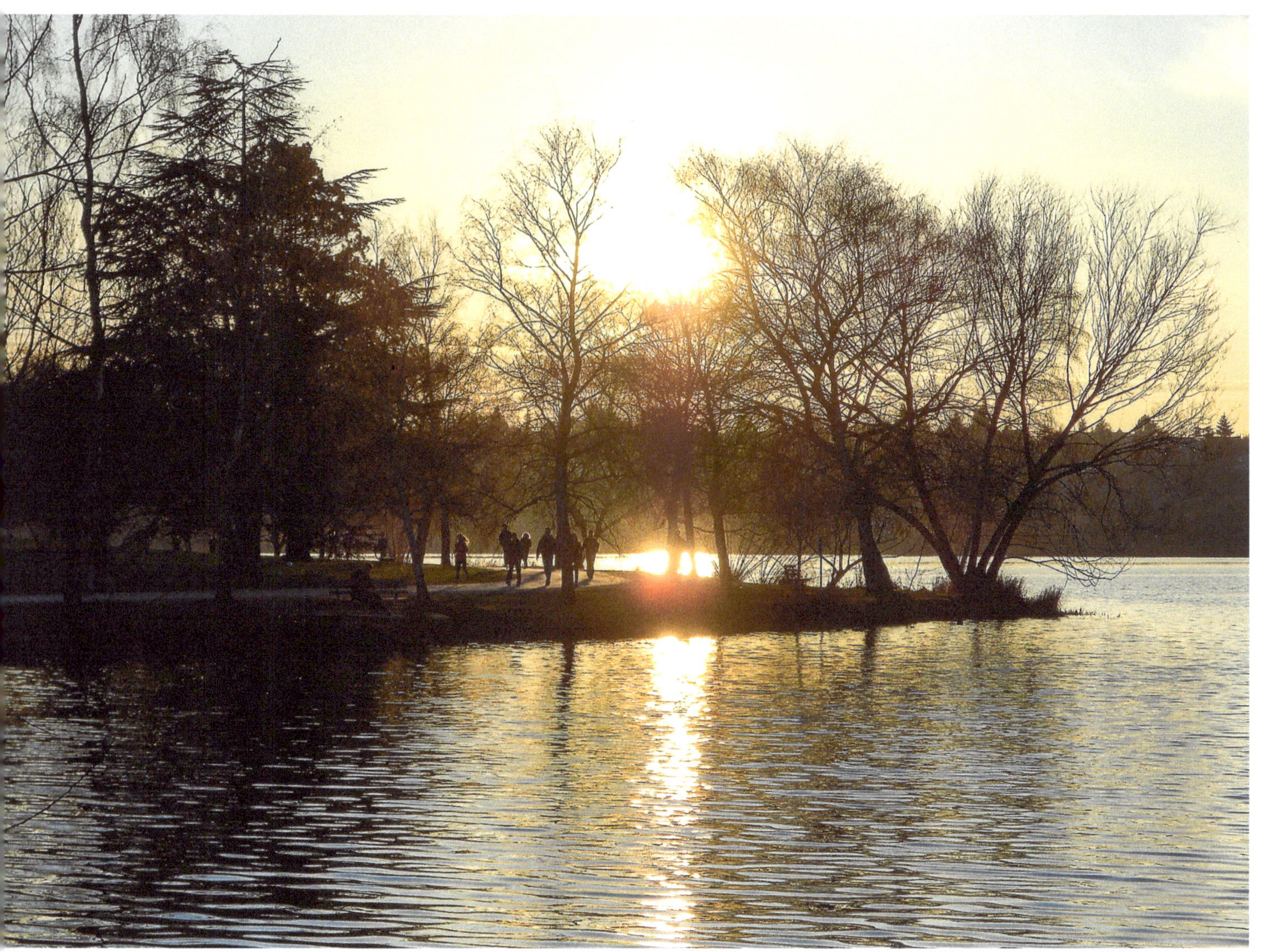

# Copper Tones

This picture was taken on a February day with the temperature in the low 50's, which is warmer than normal for that time of year and explains the number of people you see. The sun is nearing the western horizon and casting its glorious reflection on the water giving a copper touch to the scene.

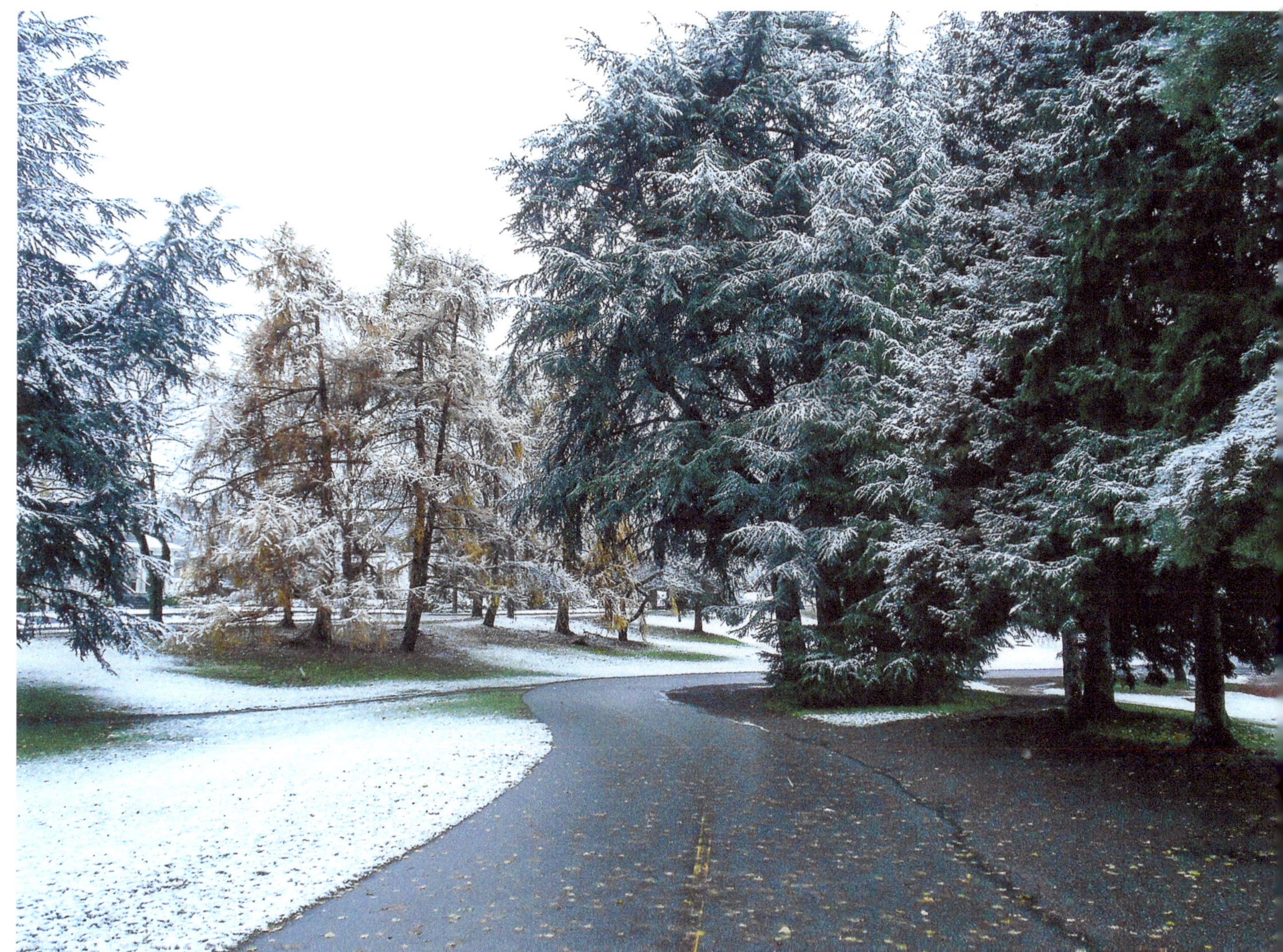

# A Dusting of Snow

A light snowfall creates a magnificent texture of white against green among the trees. It shows how beautiful Green Lake is in every season.

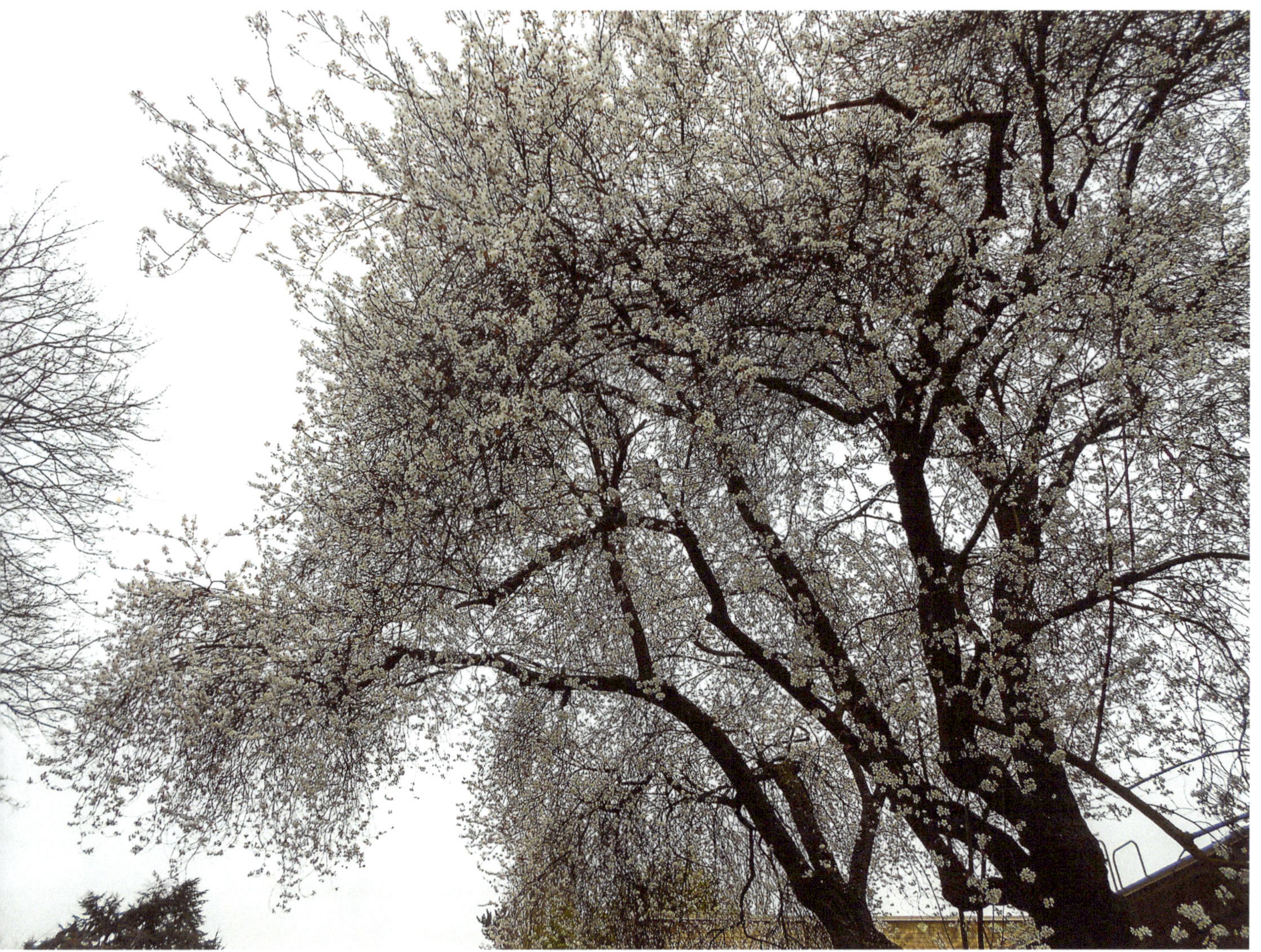

# Near Spring Time

Shown here is the early blossoming tree adjacent to the Bathhouse Theater. At this point, the blossoms are small which gives the tree a speckled look. It's seeing the branches that make this picture interesting to me.

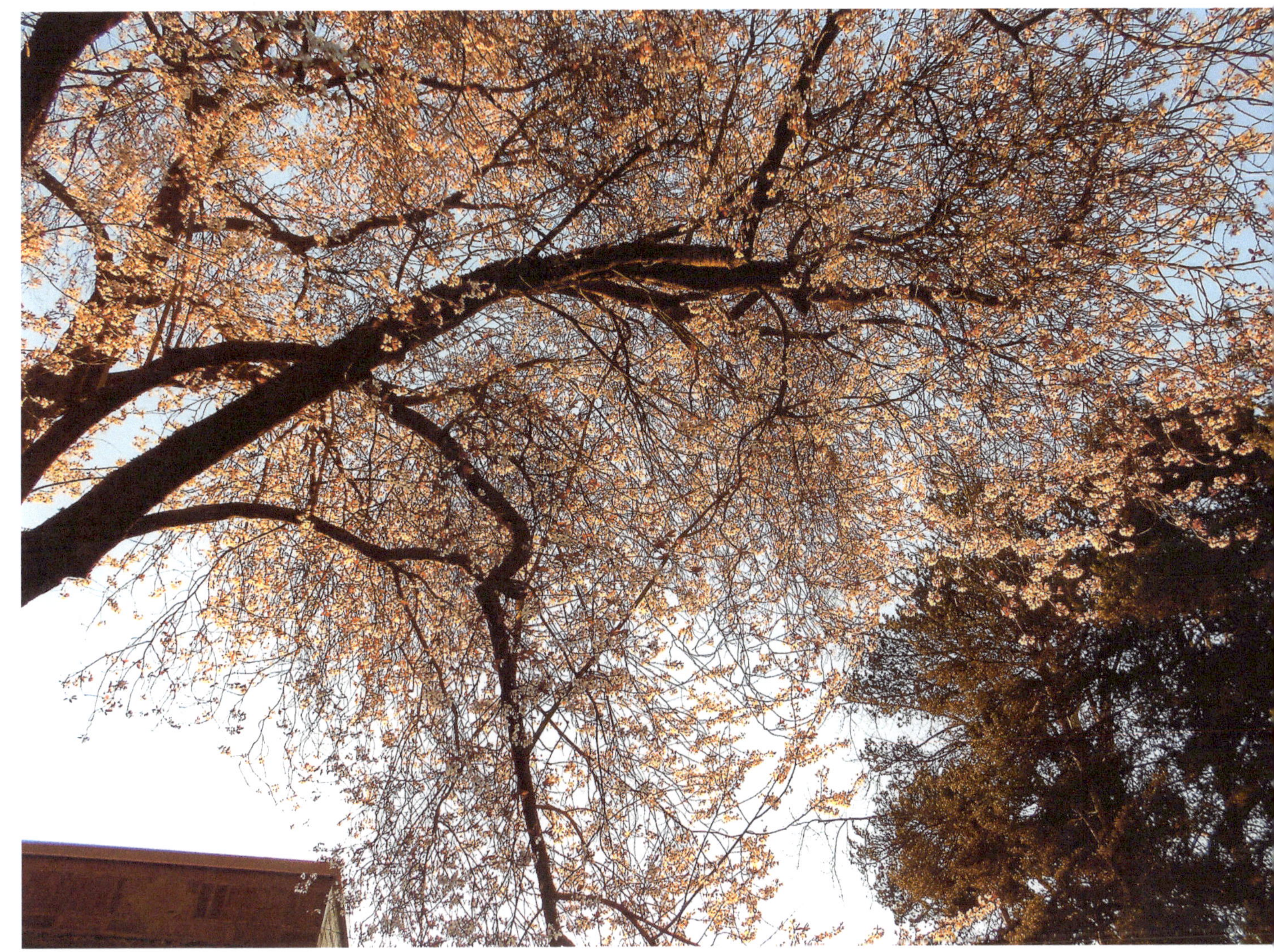

# Shimmering Tungsten

This is the same tree as in the previous scene except that it was taken early on the next day when the sun was shining brightly on the blossoms. The effect is magnificent, even dazzling, as you can see.

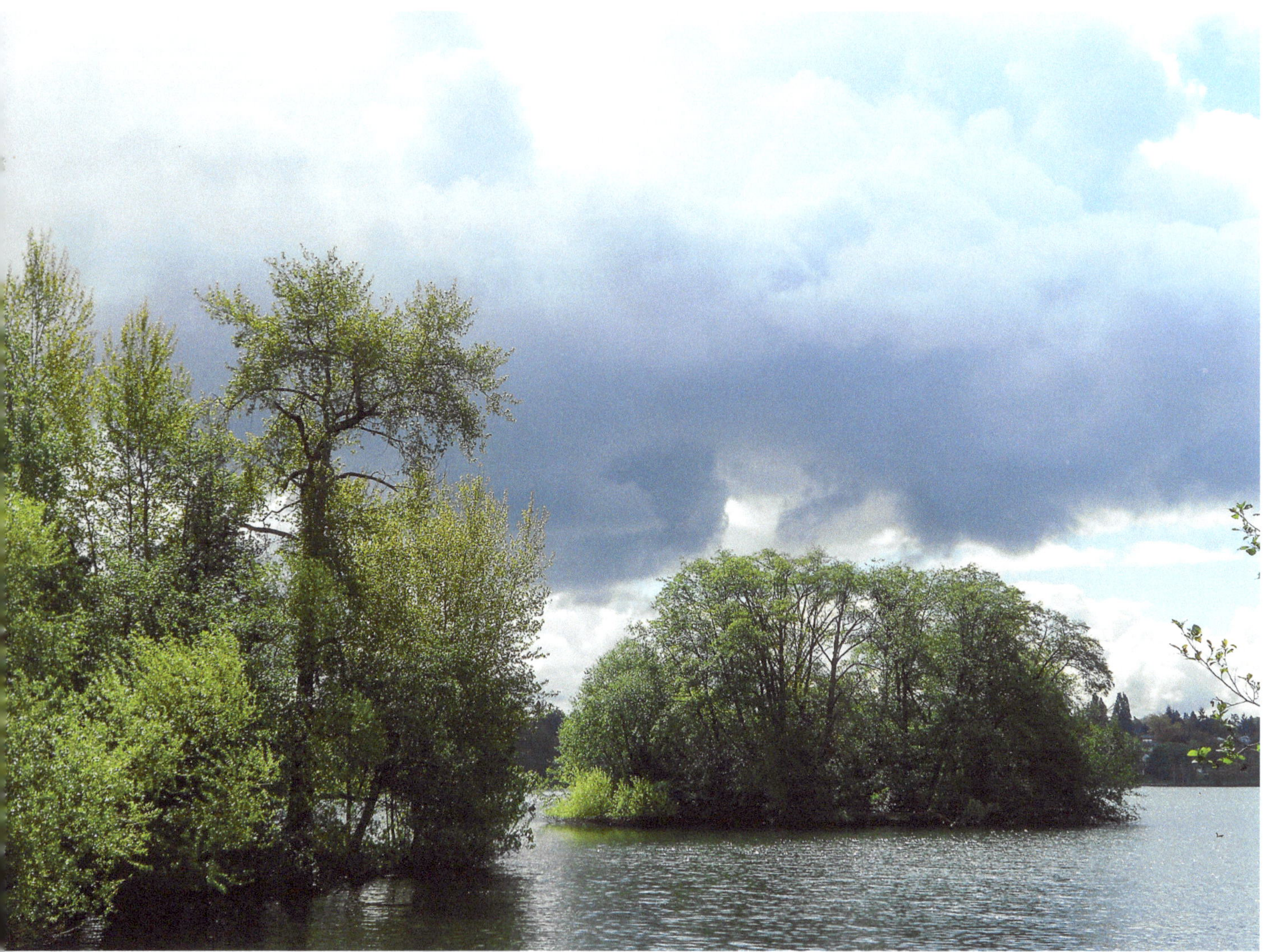

# April Setting

While the clouds are quite impressive in this scene, what I enjoy
about it is the deep greens that mark the spring season. There
is a freshness seen here —I very much like it. It is a stunningly
beautiful picture.

# Green Lake Color

## In Praise of Autumn Hues

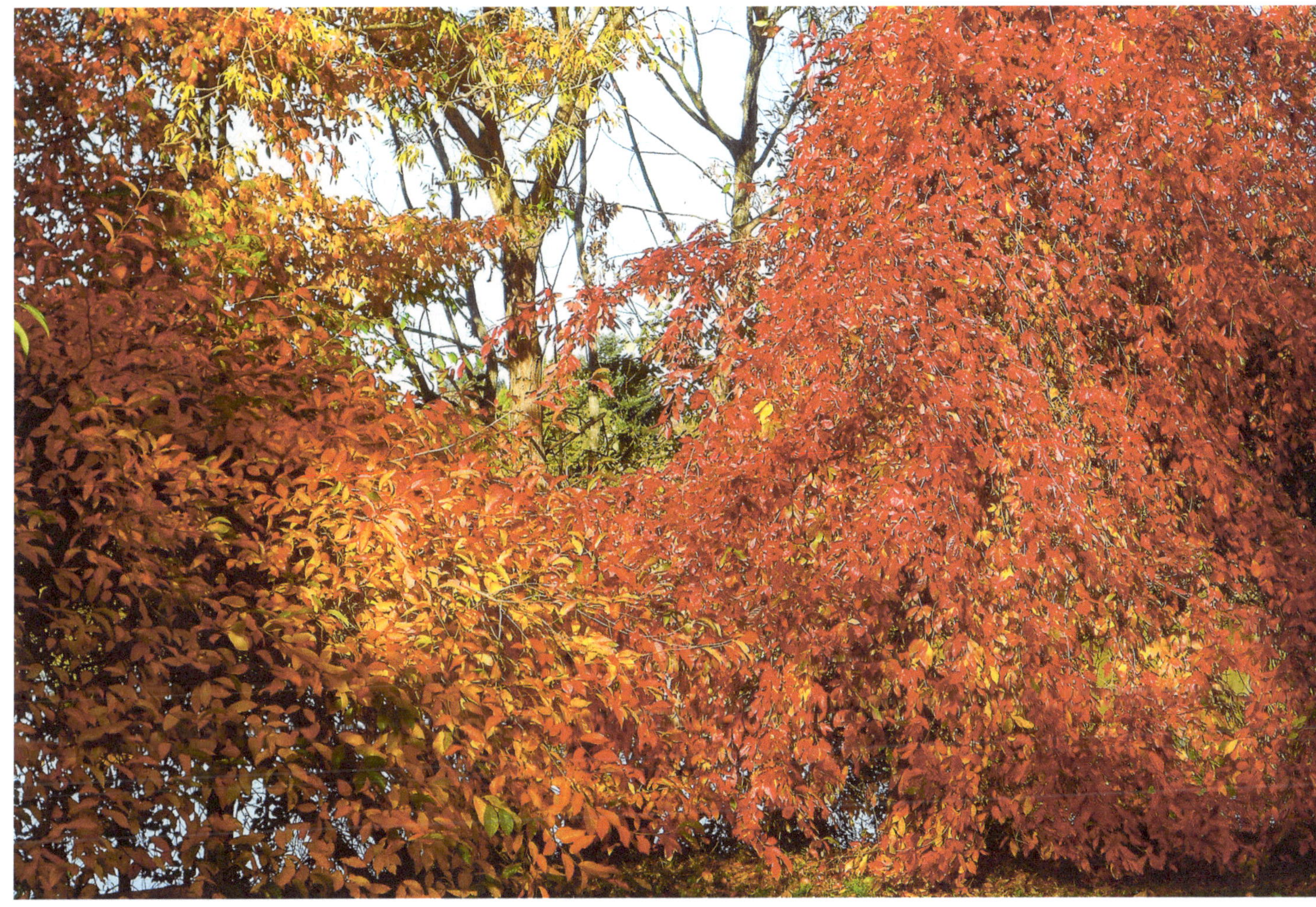

Autumn is a wonderful time of year to be walking around Green Lake if you are willing to cope with the rains that return then. As seen here, the trees are resplendent in their colorful dress before they shed their leaves. The scenes in this category deserve special attention because of their brilliance and variety of contrasting and glowing shades which mark that season. I would say that October is my favorite month of the year.

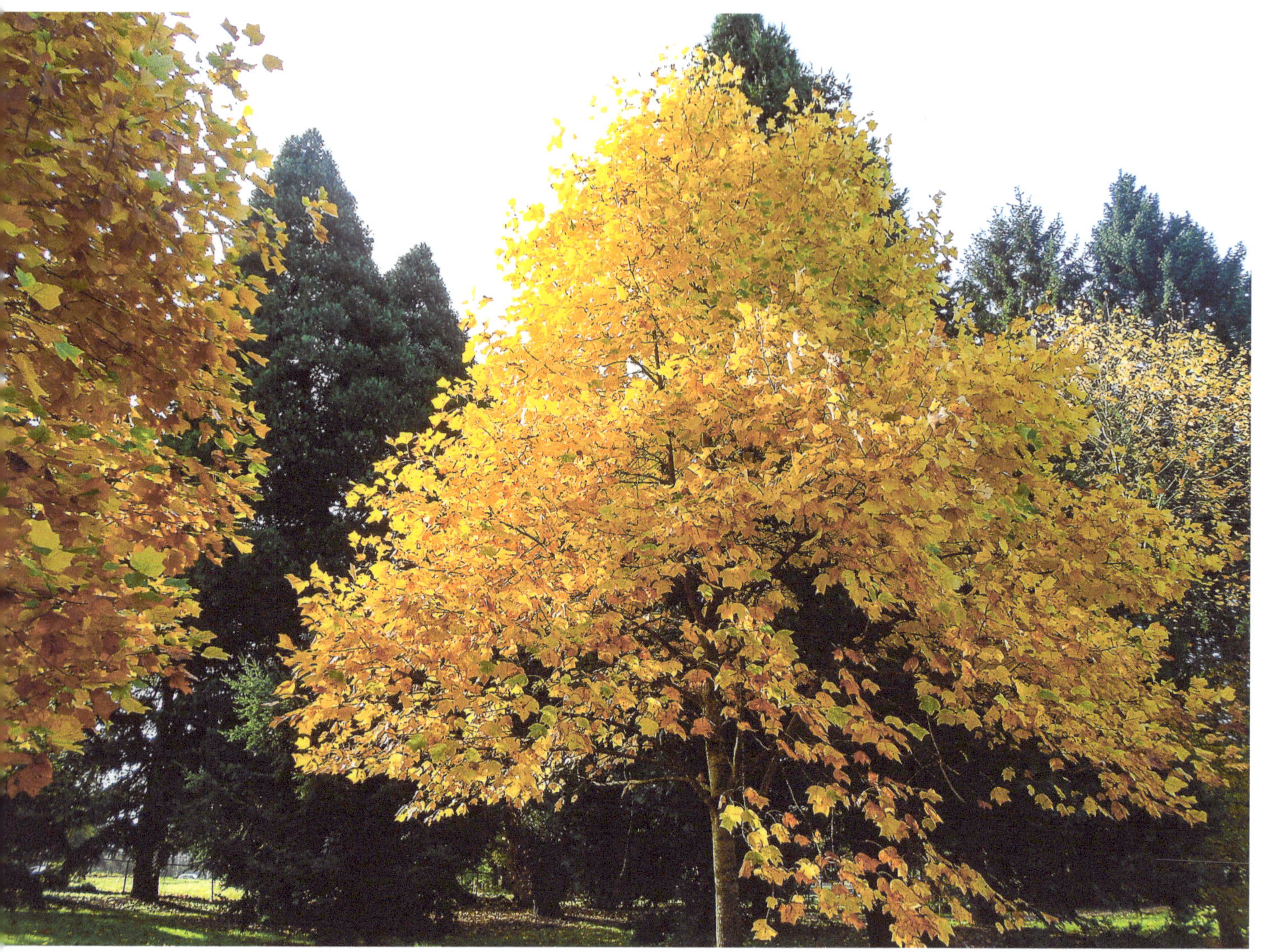

# Gold on Green

The trees change their leaves at different rates, some turning red in late September while others turn to the nice golden glow in November, giving a continuous display of splashes of color for a more than a two month period. Beauty abounds in the fall.

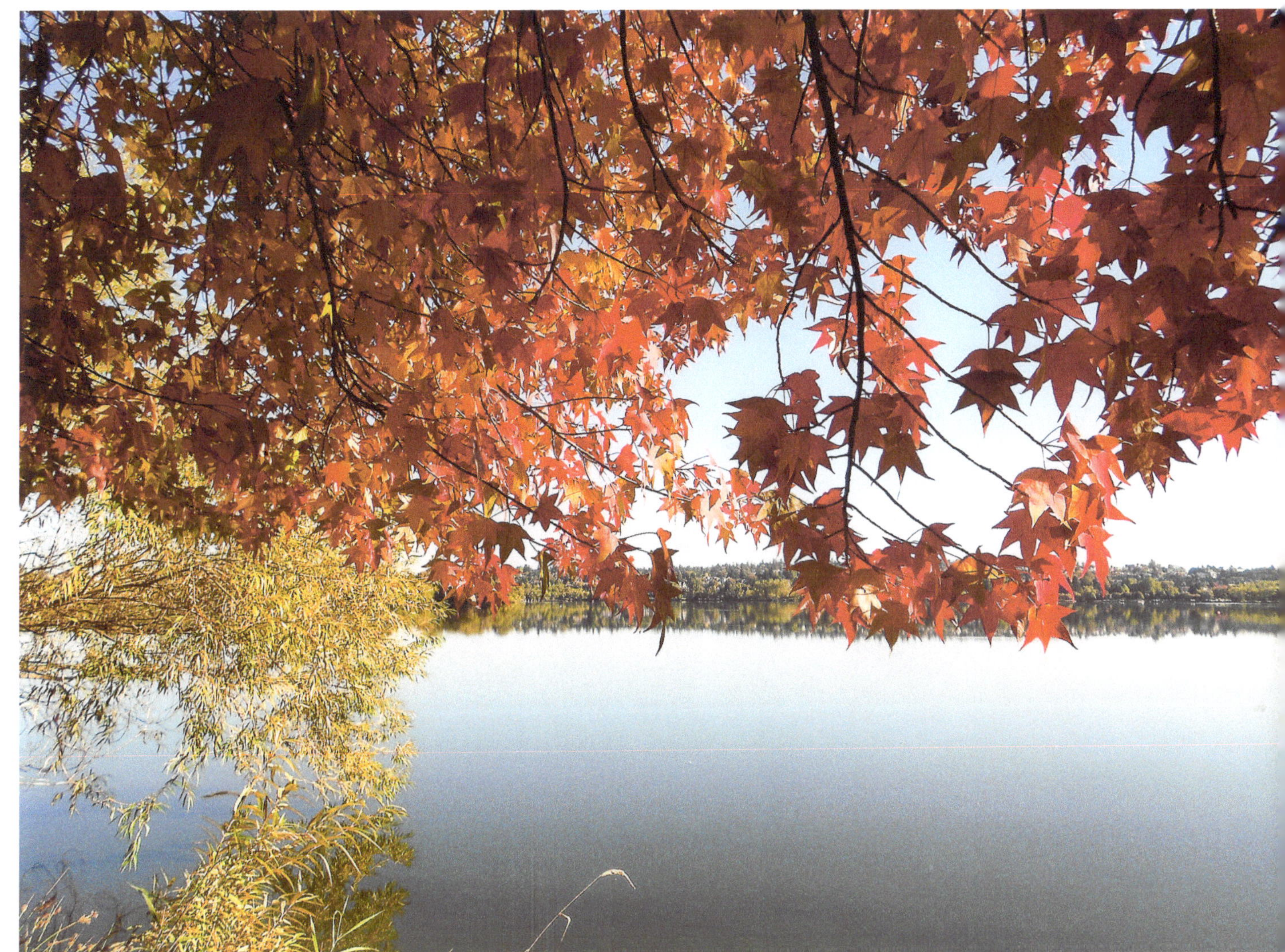

# Early Bloomer

The trees on the southwestern end of the lake by the boathouse typically are the first to acquire their fall plumage. You can contrast that with the background trees on the distant shore which are only beginning to change their summer green mantle. Later in the seasons, the shrubs also turn yellow.

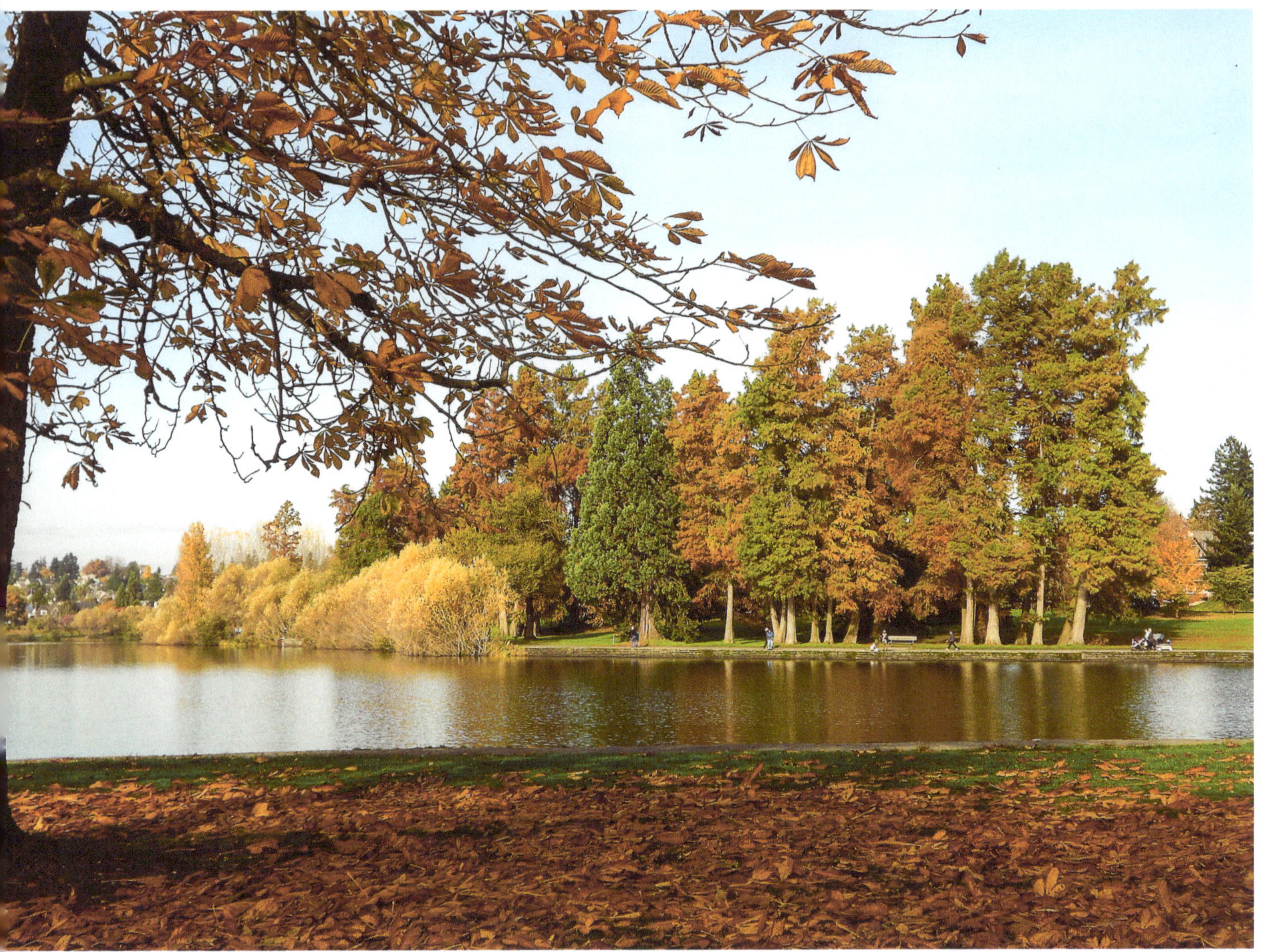

# Raking Season

The Seattle Parks Department does a good job of ridding the ground of fallen leaves so it's not that easy to capture a scene like this. When you do, it brings out the flavor of the season, enhancing it with its tawny look.

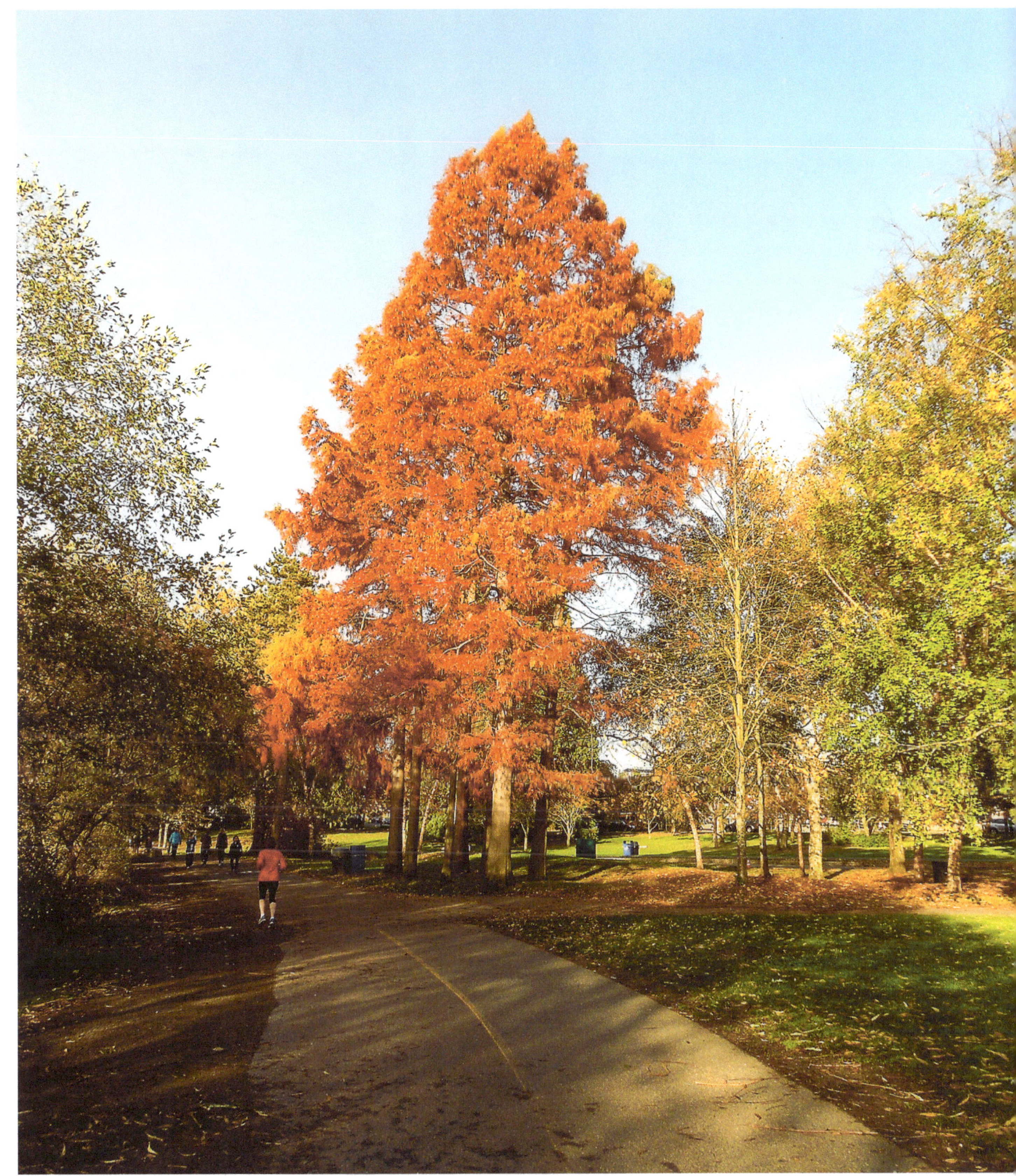

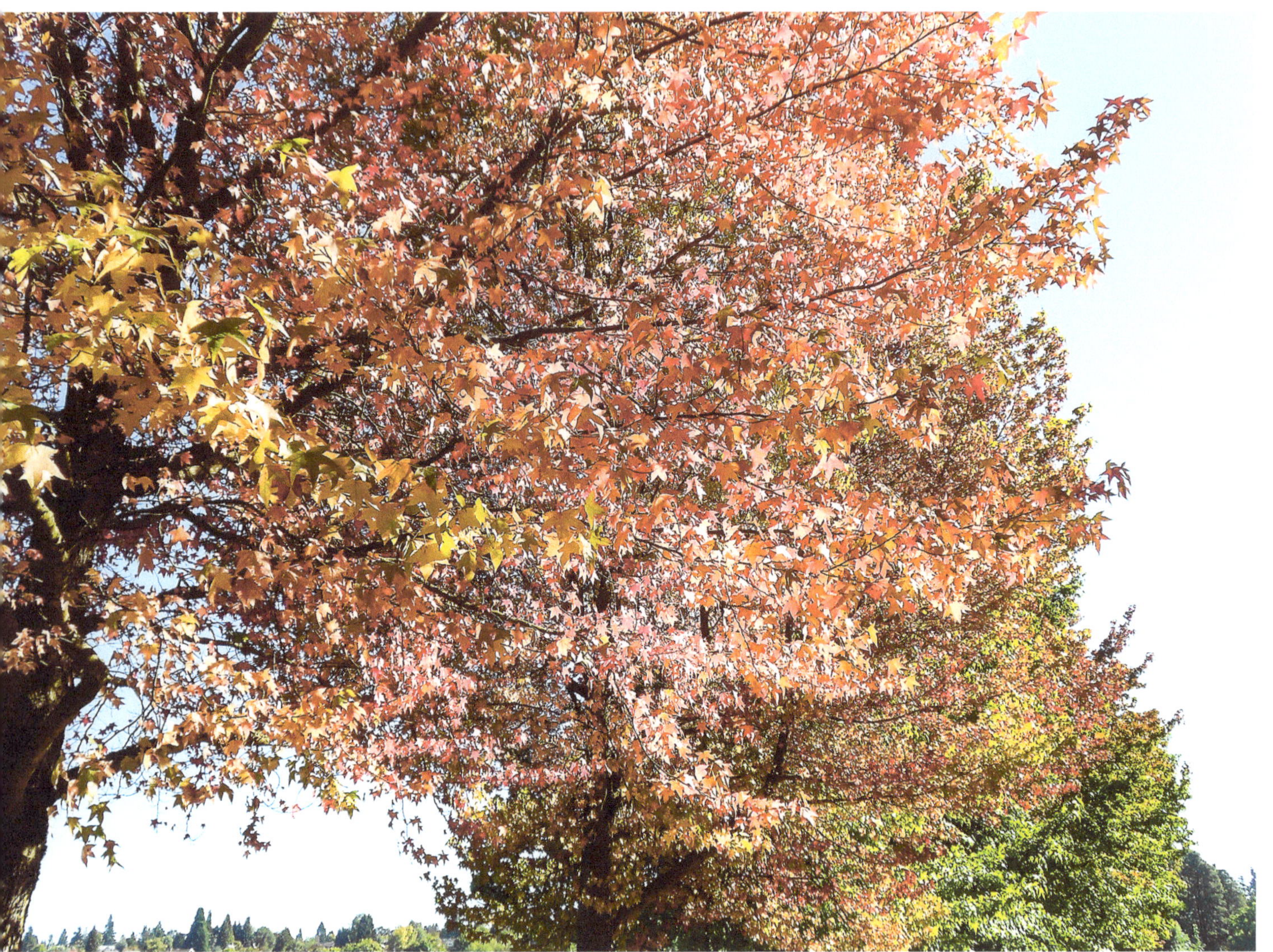

# Variations of Hues

I've noticed that trees of the same species, in this case Liquid Ambar Trees, change to fall colors at variable times, some as early as late September and others not until mid to late October. The effect of this is that the foliage remains in place over a lengthier period of time, giving autumn an enhancement of its appeal.

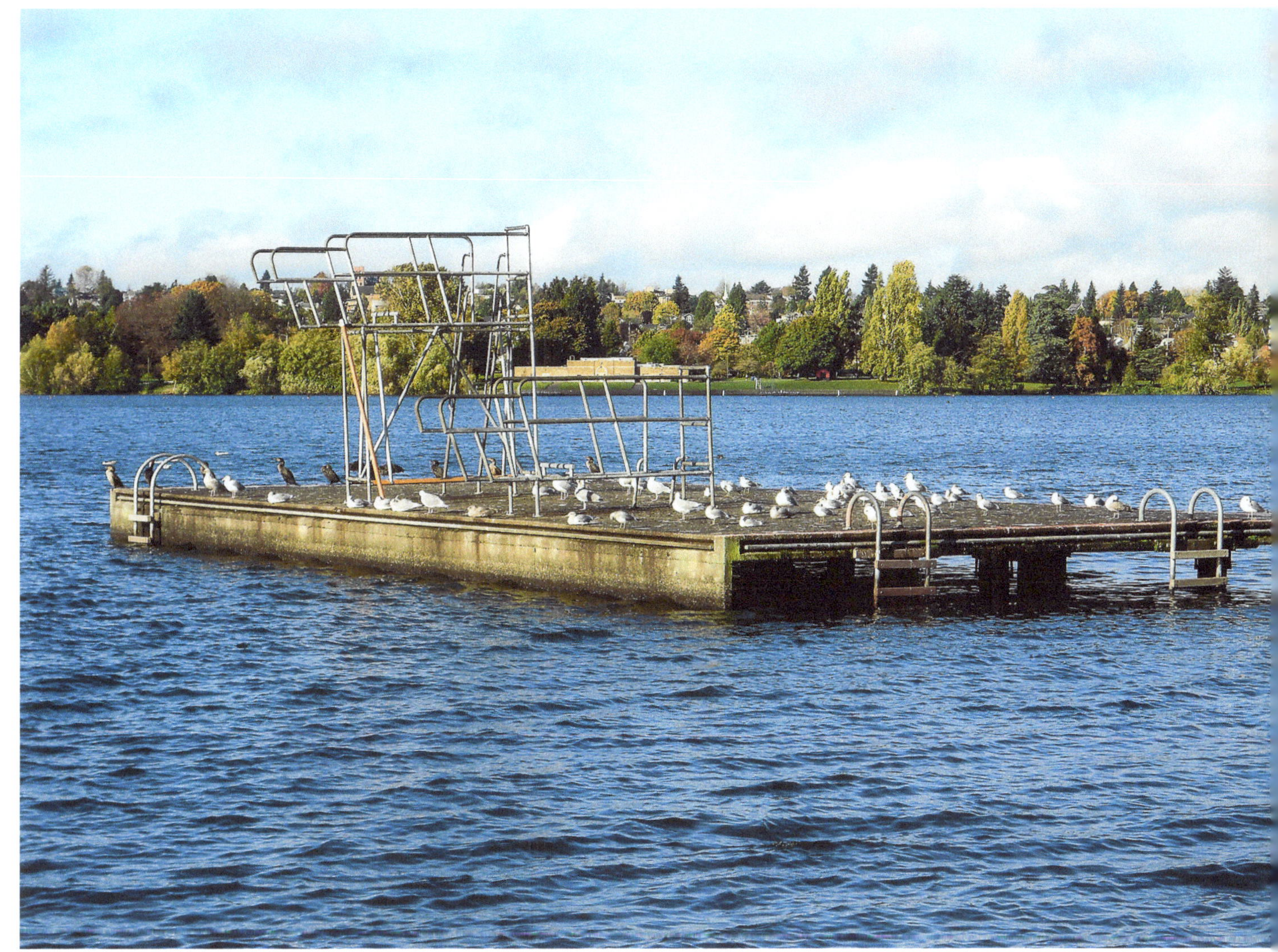

# After Swimming Season

With the passing of summer comes the closing of the swimming season and this is what happens to the docks at the lake then. The birds take over, using the facility for resting until the next summer. It must be an incredible cleaning feat to make it suitable for people again.

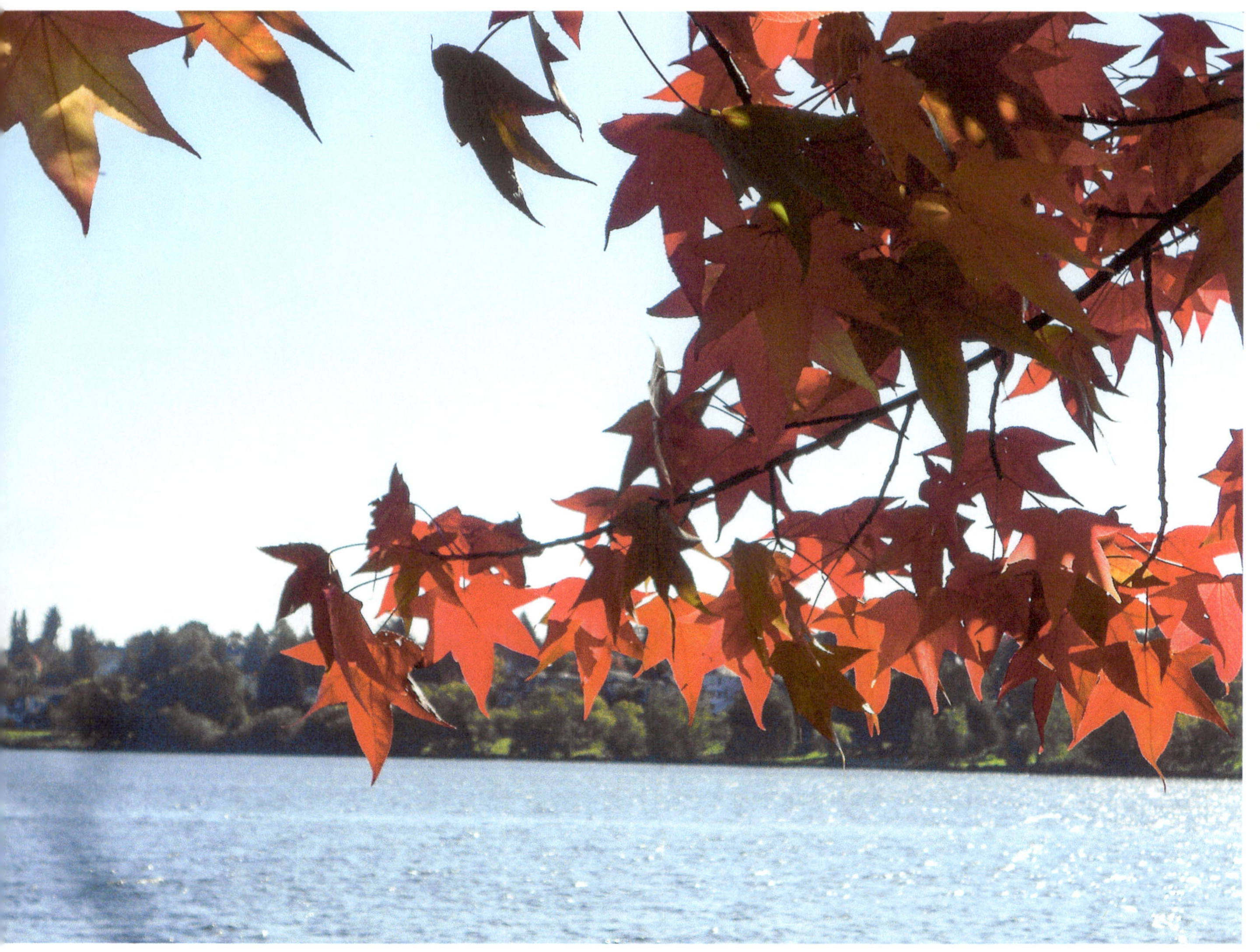

# Autumn Glory

I love the sheer beauty and simplicity of this picture, a quintessential fall scene, taken in late September. The sky is blue, the air is crisp, and you know that colder days are coming. It feels good to be outdoors on such a day.

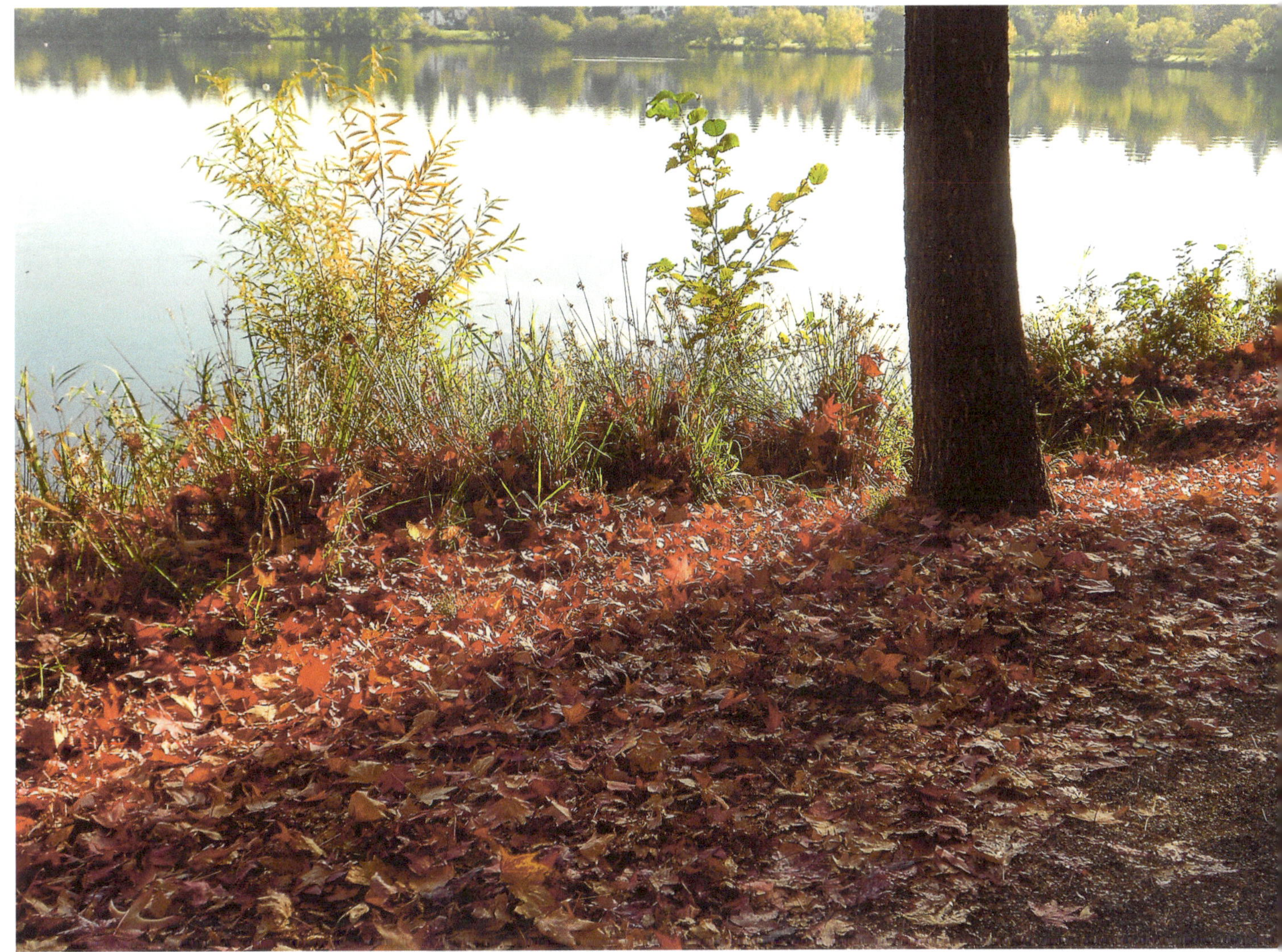

# Fallen Leaves

Even fallen leaves, retaining their myriad of colors as seen here with the sunlight at your flank and the shadow of the tree darkening the reddish glow, have a beauty to them, spread about the ground like an oriental area rug. I like this scene because you can see the southeastern shore framing the top of it.

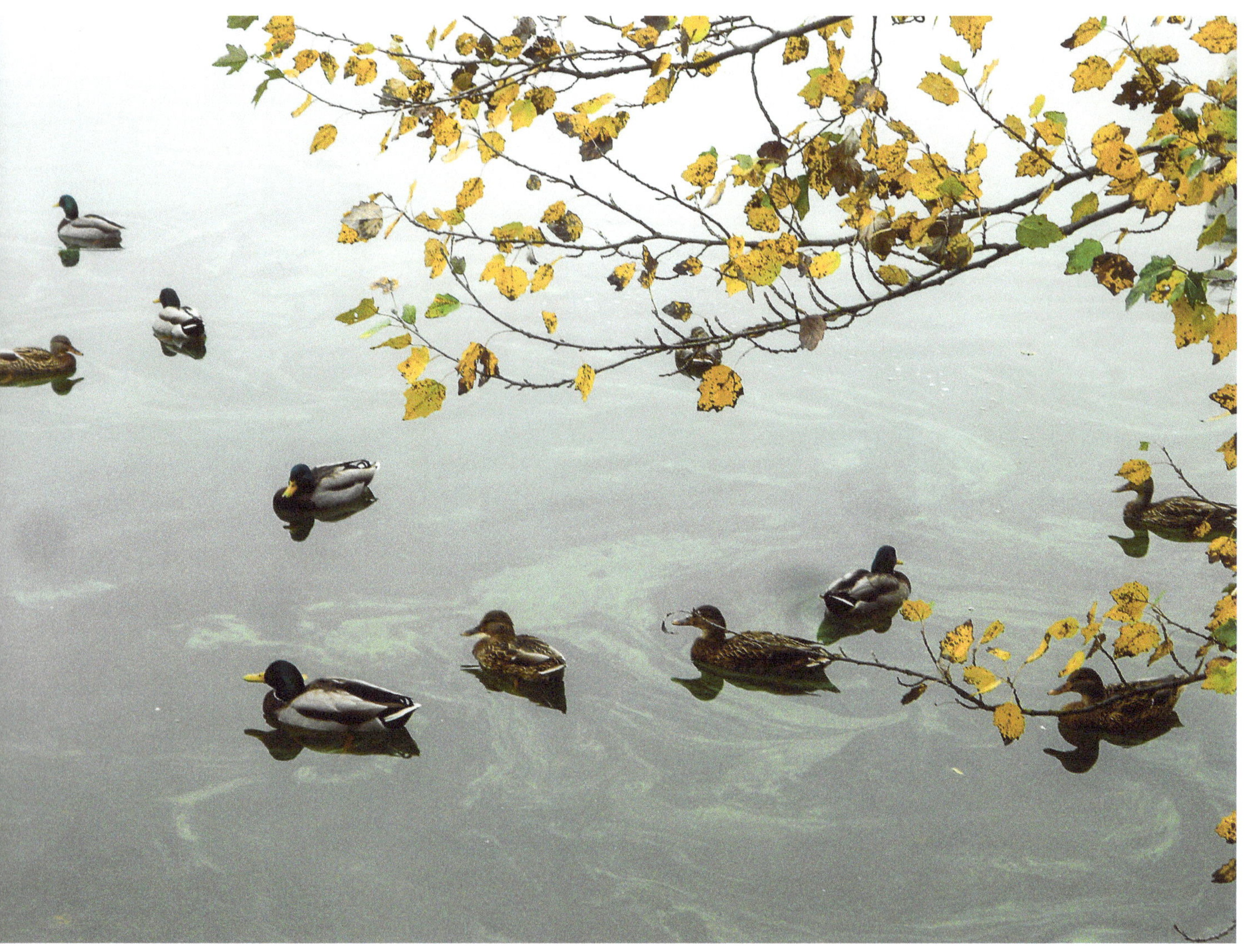

# Tranquility

What gives this picture its appeal is the overall grayish tones offset by the thinning yellow leaves. It also reveals the algae problem that occurs at Green Lake after an unusually hot summer such as we had in 2015. Some areas of the lake begin to smell, but that's cleaned up by the time spring arrives.

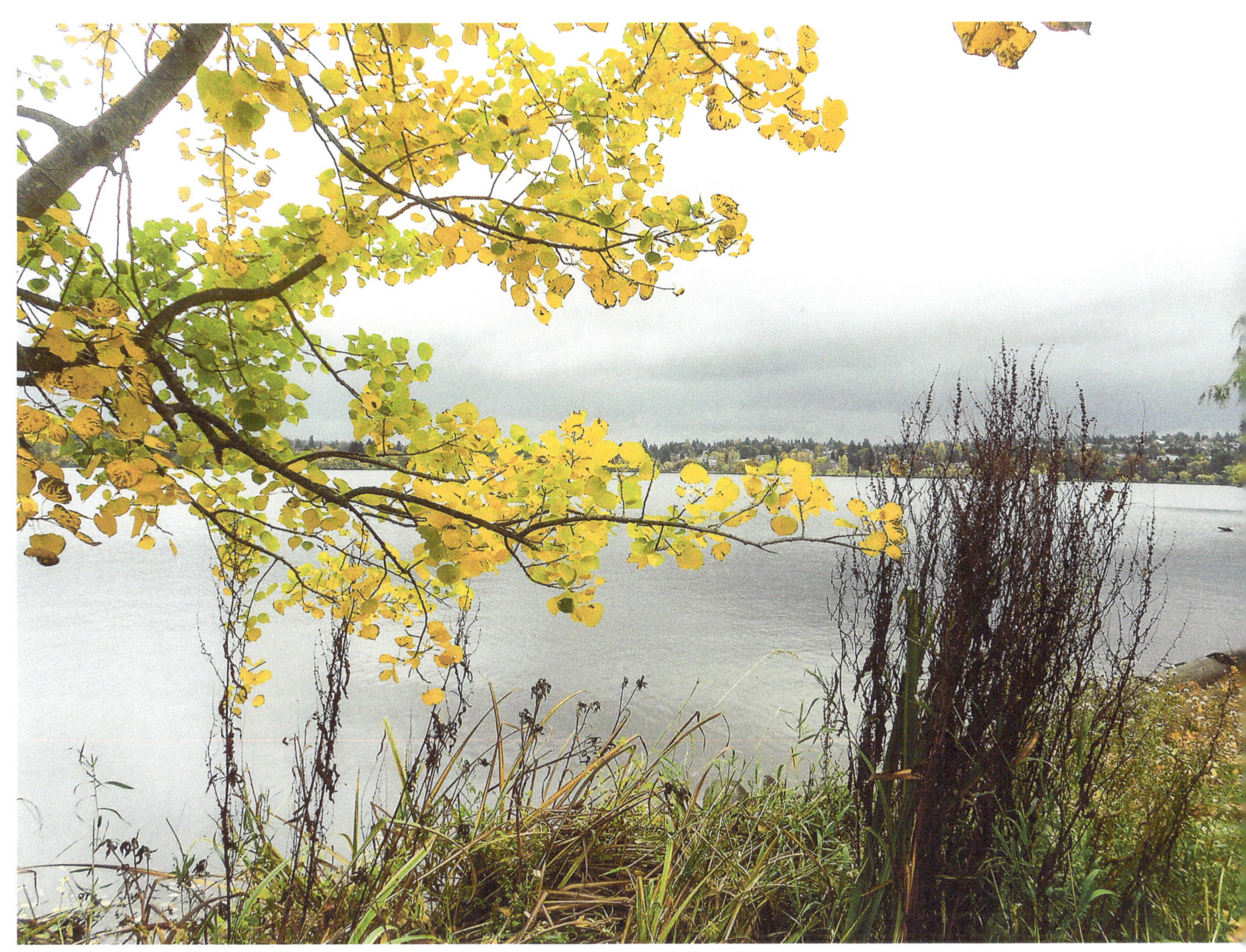

*With grayish skies and waters cold*
*Offset by autumn leaves of gold The color contrasts*
*clear and bold In serenity here unfold.*

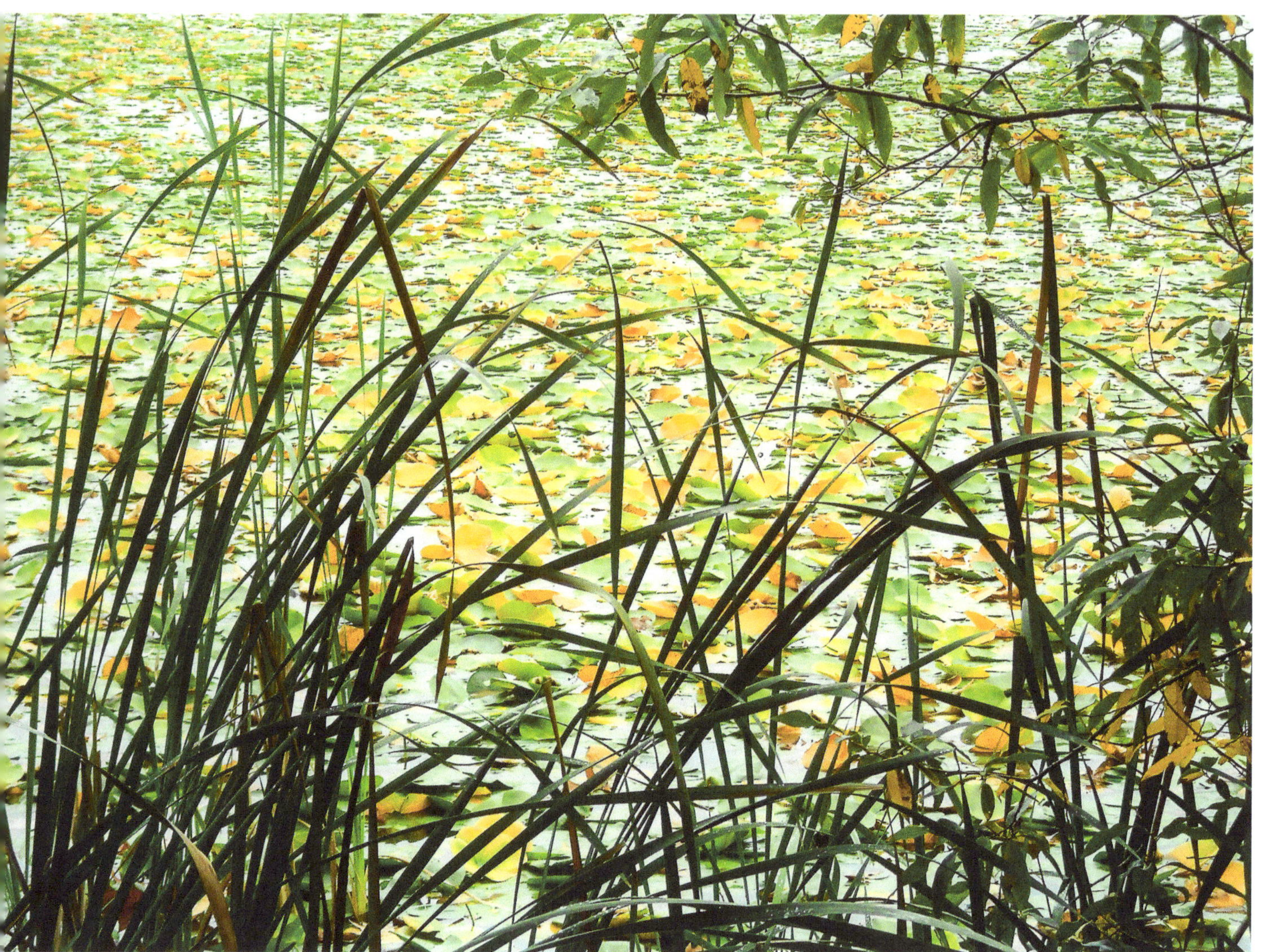

# Lily Pads

It's interesting to see that Lily Pads actually change their color in the fall season. They're found along the western shore of Green Lake and usually first appear in mid-spring and reach their maximum width in late-summer, an annual occurrence. It's among the Lily Pads where the turtles hang out.

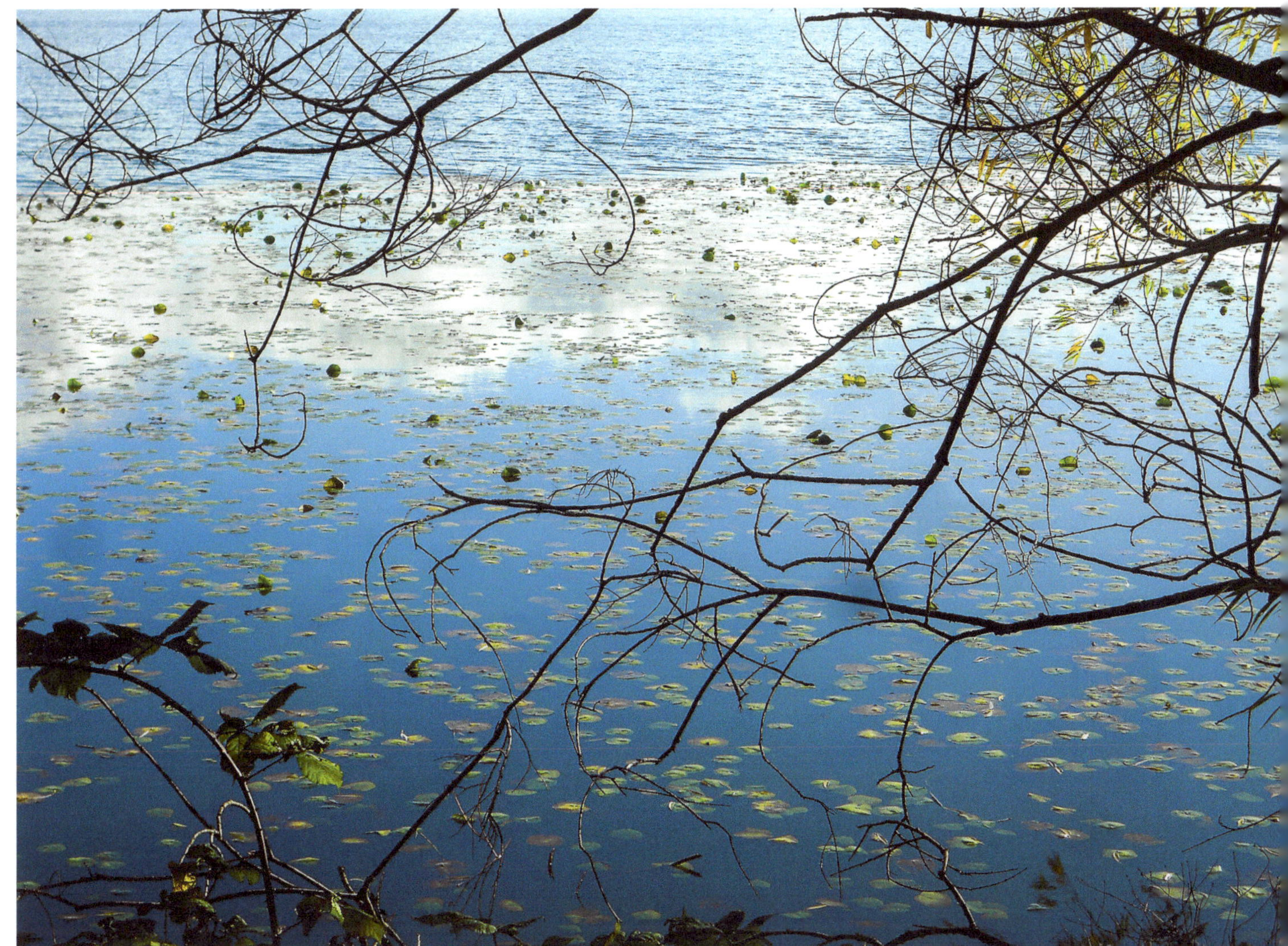

# Disappearing Lilies

Here you see what happens to the lily pads late in the fall. They shrivel up and then sink in the water, thinning them out and eventually disappearing altogether. It is now mid-November; nearly all the leaves from the trees are gone.

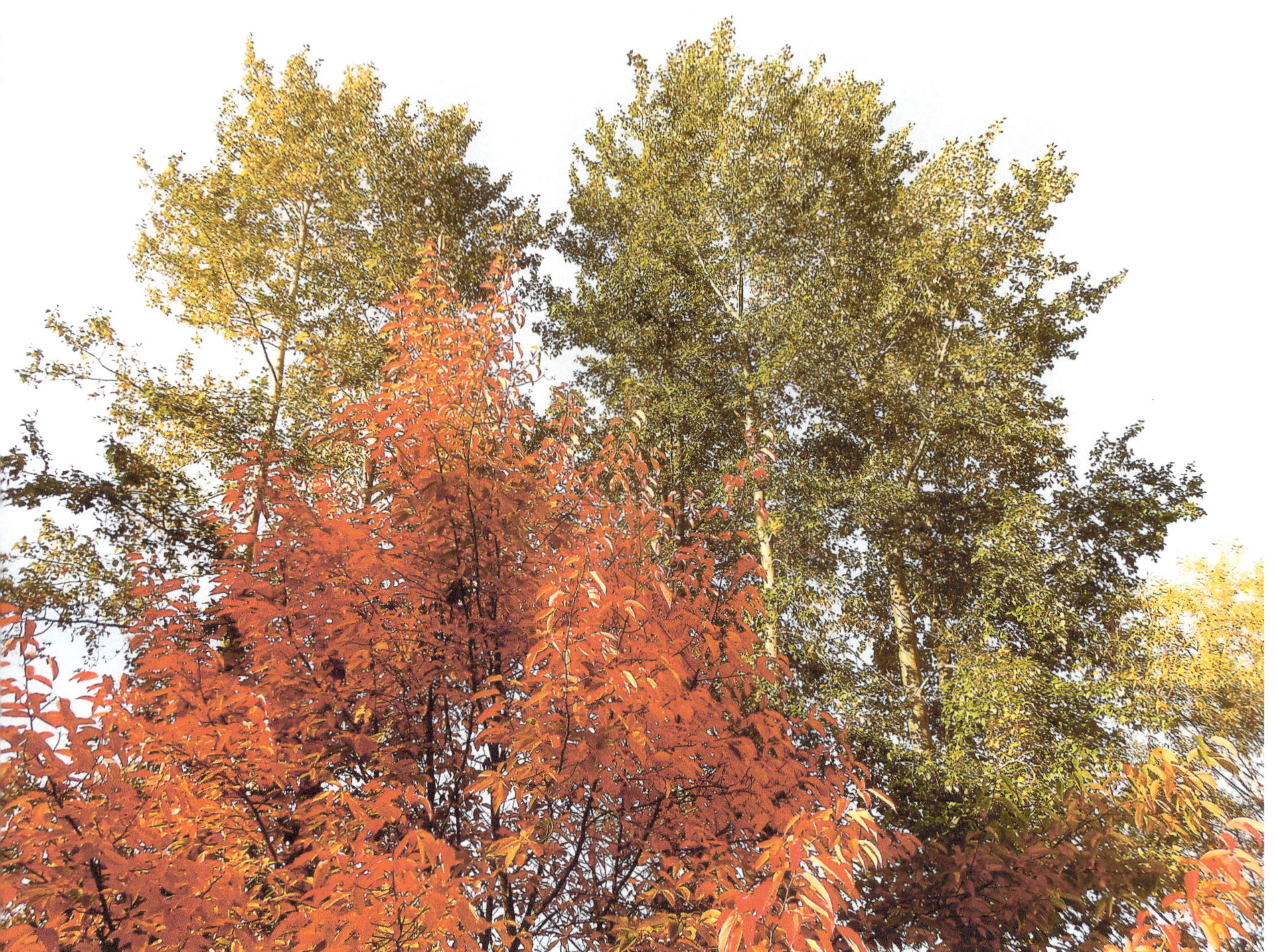

# Blazing in the Sunlight

Fall's brilliance is best demonstrated on a bright sunshiny day when the colors are at their most dazzling display. Seen here is a perfect example of this; you get the feeling it is a hot day even though such was not the case.

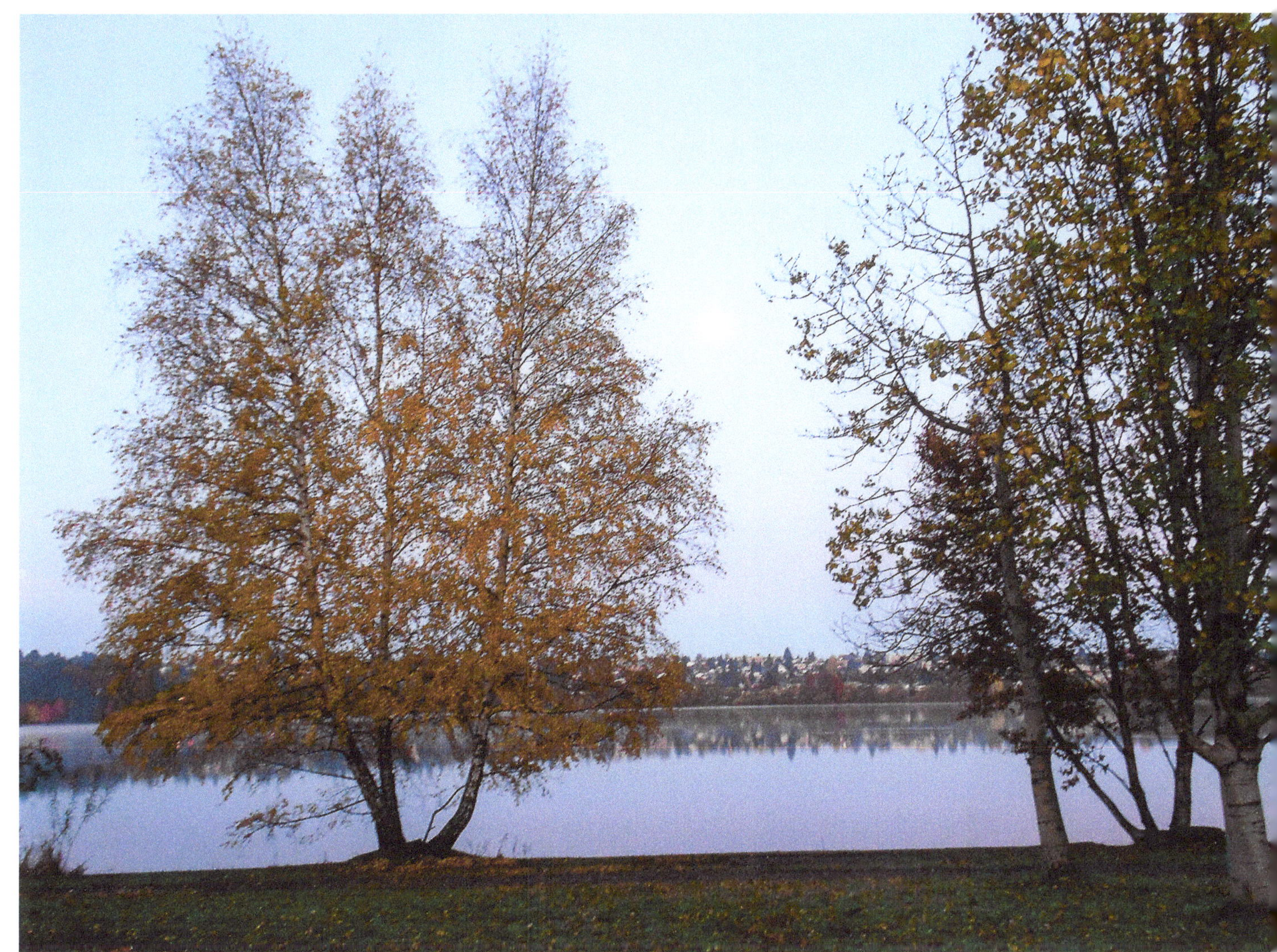

# Moon over the Lake

Here we see the moon on a Saturday morning when I walked the lake before the sun came up. The trees are balding, a sure sign colder times are coming.

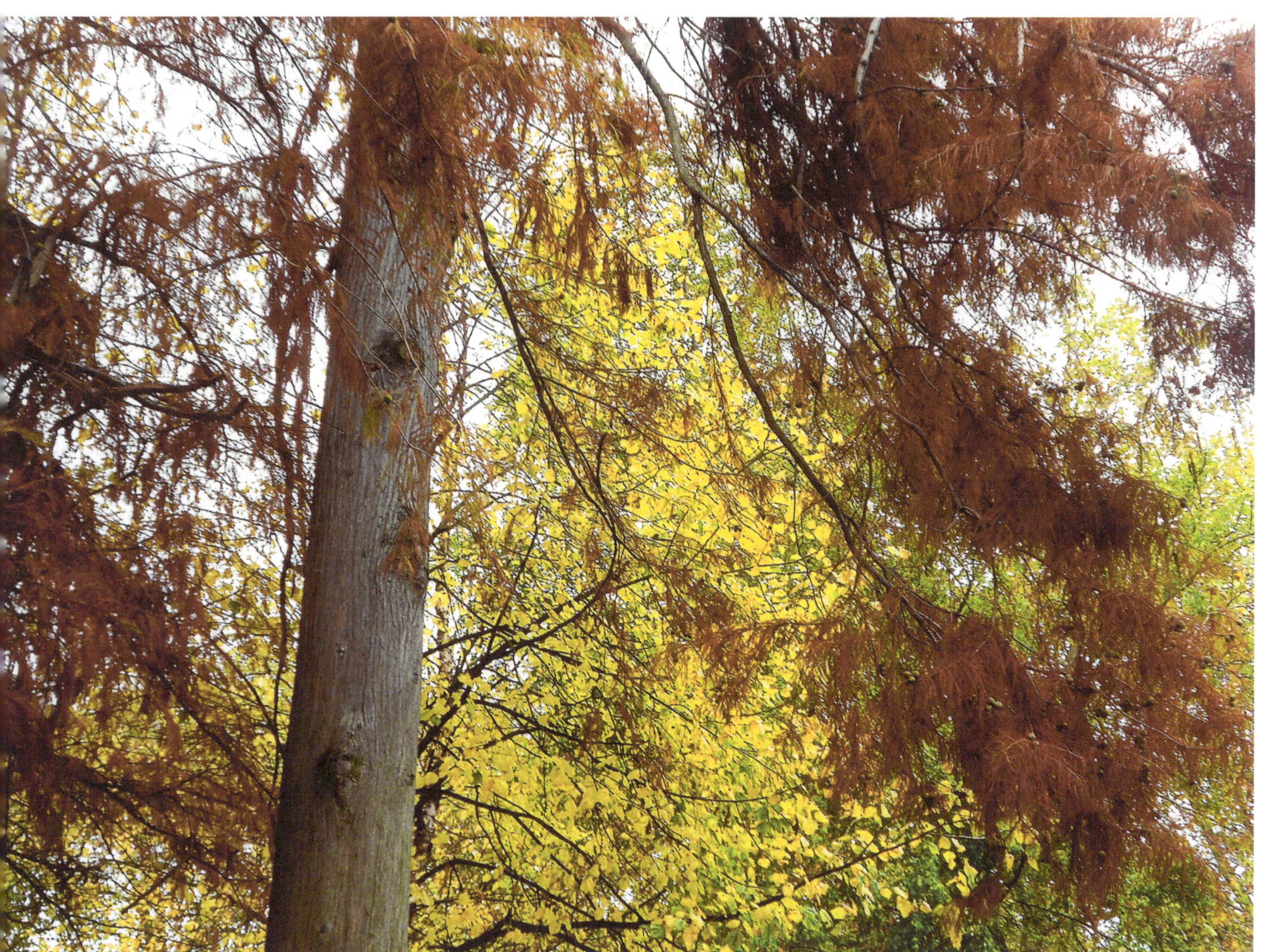

# Rusty Tones

Bald Cypresses are the most frequently seen trees on the northern end of Green Lake Park. Although they resemble Evergreens, their similar leaves turn to a rusty brown in the fall and are eventually shed.

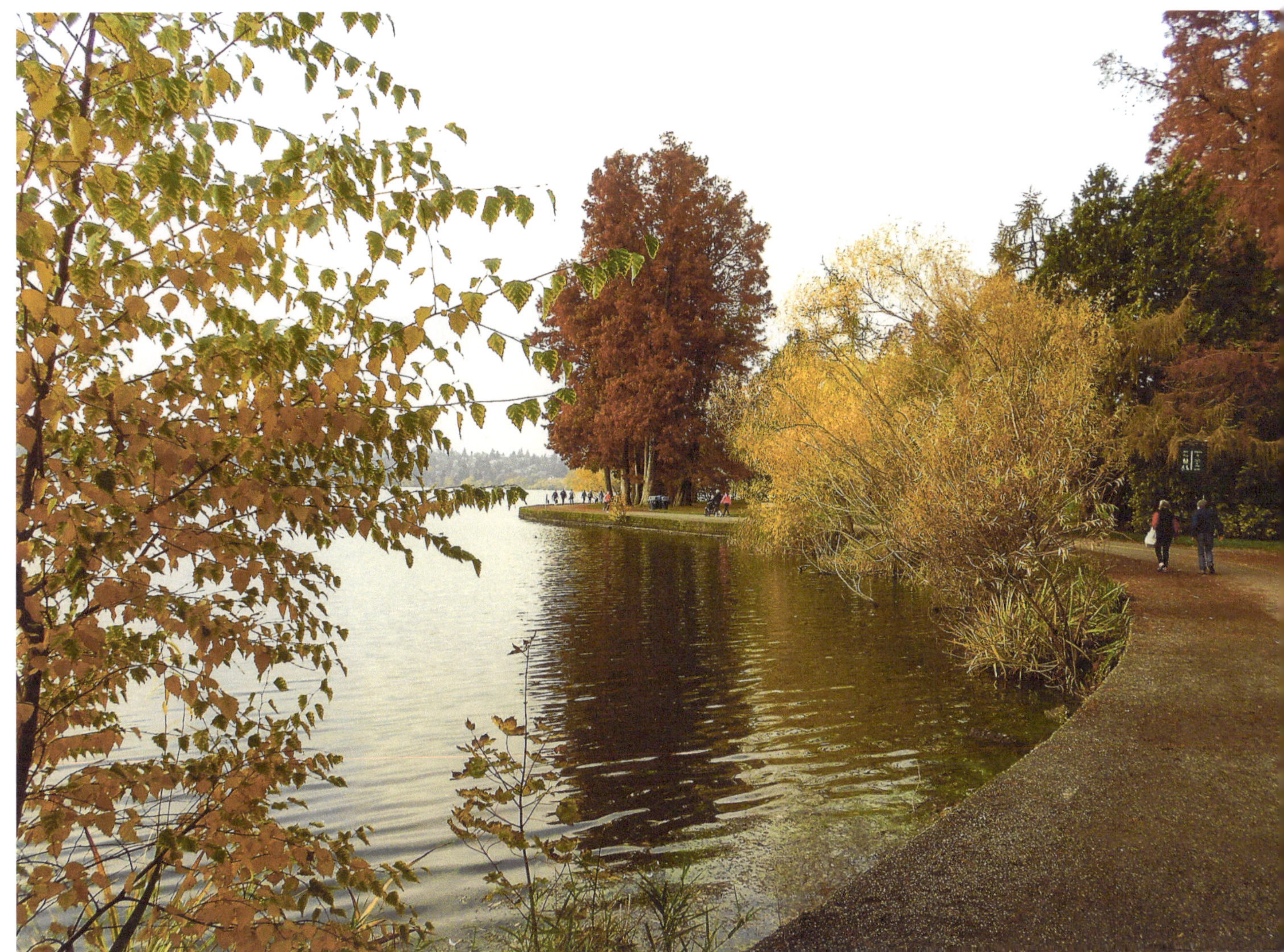

# Tawny Shades

I love this picture for its tawny colors, a transformation occurring during the fall season. Even the water has a brownish-yellow tint to it. Magnificent!

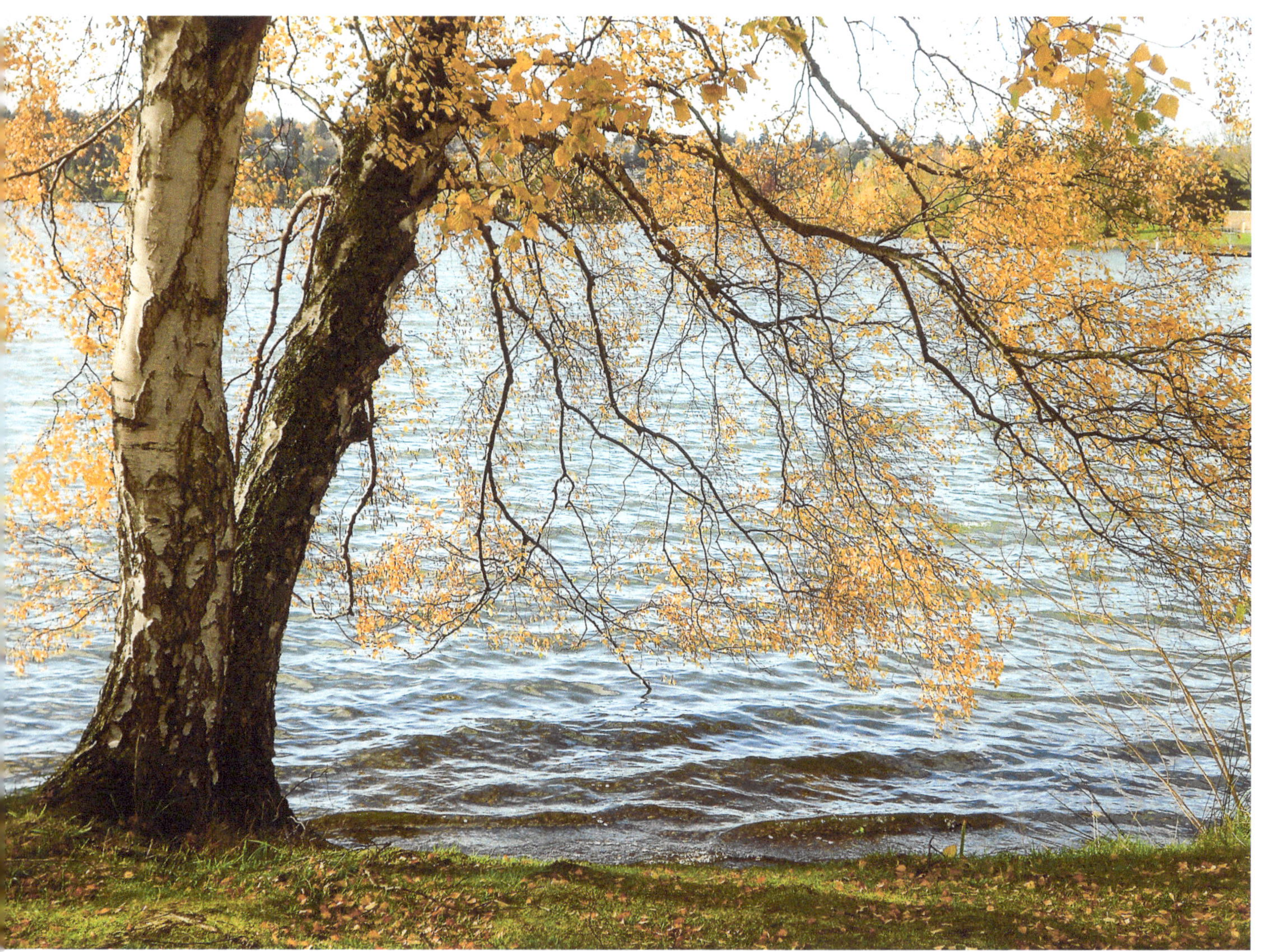

# Clinging to Life

Some leaves cling on, as if desperately trying to stay alive and not succumb to the fate that is inevitable for them.

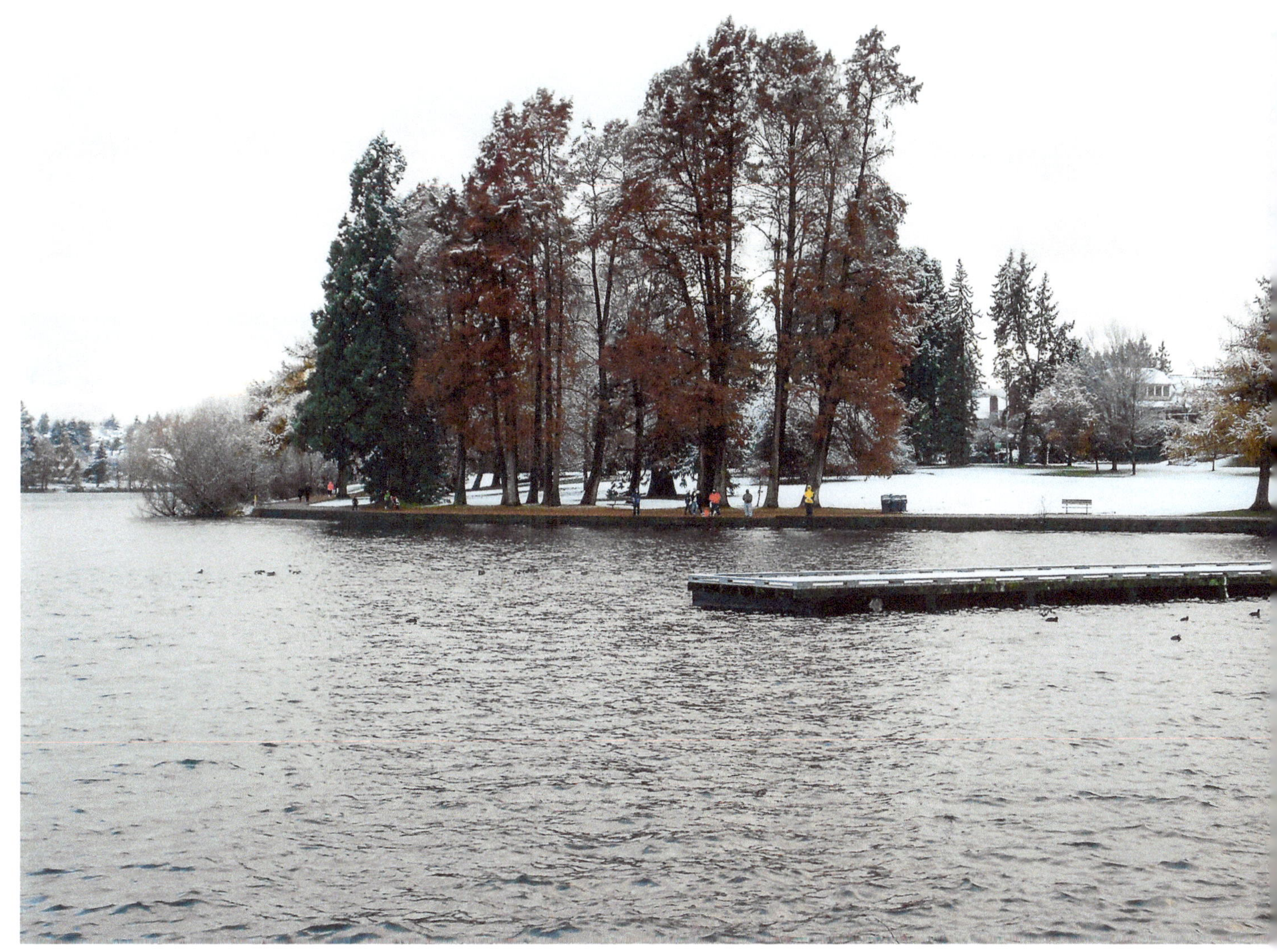

# An Early Snowfall

It is still in autumn, as can be seen by the foliage on the trees, but snow has already fallen. Such a sight is relatively rare in Seattle, where our winters tend to be somewhat mild for its latitude and we don't have much snow. Yes, we're seeing Bald Cypresses here.

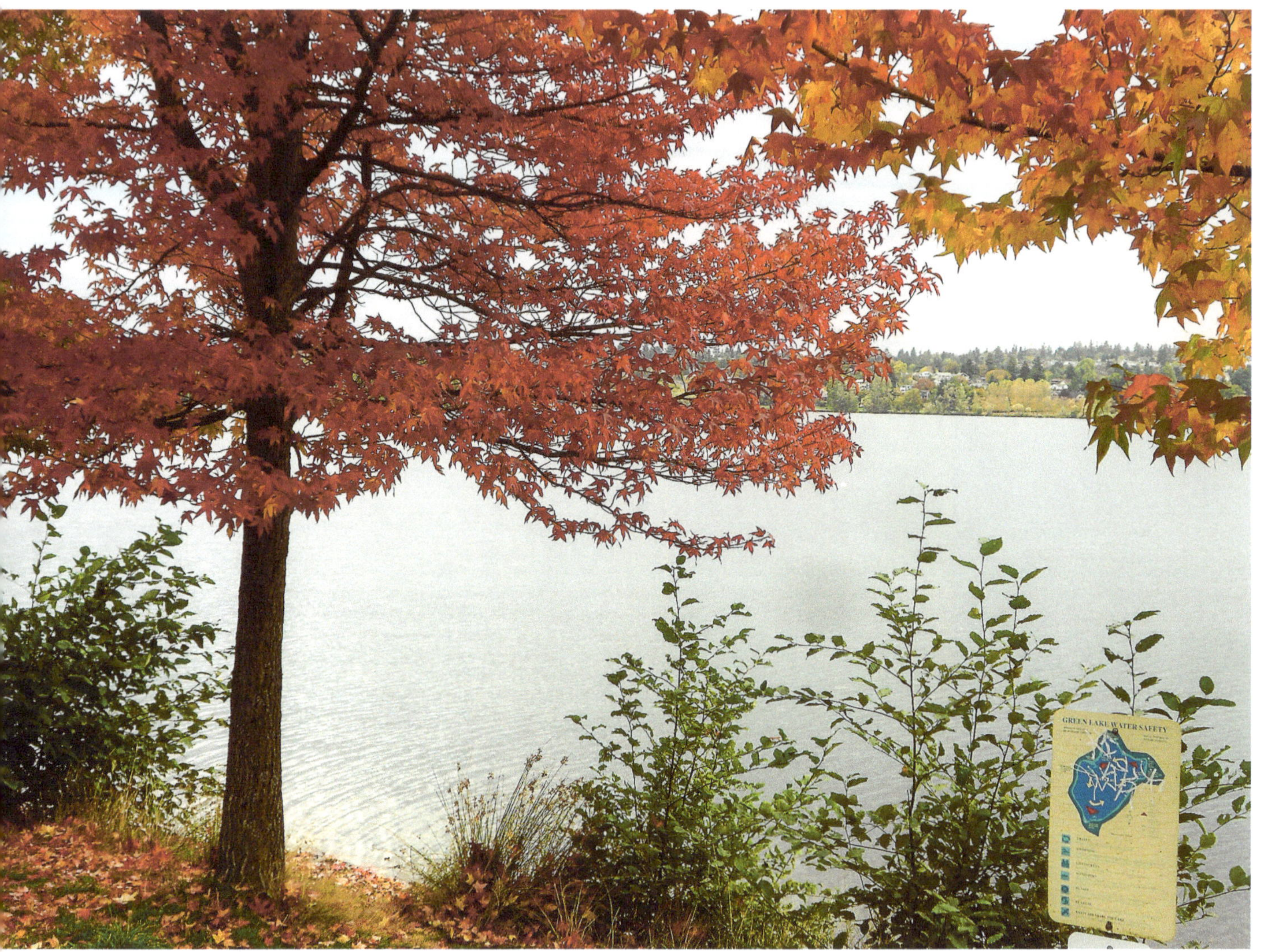



# Liquid Ambar Tree

Another splendid autumn scene; it's no wonder I consider October my favorite month of the year. Taken at the south end of the lake just north of the boathouse, this is where the season is displayed at its most glorious best.

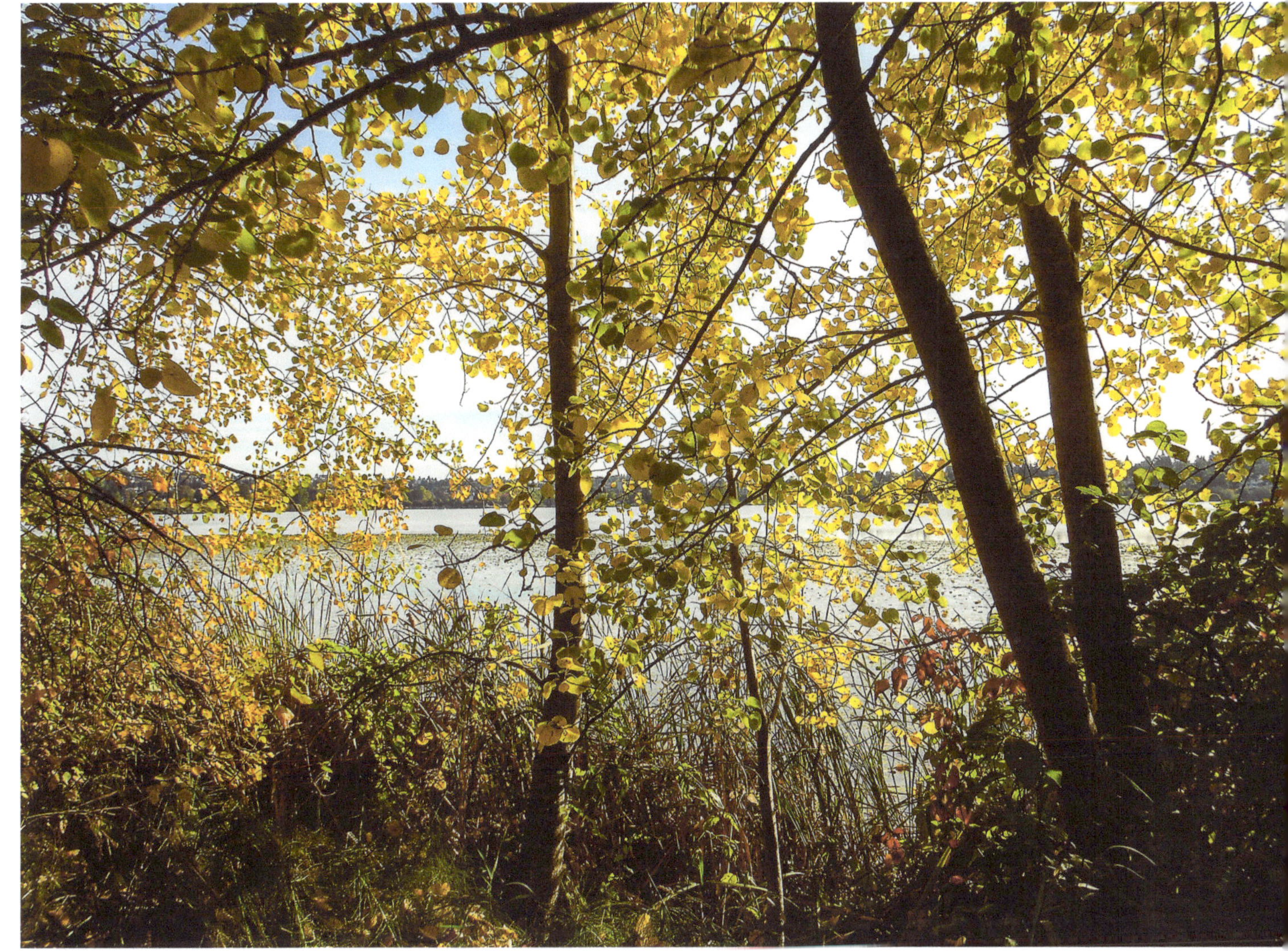

# Golden Fringes

The two most prominent fall foliage colors are red and yellow and both are displayed at their most brilliant best at Green Lake. The trees that turn red often also have yellow leaves, but the ones that turn yellow rarely have red ones.

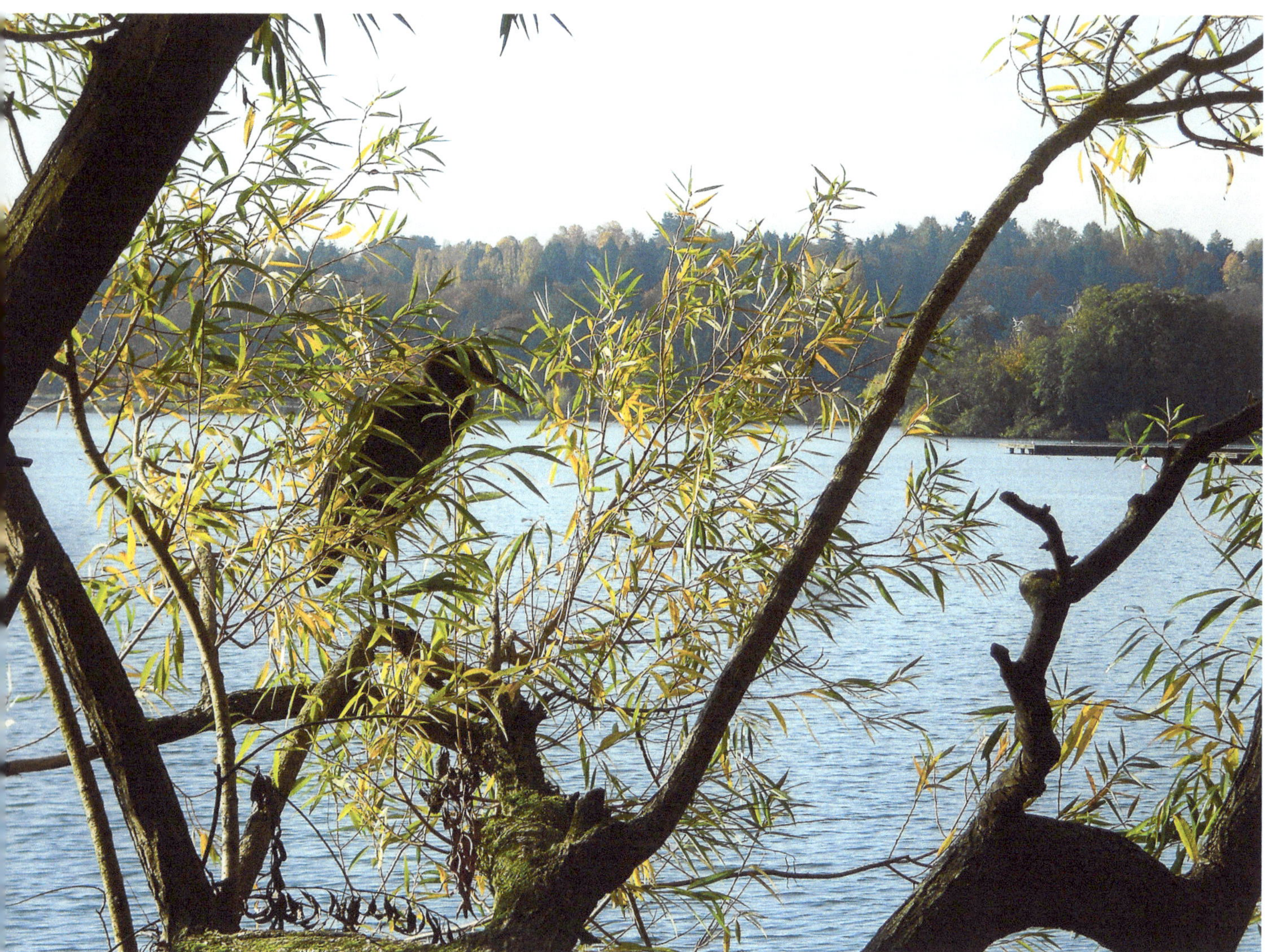

# Failing the Camouflage Test

Here is my Blue Heron friend trying to look as inconspicuous as he is able to with the thinning fall foliage. Actually he is well behind the leaves but it made for an interesting idea. It reminds of Pigpen in the Peanuts cartoons, only that it is collecting leaves instead of dirt.

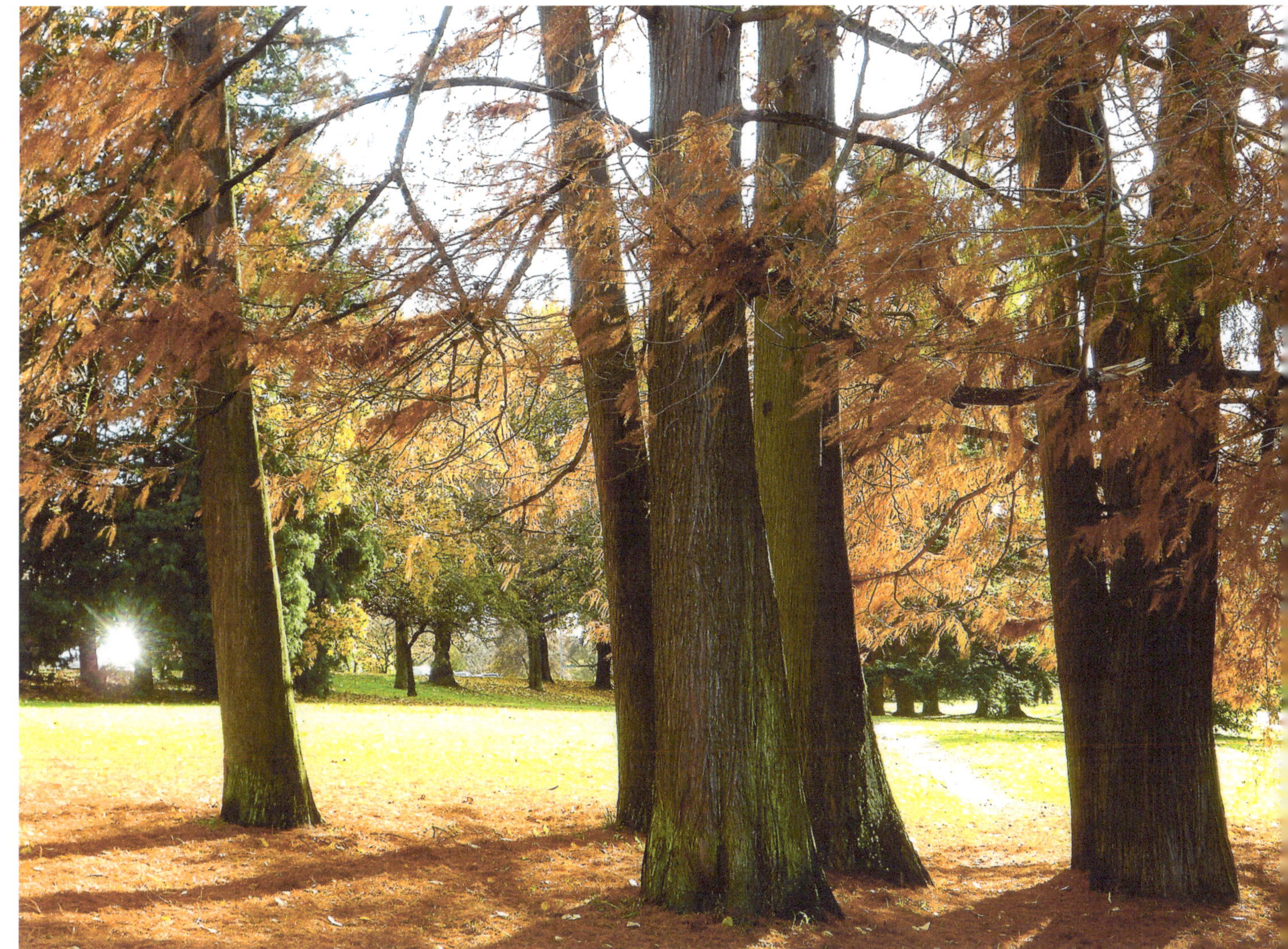

# Late Autumn

You can see that the leaves of the Bald Cypress trees are falling to the ground in this wonderfully tawny scene. I love the warm colors emitted by the sunlight, giving off a copper glow: a classic fall view.

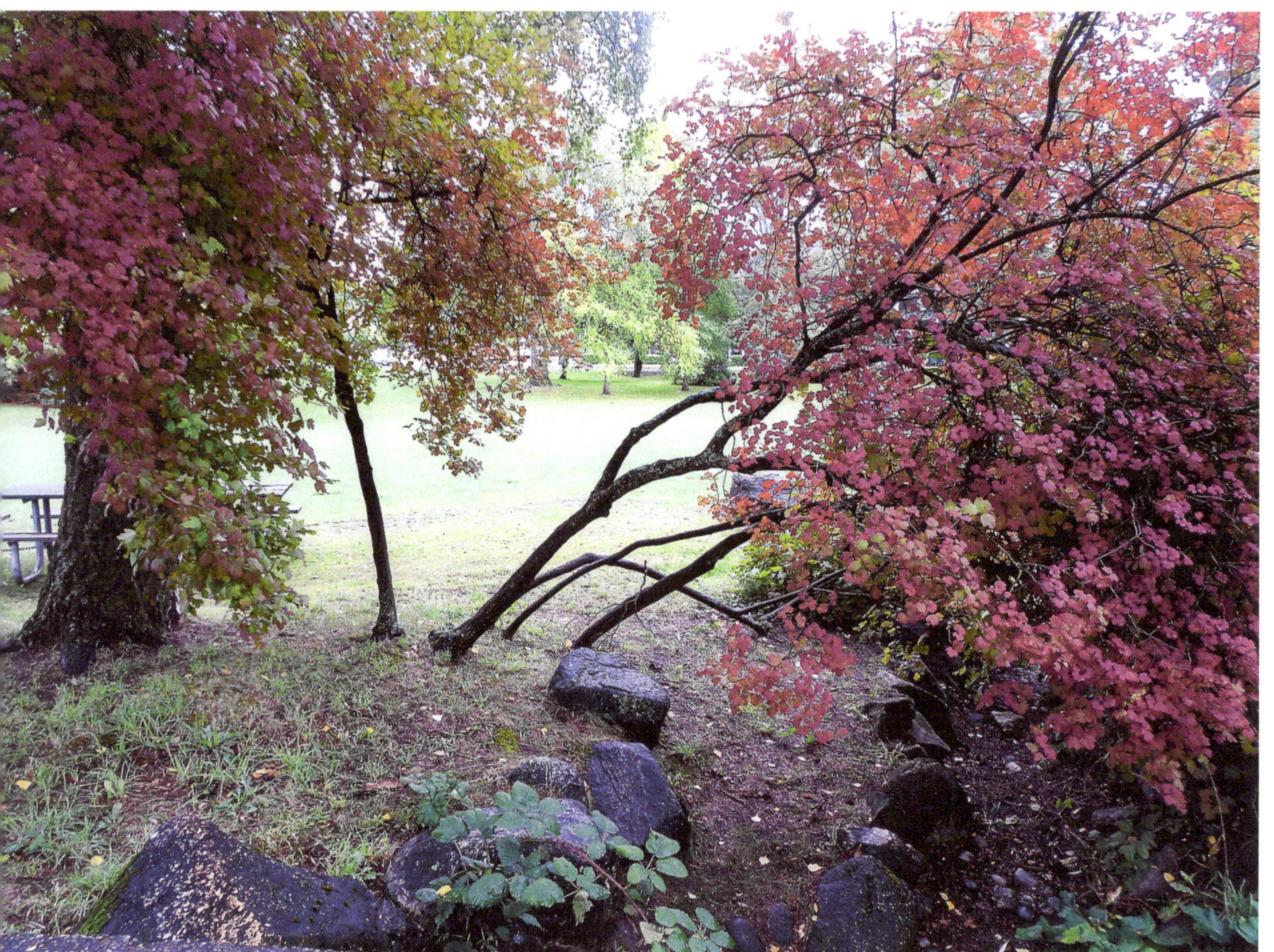

# Purple Shades

This picture was taken from the old stone bridge at the most northern point of the lake. It nicely shows the differing range of colors seen in fall foliage, in this case, a purplish shade that almost makes the rocks look the same.

# Green Lake Moods

## In praise of our emotional side

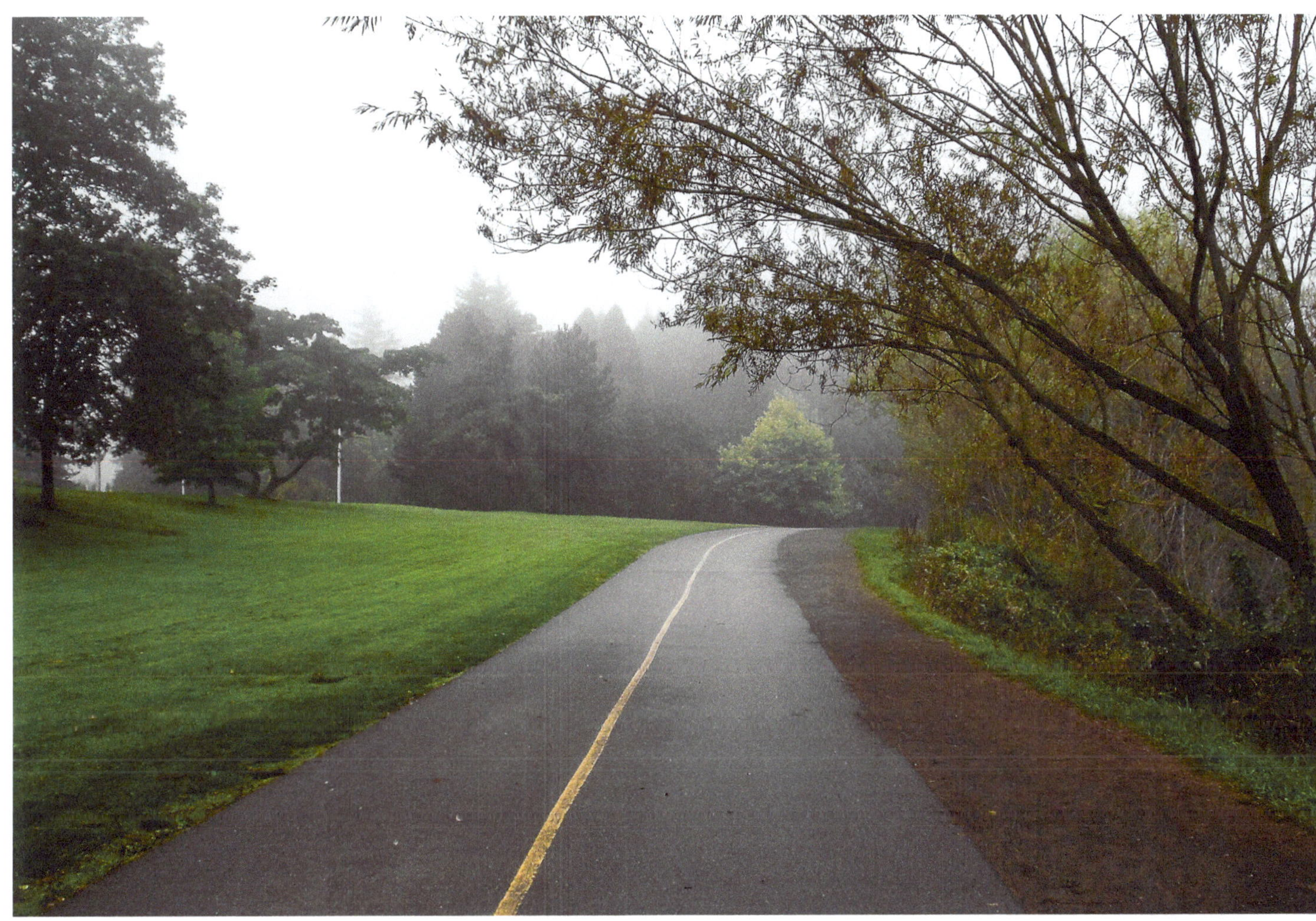

Green Lake projects certain moods depending on the way you see it and your frame of mind at the time. A good representation of that is seen above where the pathway appears utterly empty –a very rare sight– and almost intimidating, as it moves toward the distant trees shrouded in fog. A sense of isolation is evoked by this scene making the observer seem as the only one alive. Inclement weather, especially fog, helps to create such an effect.

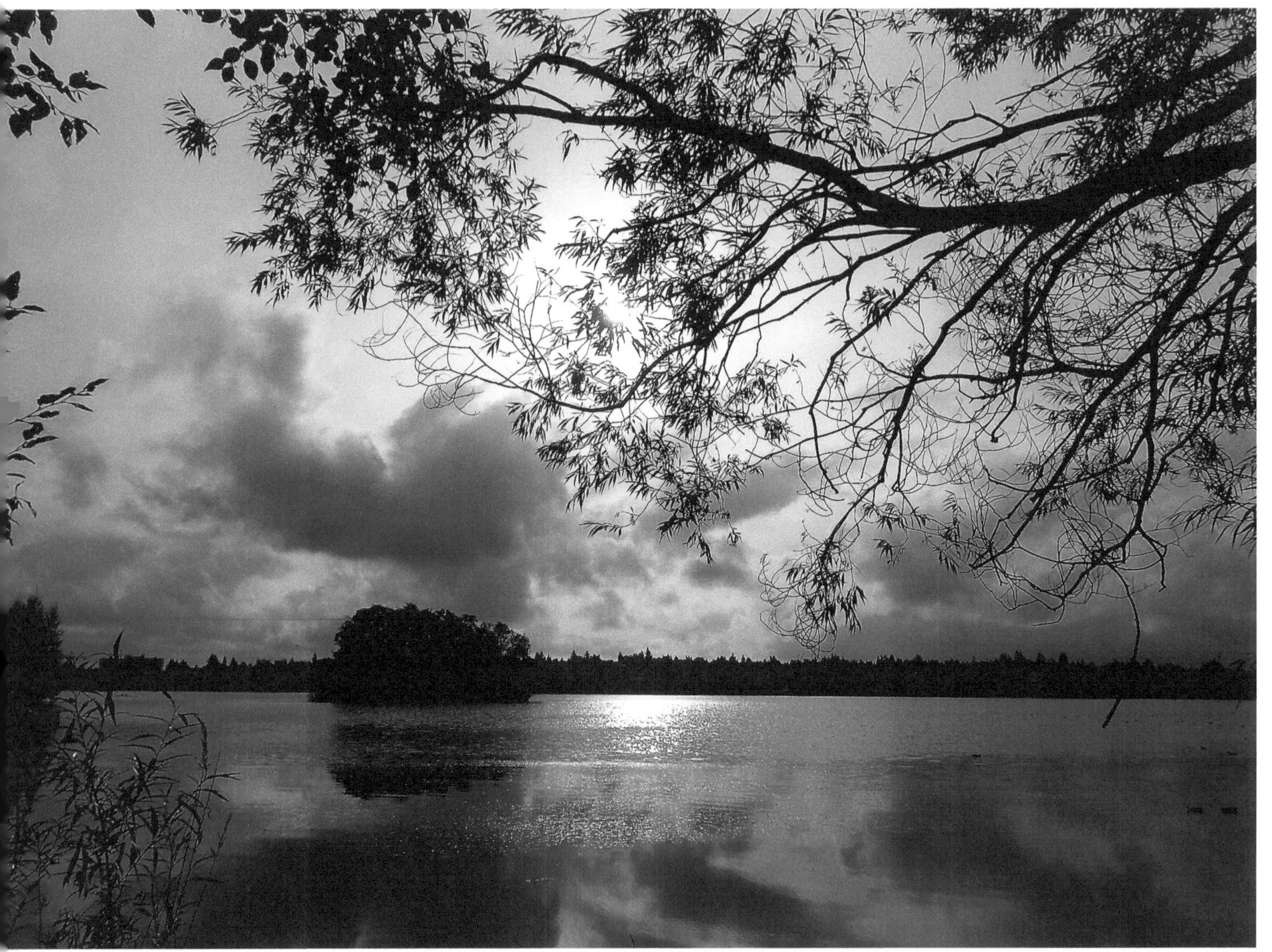

# Ghostly Night

Not really. It's a daytime shot of an overcast sky, the sun looking more like the moon. I am reminded of the opening lines of Alfred Noyes's The Highwayman: 'The wind was a torrent of darkness among the gusty trees. The moon was a ghostly galleon tossed upon cloudy seas...' It looks like a dismal swamp in an animated Disney movie rather than an actual real-life scene. It has a haunting quality about it.

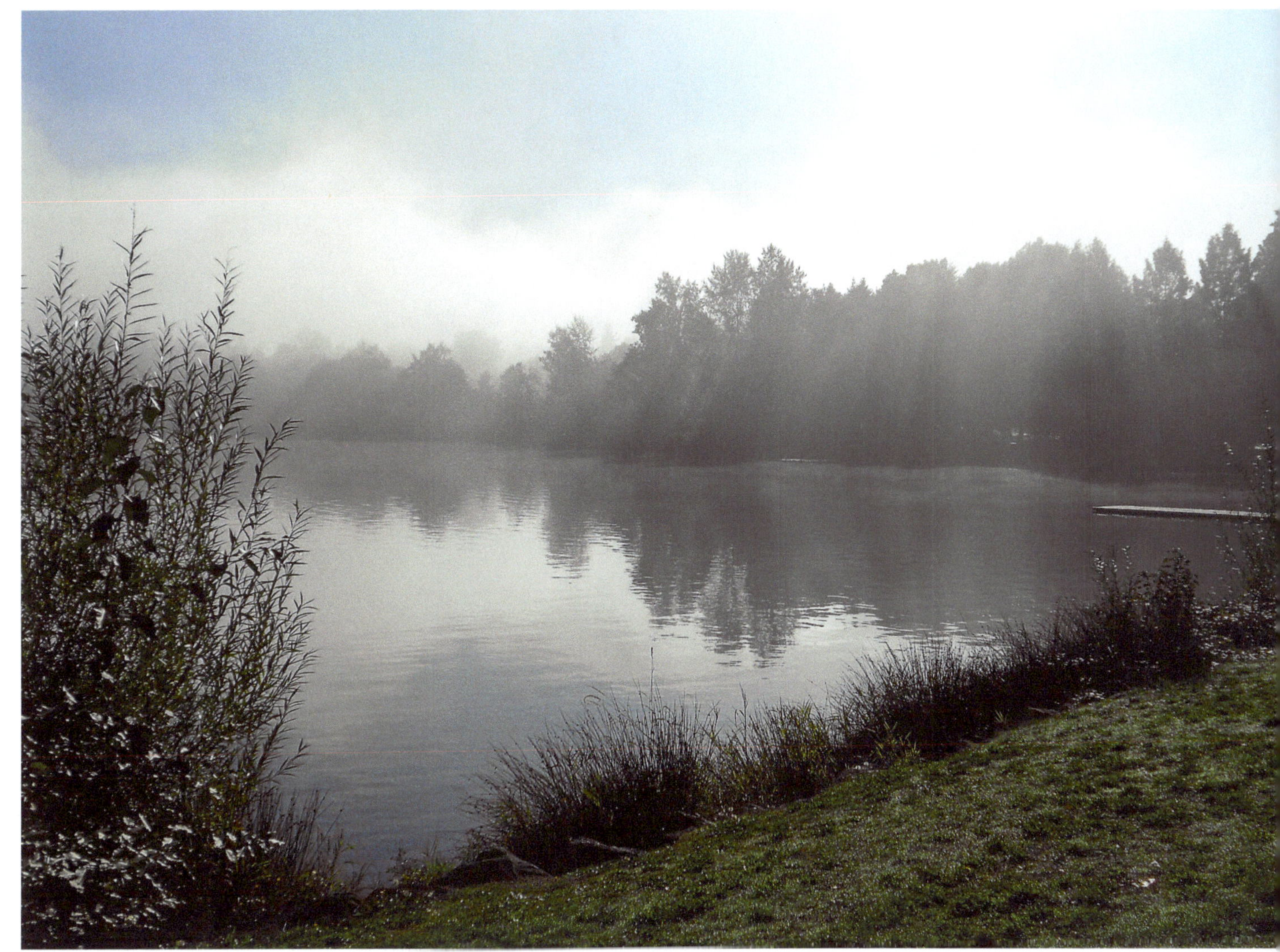

# Misty Shore

Here is a view of the south end of the lake shrouded in fog. Fog does a lot in projecting a sense of isolation, mainly because you can't see beyond a certain range and that makes you feel that you are all by yourself within a visible world that's confining.

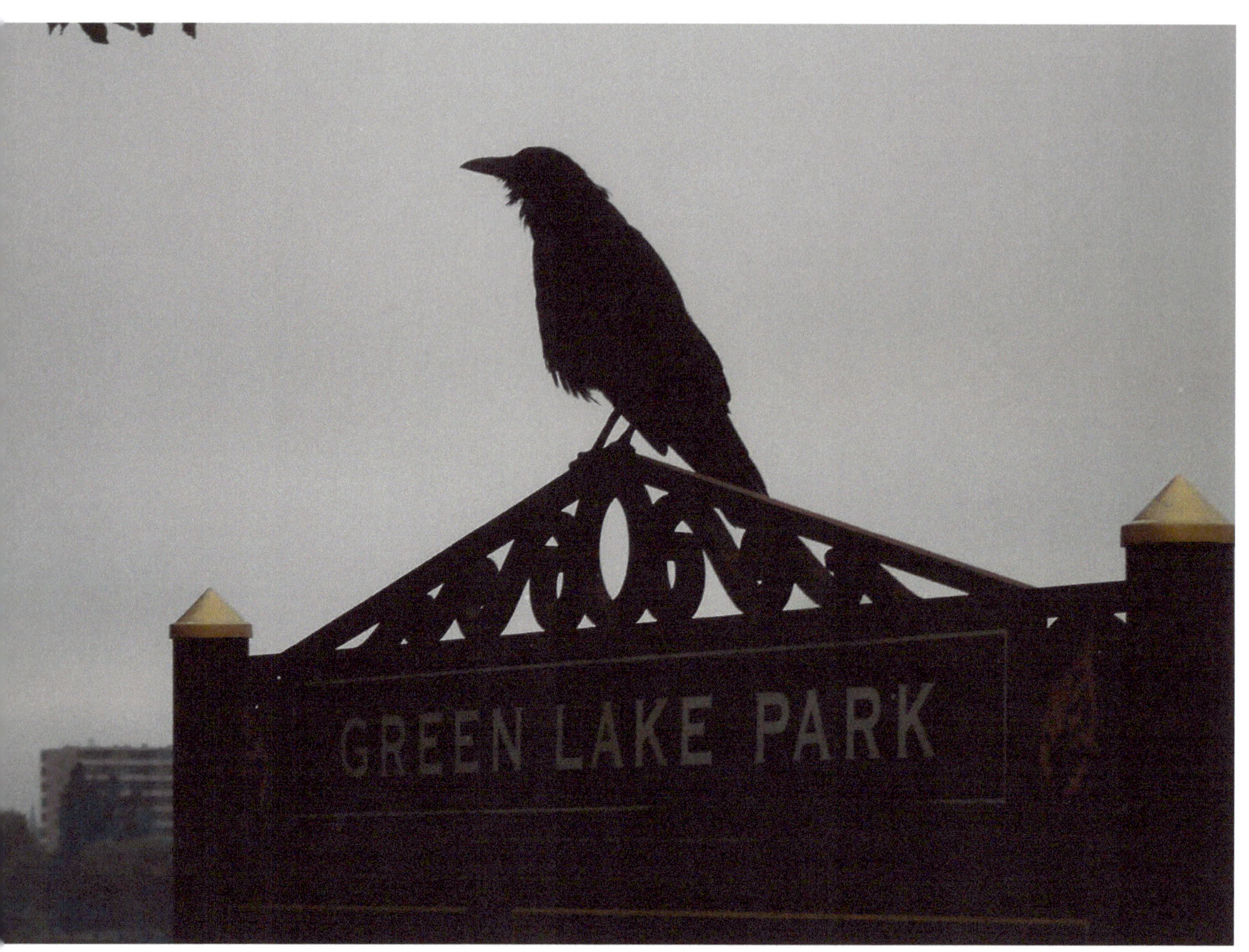


*Then this ebony bird beguiling my sad fancy into smiling,*
*By the grave and stern decorum of the countenance it wore,*
*"Though thy crest be shorn and shaven, thou," I said, "art sure no craven,*
*Ghastly grim and ancient Raven wandering from the Nightly shore—*
*Tell me what thy lordly name is on the Night's Plutonian shore!'*
*Quoth the Raven, "Nevermore."*

**–Edgar Allen Poe**

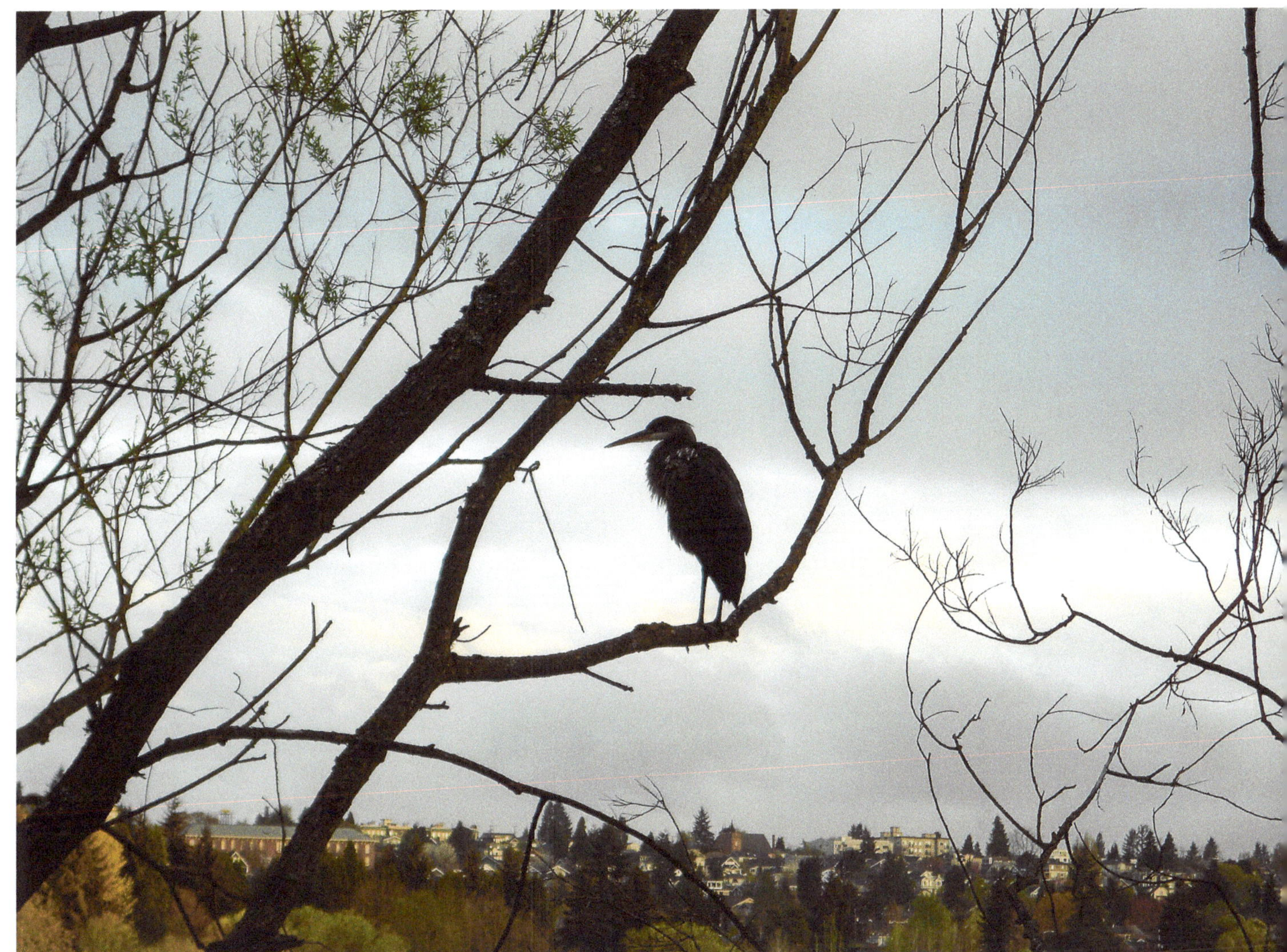

# Somber Setting

You usually don't see herons perched in trees; they are wading birds and mostly cling to the shores. There's a haunting quality about this scene, enhanced, I think, by the solitary bird offset by the gray, overcast sky and the stark barren branches of the trees. The bird appears menacing.

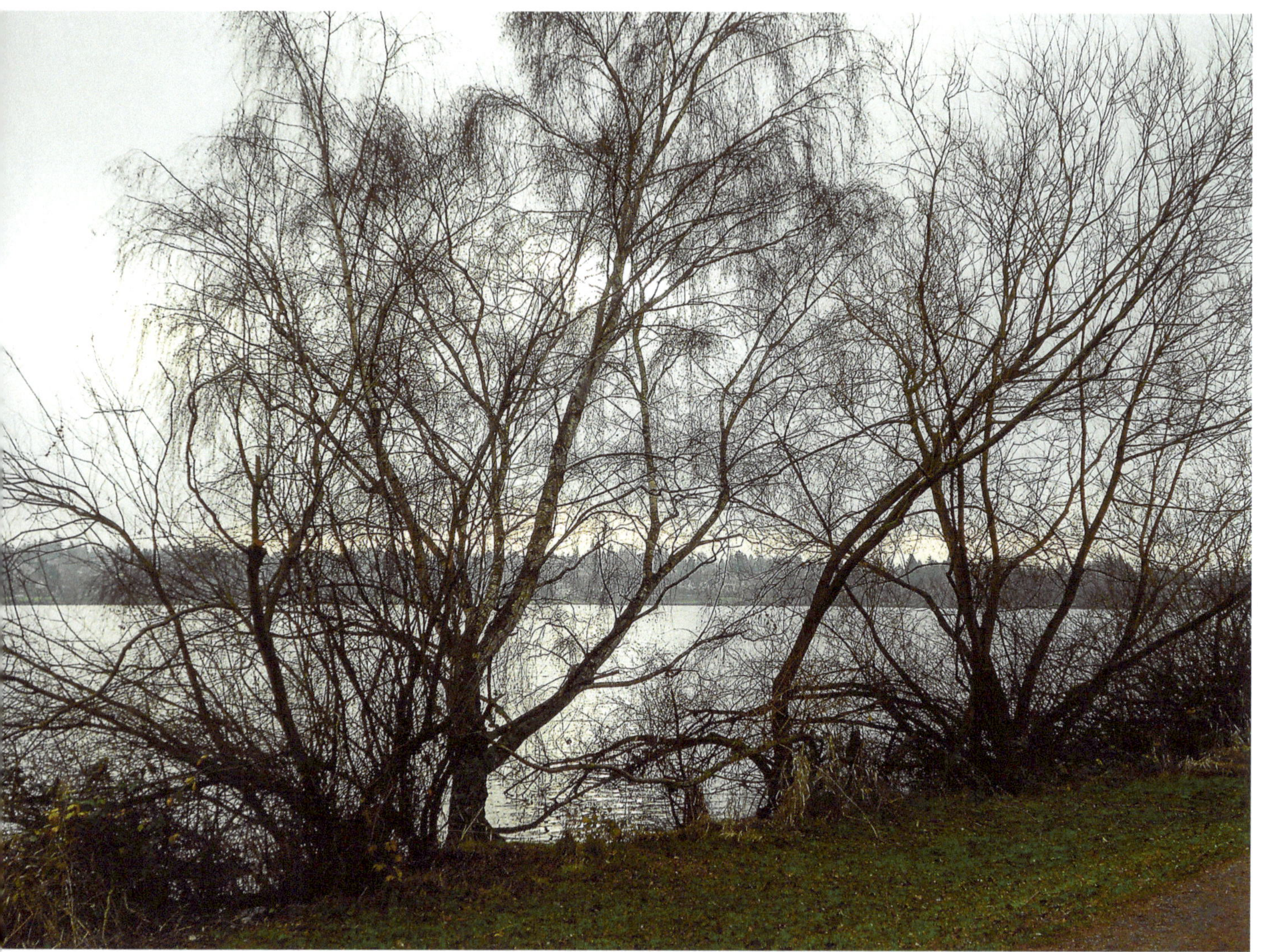

# Naked Trees

Even stripped of their leaves, trees have majesty about them.
Here we see them as they appear in the winter months, bare and
seemingly tangled up in a mesh of branches, and yet still graceful.
This strongly resembles a Corot painting.

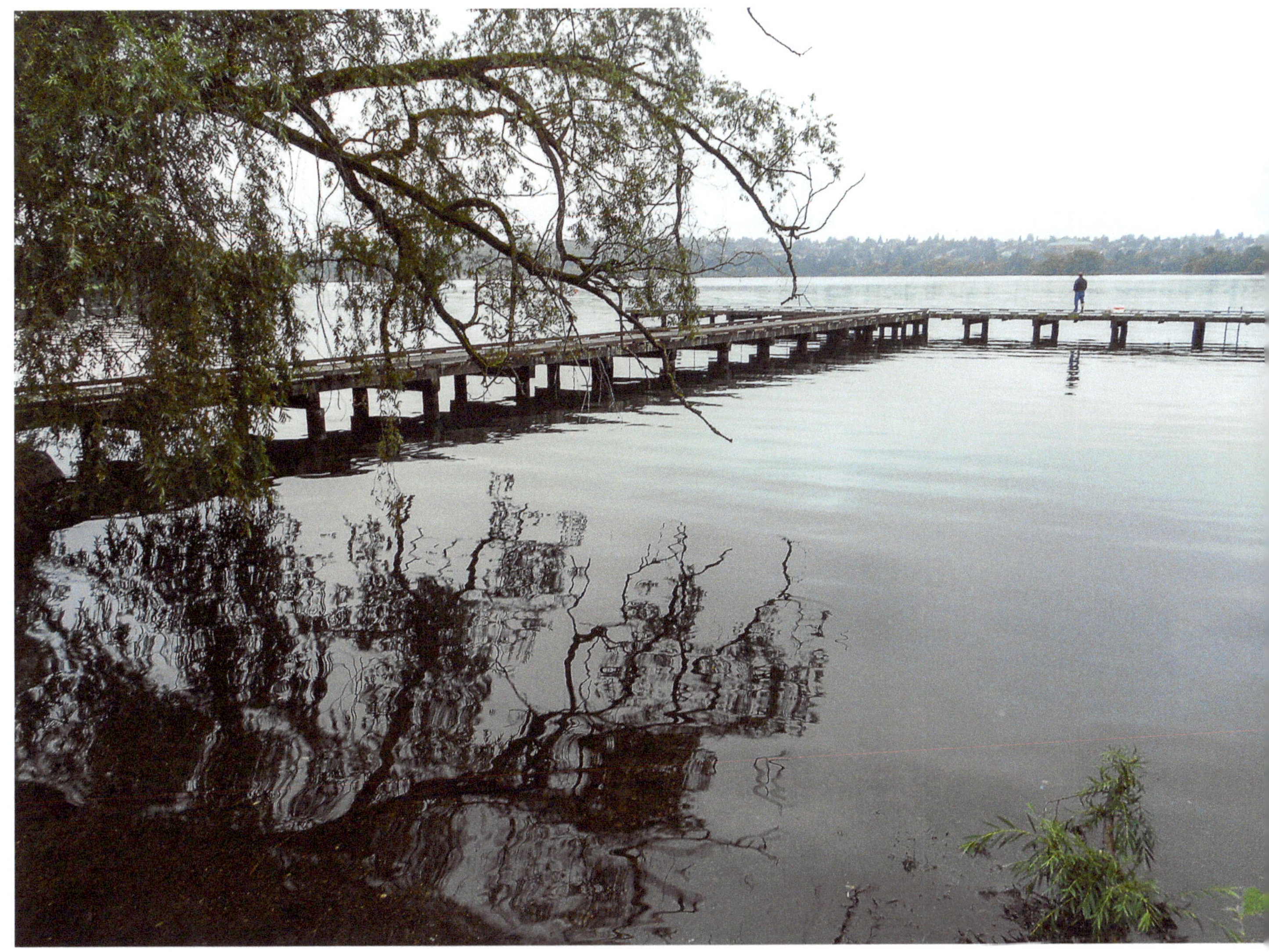

# That Eerie Feeling

There's something creepy about this picture. I think it's the reflected contorted branches reaching up as if alive and wanting to grab you and drag you under. The drab coloring helps to create a sinister setting, like it's out of horror movie.

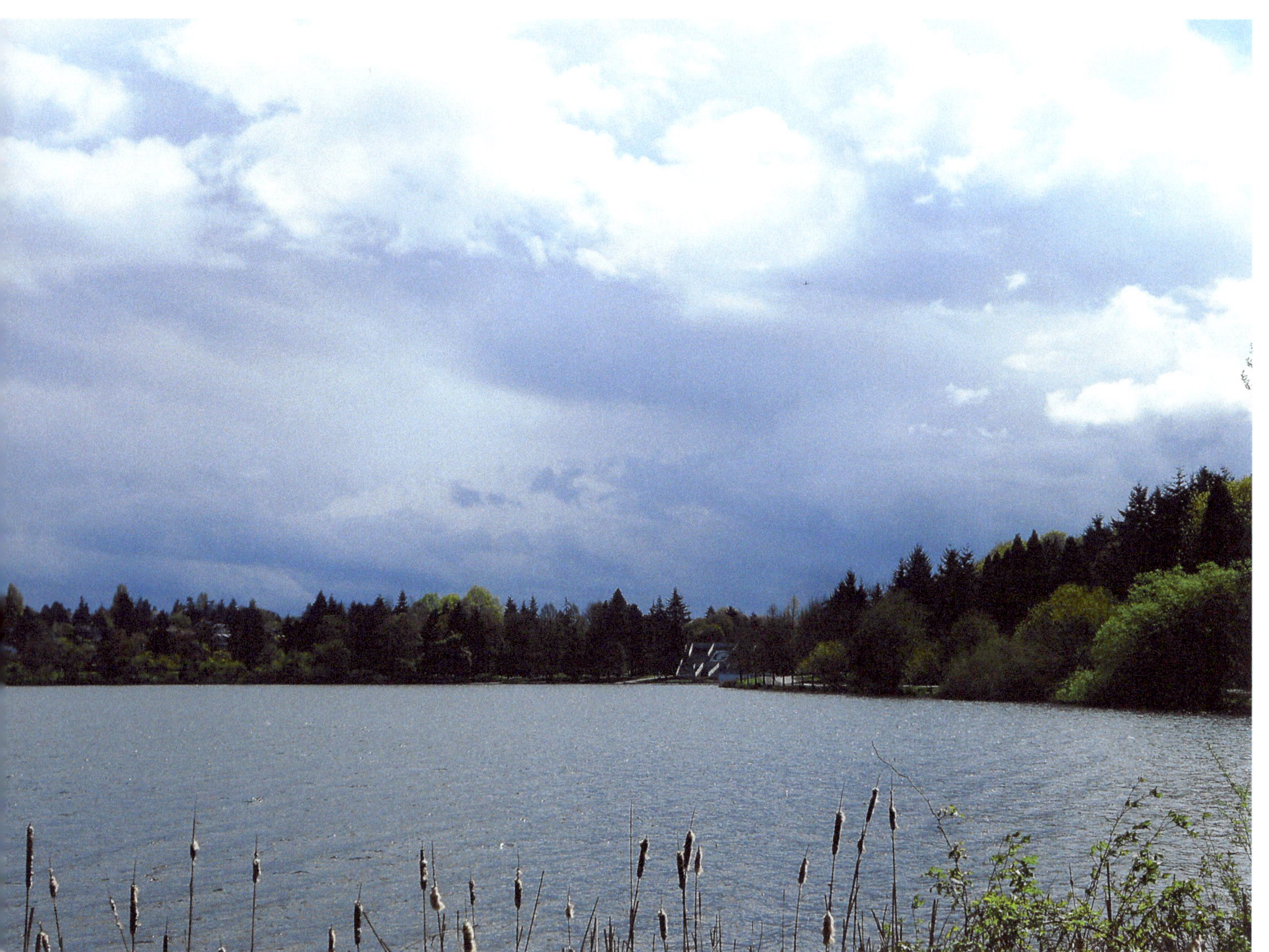

# Threatening Skies

Looking at the ominous clouds seen here makes you want to seek out a shelter of some kind to escape what is about to unfold on you. What am I doing out here? —you ask yourself. Still, I love the way the cattails appear seemingly detached from it all.

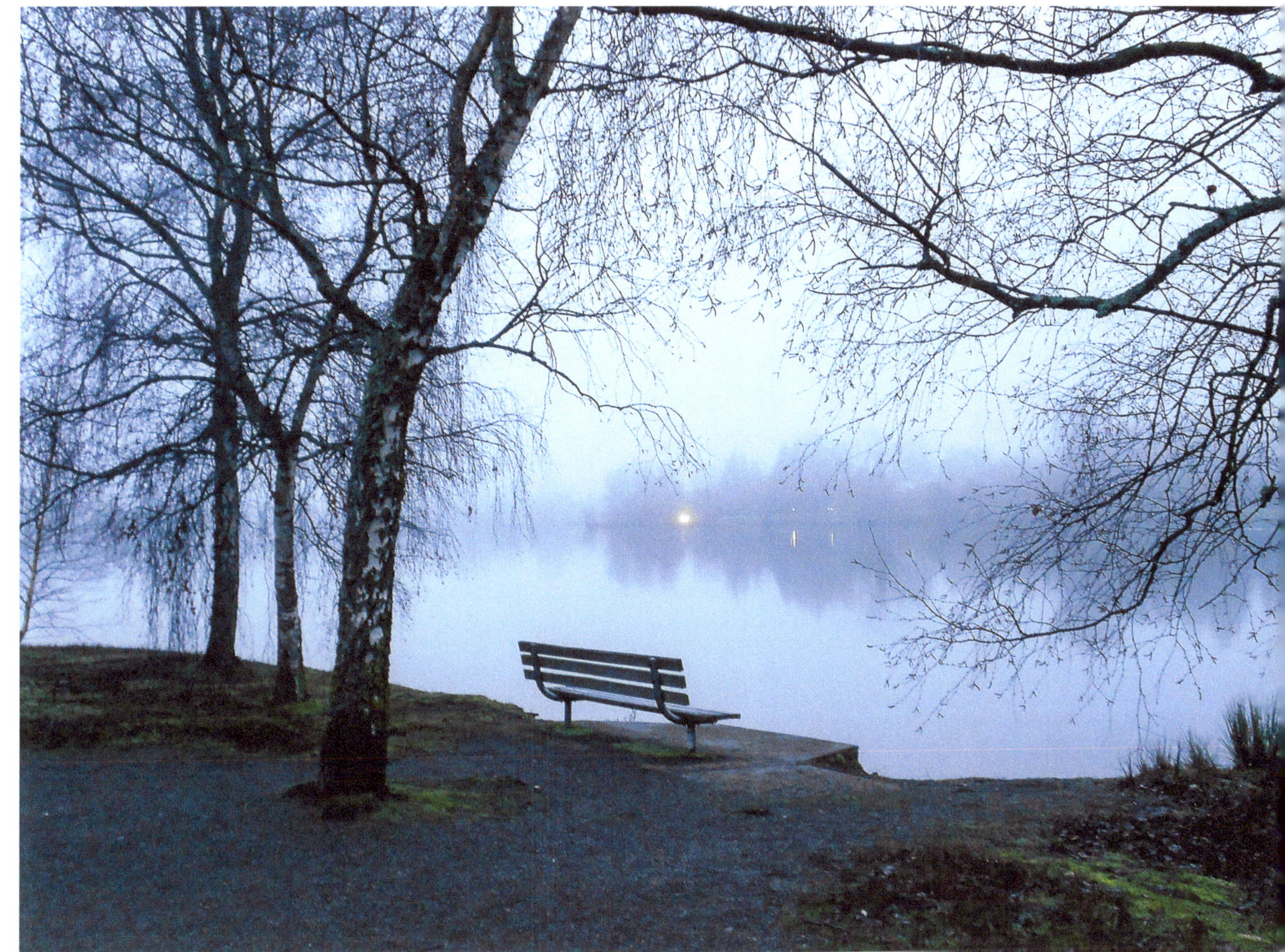

# Lonely Setting

I get a sense of seclusion looking at this picture taken on an early foggy winter morning. The distant headlights of a car exist as a somber reminder that there are signs of life in this otherwise bleak setting and that you are not entirely alone.

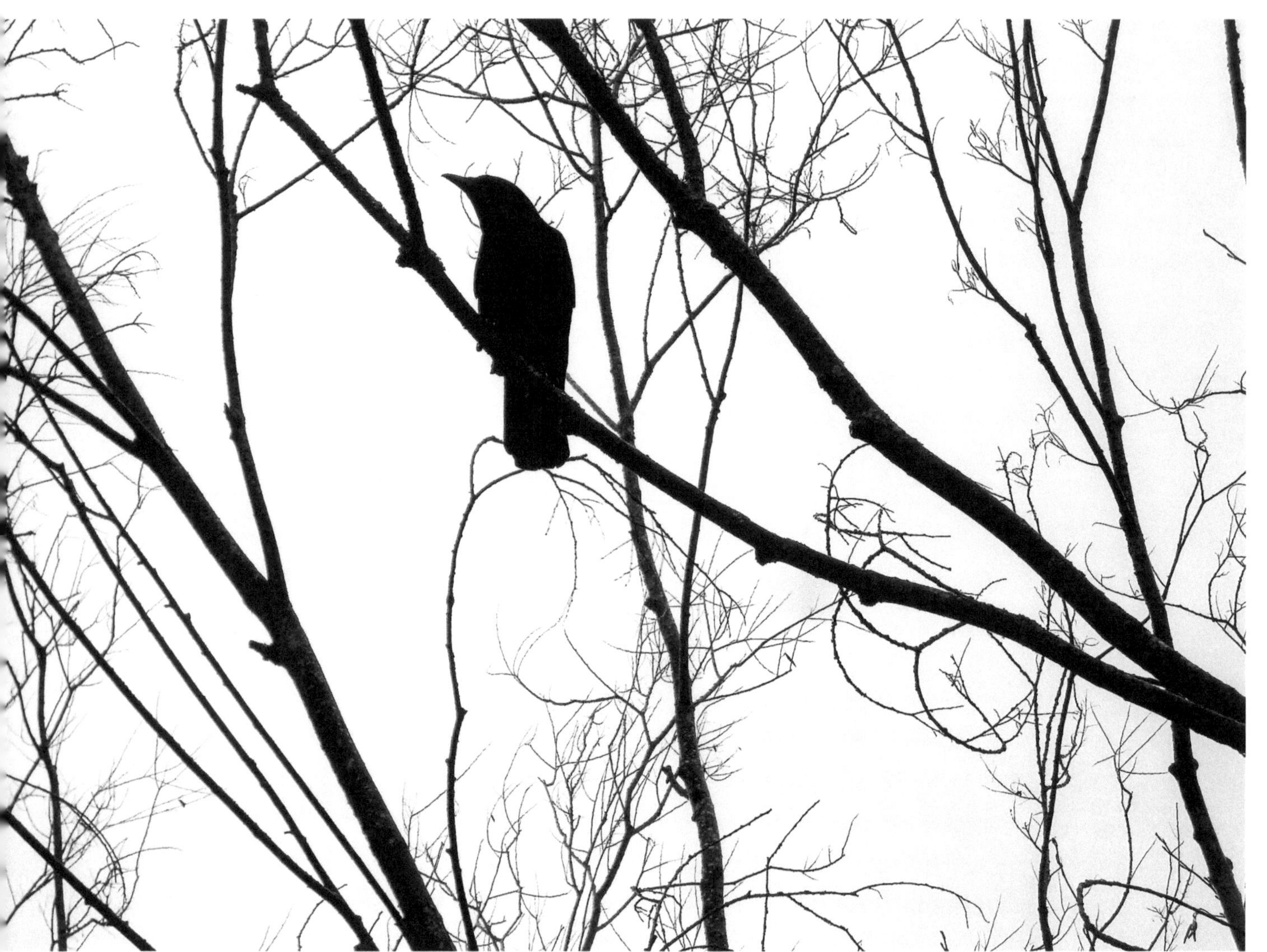

*On a withered bow*
*A crow alone is perching;*
*Autumn evening now.*

This is my favorite Haiku by the Japanese master, Matsue Basho (1644-1694). I like Haiku —a condensed poem that consists of seventeen syllables— as a literary art form and have tried to create my own compositions, which is more challenging than it appears. Basho remains the Haiku poet whose works I admire the most.

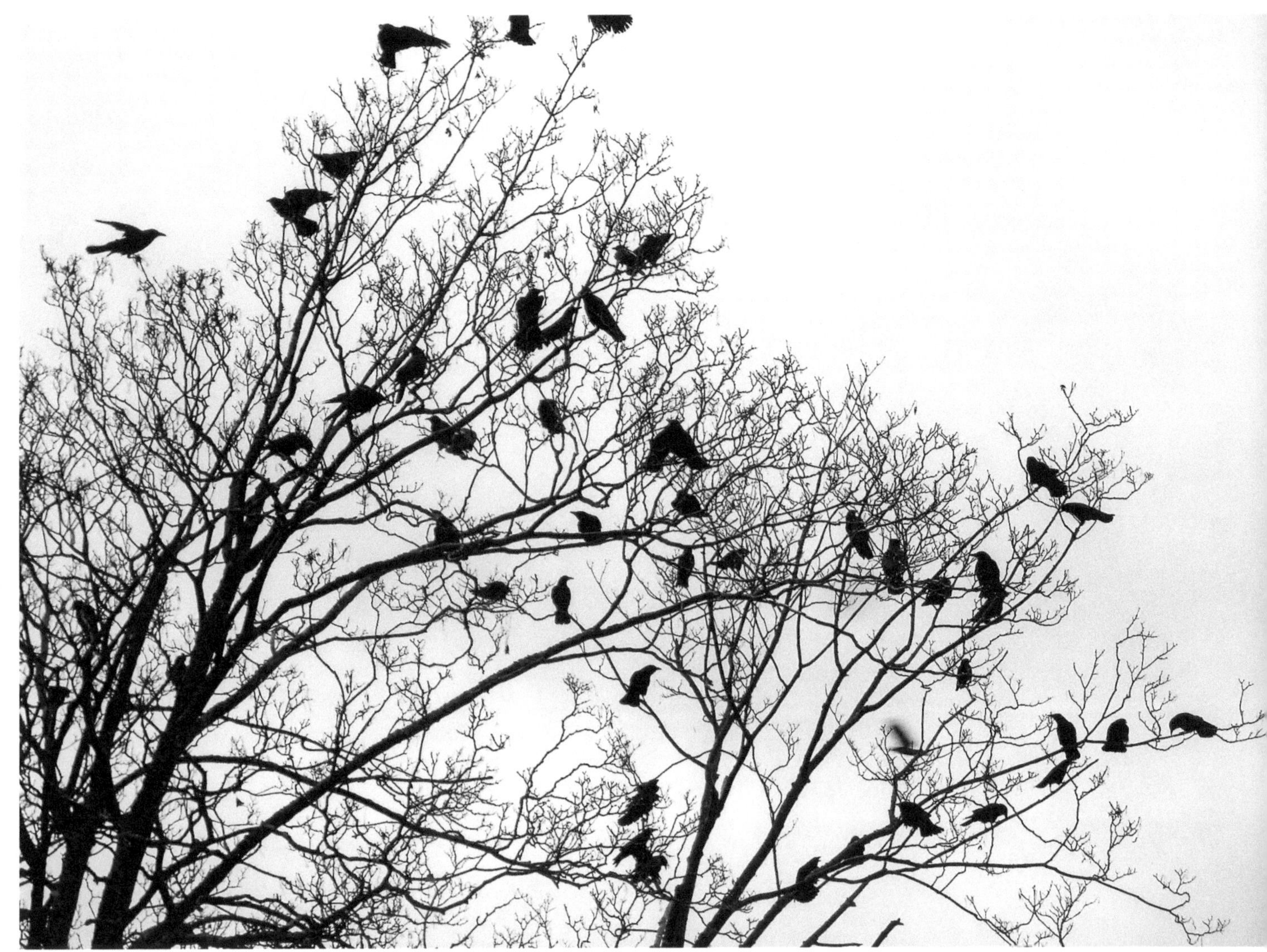

# Tree Trimmings

A murder –that's what a group of crows is called– staging for a possible attack on an unwary walker. Anyway, that's what this picture evokes, an unnerving sight that conjures up Alfred Hitchcock's movie which I remember most for its grammatically correct advertisement: The Birds is coming!

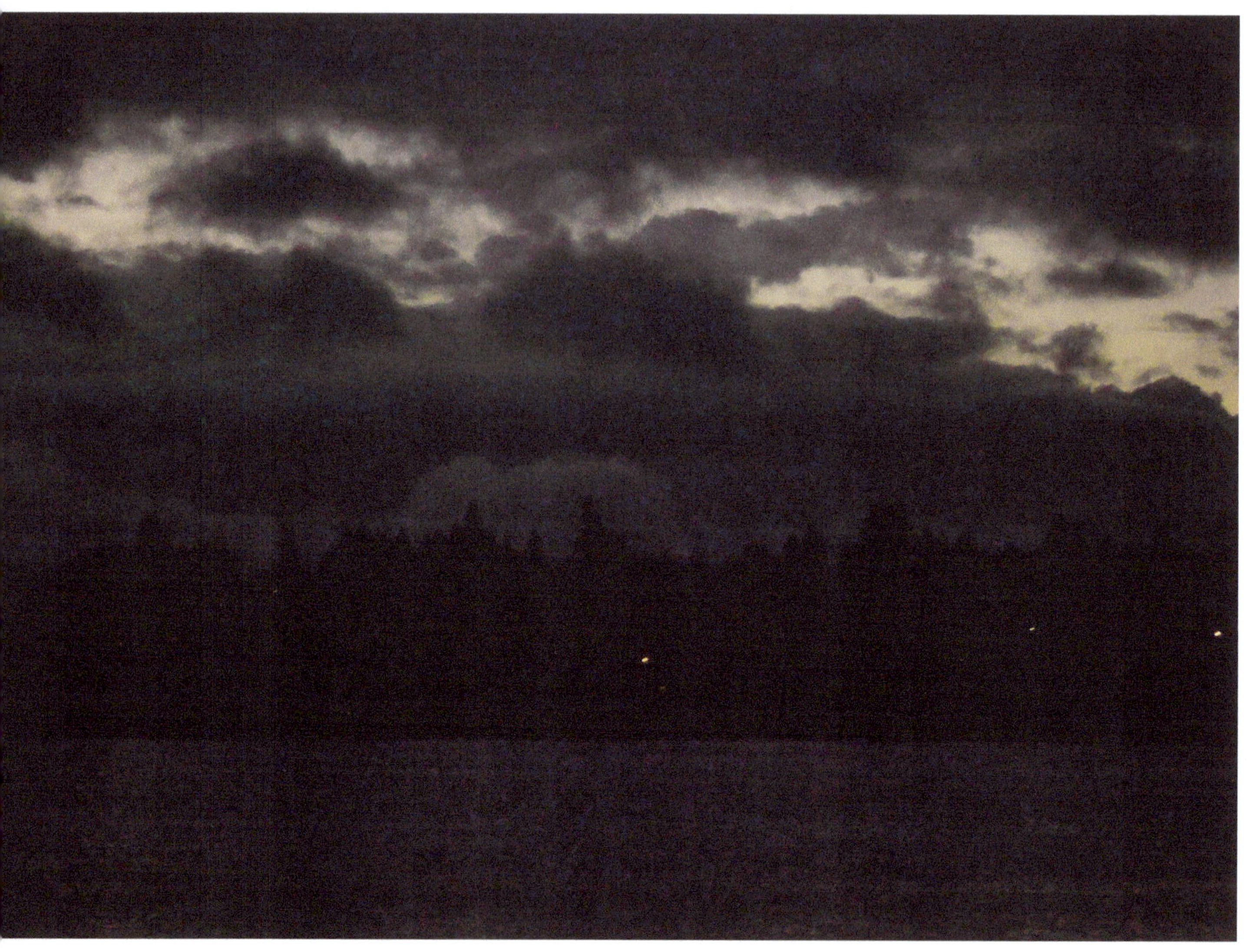

# Ragnarok

Ragnarok is the Day of Doom or of the death of the Gods in Norse mythology. It's when the last vestiges of light are overwhelmed by the forces of darkness. This might well be what that would look like; it could also be a true representation of how light, and consequently life, would be snuffed out if the Yellowstone caldera or some other super volcano erupted, spreading its ash cloud upon the world. It is an ominous scene of gloom and doom —a disturbing photo.

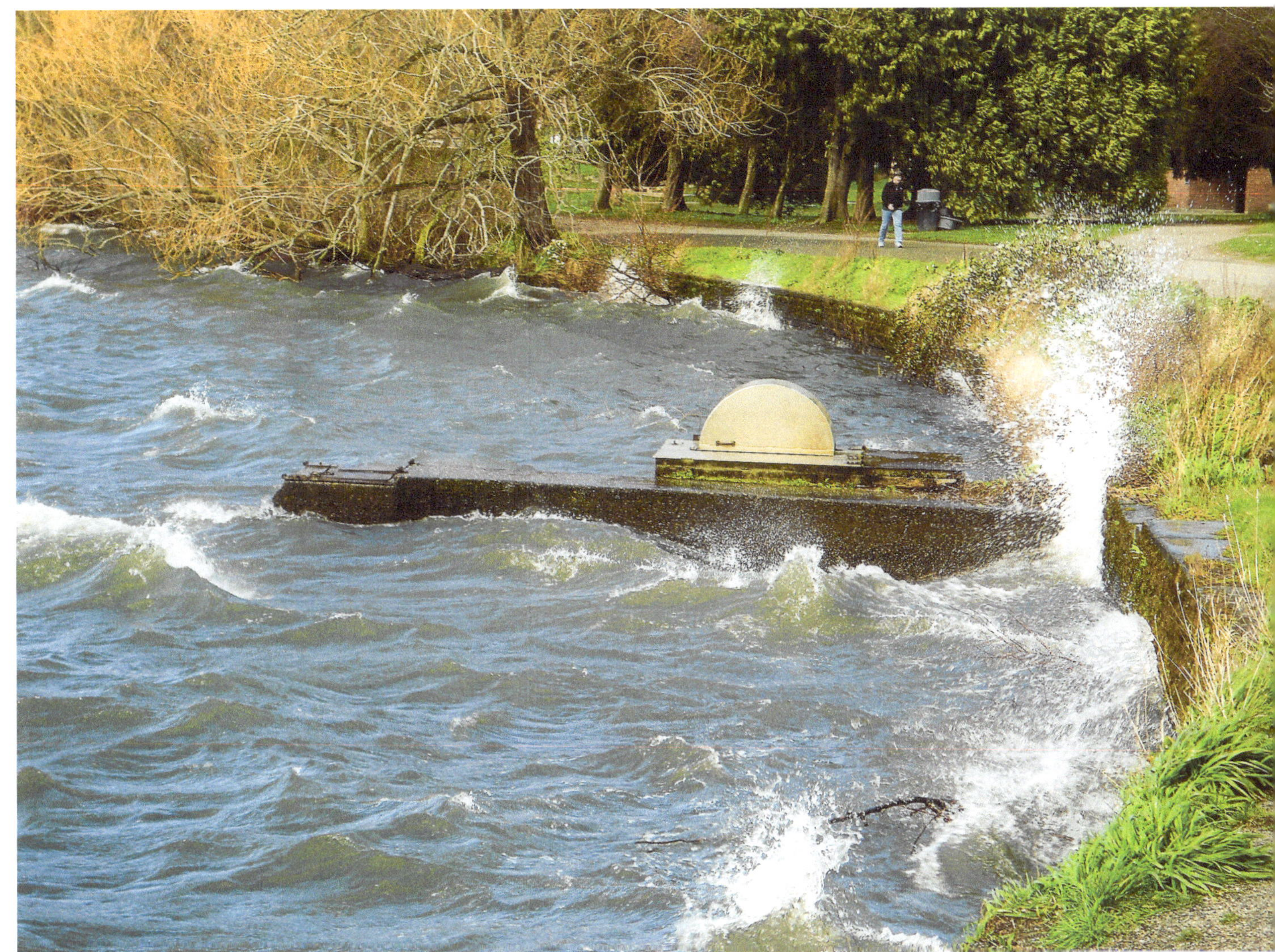

# Angry Waters

Storm tossed waves strike the northern edge of the lake in full fury on a windy spring day. Typically the worst storms move from south to north, battering the shore as seen here, with gusts probably up to 60 miles per hours, and leaving the park strewn with broken branches of trees and looking like a combat zone. Such storms are most frequent in the spring and fall seasons.

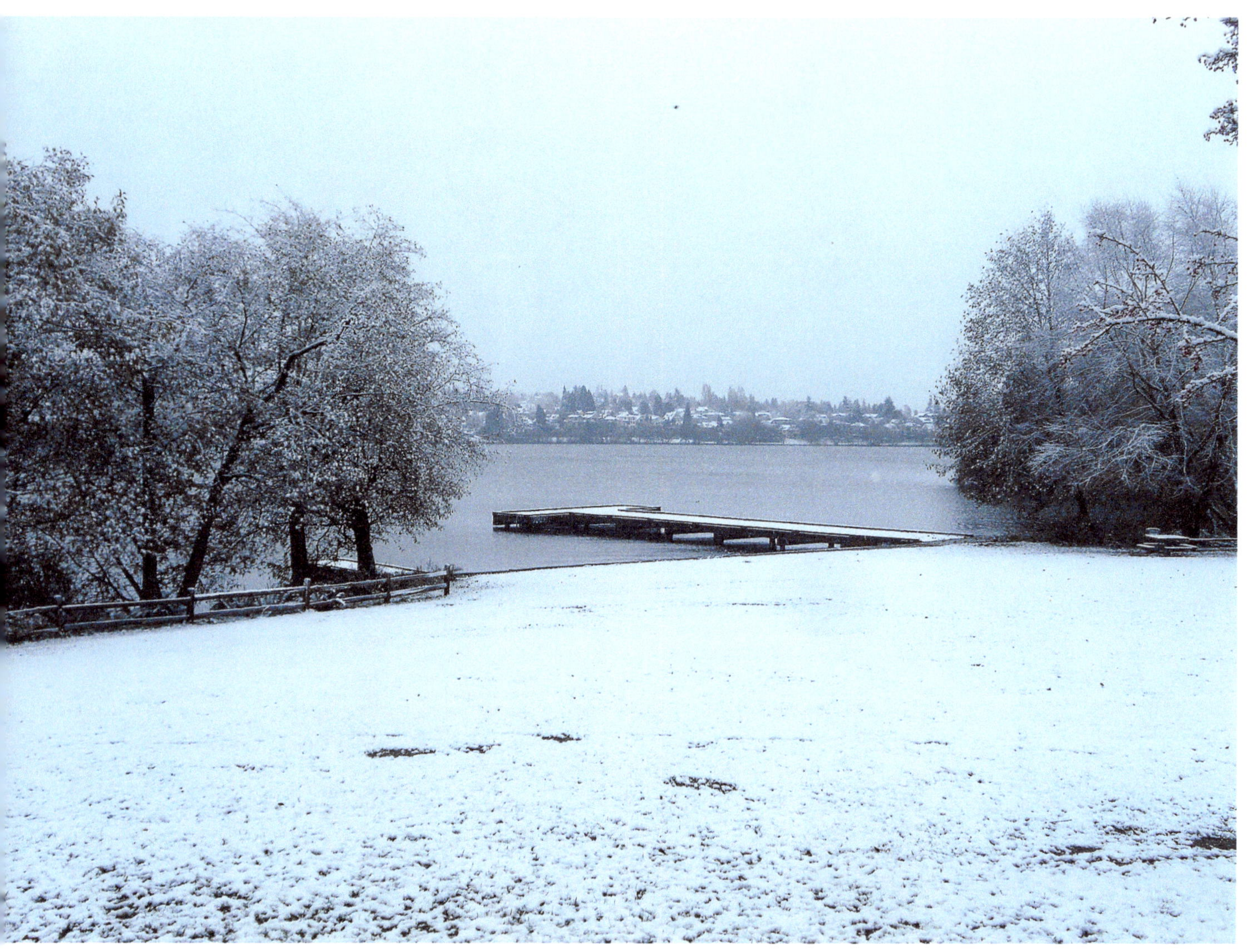

# Sounds of Silence

Nothing creates a sense of quietness more effectively than a blanket of snowfall as seen here. The seeming calmness, upon contemplation, reveals a kind of setting that is both intimidating and meditative.

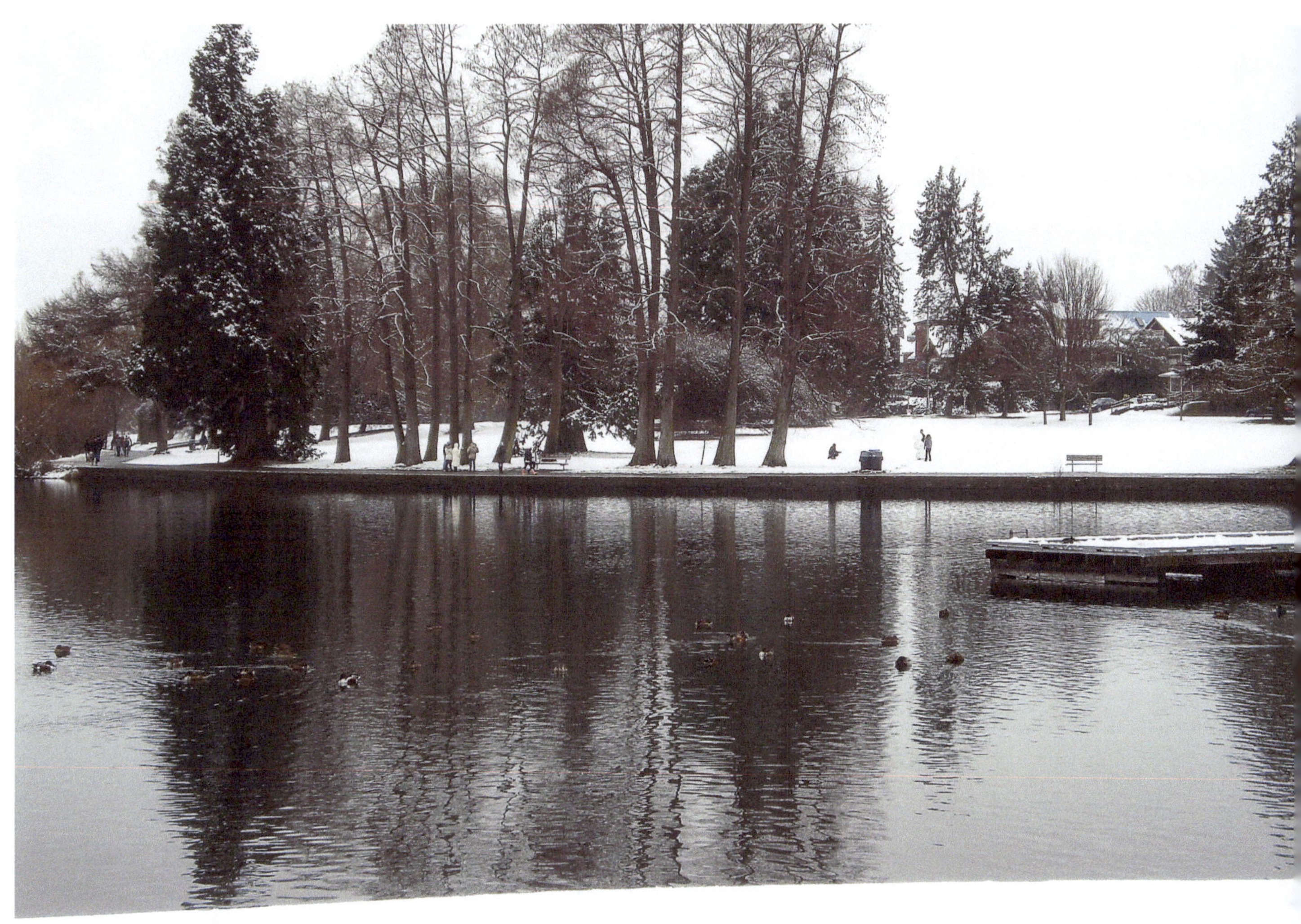

# Monochrome World

This is one of my favorite pictures at Green Lake. The longer you look at it, the more serene it becomes and seems to instill the observer with warmth despite of its cold theme. A winter morning with overcast skies reflected gray in the water, there appear to be only two colors in this world, like seen in old black and white films.

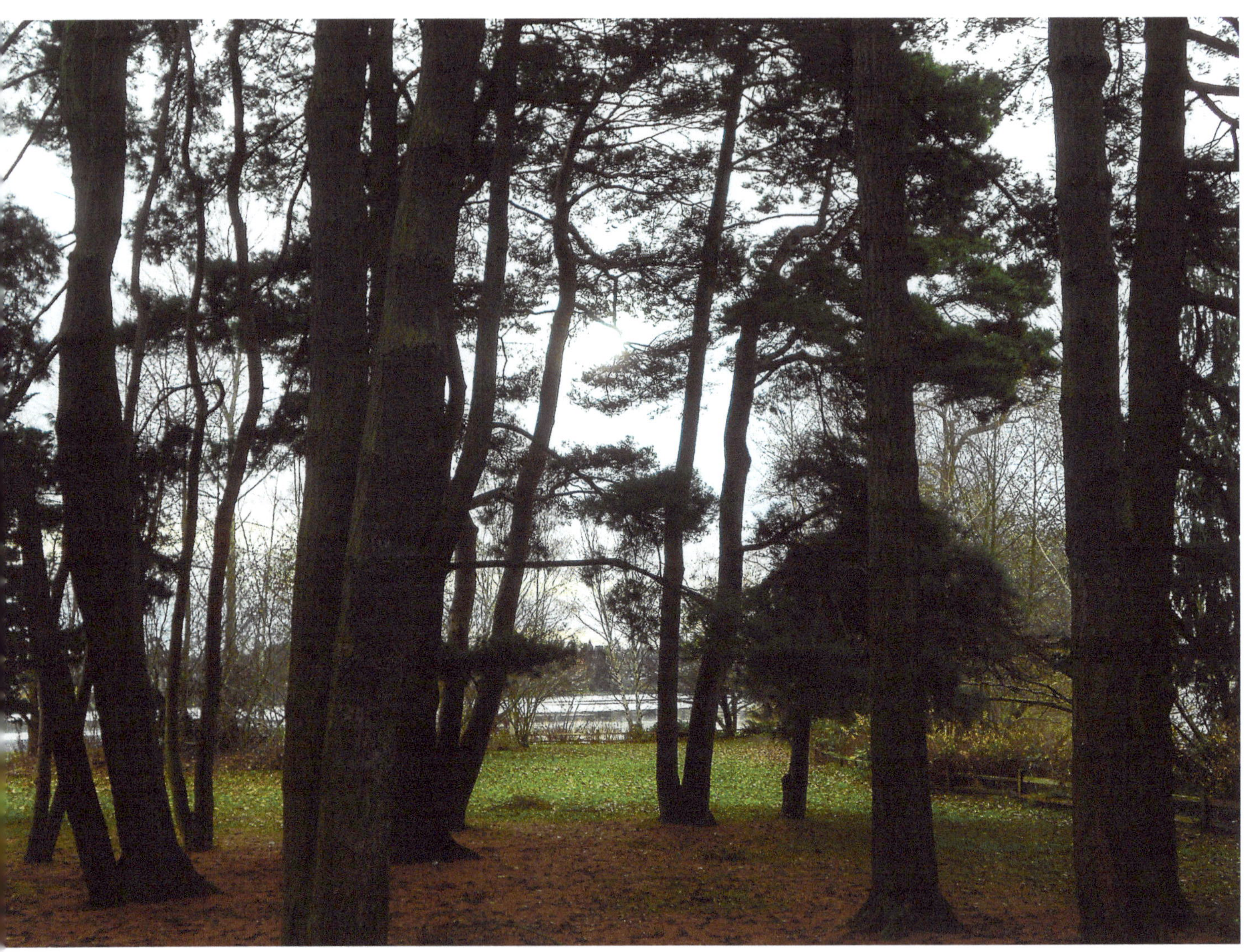

*Immediate Impression*
*"...Well I know, now, this dim lake of Auber - This misty*
*mid region of Weir- Well I know, now, this dank tarn*
*of Auber, This ghoul-haunted woodland of Weir."*

**—Edgar Allan Poe, Ulalume**

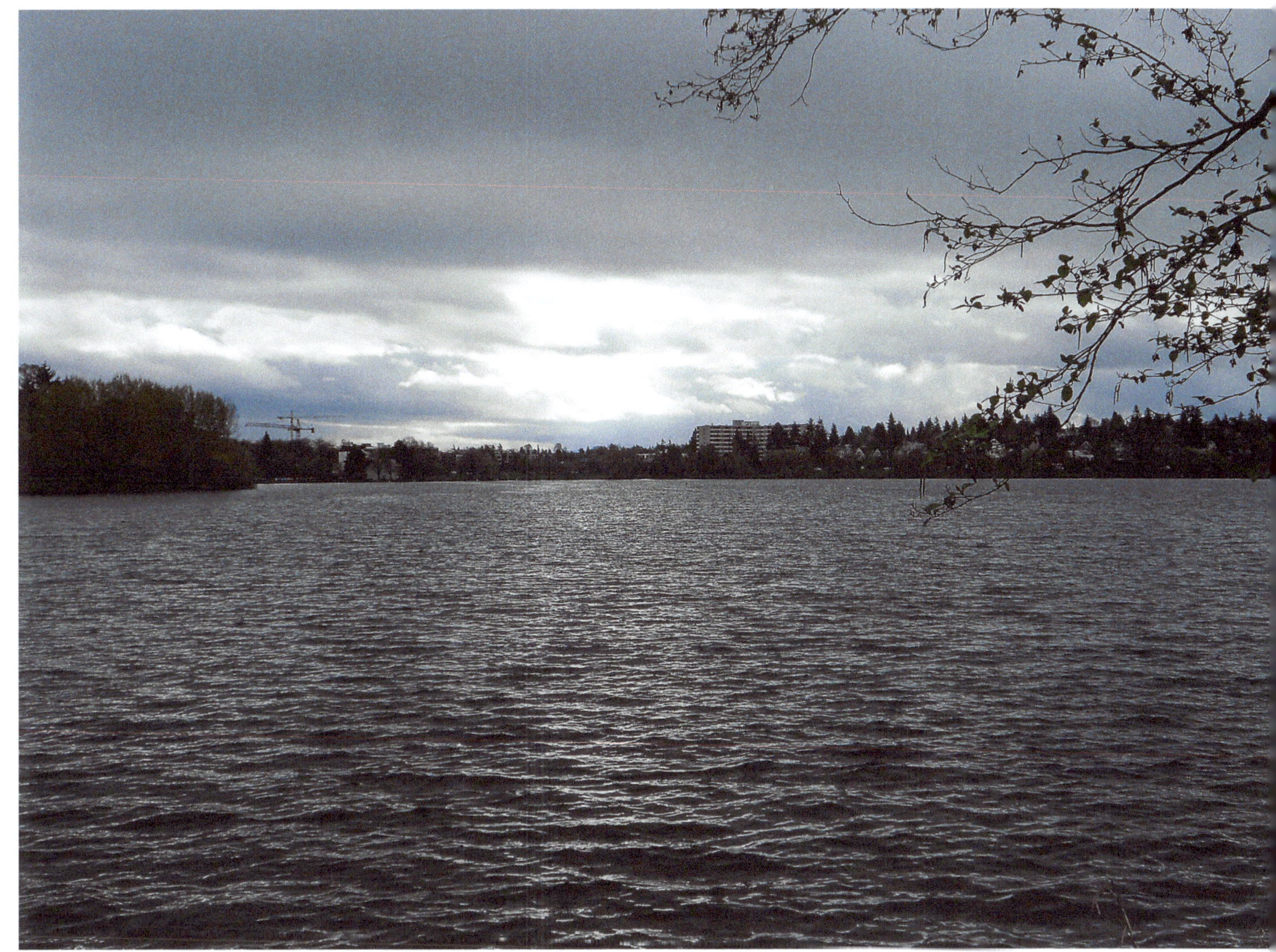

# Wide Expanse

The lake seems larger than it is in this rather grim picture. Even though the rainy day view is lacking much color, I like it for its clarity and gray-blue accents. Yet I think there is an unsettling quality about it, leaving me somewhat depressed. I can't explain why.

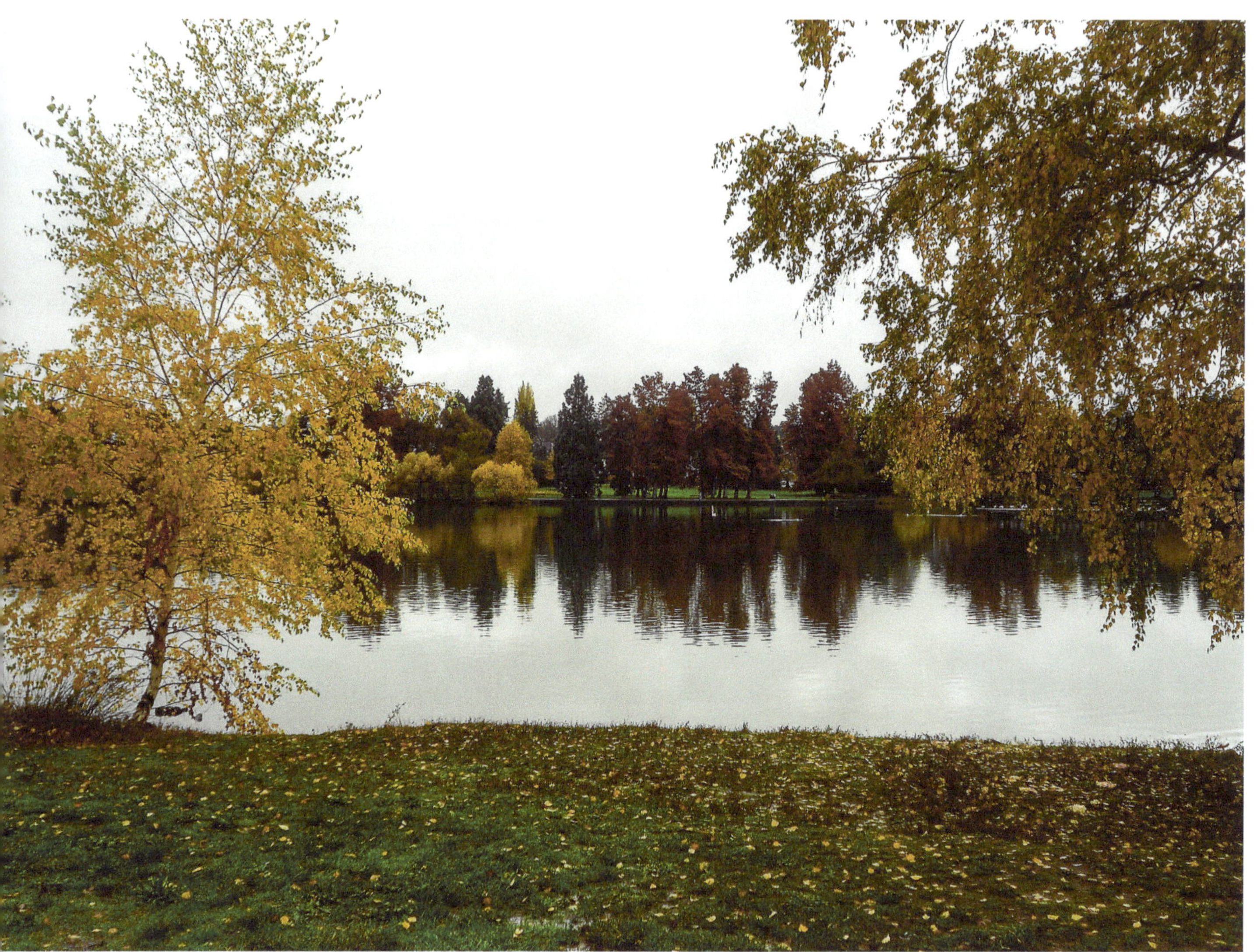

# That Terrible Beauty

A strange sensation comes over me when looking at this picture. Despite the beauty, a kind of gloominess seems ever-present here. And the more I look at it, the more pronounced becomes that feeling.

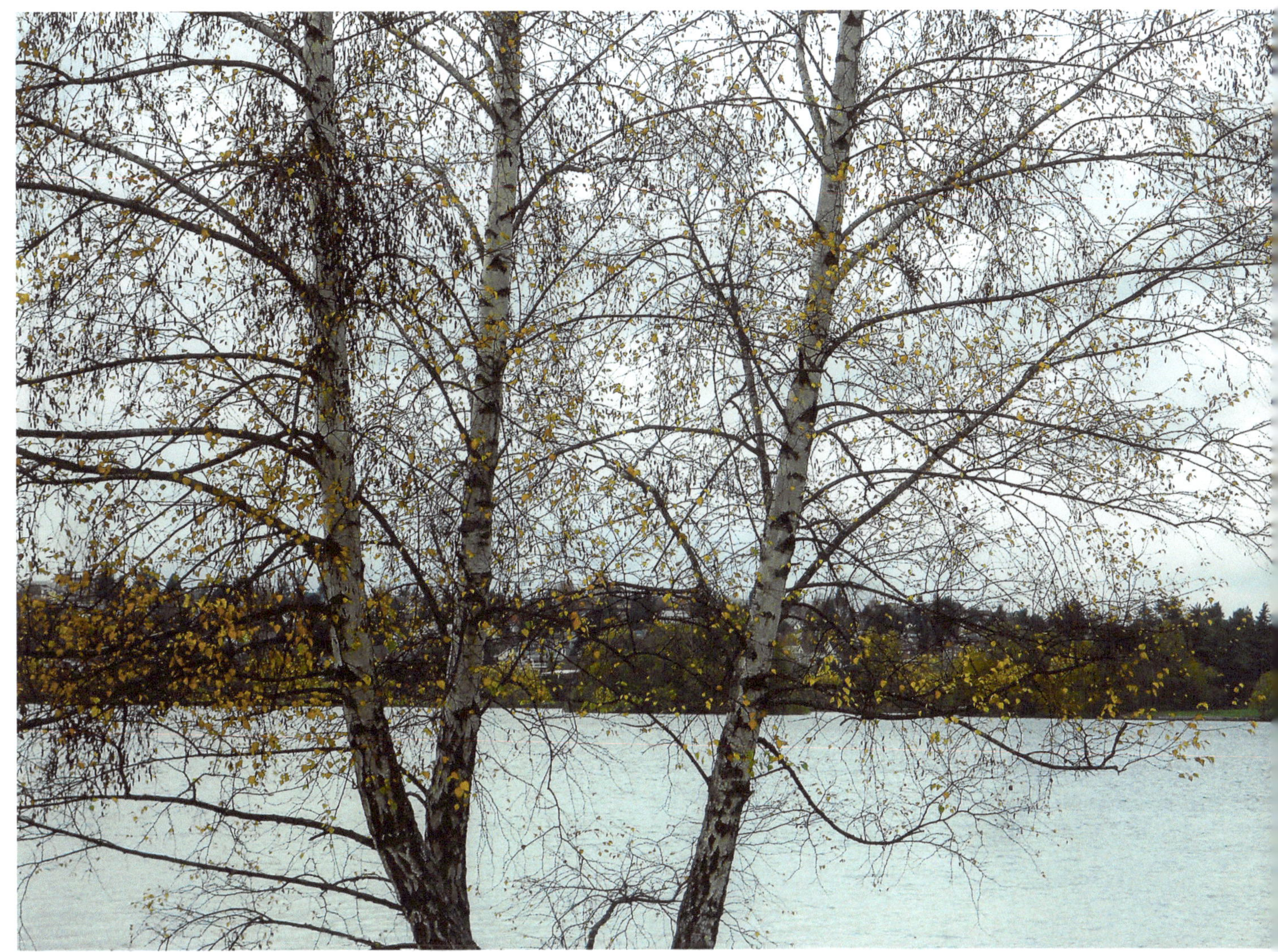

# Bleak Times

The bluish tint that predominates in this scene is somehow appropriate in signifying the colder days ahead. I like its austere simplicity, with the sparsely spaced thinning leaves and exposed twigs giving an almost lace-like quality to the picture.

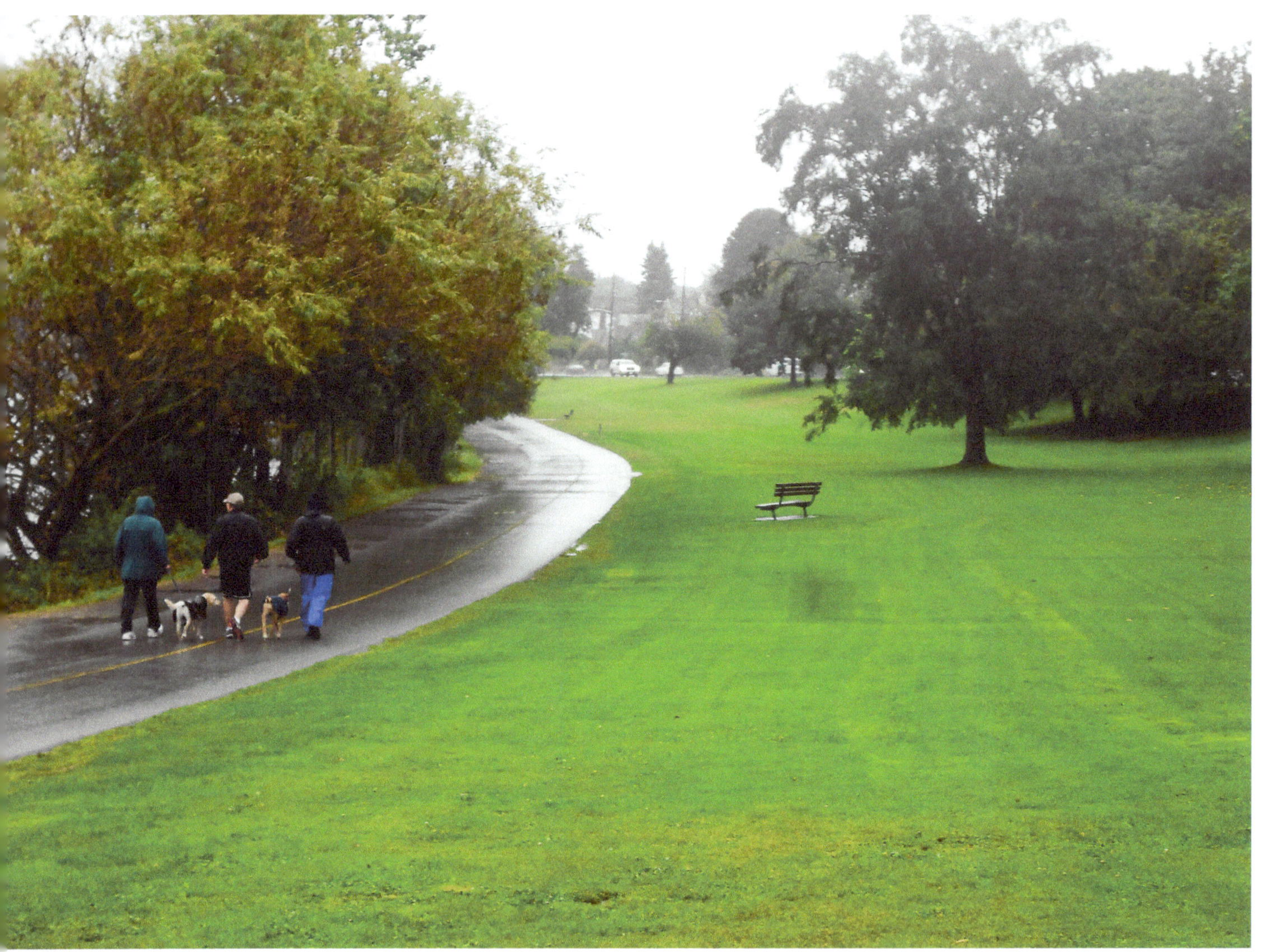

# The Quintessential
# Green Lake Walk

What I like about this picture is that it so typifies Seattle's climate, or what it is known for. People walk their dogs come rain or shine, and when it is wet, they seldom carry umbrellas. Rain makes everything smell clean and fresh. Living here, you actually come to appreciate it, as long as it doesn't pour in torrents.

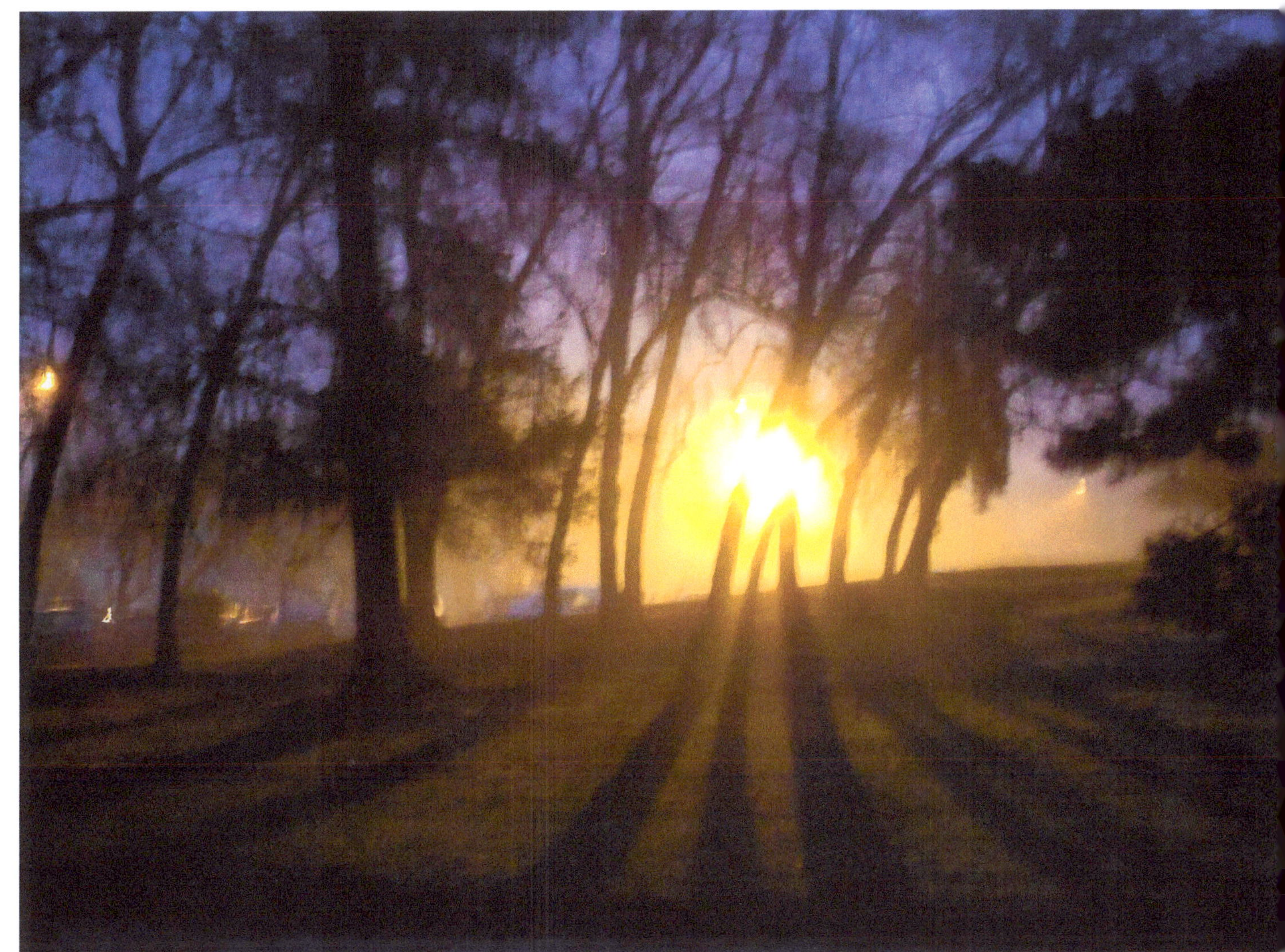

# Missing Out

In seeing this, I am reminded of being on the outside looking in. It's only a light in the north parking lot but appears, with the cars and all, as if a lot of activity is going on there and I am not part of it —a sense of separation comes over me.

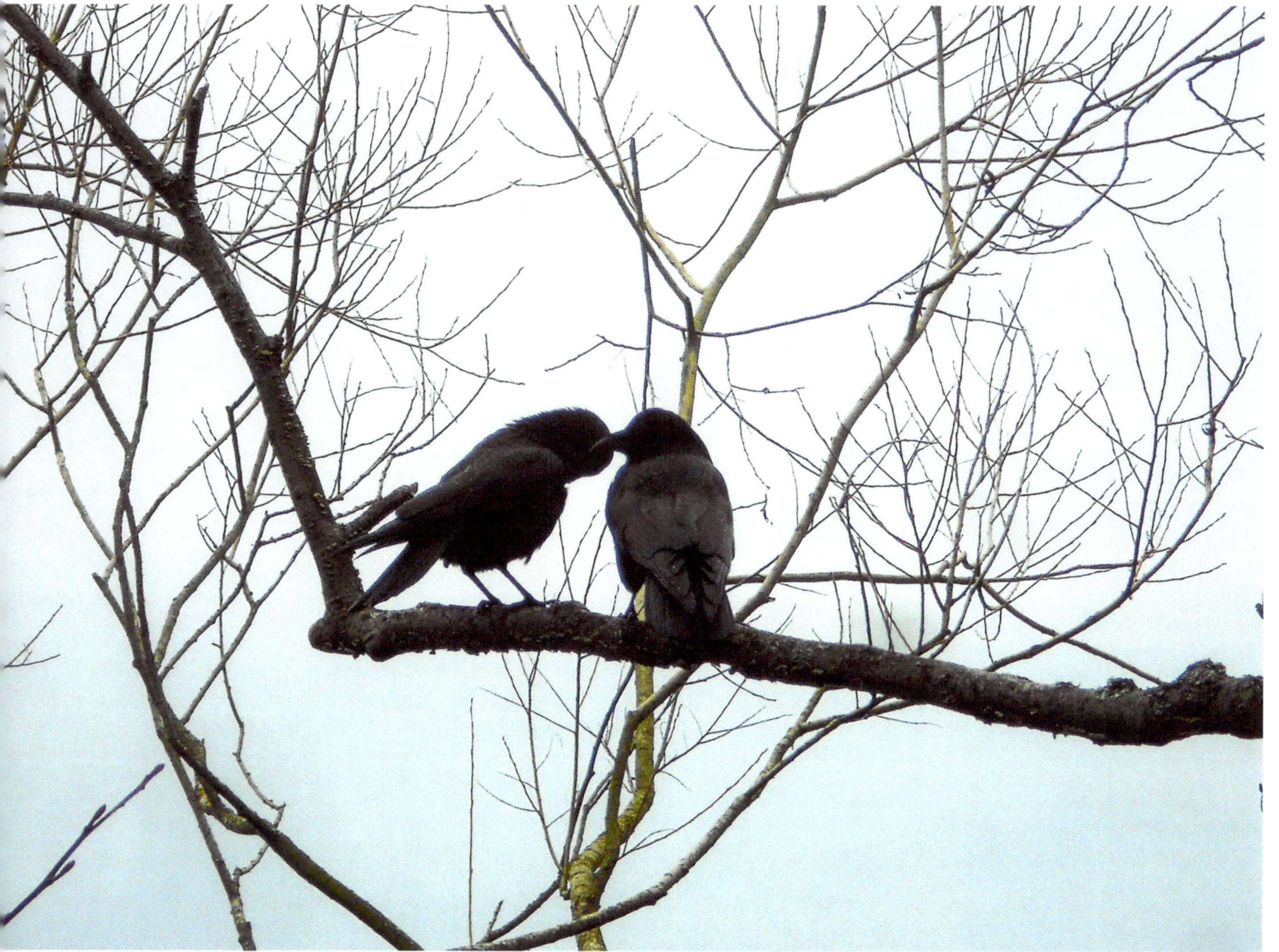

# In Love

You normally don't think of crows as love birds, but these two were quite enamored with each other and inseparable. What I find interesting is that you can tell from looking at them which is the female by her gentle bow of the head as if being coy about it —not that different from human behavior.

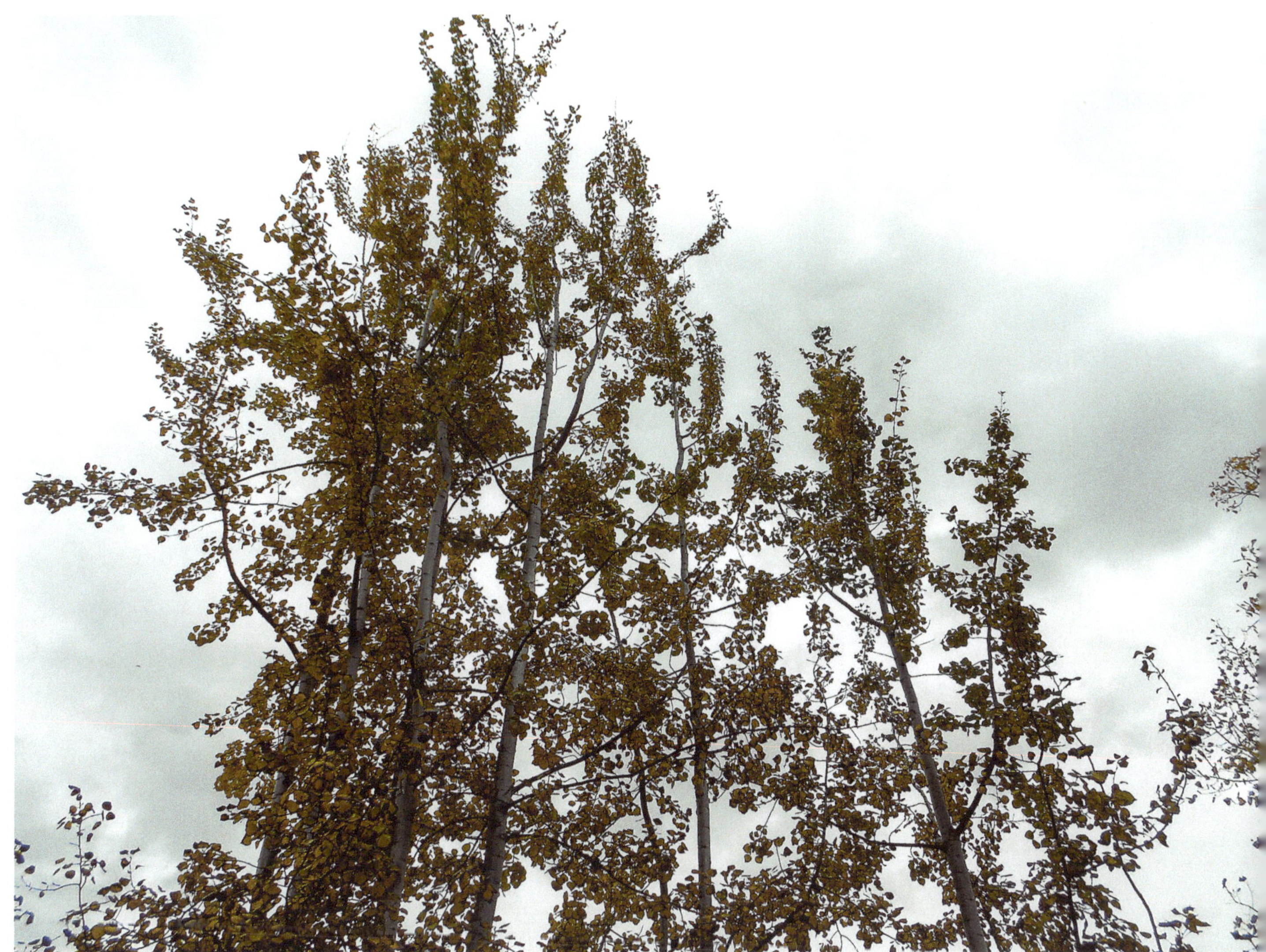

# Turbulent Skies

There's something about this picture that arouses a foreboding feeling. I think, more than anything else, it is the color contrast of the trees set against a threatening gray sky. The leaves are thinning and turning orange, marking this as an autumn scene. It also reminds me of a David Lean movie —Great Expectations comes to mind.

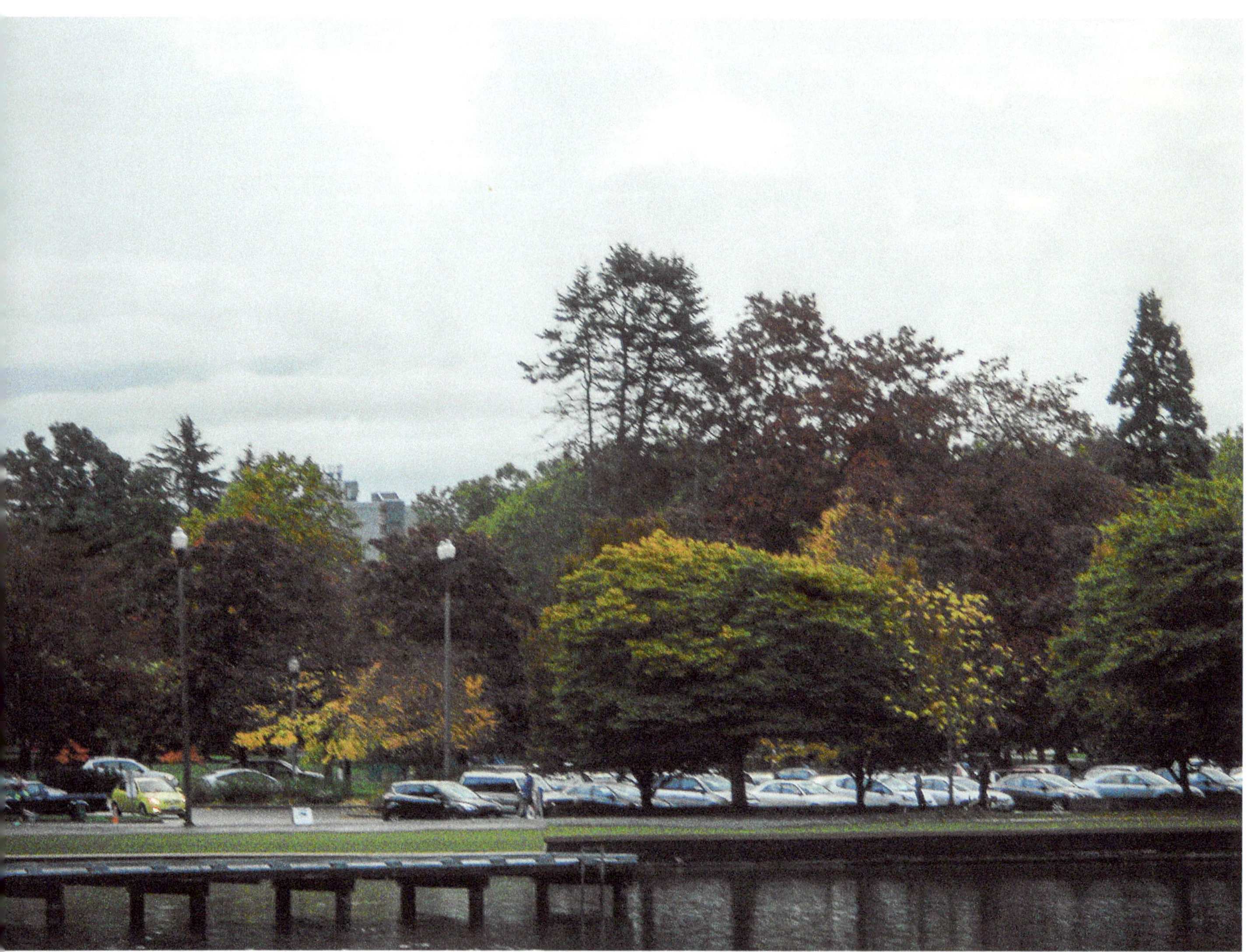

# Big Brother is Watching You

The Norse mythological giant Ymir looms over the lake keeping its eyes on what is happening below. This unusual scene conjures up that setting to me. Ymir was the God of Fire and Ice who was slain by Odin and his companion Gods and his body provided the material used to create the earth.

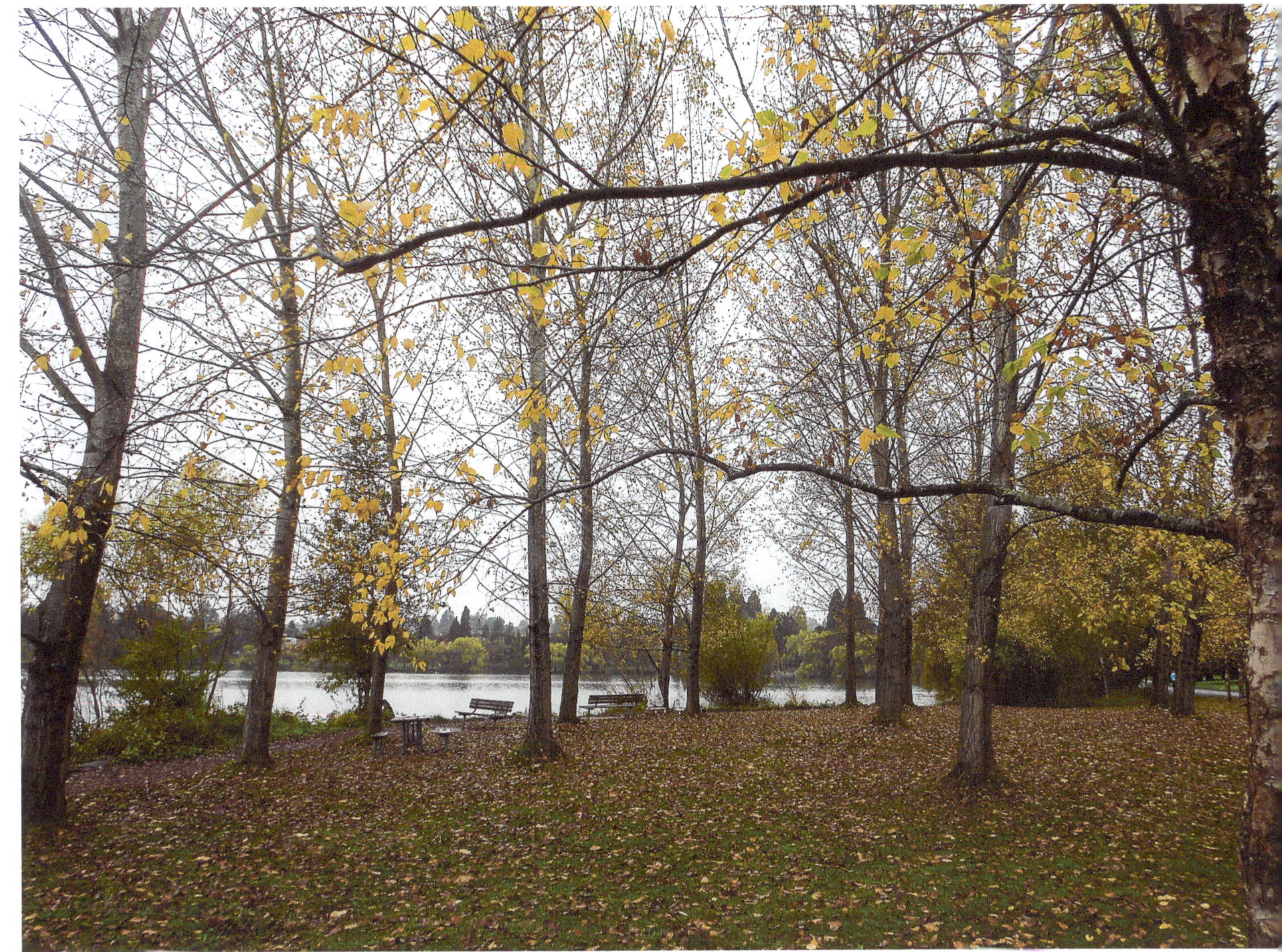

# Grim Serenity

I'm reminded of the introduction to the old television program 'Tales from the Dark Side' when looking at this. It leaves you with that same sort of creepy feeling. You feel a dread of sorts at taking a walk here, expecting something unpleasant to happen to you.

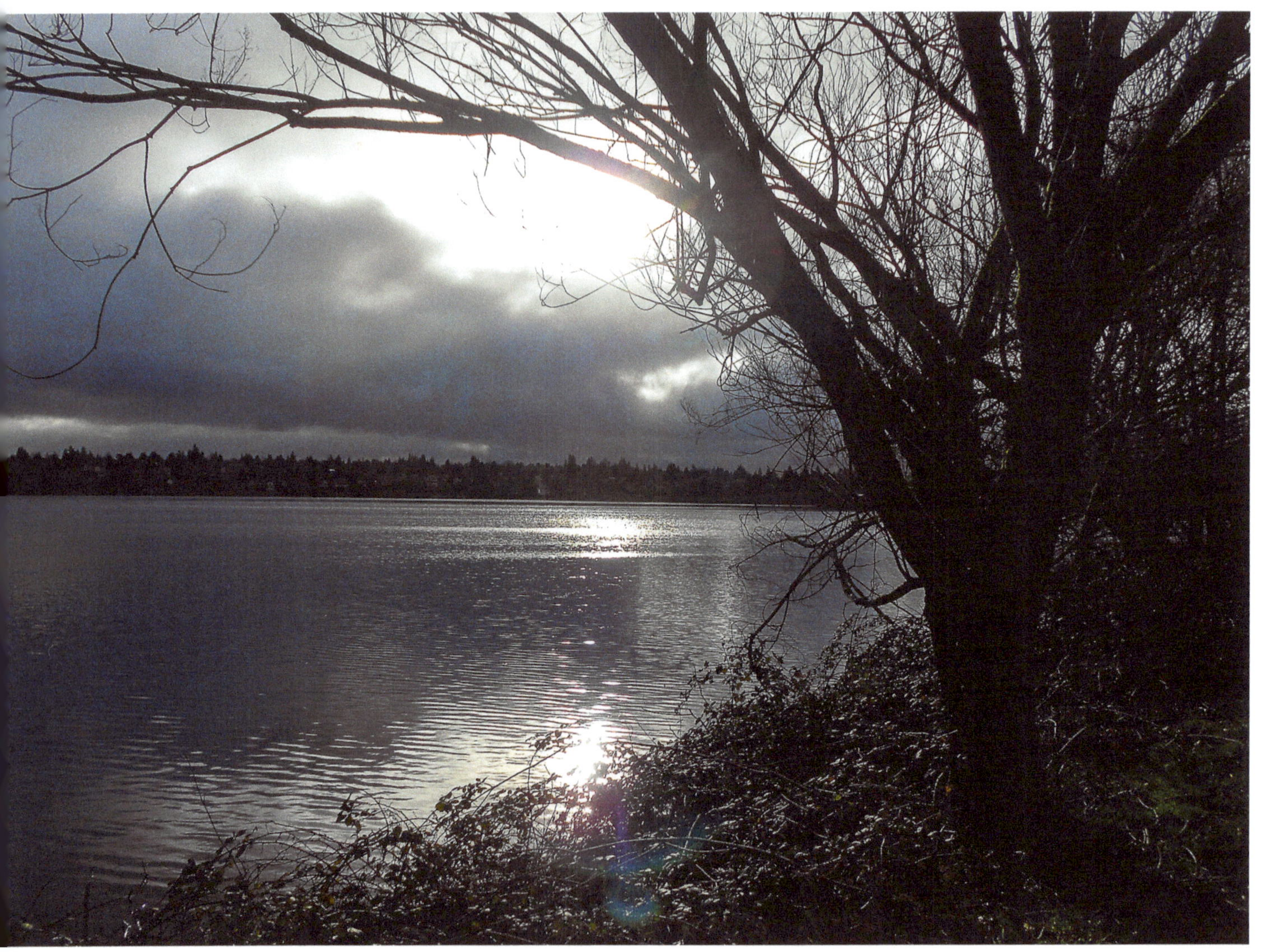

# The Edge of an Enchanted Forest

This menacing scene captures the essence of a dark fairy tale. Gloominess prevails here, and not even a glorious sunburst is enough to dispel that atmosphere. I do like it, though, and precisely for that reason. It definitely evokes an emotional response.

# Green Lake Environs

## In Praise of the Human Presence

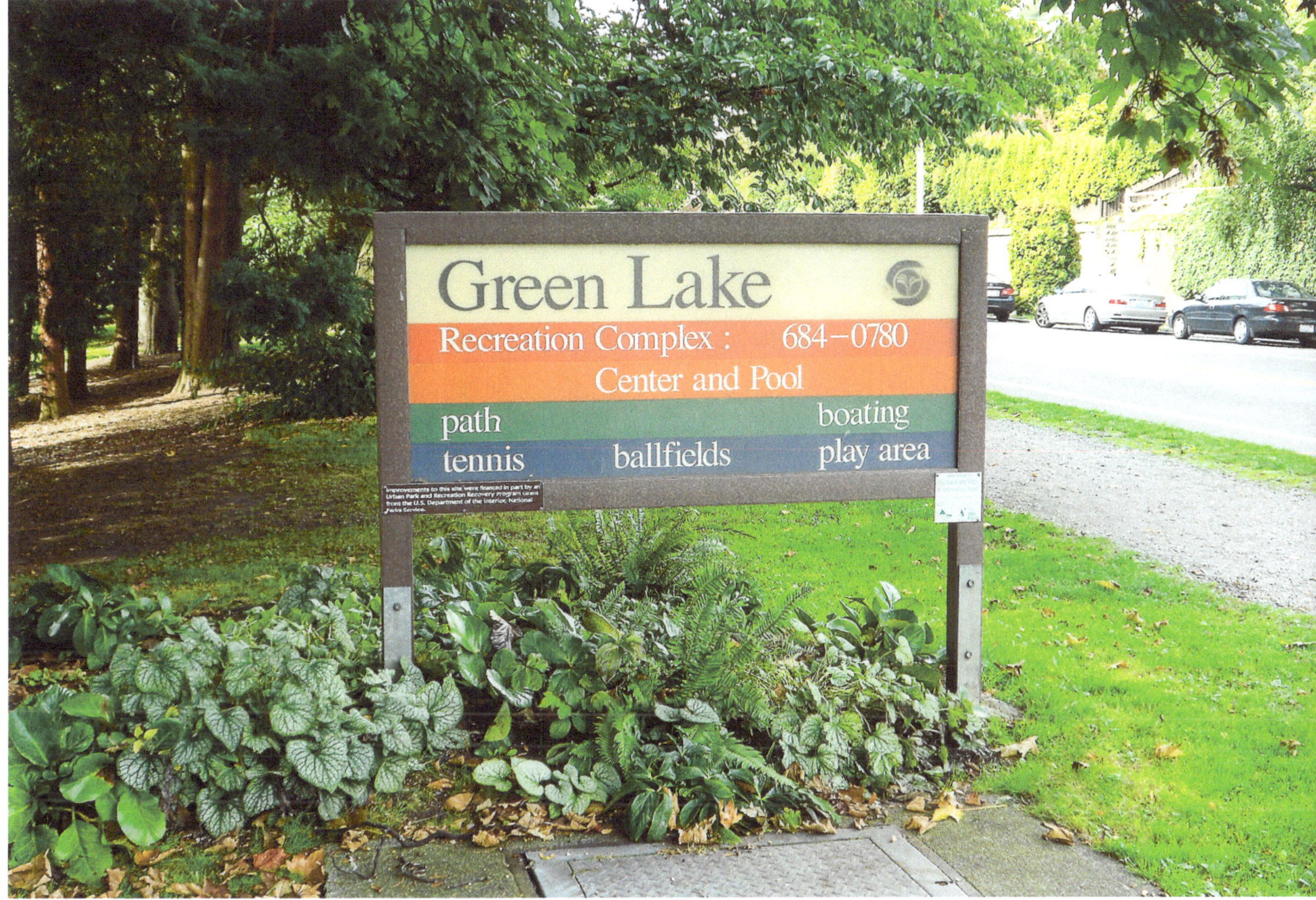



This final segment of my photographic journey is dedicated to the human presence that completes the Green Lake Park setting. It should be noted that, in a sense, the entire park is essentially man-made in that the lake was lowered by approximately seven feet to create the parkland around it in 1911. Since then, numerous facilities have been built to accommodate visitors and provide for the activities they might engage in. People make the park what it is: a fun place to be at, and for many, watching others remains a favorite pastime there.

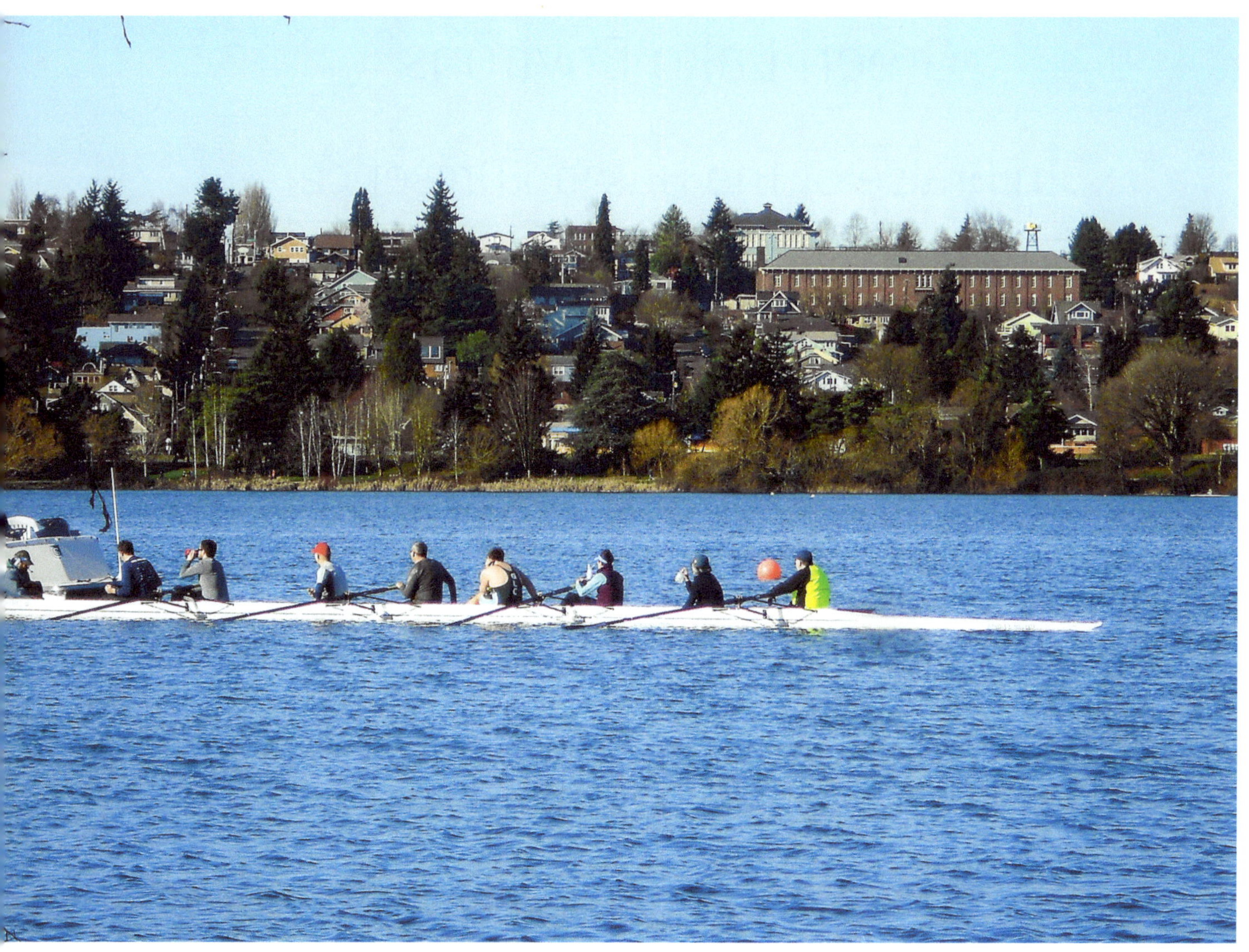

# Phinney Ridge

The Phinney Ridge neighborhood borders on the west side of Green Lake Park and is, as the name suggests, an elevated area stretching for the entire length of it and more. Numerous apartments and commercial facilities that include restaurants, shops, churches, as well as houses comprise this hill. Seen here is one of its old landmarks, Allen School, long closed and now a community center (the elongated brown structure). Boating is a popular activity at Green Lake.

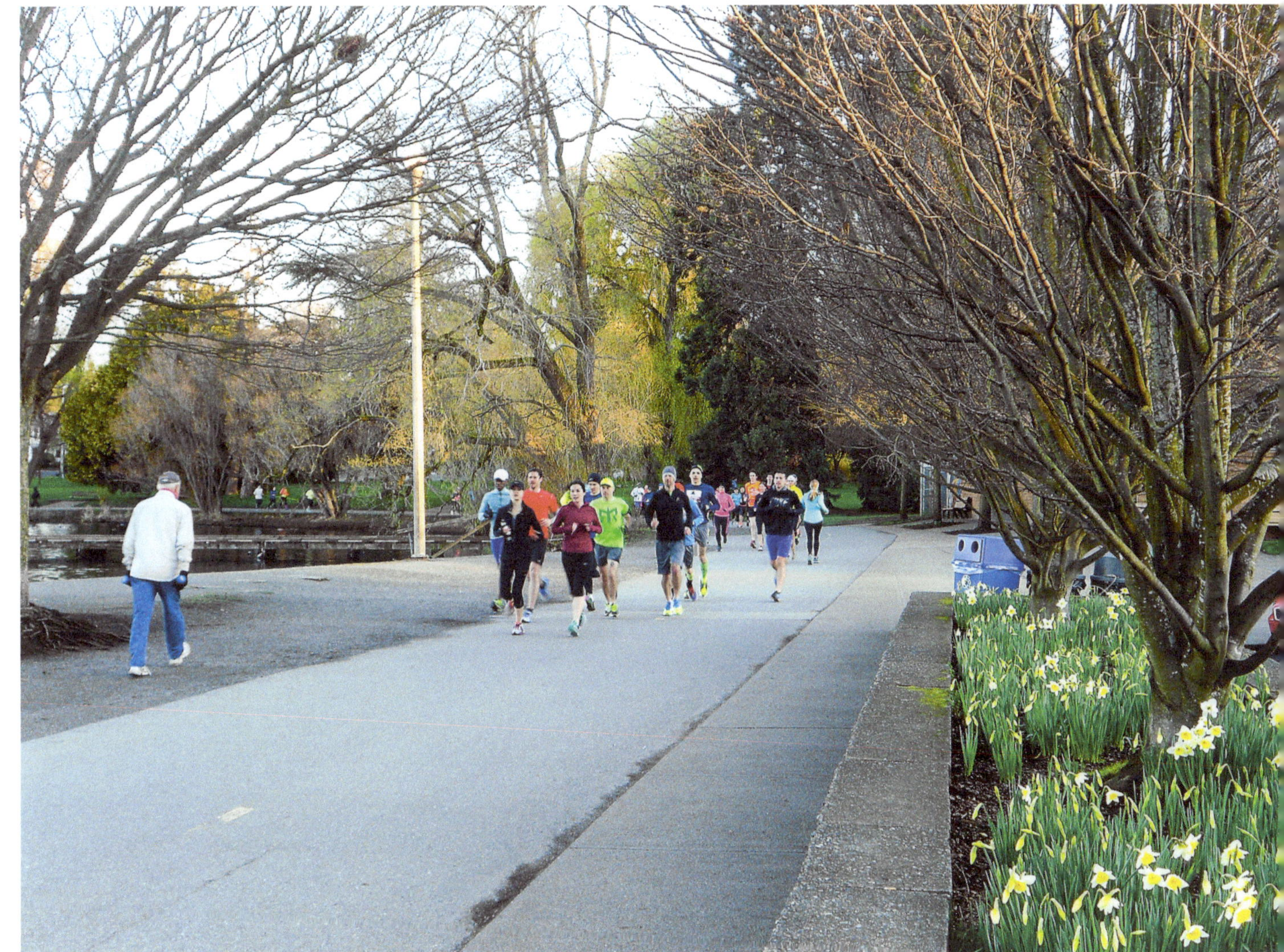

# The Morning Jog

For years, I did just that. A back injury ended my running days, but I have to say that I enjoy my walks more. Here we see a spring morning as evidenced by the daffodils; sunlight has hit the upper branches and is working its way down. Jogging is a popular pastime at Green Lake and when you joggers in groups, like above, it's usually for a charitable cause.

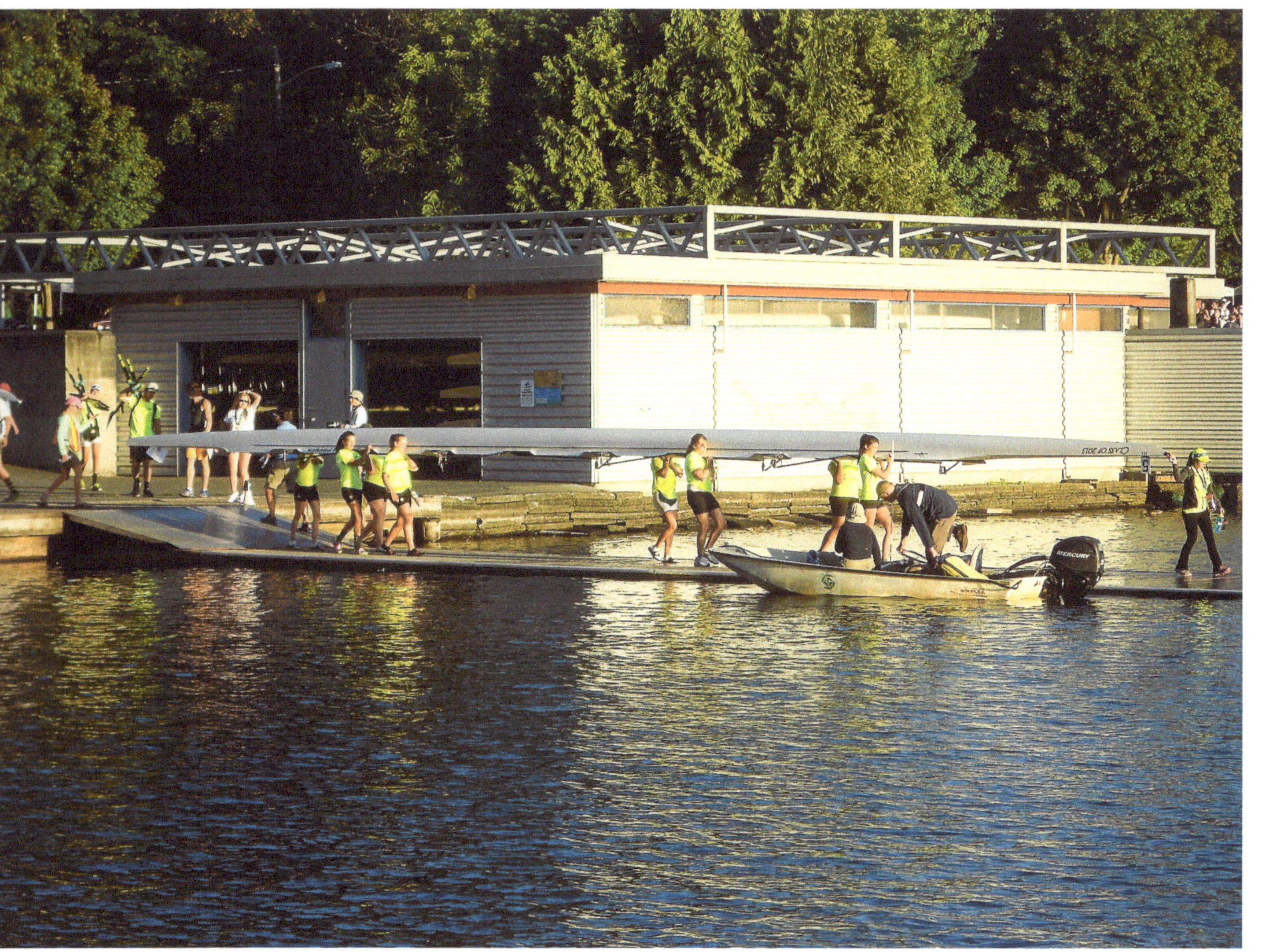

# Getting Ready to Race

A rowing crew is preparing for the day's activities at the boathouse. The uniforms of the performers indicate that a competition is taking place, which happens several times during the year. Only the coaches of these teams are permitted to use a motorized boat.

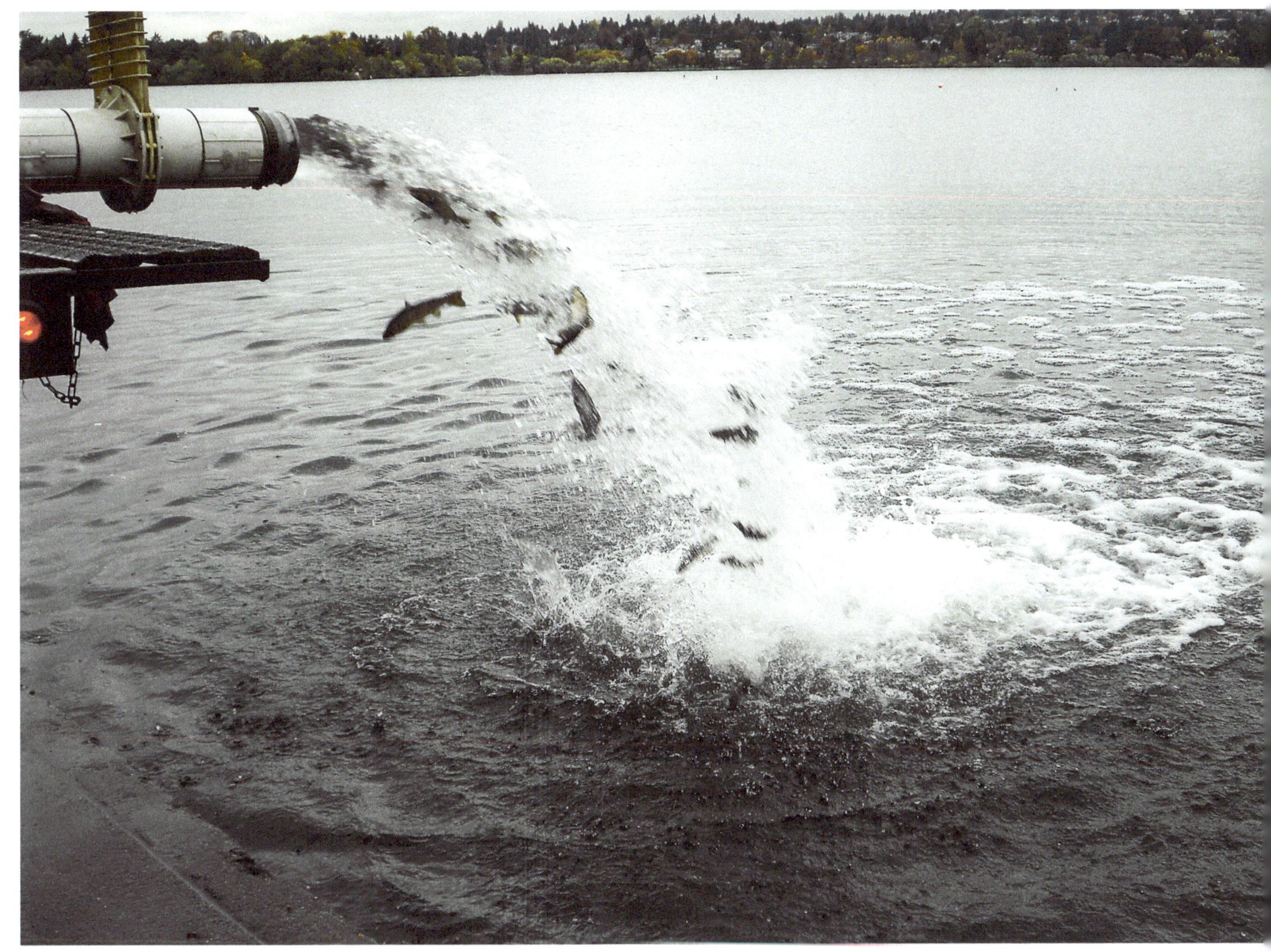

# Stocking the Lake

Fishing is a popular activity at Green Lake. It is stocked with trout, typically in the fall, with dumps of 3,500 live fish at a single truckload I was told. I have one thing in common with most fishermen —we both are early risers and enjoy our pastimes at early dawn. But here a lot of the similarity ends as many fishermen tend to be smokers. I often had to hold my breath when passing them, but in 2015 all smoking was banned in Seattle's public parks which helped a lot in being able to avoid inhaling second-hand smoke.

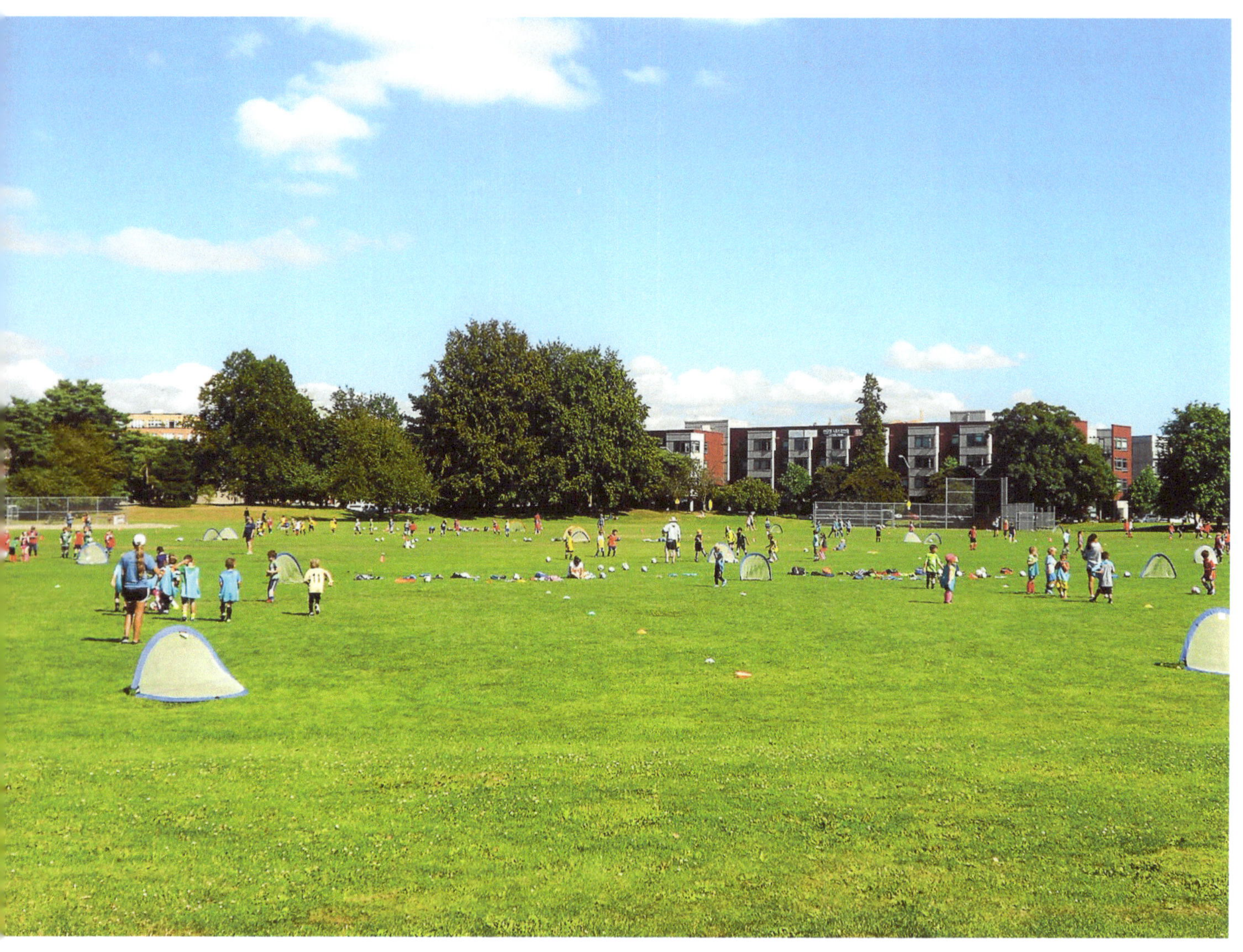

# The Park next to the Lake

Green Lake's largest commercial center is on its east side (actually more like northeast) with several restaurants, a food store, bicycle rental shop, apartment complexes, and more. Seen here is the park that extends from lakeside to this area which contains a tennis court, an outdoor basketball area, three baseball fields, a soccer field (improvised) and a kids' playground. A hubbub of activity takes place here, especially in the summer.

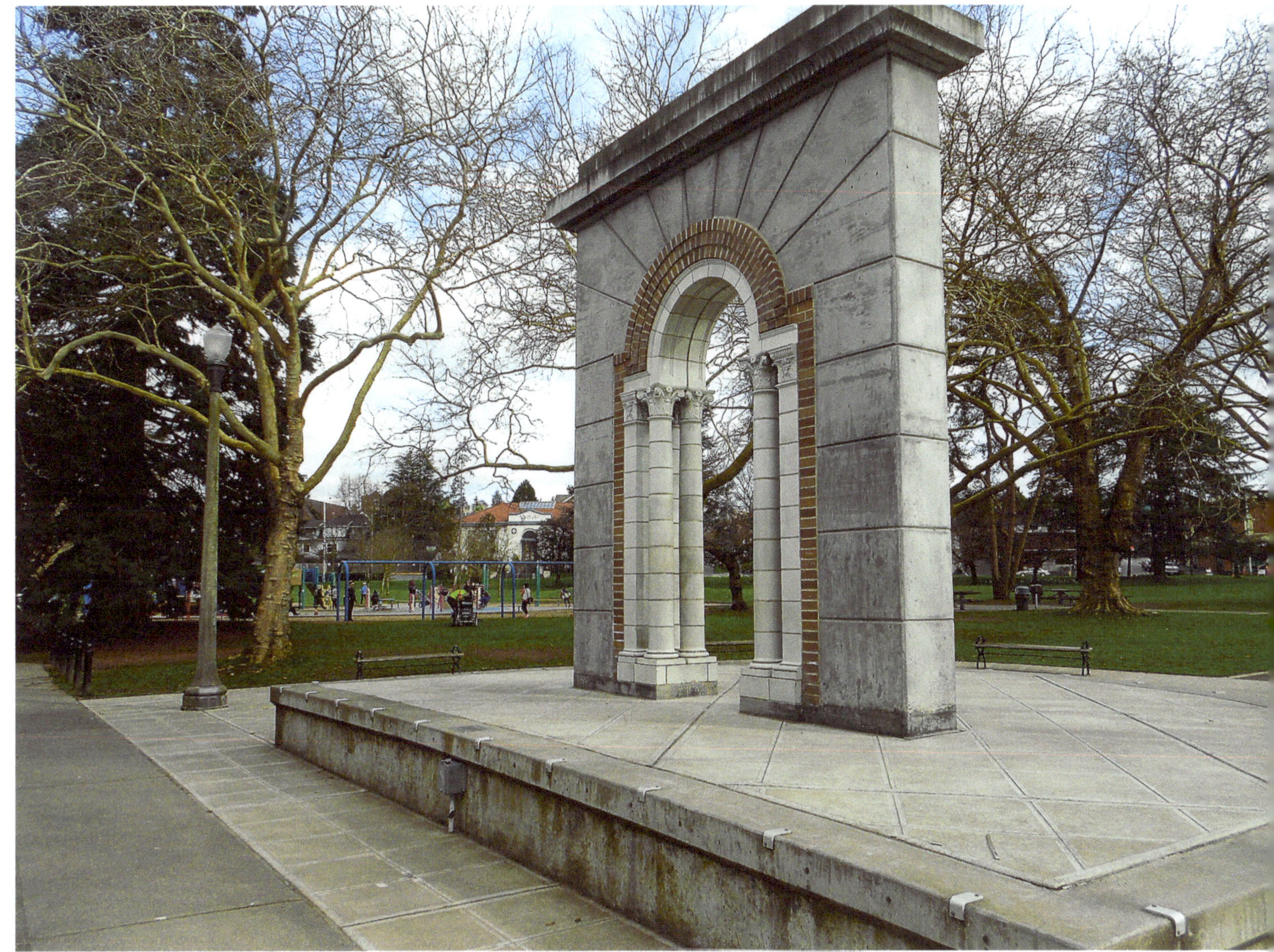

# Arc de Triomphe

Green Lake's version of the famous Paris landmark, simply called the archway, is considerably less impressive and somewhat strange with its half-hearted capitals on the columns (resembling but not quite the Corinthian ones). This monument is just in front of the Green Lake Center house as you approach it from the east. Notice the children's playground nearby.

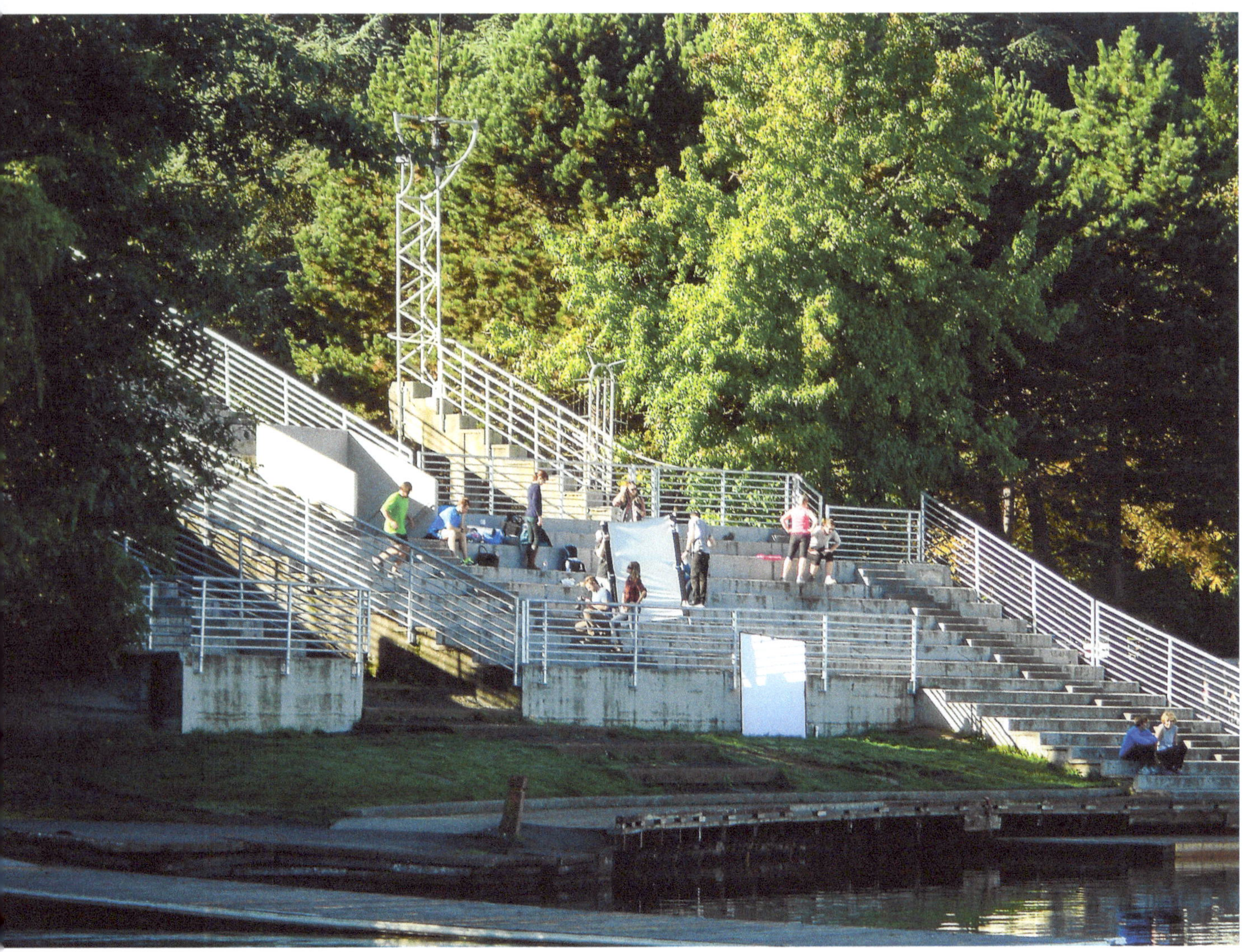

# Ruins into Sculpture

Here's what's left of the Aqua-Theater. Originally it was built in 1950 to offer an attraction called Aqua Follies which consisted of aqua ballet, stage dancing, and comedy. In its heyday, the shows drew many celebrities for its plays and musicals. After the World's Fair in 1962, its popularity waned with the Seattle Center taking over such activities. In the 70's it was dismantled except for what you see here. People are still drawn to it for exercise now, running up and down its steps. Crew shells are housed inside the facility.

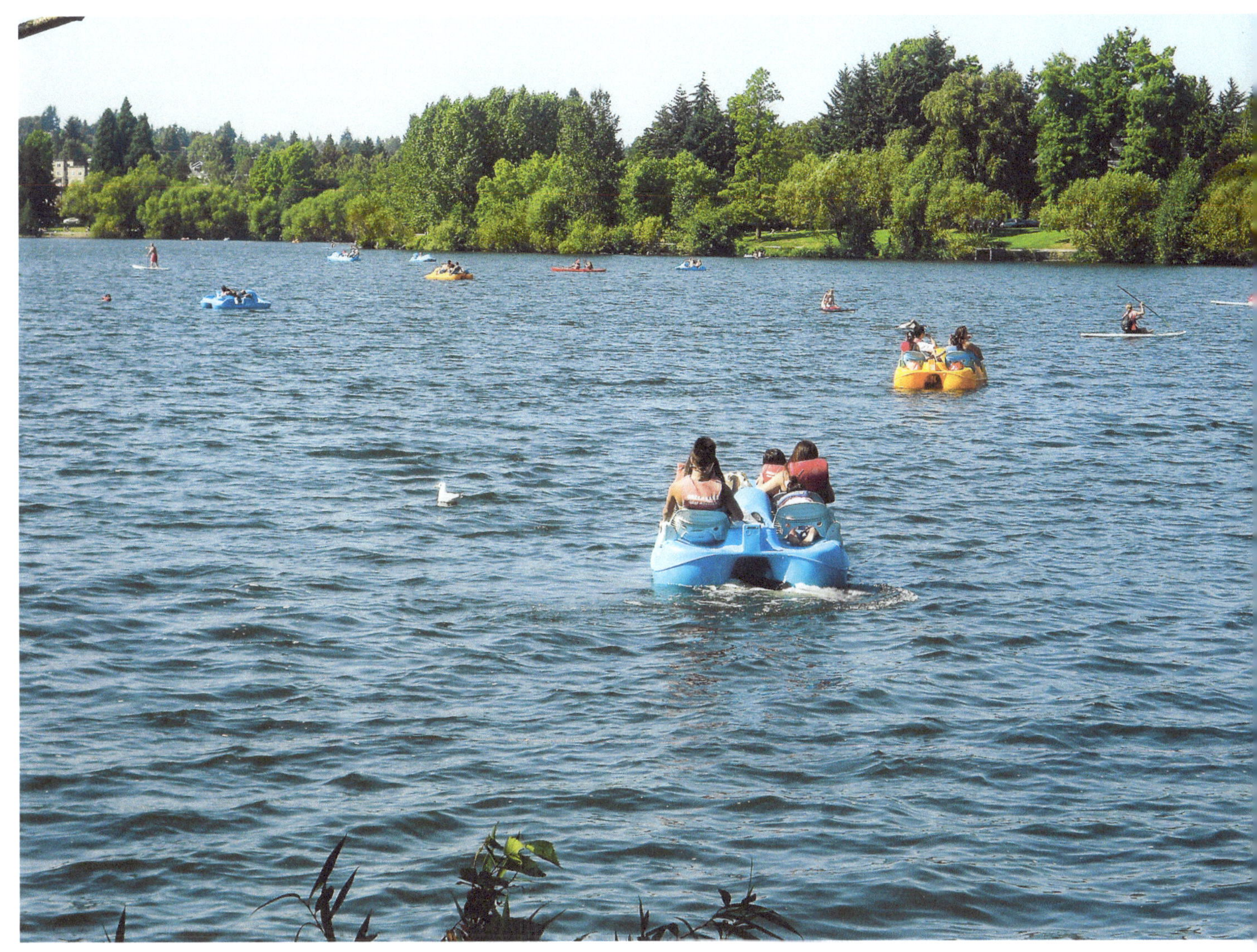

# Summer Fun

Here's what happens at Green Lake on a warm summer's day. Everyone appears to be having a good time with the floating equipment that can be rented. Motor boats are not allowed. It's interesting to note that the Gull to the left of the blue boat is totally unruffled by the human presence.

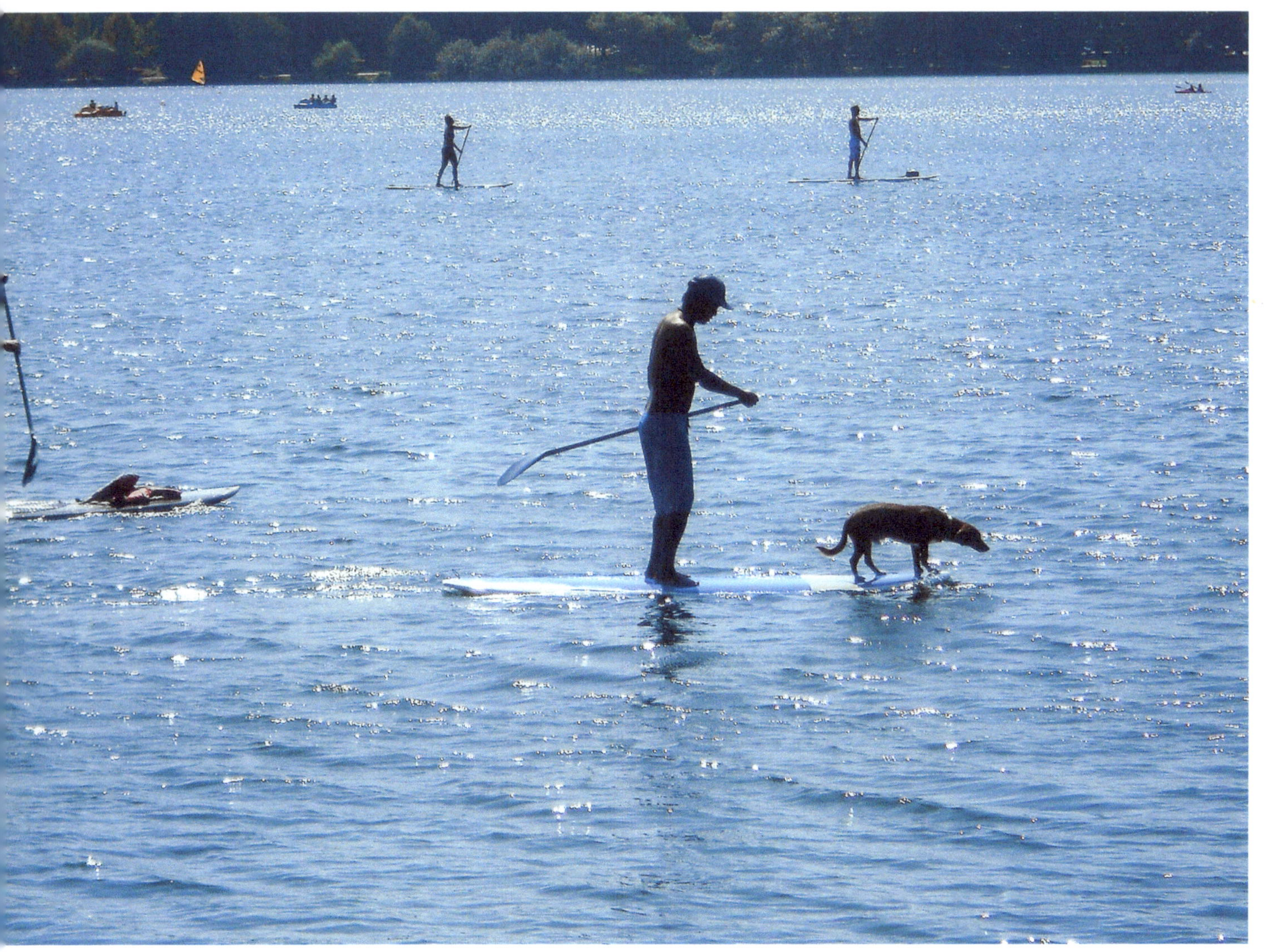

# Inseparable

A loyal dog and its master are seldom apart. You have to wonder
what goes on the dog's mind when on a paddleboard. Is it enjoying
the ride? Is it frightened? Paddle boarding has become more
popular recently with lake users able to rent them at the northeast
facility near the Green Lake Center.

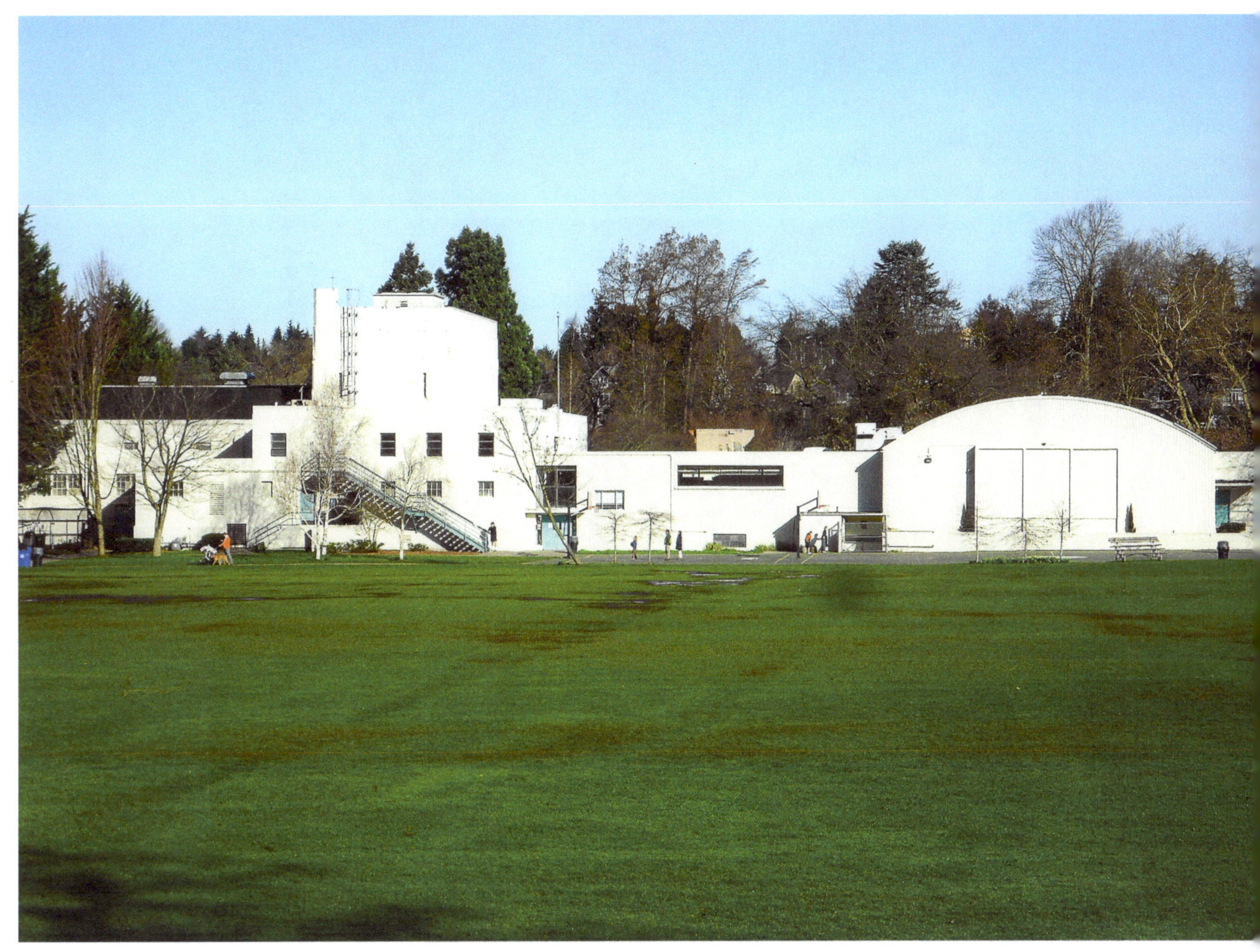

# The Center Complex

The Green Lake Center was erected in 1929 and then expanded in 1945 by adding a swimming pool (the annex on the right with the arched roof). The facility contains a gymnasium, two conference rooms, showers and bathrooms, and a stage in addition to the pool, named Evans Pool. There is also an outdoor basketball court. It is the largest structure in the park and always seems to have some activity going on.

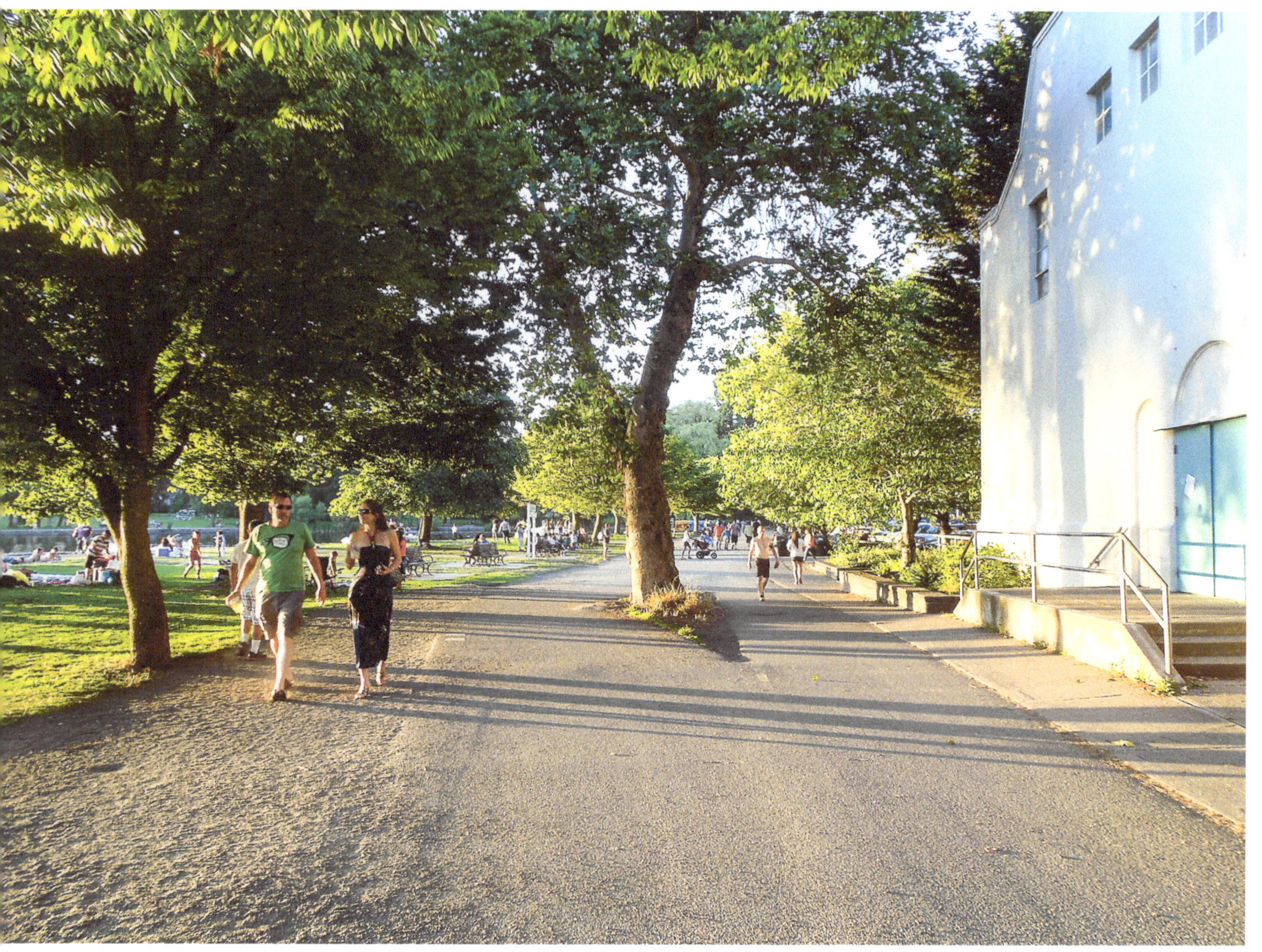

# A Warm Summer's Stroll

A view showing the western wall of the Green Lake Center behind which the gym is located. This picture was taken in late August just before sunset with the long shadows cast much in evidence. The swimming area seen here is one of two at the lake, the other being by the Bathhouse Theatre.

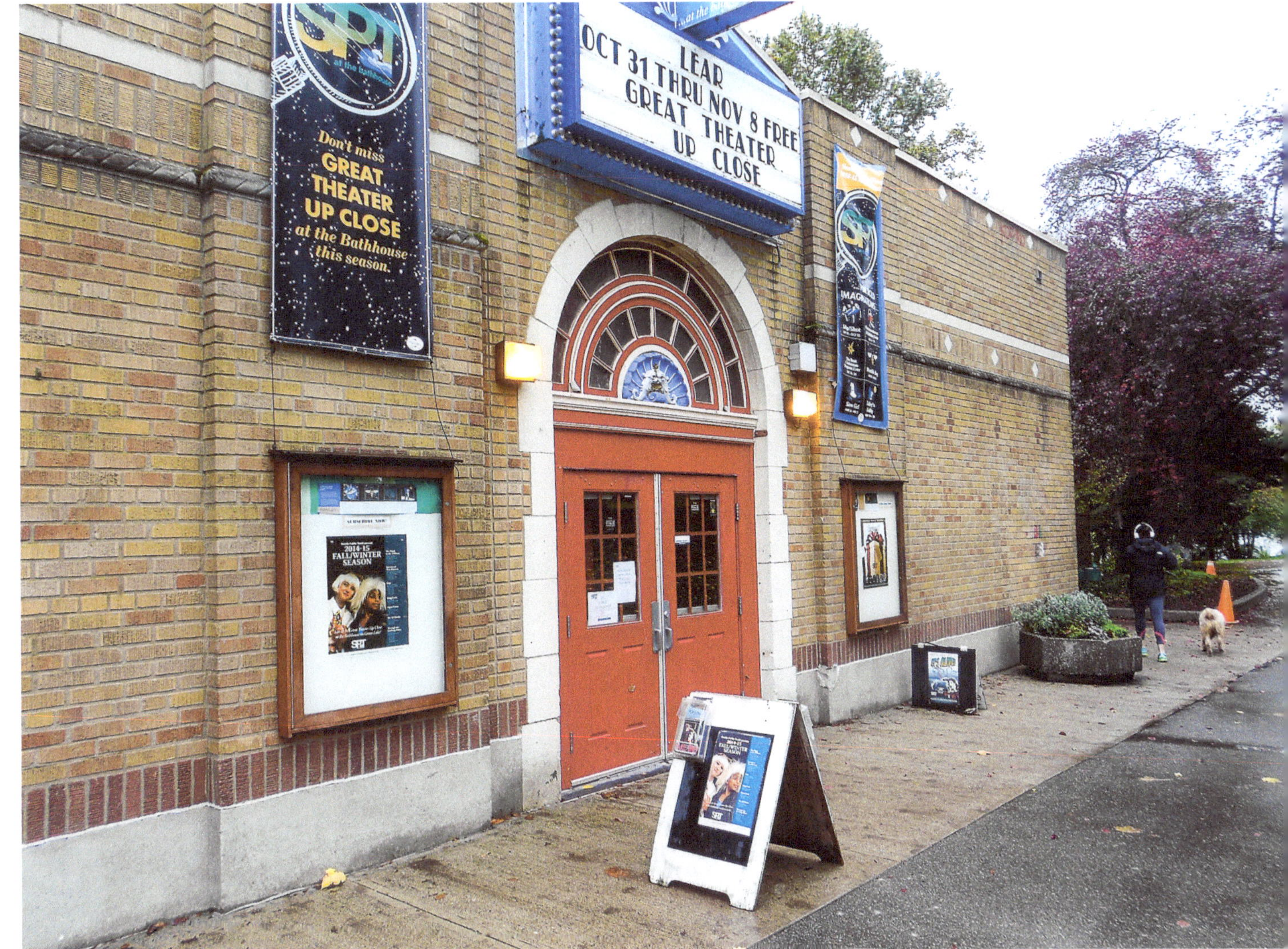


# The Bathhouse Theater

I've seen a few plays here, presented by amateur actors, some of who display real talent. The theater gets its name because the back side of it (facing the lake) is a facility for swimmers to shower and change. There is no charge for attending the performances plays but donations are asked for.

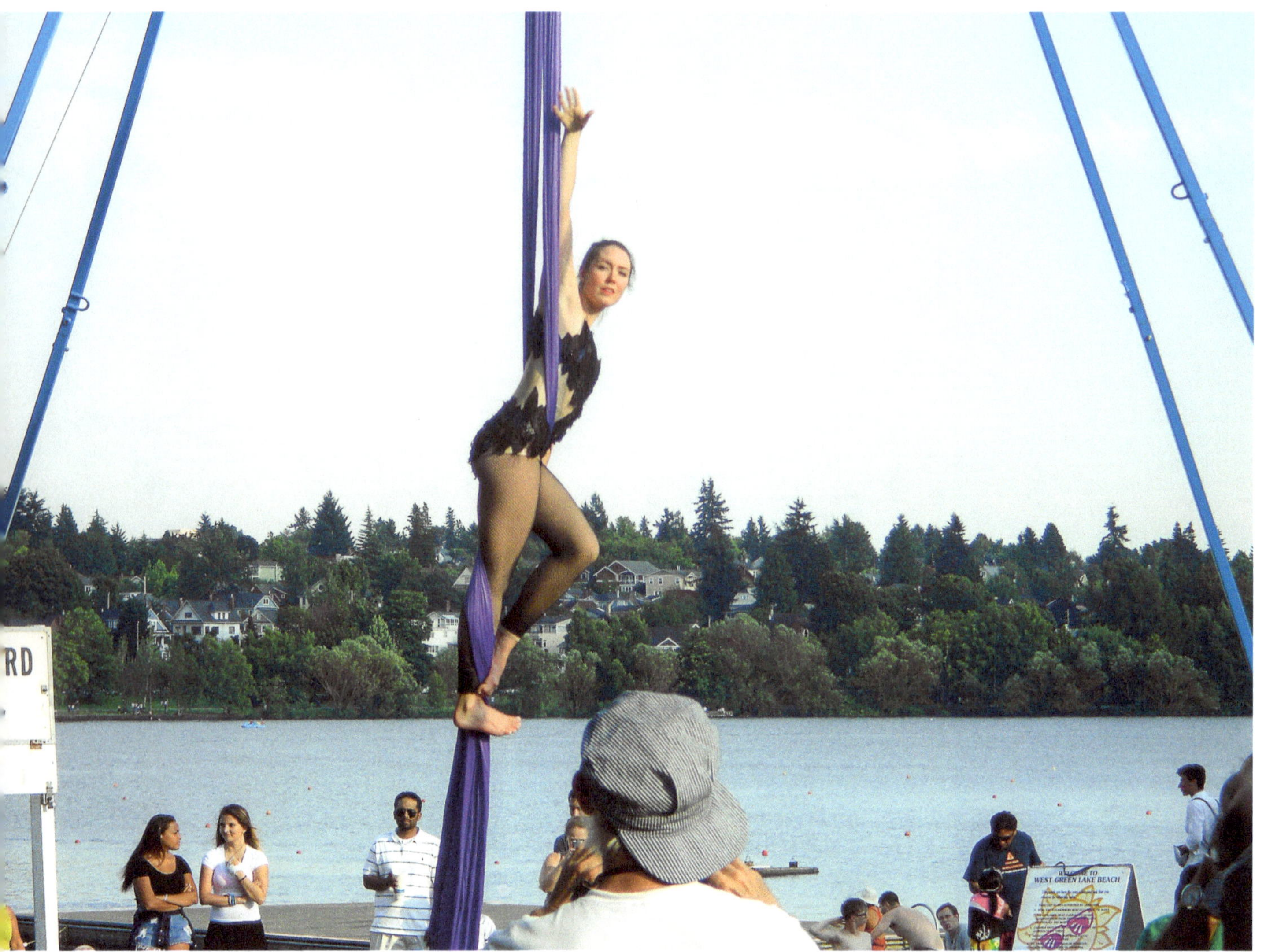

# Summer Activity

I happened to be walking in the late afternoon when I saw this acrobatic show being put on next to the Bathhouse Theater. It's unusual for me to do this during that time of day and is a reminder that I may be missing out on such activities by preferring early morning walks.

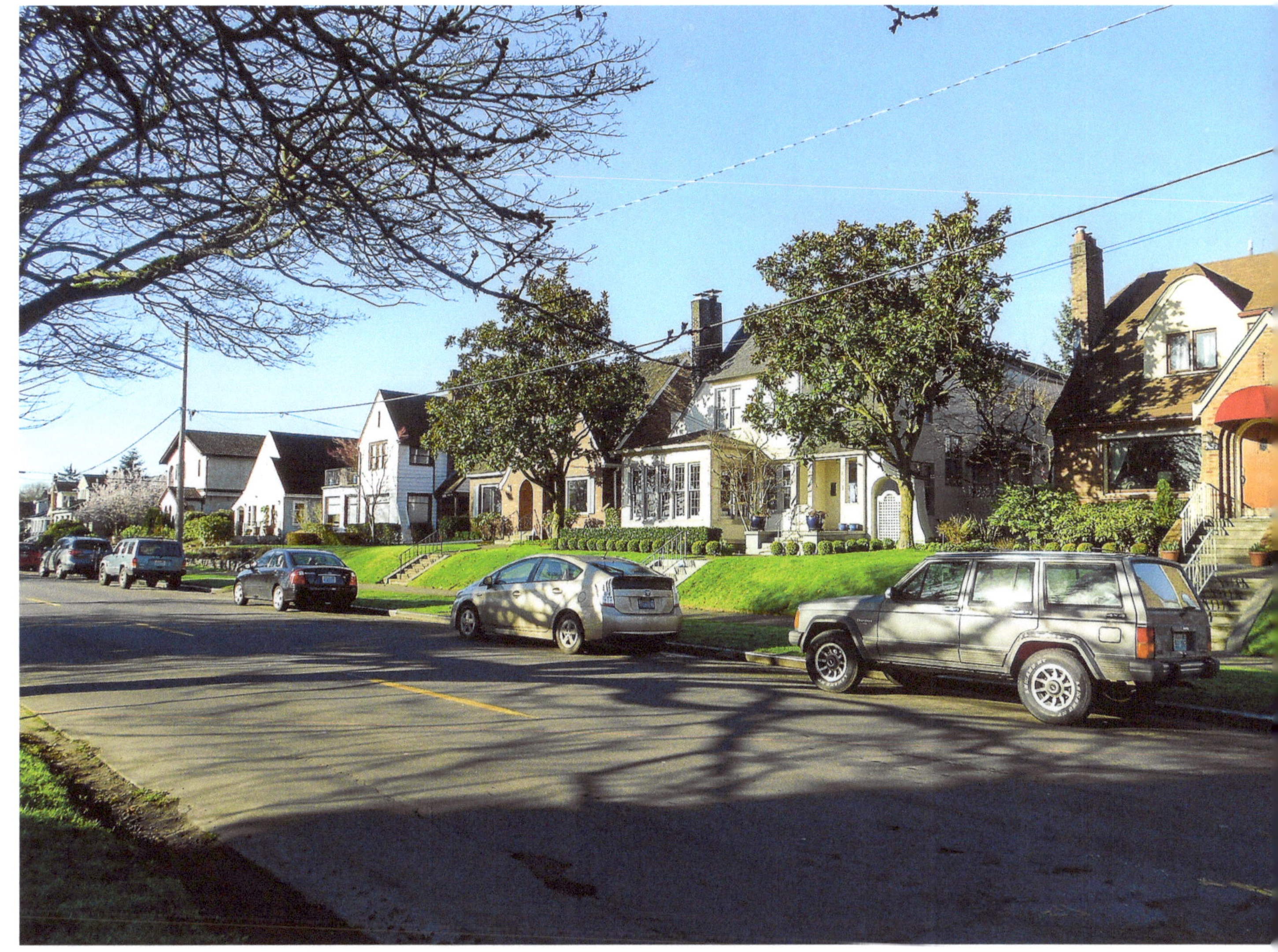

# Stately Homes

Seen here is West Green Lake Drive N at the northwest side of the lake. Typical of most residential areas in Seattle, the lots are somewhat small and the houses in close proximity to each other, but despite this, they are well maintained and the overall look is one of affluence. For me, it's the best possible place to live within the city. People living on the shores of Lake Washington, Lake Union, or Puget Sound will dispute that, of course, but they can't get their exercise walking around their waters.

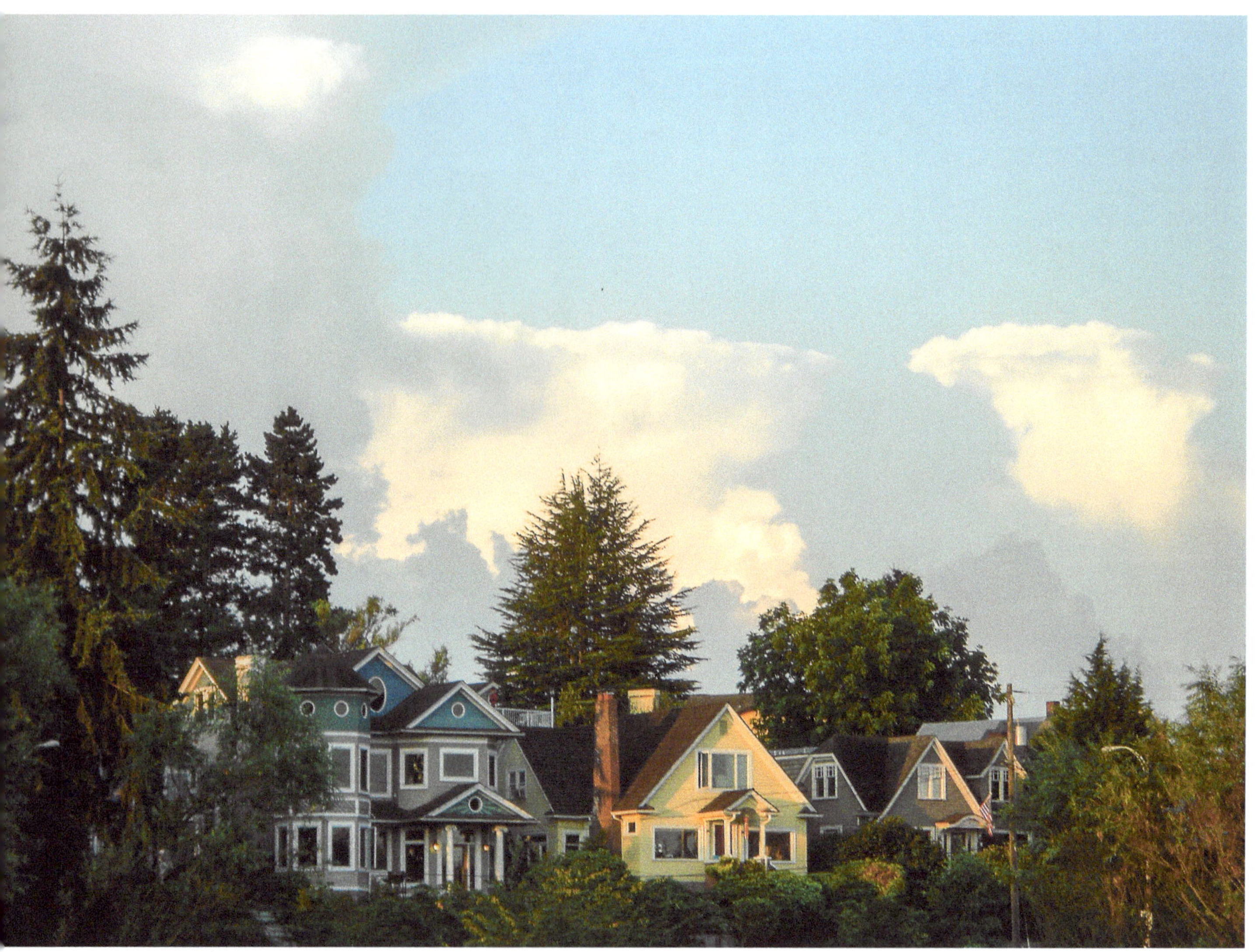

# View Looking East

A view of the attractive houses that can be seen on the east side of the lake along East Green Lake Way N with an imposing thundercloud behind them.

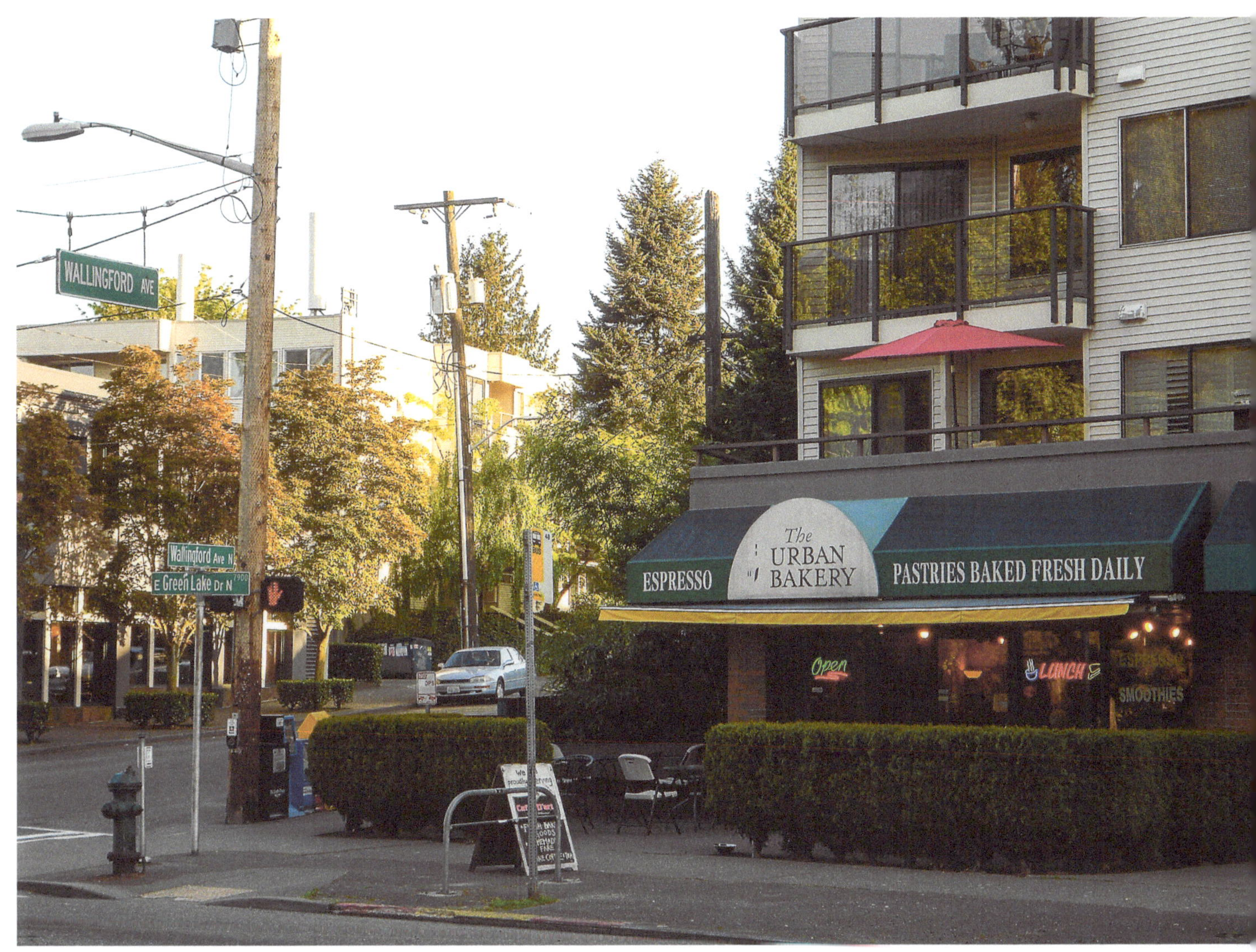


# Northernmost Point

The intersection of Wallingford Avenue N and E Green Lake Drive N marks the northern edge of Green Lake Park. The Green Lake Plaza, a small mall, is just west of this intersection. This area and the area east of the Center House are the only ones consisting of commercial property, including restaurants, shops, apartments, and other facilities.

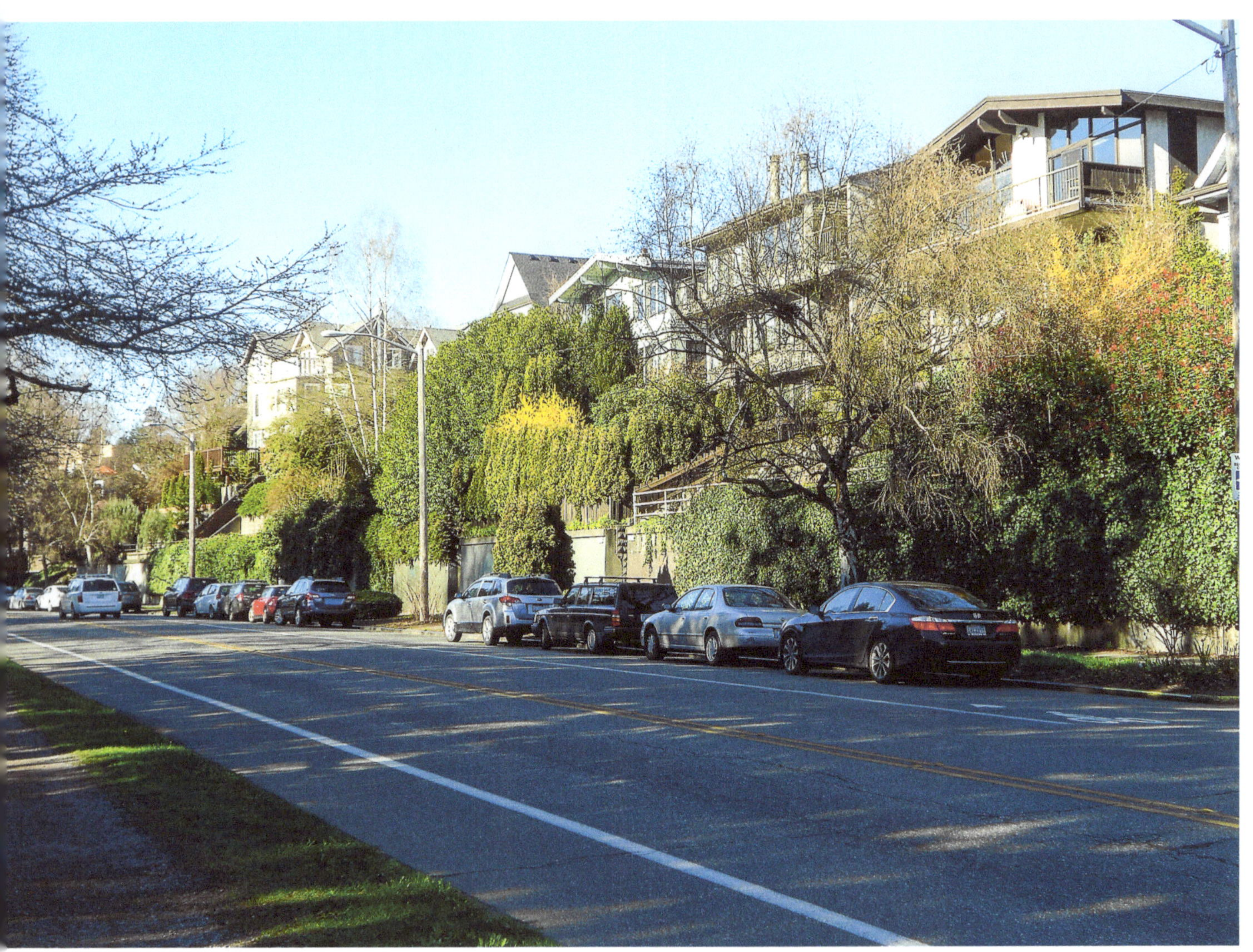

# Leaving the Park

We are looking west on East Green Lake Drive N which is what you
see when leaving the main entrance of the park. There is a traffic
light intersection there allowing for an easy exit.

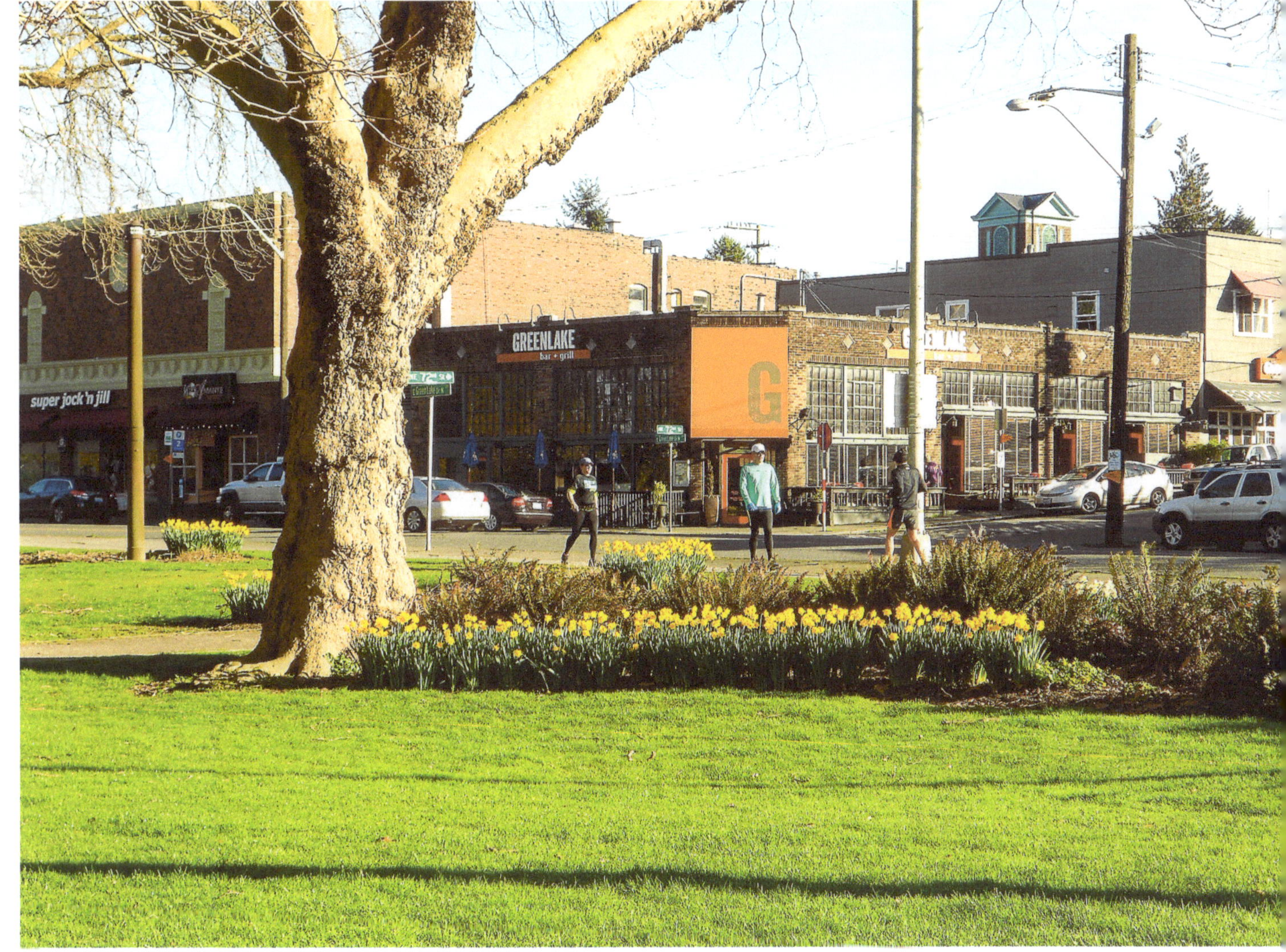

# Good Eating

The Green Lake Bar & Grill has been around for a long time. There are small tables and chairs along the sidewalk so you can dine alfresco. In the evening the place exudes a lot of ambience when its earthy tone bricks and orange awnings are under lights –warm colors that beckon you to stop by. I had a great margarita there during Cinco de Mayo.

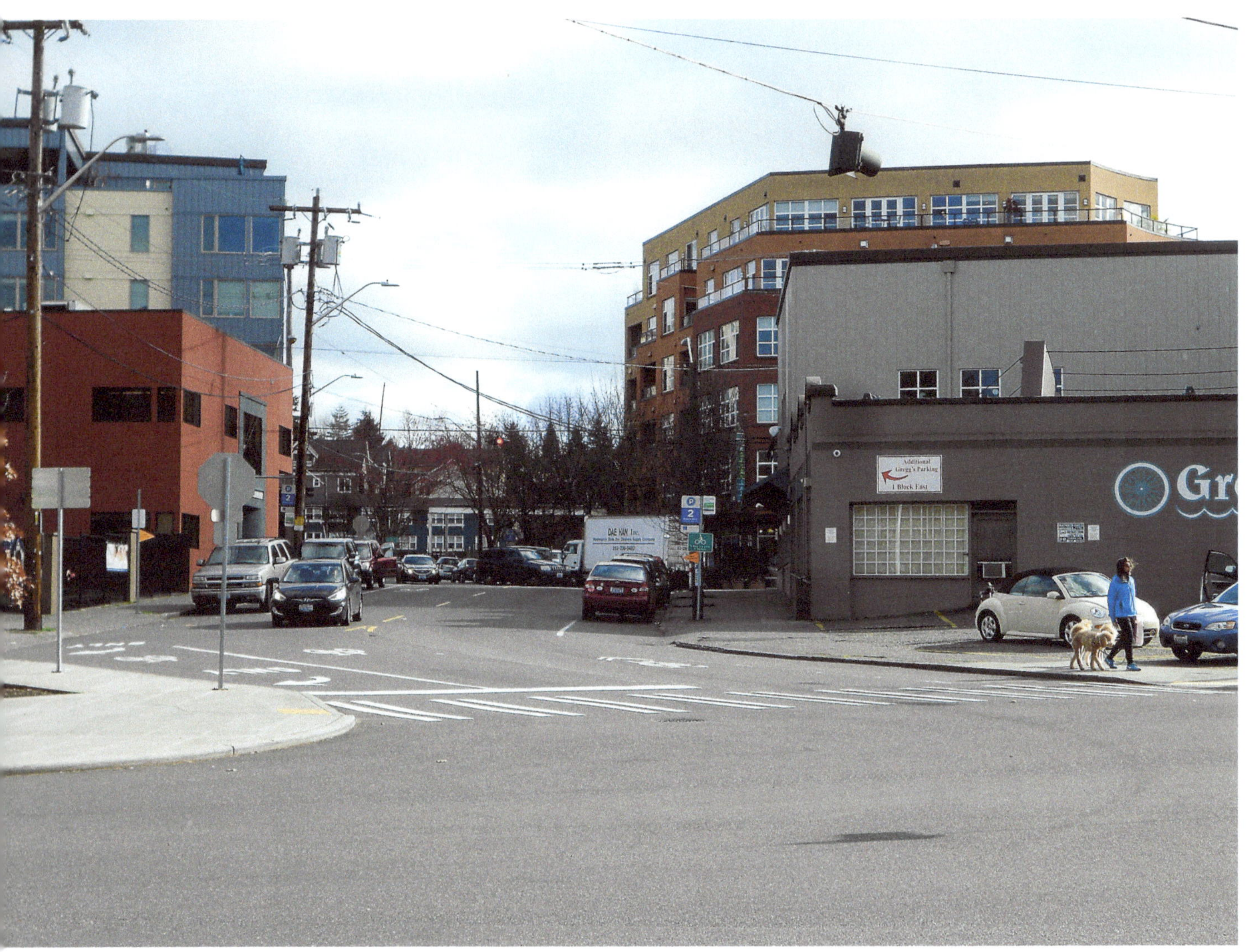

# Main Access Route to Lake

Looking up NE 71 Street, the main route I take to go to Green Lake as it appears from the edge of the park. It is just about one mile from my house to lakeside and I use this street because it has a bridge over Interstate 5 permitting direct access. The tall apartment buildings are all recently built.

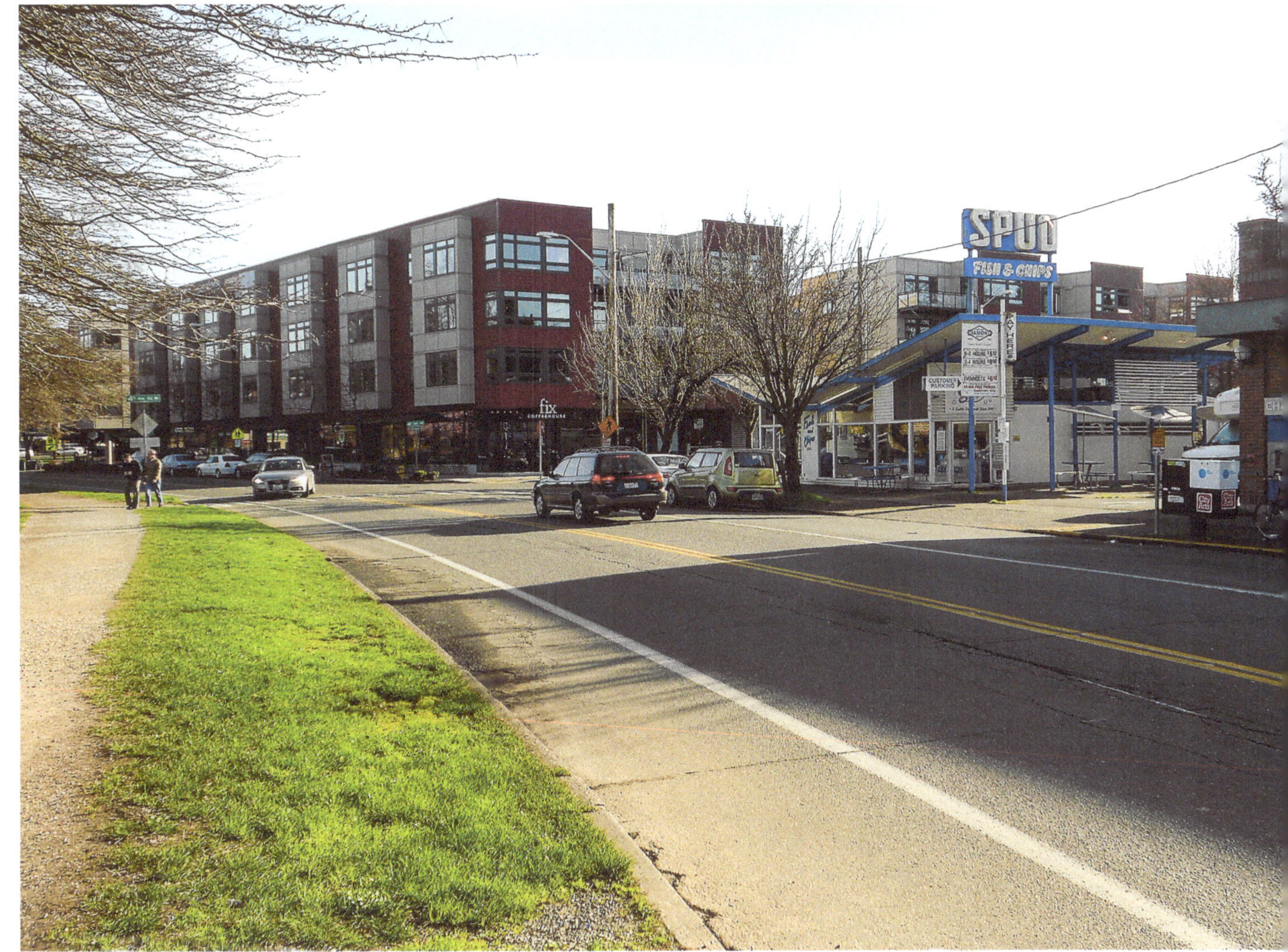



# Great for Lunch

Spud is famous for its fish and chips. I've gone there many times for lunch when I worked for the Seattle School District and our office was at the Wilson-Pacific School site only a few blocks north of the lake (now torn down to make way for a new school). The distant apartment complex has replaced what used to be an Albertson's Food store.

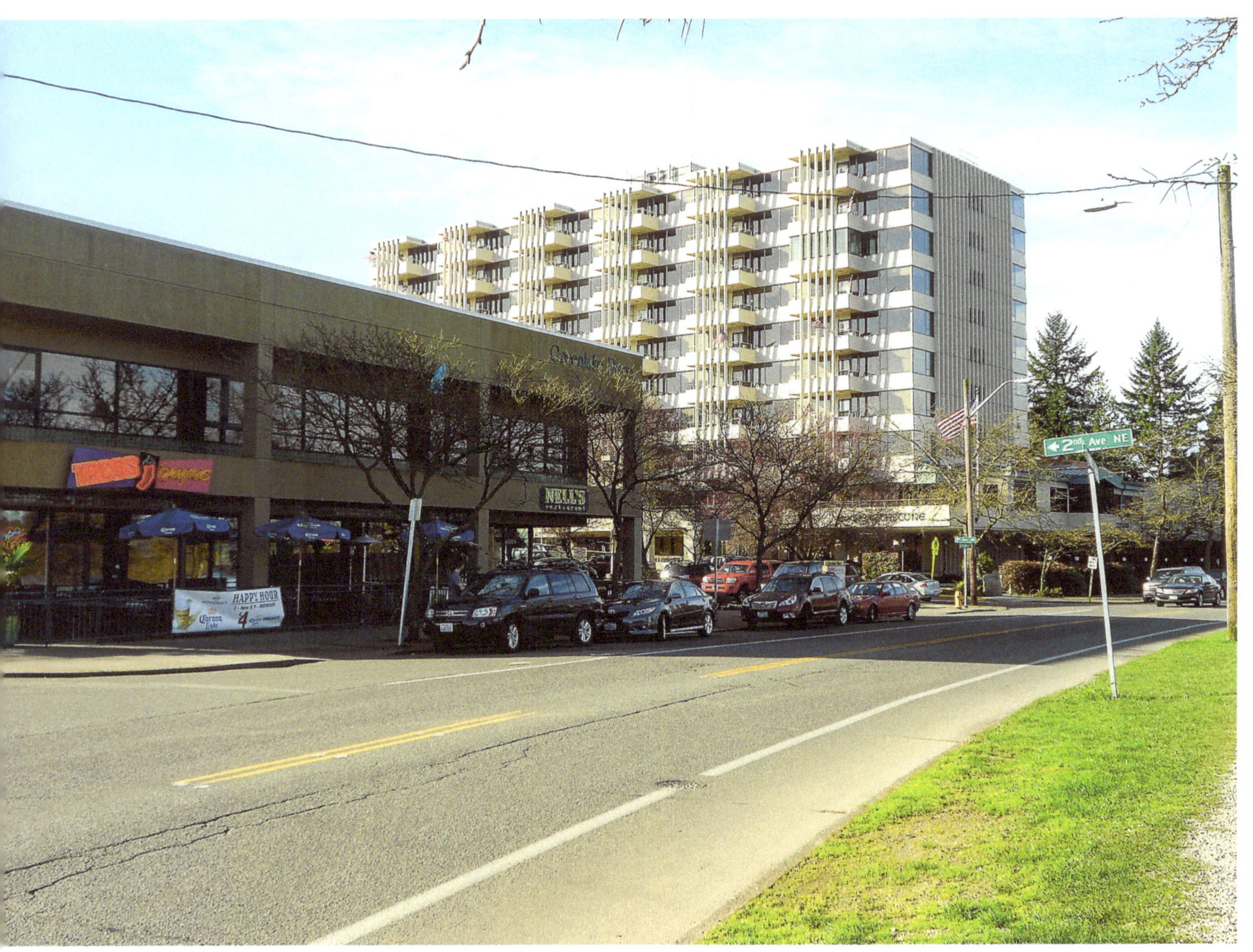


# The Hearthstone

The nine-story Hearthstone retirement, assisted care, and rehabilitation center is the most prominent building at Green Lake. I visited the place for several days when my friend was recuperating from back surgery there. It's been there ever since I first came to Seattle in 1975 —not a bad place to spend your remaining days, I think.

# Author's Afterword

This completes my photographic journey of my favorite setting in Seattle, Green Lake Park, which basically covered a one and one-half year time period, from May 2014 through October 2015. I wanted the reader to share in the beauty I see here every day, to feel the exhilaration I feel when making my walks there, and to rejoice at nature's magnificence, appreciating its diverseness in color and artistry. I never tire of doing my exercise there, as if anticipating with eagerness the new marvels that will greet me on each successive day. My thoughts whenever I do this are always the same: it's good to be alive.

2014 had to be the year of the fowl in that more ducks and gulls were seen at Green Lake than ever before, and I even believed at times that the lake would be overwhelmed by them. How different it all became going into the following year in that a great number of them have disappeared. While this in itself does not diminish from the beauty of the place, it does somehow make it seem less full of life. I enjoyed watching the wildlife —they constituted an integral part of the Green Lake experience for me. There's no need to be dismayed, however; I'm sure by the time we go into the fall season they will again be plentiful and enhance the park with their presence. It's all part of the life cycle there and I am reminded to relish it as I see it when I see it.

At first, I was tempted to add some pictures from atop Phinney Ridge and some of the side streets leading up to the lake as I alluded to these providing stunning views of it. But then I decided this would be inconsistent with the title and premise of this book, which limited my activity to the pathway around the lake and its bordering streets. I leave it to the readers to take my word for it and apply the effort to view Green Lake from these heights; they will be well-rewarded in doing so.

I am truly grateful to the city officials for having the foresight to create a public park out of this lake. How easily it could have been to have this natural setting obscured by private residences and public access to it restricted or denied altogether. How often does this happen elsewhere? I am the beneficiary of their decisions and applaud them for it every day. I continue to do my daily walks around Green Lake and will probably go on doing this until I am no longer able to —the pleasure I derive in this, as I have presented here, is immensely satisfying for me. I am lucky to live in Seattle.

I hope you enjoyed this journey.

*H. Allenger*

9 781613 398944